BEN TRAVERS: THREE FARCES AND A COMEDY

Ben Travers

# THREE FARCES AND A COMEDY

OBERON BOOKS
LONDON

WWW.OBERONBOOKS.COM

This collection first published in 2013 by Oberon Books Ltd
521 Caledonian Road, London N7 9RH
Tel: +44 (0) 20 7607 3637 / Fax: +44 (0) 20 7607 3629
e-mail: info@oberonbooks.com
www.oberonbooks.com

A catalogue record for this book is available from the British
Library.

PB ISBN: 978-1-84943-443-0
E ISBN: 978-1-84943-793-6

Cover design by James Illman

# Contents

# Foreword

Being a war baby, I never met my father until I was three years old so my grandfather, Ben Travers, became my surrogate father during that time. Consequently we had a very close and loving relationship right up to his death in 1980, aged ninety-four. He was an extraordinary man who twinkled and was full of fun and wit. I remember laughter – always laughter.

He was educated at Charterhouse but left by mutual consent in 1904 after a rather undistinguished career there. He subsequently joined the family firm – a wholesale grocery business called Joseph Travers and Sons where his superiors found him even more inept than he was at school, so it was decided that they would ship him out to the furthest point from the firm's headquarters in the City, Singapore and Malaya. It was there during the first decade of the 20$^{th}$ century that young Ben came across a uniform set of Arthur Wing Pinero's plays in Malacca Public Library. He avidly read each one and they became his guide-book to the technique of stagecraft, and he discovered the real secret of Pinero's mastery, namely his attention to every line and the importance of climax in every scene. Many years later when Ben himself had made a name for himself, he met Pinero and asked him which play was his favourite. 'My boy, the one that made the most money' was the reply.

During the First World War he joined the Royal Naval Air Service and was awarded the Air Force Cross for dropping the first ever torpedo from the air. Long before aircraft carriers were a part of the Navy, single engine seaplanes were winched into the sea off the deck of a warship. So long as the sea was calm they were able to take off and after their 'mission' was completed, they were retrieved in the same fashion. Ben later taught many future 'aces' how to fly, yet he himself was quite incapable of understanding the rudiments of the motor car and never mastered being able to drive one. He left that to his wife.

It was during the Great War when he fell in love and married Violet Mouncey. They had three children, my mother being the oldest. Their second child was a boy and as tradition dictates, the oldest son is always called Benjamin. My uncle Ben has now sadly died but his son (Ben) is now Literary Executor of the Travers Estate, and his young son is known as Ben Ten, being the tenth Ben Travers in succession. Grandpa Ben and Violet (known as 'Munga' because I couldn't say 'Grandma') were a deeply happy and loving couple. When she died of cancer in 1951 it was the biggest tragedy of his life. Apart from the theatre his other great love was watching cricket and he was a member of the MCC for nearly all his long life. He could nearly always be seen smoking his pipe at the Lords and Oval Test matches from 1896 right up to 1980!

In fact the last thing he wrote was a book about cricket reminiscences called *94 Declared*. Its original title was *94 Not Out* but he died just before its publication so one of my first duties as his then Literary Executor was to change its title. Ben saw WG Grace make a century and Jessop's historic innings at the Oval in 1902. He also accompanied the great English 1928-9 team on their tour of Australia. In those days they went by boat, and he made friends with most of the eminent cricketers of the day including Jardine, Hobbs, Sutcliffe, Hammond and Larwood.

By 1922 the Aldwych Theatre had become home to two comedians, Tom Walls and Ralph Lynn and their success was fast becoming a regular theatrical institution. But they had a problem. They needed a new farce. The current production was no longer playing to big audiences and so Ben's *A Cuckoo in the Nest* was chosen to replace it. It was directed by Tom himself. By the end of the second week of rehearsal the first two acts had been cut, reinvented and tinkered into shape which resulted in the third act not making any sense whatsoever. Tom handed him the script on the Monday of the final week of rehearsal – 'Go back to your room and re-write the whole bloody thing. Thursday morning will do, so long as you get it right.'

After fifty-four hours of hard work Tom was handed his re-written (and in fact completely re-devised) third act, and very successful it proved to be. This was the start of an amazing period. Ben wrote a total of eleven plays which were produced at the Aldwych between 1925 and 1933. The tally reads –

A Cuckoo in the Nest
Rookery Nook
Thark
Plunder
A Cup of Kindness
A Night like This
Turkey Time
Dirty Work
A Bit of a Test

Most of these titles became successful films, or rather successful at the time. Nowadays they are almost unwatchable except for their historical interest. Tom Walls and the Company knew where the laughs were and paused for what now seems an eternity before continuing with the next line.

However the plays still continue to be successfully produced, especially *Rookery Nook*. The reason for this is probably because it has a smaller than average cast and there is only one set, so this makes it much more attractive to producers. In fact *Rookery* has earned more money in royalties than all the other plays put together. *Thark, Plunder and Cuckoo* have all had West End revivals and the National Theatre's production of *Plunder* was one of the first plays to be performed in the Lyttelton Theatre. It starred Frank Finlay and Dinsdale Landen. In my opinion the Scotland Yard scene is probably the funniest and most beautifully crafted scene Ben ever wrote and it remains a classic in the art of scripting farce. *Plunder* would have enjoyed many revivals had it not required four sets and a huge cast (Twenty-seven parts in the National Theatre production).

*Thark* had a successful revival at the Lyric, Hammersmith starring Gryff Rhys Jones and was set to transfer to the Savoy but unfortunately a disastrous fire there prevented the play from opening. Recently Clive Francis, an old friend of Ben's, wrote a new adaptation of the play which was produced at the Finsbury Park Theatre and received wonderful notices. I also remember a revival of *A Cuckoo in the Nest* at the Royal Court Theatre with Arthur Lowe, and John Osborne playing a small part.

After a long period of thriving on revivals interspersed with the odd success such as *Banana Ridge* Ben remained a successful playwright but he never reached the giddy heights of the Aldwych heyday, but - roll on to the 1970s. Censorship had at last been disbanded and Ben was now free to write what he wanted (he had always had difficulties with the Lord Chamberlain's office, especially over innuendo and double entendres). *The Bed Before Yesterday,* produced by Helen Montagu and directed by Lindsay Anderson, opened on 9 December 1975. Ben was very nervous because he felt the contents might well shock his family and friends. He anticipated the critics would pour scorn on him and pity the foolish old playwright revelling in permissiveness. The play is about a middle-aged woman discovering the pleasures of sex for the first time, revelling in the delights of the orgasm, and driven almost to the verge of nymphomania. Good comic material and Joan Plowright was brilliant in the leading role. The comedy was a resounding success and is now ripe for a revival. The then unknown Helen Mirren was excellent in a supporting role. When asked if he didn't think he was a bit old for writing sex romps, he replied – 'Ah yes but you see, I have an awfully good memory'.

Ben's abiding principle was, 'The situations may be unreal but the players must always be true to themselves and never step out of character'. This is the key to playing farce and many actors have rued the day when they tried to ignore this advice.

He was awarded a CBE in the Queen's Birthday Honours in 1976 and during the last few years of his life, Ben came back to live in a self-contained flat in our house near Baker Street. My wife looked after him and either drove him to and from his various appointments with his agent, Robin Dalton, or to the Garrick Club. He was made a life member and greatly enjoyed the company there. His other great love was the Fishmongers' Company, one of the Great Twelve Livery Companies situated on London Bridge. He had been Prime Warden in 1946 and was by now the Senior Member of Court and was enormously popular as a raconteur. He always had a wonderful memory. One of his favourite pastimes was reading the obituary columns in the *Times* and was delighted to note that he had outlived a contemporary. 'Ah-ha I've beaten him,' he used to say with glee.

Ben was a staunch Christian although he preferred to worship in private. His epitaph on his gravestone reads – 'This is where the real fun begins'.

*Andrew Morgan, 2014*

ROOKERY NOOK

*Rookery Nook* was produced on 30 June 1926 at the Aldwych Theatre, London, with the following cast:

| | |
|---|---|
| GERTRUDE TWINE | Ethel Coleridge |
| MRS LEVERETT | Mary Brough |
| HAROLD TWINE | J. Robertson Hare |
| CLIVE POPKISS | Tom Walls |
| GERALD POPKISS | Ralph Lynn |
| RHODA MARLEY | Winifred Shotter |
| PUTZ | Griffith Humphreys |
| ADMIRAL JUDDY | Gordon James |
| POPPY DICKEY | Ena Mason |
| CLARA POPKISS | Stella Bonheur |
| MRS POSSETT | Vera Gerald |

The action takes places in the lounge-hall of *Rookery Nook*, Chumpton-on-Sea, Somerset. It begins on a night in Summer.

# Act One

*The lounge-hall of 'Rookery Nook' is in darkness as it is late on a summer
night. There is a trace of daylight left, and as the front door stands open
facing the audience R. C. of the back wall, the shrubbery across the drive
can be faintly seen. As the Act progresses the moon rises. From the hall
the staircase runs up L. and the balcony for landing in each case is seen.
On this balcony is a door L. (and, if the balance and appearance of the
set requires a second opening, that which leads to the back stairs which
are not shown). The balcony runs off the set R. and L. On the R. there
are two doors which lead to other bedrooms. On the ground floor are
two doors on each side of the hall. These, as explained later, lead R. to
drawing-room and study, L. to kitchen quarters and dining-room. The
electric light switches operating the hall lights are just inside the door,
D. L. The hall is well furnished with a very fine hall table slightly R.
of C., a Chesterfield sofa and hall chairs. A parquet floor with rugs: in
the back wall are large windows.*

*GERTRUDE TWINE discovered C. above table.*

GERTRUDE: Mrs Leverett! *(Raps on table.)* Mrs Leverett! *(No
answer. She is a woman in the thirties, a critical, suspicious type
of seaside resident. She is in semi-evening dress with a wrap. Calls
again.)* Mrs Leverett!

MRS LEVERETT: *(Heard off.)* Oh, is that Mrs Twine? Very
good; I'll come.

*GERTRUDE C. MRS LEVERETT enters from down left. She is a stout
person wearing a striking tartan blouse, tweed skirt and no hat;
leaves door open, through which a strong light shows.*

GERTRUDE: Hasn't he arrived? *(Moves to MRS LEVERETT.)*

MRS LEVERETT: *(Querulously.)* No, he has not, Mrs Twine, and
look at the time. I may say I was engaged by the day and
not by the night.

GERTRUDE: *(Freezingly.)* All right, all right. 'Has he arrived? –
*No.'* That's all I wanted. *No.*

MRS LEVERETT: *(Getting rattled.)* I suppose there is no
question he *is* coming to-night?

GERTRUDE: Of course he is. That's why you're waiting here.

MRS LEVERETT: Yes, but I should never have consented to wait had I known he was going to keep me here at improper hours. *(Cross L., switch on lights.)*

GERTRUDE: You must make allowances. In the ordinary way the whole party would have been here by this time.

MRS LEVERETT: H'm. I prefer to work for parties of regular habits.

*Waves imaginary cat into kitchen and closes door.*

*This fires GERTRUDE. A breeze springs up.*

GERTRUDE: My sister is a most considerate person. Was it *her* fault that my mother was taken ill at the last moment? *(Crosses L. of table to front.)*

MRS LEVERETT: I'm not saying – *(Crosses to GERTRUDE L. C.)*

GERTRUDE: And couldn't be brought here?

MRS LEVERETT: I know, madam, but – I can't worry about their troubles.

GERTRUDE: Don't talk like that of your betters, please.

MRS LEVERETT: I'm not talking like that of my betters.

GERTRUDE: Yes, you are. *(Slight pause as they glare at each other.)* My sister did the only possible thing – stayed and looked after my mother. *(Crosses to front of table.)*

MRS LEVERETT: Madam! I am not making any complaint about your sister. But her husband was coming here alone –

GERTRUDE: It isn't 'he *was* coming'. He *is* coming.

MRS LEVERETT: When?

GERTRUDE: I only know he's coming to-night. *(This as if trying to drum home a thing for the twentieth time.)*

MRS LEVERETT: Yes, but *when* to-night?

GERTRUDE: Oh, how can I tell? *(Breaking off with a little 't'ck' of annoyance, cross R. in front of table.)* When a man gets left alone with a car, there's always trouble. If the car doesn't go wrong, the man does.

MRS LEVERETT: *(Much more patiently.)* Well, excuse me *(Cross D. L. and come back.),* but can't you wait here for him, madam? Or can't Mr Twine?

TWINE: *(Appearing at front door.)* Yes. Hallo! What's that?

*TWINE is a short, feeble man of about forty in a dinner suit and straw hat.*

GERTRUDE: Oh, there you are, Harold.

TWINE: *(Coming down.)* Yes, dear.

GERTRUDE: Gerald hasn't arrived.

TWINE: No, dear.

GERTRUDE: How did you know?

TWINE: I didn't dear.

GERTRUDE: Then why say 'no' like that?

TWINE: Like what, dear?

GERTRUDE: Is Clive there?

TWINE: Yes, dear.

GERTRUDE: Call him in.

TWINE: Yes, dear. *(Crosses to door – at door R. C. calling.)* Clave! Clave!

GERTRUDE: Where is he?

CLIVE: *(Calling.)* Clave! Clave!

GERTRUDE: Clive!

TWINE: Clave!

CLIVE: *(Appearing at front door.)* All right; don't make an anthem of it.

*CLIVE is a sport in the thirties. He wears a dinner suit.*

*TWINE crosses L. to MRS LEVERETT, and she tells him of her troubles at CLIVE comes down R. C. to GERTRUDE.*

GERTRUDE: Come in. Come in.

CLIVE: Oh, so this is the house you've got for them, is it? What a nice house! Nice, peaceful atmosphere for a change.

GERTRUDE: What do you mean – for a change?

CLIVE: For them. For Gerald and Clara. They're coming here, aren't they?

GERTRUDE: I don't see why you should say they want a peaceful atmosphere for a *change*. They've only been married six weeks.

CLIVE: I don't mean that.

*CLIVE R.C., GERTRUDE C., TWINE L.C., MRS LEVERETT L.*

GERTRUDE: Well, what *do* you mean?

CLIVE: *(Long-suffering, stifling his impatience.)* They're on a holiday, aren't they?

GERTRUDE: Well?

CLIVE: Just like I'm on a holiday – *(Cross to GERTRUDE.)* – staying with *you*.

GERTRUDE: Well?

CLIVE: Yes – well, I say – what a nice house they're coming to. Lucky people.

GERTRUDE: *(A little jealous.)* Haven't you come to a nice house? Isn't mine nice?

CLIVE: *(Getting past his patience.)* Oh, very. There can be two nice houses, can't there?

GERTRUDE: *(Who shines at females' argument.)* You don't suppose I'd have got them a house that *wasn't* nice *(Turning away L.)*, do you?

CLIVE: *(Turning, cross D. R. desperately, speaking to himself.)* Oh, hell!

*TWINE crosses to GERTRUDE.*

TWINE: Dearest!

GERTRUDE: What do *you* want?

*CLIVE watches them, listening.*

TWINE: It isn't I that wants anything.

GERTRUDE: Well, who is it that wants what?

TWINE: *(Apologetically.)* Mrs – er – em –

GERTRUDE: Yes. I know what she wants. She wants to go home.

MRS LEVERETT: Quite right.

*CLIVE moves towards C.*

TWINE: She was asking me what time I thought Gerald would arrive.

GERTRUDE: *(Very annoyed.)* Well, gracious me, how can I tell? I've been asked that twenty times. Don't ask me again.

TWINE: *(Very subdued.)* He only had to come on from your mother's at Bath. Bath isn't far – a matter of two hours. He ought to have started –

GERTRUDE: Started! He ought to have been here hours ago.

*TWINE goes up L.*

MRS LEVERETT: Well, something's got to be done about it.

CLIVE: *(Sauntering back to GERTRUDE C. with malice aforethought.)* I say, Gertrude –

*(Table)*

*TWINE L.C., CLIVE R.C., GERTRUDE C.*

*(Settee)*

*MRS LEVERETT L.*

*(Airily, crosses to GERTRUDE.)* About what time do you suppose old Gerald will breeze along?

GERTRUDE: Clive, you're trying to annoy me.

CLIVE: *(With injured innocence.)* Annoy you, Gertrude? I like that. I wouldn't do such a thing. I was going to suggest something.

GERTRUDE: I shouldn't think *that* would be likely to help.

CLIVE: Oh, all right. I was only going to suggest a suggestion.

*(He crosses L.C. to MRS LEVERETT.)* P'r'aps you might like to hear it. It's a really good one.

MRS LEVERETT: I have no time to listen, sir. I must be *off.*

CLIVE: Oh, don't be that.

MRS LEVERETT: If you knew in what a hurry I was to get home, sir, you'd offer to wait here yourself for the coming gentleman.

CLIVE: You must be psychic.

MRS LEVERETT: *(Obviously shocked.)* I *beg* your pardon – I'm nothing of the kind.

CLIVE: We've got the same idea. *(Turning to GERTRUDE.)* There you are. We've fixed it. I'll stay here till Gerald comes, and Mrs Flannelfoot will waddle off home.

GERTRUDE: *(Considering this.)* Oh – I see.

MRS LEVERETT: *(Briskly.)* If the gentleman is willing, that settles it. I'll get me hat. *(Goes off D. L.)*

*TWINE comes down L.C.*

GERTRUDE: Oh, well, if you're going to be left here alone, I hope you're to be trusted. You'll be responsible for the house, not only to Gerald, but also to the Mantle Hams.

CLIVE: *(Crosses to GERTRUDE.)* To the who?

GERTRUDE: The Mantle Hams. The people this house belongs to.

CLIVE: Oh, the Mantle Hams. That's a good one. But I fail to see what trouble I can get into here alone for a few minutes. *(Sits on table C.)* If you can think of any, I wish you'd let me know.

GERTRUDE: *(Decisively.)* Someone's got to hang about here, so I suppose you'd better.

CLIVE: Righto then. I'm very good at hanging about.

TWINE: *(Tentatively.)* Erm –

CLIVE: *(Looking at TWINE curiously.)* Yes?

TWINE: *(Looking at GERTRUDE.)* Erm –

GERTRUDE: *(Who has turned towards the door, looking around again.)* Well, what's the matter?

CLIVE: Shh! Don't discourage him. I think Harold is going to lay an egg.

GERTRUDE: Clive, don't be coarse.

TWINE: No, I only thought –

GERTRUDE: You thought what?

TWINE: Wouldn't it be as well for me to stay as well?

GERTRUDE: What?

CLIVE: Now, old sportsman, sort yourself out. *(Patting him gently)*.

TWINE: *(Precisely.)* Shall I stay too?

CLIVE: No.

GERTRUDE: No.

CLIVE: Carried.

GERTRUDE: Why do you want to stay?

TWINE: I don't, dear.

GERTRUDE: Then why say you did?

TWINE: I didn't mean I did. I meant if you'd rather I did, should I?

CLIVE: The answer is a sponge cake.

GERTRUDE: Oh, come home. *(Cross U. R.)*

TWINE: Yes, dear.

*CLIVE trips him playfully as he crosses.*

*(Apologizes.)* I'm sorry.

CLIVE: Oh, it's all right.

*GERTRUDE turns back; TWINE is following close on her heels: he drops down R. and starts to nibble his straw hat.*

GERTRUDE: *(To CLIVE.)* Let me know directly Gerald arrives. I've got several things to see to at home, or I'd wait myself. Tell him I may be able to come over and see him later.

CLIVE: That'll amuse him.

GERTRUDE: What?

CLIVE: Oh, nothing.

GERTRUDE: *(Is going.)* Harold! Don't stand there nibbling your straw hat. I'm always telling you about that. Put it on your head.

TWINE: Yes, dear. *(D.R.)*

*The TWINES depart up R.*

CLIVE: And those whom the gods love die young.

*He gives an elaborate gesture of pent-up fury. Then he turns and crosses to the door D.L., which he opens.*

I say, haven't you gone – ?

*The noise of a cat is heard. He steps back quickly.*

Oh, sorry.

*He steps out again into the hall. MRS LEVERETT, now wearing a hat, follows him.*

MRS LEVERETT: Was that you, sir?

CLIVE: Yes

*MRS LEVERETT shoos cat away, and shuts door D.L.*

I'm afraid I trod on the cat. *(Cross to L.C.)*

MRS LEVERETT: Then kindly do not do so.

CLIVE: Ah, too late. I've done it now. *(Up L.C.)*

MRS LEVERETT: You know this gentleman, I take it?

CLIVE: Who? Mr Popkiss? *(Behind table C.)*

MRS LEVERETT: Yes. The one that's expected.

CLIVE: Oh, rather. He's my cousin. My name's Popkiss, too.

MRS LEVERETT: Oh, I see. Then you're also related to Mrs Twine?

CLIVE: No, that I'm not. He's my cousin and he married Mrs Twine's sister; that's all.

MRS LEVERETT: Oh, is that all?

CLIVE: Yes, quite enough. And Mrs Twine *(Cross back of table to R. and looks at knick-knacks on the desks.)* very, very kindly invited me to stay down here. And knowing my cousin was coming here, I like a fool fell for it.

MRS LEVERETT: *(Cross R to CLIVE.)* Oh! Yes, I know Mrs Twine's house well enough – Frascati. A very nice house.

CLIVE: Personally, I'd much rather be in this one. *(Cross D.R.)*

MRS LEVERETT: *(Betrayed from her hurry into the love of gossip cross R.)* Yes? Well, this house – Rookery Nook – now, I reckon it's in the wrong part of Chumpton.

CLIVE: Not for me.

MRS LEVERETT: I mean, this here Lighthouse Road don't lead anywhere.

CLIVE: No I've noticed that. *(Cross in front of table C., sits.)* Not even to the lighthouse. But *all* this place is exceedingly quiet. There's nothing doing – you know what I mean – no amusement – no fun.

MRS LEVERETT: *(Cross to table.)* No. I'm glad to say Chumpton is a very respectable place – for the *most* part.

CLIVE: In which direction lies the *least* part?

MRS LEVERETT: Though I suppose every place has its black mark. *(Cross to L. of table.)* Well, I must really be getting home, sir.

CLIVE: I say, where is the black mark here?

MRS LEVERETT: *(Again lured into gossip, crosses to CLIVE, returning in a more confidential manner.)* Well, sir, just what I was saying about this particular part of the place – one of these houses nearby here, for instance, has a most improper reputation.

CLIVE: No?

MRS LEVERETT: Yes.

CLIVE: *(With interest.)* Really! Oh, go on. Where and what?

MRS LEVERETT: Meself I wonder Chumpton puts up with it. A foreigner living here, with a step-daughter. So-called. Huh!

CLIVE: Oh? And – isn't she really his step-daughter?

MRS LEVERETT: *(Decidedly.)* No, sir.

*Warning for car.*

CLIVE: How do you know?

MRS LEVERETT: Well, Mrs Twine knows most things.

CLIVE: You're quite right, she does.

MRS LEVERETT: And her cook told me that the story of the step-daughter was all sheer hullaballoo.

CLIVE: Is that so?

MRS LEVERETT: Yes. Well, the very name of the house is enough. Malmaison Cottage. And you, sir, being a scholar, will know that that is French, and *means* 'a bad house'.

CLIVE: I see, a sort of advertisement on the gate.

MRS LEVERETT: Yes. And now, sir, reely, I must hurry away.

*(Cross L.)*

CLIVE: What, again? All right. Off you trot.

MRS LEVERETT: *(Cross L.C.)* Mind you, I don't actually know these persons. At least, I know them both by sight very well, but that's all. And that's enough, seeing he's a foreigner and she as good English as what I am.

CLIVE: Yes. But she might still be his *step-*daughter.

MRS LEVERETT: Why, sir?

CLIVE: Her being English wouldn't stop her being his *step-*daughter.

MRS LEVERETT: Oh! Then all I can say is it's a very slippery step. Now, sir, if you please. I cannot remain and let you talk to me any longer.

CLIVE: Quite right. We must be careful, or Mrs Twine will be saying things about us. *(Pushes MRS LEVERETT playfully – L. – goes up towards door R. At front door looking off L. hears a motor-horn and sees reflection of car lights through window with sudden exclamation.)* Hallo! Wait a minute; here is my cousin.

MRS LEVERETT: *(Pausing.)* At last.

CLIVE: I'll go and help him.

*GERALD is seen driving past the windows from L. to R.*

MRS LEVERETT: *(Cross R. going to door.)* The garridge doors is open. *(Cross to L.C.)*

*The car is heard to stop.*

*MRS LEVERETT comes C. and stands facing door.*

*GERALD enters, a young, smiling and cheerful man, in a travelling outfit, and carrying a handbag and a light overcoat. He wears a cap.*

GERALD: *(Taking his cap off.)* Rookery Nook?

MRS LEVERETT: *(Snappily.)* Yes.

GERALD: *(Putting down bag.)* Good. I'm coming here.

MRS LEVERETT: You've bin coming for some time.

GERALD: A month. I was told I should be met by a daily woman. Are you it – the daily woman?

MRS LEVERETT: *(With a sniff.)* H'm. I'm not so sure that I *am* now.

GERALD: Well, perhaps you could find out. *(Puts bag on table.)*

MRS LEVERETT: I am a working wife and mother, and there at home waiting for me is my five children and cetera, not to mention my husband and what not.

GERALD: Oh, you've got five children and a what-not – I wonder you can find time to be daily.

MRS LEVERETT: 'Owever now you have come, I may as well show you the house and quit.

GERALD: Where's the quit?

MRS LEVERETT: Quit. Go. I'll go.

GERALD: Oh, go. You'll go. Good! Yes, thanks very much. I see. Quit – I thought you meant the quit was some sort of – well I mean quit – it might be anything.

MRS LEVERETT: Well, this is the main 'all.

GERALD: Oh, this is the main hall, is it?

MRS LEVERETT: *(Cross up L.)* This is the dining-room. *(Indicating off up L.)* I suppose you've had all the food you need to-night.

GERALD: Yes, I had something on the way.

MRS LEVERETT: Yes, I should think you *did. (Indicating off L.)* The dining-room.

GERALD: *(Looking in.)* Oh, a nice square room; thanks very much.

*CLIVE enters R.C.*

CLIVE: I say, Gerald, you didn't leave me out there with the idea that I was going to wash the car and put it away for you, did you?

GERALD: No. Have you unstrapped the trunks?

CLIVE: Yes, I've done that.

*MRS LEVERETT crosses to study door D.R., which she opens. Throughout this scene she hustles GERALD unwillingly from room to room.*

MRS LEVERETT: The study! *(Impatiently.)*

*CLIVE crosses to back of table.*

GERALD: *(Turning to study.)* The study? That's very nice. *(To CLIVE.)* We might go and sit in there –

MRS LEVERETT: *(Closing study door.)* I can't sit anywhere.

GERALD: Why, what have you done to yourself?

MRS LEVERETT: *(Looking fiercely at GERALD and crossing up R., opening drawing-room door and immediately closing it again.)* Mrs Mantle Ham's drawing-room.

*CLIVE crosses to R. front of table.*

GERALD: Oh! *(She closes door.)* Very nice outside.

MRS LEVERETT: *(Cross L. in front of settee, followed by GERALD; opens kitchen door D.L.)* The kitchen and so on. Those are my quarters. You don't want to see them, do you?

GERALD: *(To CLIVE.)* I don't think we want to see her quarters, do we? No, we won't.

MRS LEVERETT: *(Pointing up R.)* The stairs.

GERALD: Oh, impossible!

MRS LEVERETT: The door there is the main bedroom. The bed is made. The bathroom is next door. The other bedroom is elsewhere.

GERALD: *(To CLIVE.)* I wonder who thought of that.

MRS LEVERETT: *(Crosses to kitchen.)* I must get back now hurried. *(Cross to GERALD.)* Oh, here is the front-door key. I have the back. I will come at eight-thirty in the morning. Earlier than that I cannot be. And good night to you. *(Turns towards kitchen door.)*

GERALD: Yes; but, I say, hold on one moment.

MRS LEVERETT: What, sir? Quickly, please.

GERALD: There were just one or two things I wanted to ask you.

MRS LEVERETT: What was it you wanted to know, please?

GERALD: It's all right. Only I thought there were to be some other girls here besides you. You know – maids.

MRS LEVERETT: Ah! *(Crosses to GERALD.)* But not yet, sir. Mrs Twine put them off directly she heard you were coming alone.

GERALD: Why? *(MRS LEVERETT gives an elaborate shrug.)* Oh, I see. *(To CLIVE.)* You hear that?

MRS LEVERETT: Good night then. And eight-thirty in the morning. *(Cross L. at kitchen door.)* Oh, and there is also a cat. It lives in the kitchen. *(Coming back L.C.)*

GERALD: It had better.

MRS LEVERETT: Kindly mind out for it. It's been trod on once to-night already *(Looks at CLIVE freezingly.)* even in there.

*She goes off D.L., closing door.*

GERALD: Well, here we are. It was very nice of you to be over here to meet me, old boy.

CLIVE: You needn't flatter yourself. I only stayed over here away from those blasted Twines.

GERALD: *(Laughs.)* Yes, I wanted you there.

CLIVE: Dash it, what have I ever done to you?

GERALD: I wanted *you* there, so that I shouldn't have to go about with Harold.

CLIVE: Well, anyway, I'm very glad you've come.

GERALD: Yes, and I'm very glad you're here. You can help me in with my portmanteau. *(Cross R. back of table.)*

CLIVE: Oh, hell! Is it heavy?

GERALD: Yes, it is very. Come on, old boy. *(Going to door.)*

CLIVE: *(Going reluctantly up R.C.)* All right. If I'd only known, I'd have had Twine over to do it.

*They go out R.C. together and can be heard getting the portmanteau off the car.*

GERALD: *(Off.)* Stand there. I'll give it a heave.

CLIVE: All right. Go on then, you go first. You can be the one to go backwards.

*They reappear carrying the portmanteau, GERALD walking backwards.*

GERALD: *(R.C., looking up L. over his shoulder.)* I suppose that's my room.

CLIVE: I don't care. I'm not going to carry it upstairs.

GERALD: Righto. Put it down.

*They put it down up stage L.C.*

CLIVE: Too hot for that stuff.

GERALD: Yes. You're quite right. We ought to have had Harold.

CLIVE: I suppose you've got a bottle in it?

GERALD: That's in that one. *(Indicating suitcase R.)*

CLIVE: *(Cross R. to suitcase on table.)* Then why not say so? We need never have got the portmanteau.

*He opens suitcase; pushes several miscellaneous contents out on the floor, handkerchiefs, etc.*

GERALD: I say, Clive, careful, old boy.

CLIVE: *(Picking things up.)* I'm sorry, but you had to unpack, didn't you?

GERALD: *(Taking whisky bottle from the suitcase.)* There you are, old boy. *(Handing it to CLIVE.)* Shall I get some glasses? *(Goes to kitchen.)*

CLIVE: Yes, I hate drinking out of the bottle.

GERALD: I'll get some glasses. *(Opens door down R. and bus. driving imaginary cat away.)* Go out – I mean – don't do that – stay in – Pss!

CLIVE: What's up?

GERALD: *(Off.)* Cat.

CLIVE: Did you tread on it?

GERALD: No. I missed it.

CLIVE: Oh, pity. *(Puts bag back R. and comes back to table C.)* And see if that fellow left any soda.

GERALD: What fellow?

CLIVE: The owner of the house. You know – Brindle Stag or whatever his damn silly name is.

GERALD: Yes. Oh, here's some water, I'd better bring that.

*He returns, carrying two large glasses and jug of water. Kicks backward to scare the cat and shuts the door with his foot.*

Get back there – shoo! I hate cats.

CLIVE: That's better *(Leaves GERALD to mix drink at table and strolls over L.)* Ye Gods, if you knew what it was like over at those two teetotal Twines'!

GERALD: *(Pouring whiskies, one strong, one weak.)* Well, think of me, old boy. How different from dear little Clara. Queer thing that – two sisters so unlike.

CLIVE: *(Looking at the drinks.)* Gerald, which of these is mine?

GERALD: Just as you like it. *(Looks carefully at the drinks.)* Take that one. *(Pushes small one to CLIVE – turns to portmanteau.)*

*CLIVE changes tumblers. GERALD sees him. GERALD returns from portmanteau to re-change tumblers. Meanwhile these lines are spoken.*

CLIVE: Righto. Shall I do this for you? *(With water jug.)*

GERALD: Yes, please.

*CLIVE pours water in each glass and changes them again, taking the strong one.*

CLIVE: Yes, poor little Twine. At time he must long for death – probably Gertrude's.

*GERALD takes drink, takes more whisky.*

What's the matter – too strong?

GERALD: Not yet. I'm afraid Harold will never assault Gertrude. *(Crosses to L. front of table.)*

CLIVE: No. I might. *(Crosses to R. front of table.)* Poor little Twine. The way she dosses him up, and makes him trot about after her, wearing his little straw hat and looking like a rabbit at a stoat's tea party!

GERALD: Well, you'll have me and Clara here now. *(Crosses to portmanteau.)*

CLIVE: When's Clara coming? *(Crosses behind table.)*

GERALD: *(Returning to his unpacking.)* Oh, she'll bring the old woman along pretty soon. *(Places ties on table C.)*

*Bus. CLIVE walks with GERALD each time backwards and forwards, getting in his way each time.*

CLIVE: What's the matter with the old woman?

GERALD: I don't know. *(Pushes CLIVE gently.)* She didn't say much. *(Putting bottle encased in wood with screw top on table, also pyjamas and loofah on table C. front.)*

CLIVE: Didn't she? That sounds as if she were dying. *(Getting between GERALD and the table.)* Well, couldn't we wangle that I come and put up here with you? *(At portmanteau L.)*

GERALD: I don't know, old boy. Rather impossible if you're staying with Gertrude. Clara might be able to get you over. *(Crossing to table with bath gown.)*

*CLIVE is standing in his way.*

Get out of the way, old boy. *(Pushing him.)*

CLIVE: Couldn't I stay here now – I mean – before Clara comes? *(Has picked up a tie and is toying with it.)* How do you do these things?

*GERALD takes it and pushes him gently away.*

I mean you do want me here, don't you?

GERALD: Do I? *(Going to portmanteau.)*

CLIVE: If you only knew what I've suffered at the hands of those relations of yours.

GERALD: It doesn't worry me. I'm not there.

*Bus. CLIVE is now toying with a screw stopper on the bottle.*

*(Taking it from him.)* Don't do that, old boy; if you want to play with one of these, that's the place to get them. *(Pointing at name.)* The name's at the bottom. *(Crosses to portmanteau and brings other things back.)*

*By this time CLIVE has picked up a bath gown.*

*(Taking it from him.)* Don't mess that gown about, old boy, you'll get it all creased.

CLIVE: It's a lovely colour.

GERALD: Yes. All the more reason not to mess it about.

CLIVE: Well, what am I to do?

GERALD: You must find something else to do. This is my favourite garment. I'm very fond of that.

CLIVE: I mean about getting away from Gertrude's. *(Crosses R.C. to R. front of table.)*

GERALD: You can't; that's all.

CLIVE: *(Strolling around R. of table to front.)* No, I suppose not. After all, I suppose when you've been married six weeks you don't want other people knocking around all the time.

GERALD: *(Coming round L. of table to front, grins.)* Very little of the time.

CLIVE: How's it going? *(Sitting on table.)*

GERALD: Marriage? Oh, fine, old boy.

CLIVE: A veil is drawn over the past, eh?

GERALD: What do you mean?

CLIVE: *(Taking whisky.)* Well, dash it, we had a few bright adventures in our time, didn't we?

GERALD: Oh, a veil. Yes, a very thick veil. *(CLIVE pours out whisky.)* You'll help yourself, won't you?

CLIVE: Yes, I will, old boy. Do you remember –

GERALD: *(Quickly.)* No, I don't. And look here, I say, Clive – while you're staying in this place – I mean with the relations here and that sort of thing – don't go and get into trouble, will you? You know what I mean – with anything *local.*

CLIVE: You needn't be afraid. There's nothing to be found in this place.

GERALD: How do you know?

CLIVE: I've been here a whole week and drawn a complete blank. There's nothing here at all.

31

GERALD: Oh, that's a pity.

CLIVE: Yes, well, I suppose we shall have to play golf, that's all.

GERALD: Don't give up hope. We thought we were going to play golf that time at Bognor, d'you remember?

CLIVE: Oh yes. That was the time we met Annie and Winnie.

GERALD: Oh, Annie and Winnie. Yes. What a memory you've got! Annie was the stout one and Winnie was the pretty one.

CLIVE: Yes.

GERALD: You, you old devil. You pinched Winnie.

CLIVE: Oh, I pinched old Annie too.

*Warning – distant door bang and short bark of dog – O.P.*

GERALD: Well, as I say, none of that Annie and Winnie stuff this time.

CLIVE: As I say you needn't worry, there's nothing here at all. Gertrude only lives in this place because here she's comparatively good-looking.

GERALD: Of course, so far the only one I've seen is the daily one. And she looks like a non-swimmer in deep water.

CLIVE: You've only got to look at this place. *(Cross R.C.)* Look at it now. Only just dark and you can hear the silence.

GERALD: Yes. *(Cross to CLIVE.)*

*Bang.*

*Dog and bang of door in distance.*

CLIVE: What was that?

GERALD: A dog, I think.

CLIVE: Yes, but there was a sort of bang.

GERALD: Oh, then perhaps somebody shot the dog.

CLIVE: It sounded more like a door bang.

GERALD: Somebody letting out the dog.

CLIVE: Why should he bang the door like that?

GERALD: He probably ought to have let the dog out sooner. *(Pause.)* You can't see anything from there, can you?

CLIVE: Well, you don't want to see a dog being let out. Now are you going to start clearing up this ghastly mess?

GERALD: I haven't begun yet. I've more things in the car. *(Turns.)*

CLIVE: Well, you'd better hurry up or you'll have Gertrude round.

GERALD: Why, she's not coming over, is she?

CLIVE: You bet she is – she'll come along, nosing about like an old hen that's had her run dug up. *(Flapping his arms and scratching his foot as a hen.)*

GERALD: Well, go and tell her I haven't arrived.

CLIVE: But, you silly old fat-head, I've only been left here till you did.

GERALD: Oh, I see. Well, tell her I'm too tired.

CLIVE: All right. I'll do my best, and then come back. Don't take that up to your bedroom. *(Indicating whisky. Turns towards door R.C.)*

GERALD: If you're coming back, there won't be any to take.

CLIVE: Well, I'll try and put the lid on Gertrude.

GERALD: And Harold.

CLIVE: If I get the lid on, he can sit on it.

*Exit up R.*

*GERALD tidies the table and looks about for something in his portmanteau L. and goes out R.C.*

*The figure of RHODA, a young and very pretty girl in pink silk pyjamas, passes window L., just glancing in. She then comes to door R., pauses, looks around, crosses to L. in front of table, looks up to balcony L., then sees bath gown on table C. and sits on table drying her feet with the bath gown; she is facing half L.*

*GERALD returns with a case and golf clubs; he puts them down R., clubs R. of case; he sees her, then picks up bag and clubs, goes out again to make certain he's made no mistake about the house. He comes back, puts things down again, looking at her in a dazed way, shutting and opening his eyes. He then goes to the door R.C., calling helplessly.*

GERALD: Clive!

RHODA: *(As she turns and sees him.)* Oh! Er – is this your house?

GERALD: Yes, I think so.

RHODA: I mean, you've just got here, or something?

GERALD: Yes, but haven't you, or something?

RHODA: Yes. My name's Rhoda Marley. I come from up the road. I live there with my step-father.

GERALD: Oh, did you? – I mean, do you? Is he ill, or is your house on fire?

RHODA: No, It's nothing like that, but – shall I tell you?

GERALD: *(Getting closer.)* Yes, please, I wish you would.

RHODA: Oh, thank you. Only – excuse me a moment.

*She shifts her sitting position and extracts a loofah. She smiles half-bashfully.*

It was pricking me rather.

GERALD: Oh, was it? It should only scratch. Hadn't you better sit on something softer?

RHODA: I sat up here to dry my feet. I had to come through some very long grass to get here.

GERALD: Yes, I see – the ends of your –

RHODA: Pyjama trousers –

GERALD: Pyjama trousers – oh yes, I couldn't remember the name.

RHODA: Yes, I know. They're very damp too. There's a heavy dew, you see.

GERALD: Yes. I can see there is. *(Getting closer.)* Still, it's supposed to be a sign of fine weather, isn't it?

RHODA: Yes. *(Embarrassed pause.)* Well, I'd better tell you why I've come.

GERALD: Do, will you, please?

RHODA: Well, it's a rather long story.

GERALD: Oh, it can't be. I mean, here you are in pyjamas on my table.

*RHODA slips off table.*

Oh, that's all right. But why? That's all – why?

RHODA: *(Appealingly.)* It's all quite harmless. But I'm in such trouble. Oh, please, do be kind to me.

GERALD: *(Softening.)* Kind to you? I'd do anything. But that's just it. What do you want me to do?

RHODA: Well, first of all – could you lend me a dressing gown?

GERALD: Oh yes – *(Doubtfully.)* – a dressing-gown? Certainly. *(Cross L., puling dressing-gown from trunk and holding it up for her.)* Here you are. This one's rather short.

RHODA: *(Notices pyjamas on table, getting into dressing-gown.)* Thanks awfully. I'm afraid I've rather spoilt that bath wrap.

GERALD: Oh, never mind about that rotten old thing. *(Throwing it down and kicking it.)* Only that wasn't why you came here, to borrow a dressing-gown?

RHODA: No, I'll tell you everything. *(She shivers.)*

GERALD: You're cold. *(Nearly touches her.)*

RHODA: No, it's all right. It's only that wet grass.

GERALD: Here, drink this. *(Taking up whisky and changing it for the jug of water.)*

RHODA: No, I don't want that.

GERALD: Well, what else can I do?

RHODA: *(Hesitating, rubbing one leg on the other.)* I hardly like to ask. *(Smiling.)*

GERALD: Don't be afraid. What is it?

RHODA: *(Taking a pair of his striped blue pyjama trousers from the table.)* The ends of mine have got so awfully damp.

GERALD: You – you want to put on those of mine? *(She nods.)* But – are you going to be here long?

RHODA: Well, I'm afraid that depends on you.

GERALD: Oh, does it? Well, then, you'd better put on those of mine.

RHODA: I'm honestly in great trouble. *(In a little outburst, getting a little closer to GERALD.)* You do trust me, don't you?

GERALD: Of course. *(Making shapes with his hands.)* Only can't you give me just a hint of what it's all about, before you put on my trousers?

RHODA: I shouldn't be a minute in putting them on.

GERALD: No, I don't take long putting them on – well, you'd better put them on.

RHODA: Yes – but – *(Looking around at door on balcony L.)*

GERALD: Oh yes. Here you are. *(Opening door R. and switching on light.)* The study.

RHODA: Thanks awfully. I think you'd better shut the door.

GERALD: Oh, I was – *(Holding door open D.R.)* – I'm going to shut the door.

RHODA: No – I mean that front door.

GERALD: Oh! Why?

RHODA: You'll understand when I tell you.

*She goes into study.*

*He shuts study door, crosses to table, takes cigarette case from his pocket and puts cigarette in his mouth deep in thought; he takes his match-box out of his pocket, strikes a match and lights cigarette; still gazing at door D.R., he absent-mindedly throws cigarette away and puts the lighted match almost in his mouth. This brings him back to earth, he picks up his cigarette and starts to smoke; he looks thoughtfully straight in front and whistles quietly to himself.*

*From outside comes the sound of the dog barking. This is checked by a weird foreign command in the distance: 'Hoi – Na-na-na-na!' GERALD picks up bath gown and throws it on portmanteau L., goes to door R.C., opens it. There is the sound of a blow.*

*RHODA enters from study on the sound of whip – blue striped pyjamas – trousers over her feet; she wears the dressing gown. Then the voice again: 'Zo! Na-na!' – whip again. GERALD closes the front door.*

GERALD: Are those noises anything to do with you?

RHODA: Yes *(Cross to front of table nervously.)*; that's my step-father and his dog Conrad.

GERALD: *(Cross C. above table.)* Oh, really! It doesn't sound too good, does it?

RHODA: *(Nervously.)* No, I'd better tell you everything. *(Sits on table C.)*

GERALD: Oh, don't sit on that. *(Indicating settee L.)* This is softer.

RHODA: Thank you. *(Crosses to settee L.)*

GERALD: That's all right.

RHODA: As I say, *(Sitting on back of settee.)* that's my step-father; he's a German. His name is Putz.

GERALD: Putz? *(Sitting on settee up stage.)*

RHODA: Yes. P-u-t-z. I live with him and a housekeeper. Her name is Nutts – Mrs Nutts.

GERALD: Putz and Nutts?

RHODA: Yes.

GERALD: Is this quite true?

RHODA: Yes.

GERALD: Oh! Well, go on.

RHODA: Well, first of all, I'll tell you what's happened tonight. That's easily told. My step-father has run me out.

GERALD: What?

RHODA: That's his own expression for it. I annoyed him; so just after I'd gone to bed he came up and took me up in his arms and ran me out. *(She demonstrates this with a little sound,* 'Ph't!'.*)*

GERALD: You mean to tell me he ran you out in your pyjamas – ph't?

RHODA: Yes, and slammed the door on me. He wouldn't let me stay in the house any longer.

GERALD: He must be very hard to please.

RHODA: Yes, that's his way. He makes rules, and if I disobey them that's how he treats me. He did it once before. But he came and took me back then.

GERALD: But what did you do tonight?

RHODA: Oh, nothing really. Simply a trifle. Only it was against his orders. He wouldn't have found out only Nutts split.

GERALD: But what was this forbidden thing?

RHODA: I ate wurts.

GERALD: You did what, in heaven's name?

RHODA: I ate wurts – wurtleberries – a local Somerset fruit – wurts.

GERALD: You ate wurts and Nutts split? It sounds like a fruit salad. But you mean to say that when Nutts split to Putz he ran you out for eating wurts?

RHODA: He dislikes wurts.

GERALD: Dislikes them! He must loathe the very sound of wurts! *(Goes up C.)*

RHODA: They leave a nasty stain on the face.

GERALD: You ought to have put them in your mouth.

RHODA: Well, that is all it was. He found I'd disobeyed him and eaten the forbidden fruit. So he ran me out.

GERALD: *(Closing portmanteau.)* Is he quite sane?

RHODA: Oh yes. But very Prussian and masterful.

GERALD: But why do you stay with him?

RHODA: *(Stepping off settee and cross to face back of settee D.L.)* Because I promised my mother before she died that I'd stick to him.

GERALD: Not a very easy promise to keep if he runs you out.

RHODA: No. I'm through with it now. When he recovers his temper he'll try and get me back. But I'm not *going* back this time.

GERALD: Quite right. Don't you. I never heard of such a thing. Wurts. But – where will you go tonight?

RHODA: *(Softly, quite genuinely at a loss.)* I don't know.

GERALD: Don't you know anyone here you can go to?

RHODA: *(Shaking her head.)* None of the people here will have anything to do with *me.*

GERALD: Why?

RHODA: I don't know them. Besides, one of them invented a scandalous story about me.

GERALD: *(Cross to above settee L.)* About *you* – a dear little innocent girl like you?

RHODA: Yes. A woman here started the rumour that I wasn't really his step-daughter, but – something else.

GERALD: What woman said that? *(Moves towards RHODA.)*

RHODA: Oh, one of these seaside residential cats.

GERALD: Was it Mrs Twine?

RHODA: Yes. How did you know?

GERALD: By experience. Mrs Twine is my sister-in-law.

RHODA: Oh, I'm sorry. *(Apologizing.)*

GERALD: Oh, don't apologize. I'm delighted to hear nasty things about her. So Mrs *Twine* said that about you, did she? *(Crosses to front of settee.)*

RHODA: Yes. The whole place believes it now.

GERALD: Right. *(Crosses to C.)* If Mrs Twine said that, I'll do anything in the world to help you. There!

RHODA: *(Crosses to Gerald with a little run.)* You're very kind, but if it's going to mean any bother to you –

GERALD: I don't care. Now this man Putz. You must go back there tonight, of course. But come here in the morning.

RHODA: *(Nods, crossing to L.C.)* I'll do whatever you think right. I have been lucky to meet *you. (Moves close to GERALD.)*

GERALD: *(Smiles, pleased.)* Yes.

RHODA: But I'll only go back there for one reason, and that's because you ask me to.

GERALD: Yes. It's very nice of you to say that about me.

RHODA: Perhaps he won't take me back now. *(Nervously.)*

GERALD: Oh, I'll soon see to that. I'll come over with you and talk to Mr Putz.

*A loud rap at the front door up R.*

RHODA: I think he's saved you the trouble. *(Crosses to behind settee.)*

GERALD: Wait there. I'll see. *(Cross to door R.C. calls.)* Who is it? *(Very nervously, but trying to put on a bold front.)*

PUTZ: *(Heard outside.)* Open, please.

RHODA: Yes. That's him.

GERALD: *(She crosses up L.)* Come in. The door's not locked.

*The door is opened, but only slightly. PUTZ enters backwards, keeping his dog out. He is a finely built German, wearing loose cloth trousers and a white alpaca coat like a dentist.*

PUTZ: *(To the dog, as he enters R.C.)* No, no. Hoi! Stay out from heah!

*He gets in, closes door, turns and, taking horn-rimmed glasses from his pocket, takes stock of GERALD. His manner is quarrelsome. He sees RHODA and exclaims.*

Ah! Alzo!

GERALD: Are you Mr Putz?

PUTZ: You are who? *(Cross D.R. to GERALD.)*

GERALD: I've just been told –

PUTZ: You are who? Speak it out.

GERALD: How dare you run this girl out. Take her back at once.

PUTZ: I do not care for you.

GERALD: I don't care very much for you – take her back.

PUTZ: *(Advancing angrily, at which GERALD retires a little.)* You are who to say of what I shall make?

GERALD: I beg your pardon?

PUTZ: You are who – ?

GERALD: Eh?

PUTZ: You are who?

GERALD: Don't bark at me like that. You ran her out in her pyjamas.

PUTZ: Vell? *(Becoming still more threatening.)*

GERALD: Vell, I mean – I mean – you mustn't do things like that. It's –

PUTZ: *(Advancing again, loudly.)* It is *vot?*

GERALD: *(Stepping away.)* Well, it's – it's very naughty.

PUTZ: You – are – who? *(Slowly.)*

GERALD: Yes – I – am. But I don't see it comes into it at all.

PUTZ: Speak!

GERALD: Dash it. I'm speaking as quick as I can. Just because she ate a few – wu –

RHODA: *(Prompting him.)* Wurts.

GERALD: Wurts.

PUTZ: It is not only that she eat die vurrt. It is that she disobey me to eat die vurrt. *(Crosses door R.C.)*

RHODA: I've had enough of your orders. I'll come back tonight and I'll leave tomorrow.

PUTZ: Zo? You t'ink? Eh?

RHODA: Yes. I've kept my promise long enough. When I go, my mother's money goes with me.

PUTZ: *(Furious.)* Too much. You t'ink you can command me. *(Advancing towards her.)* Herr Gott! I show you –

GERALD: *(Stepping between them.)* Stop that, you rude – rude Putz. *(Takes a drink of whisky.)*

PUTZ: *(Challenging him, quivering.)* What you make?

GERALD: I'll show you what I make. Now, you – please – step-daughter –

RHODA: Yes?

*GERALD still facing PUTZ. PUTZ walks up and down furiously.*

GERALD: *(Pointing to door on balcony L.)* That room up there – that's your room. The bathroom's next door and the other bedrooms is elsewhere. You'd better go up at once.

RHODA: Very well. *(To the stairs L.)*

GERALD: If there's anything else you want, let me know.

RHODA: Thank you.

*Exit up stairs L.*

*PUTZ turns his head to watch her enter the room, so does GERALD. She goes in.*

GERALD: *(To PUTZ.)* You hear that. Zo! And now I'll come to your house and get some of her clothes.

PUTZ: No.

GERALD: Yes. *(Leaning his elbow on table for support.)*

PUTZ: Nein.

GERALD: Ten.

PUTZ: Finish.

GERALD: Good!

PUTZ: If you come to my house I will call my dog and have you run out.

GERALD: If you go on like this I'll call the police and have you run in.

PUTZ: Nah! *(Crosses D.R.)*

*GERALD takes another drink.*

GERALD: *(With an effort.)* Now don't be a naughty boy. *(Going to door R.C.)* Come on.

*PUTZ stays still R. As GERALD opens door R.C., PUTZ makes a sudden ejaculation to the dog outside.*

PUTZ: Tzt! Putta-putta!

*There is a sound of furious canine attack from outside. GERALD hastily closes the door again.*

GERALD: I see. You have to be protected by a dog, do you?

PUTZ: *(Feeling his biceps.)* No, no. Also Swedish drill – first certificate. *(He starts to do Swedish drill.)* Ein, zwei, drei, vier – Frisch, from, frühlisch, frei.

GERALD: I don't care about your fried fish. Give me her clothes or I'll keep her as she is.

PUTZ: Das ist mir egal.

GERALD: All right –

PUTZ: Finish. I go.

GERALD: In that room.

PUTZ: Das ist mir schnuppe.

GERALD: Half in her pyjamas and half in mine.

PUTZ: Too much. Finish. *(Opening door.)* Und if you follow my dog shall run you out. *(He goes, slamming the door behind him, shouting at dog.)*

*Pause and bus. GERALD smells whisky as a tonic – cue for RHODA – she opens bedroom door again.*

GERALD: All right, he's gone; come down.

RHODA: What happened – was he very cross? *(She comes down L.C. a little nervous.)*

GERALD: I ran him out. I don't mind doing that sort of thing. Do you mean to say that man is content to leave you here all night long with a stranger?

RHODA: That's just like him. *(Leaning on table C.)* Anything rather than give way and say he was in the wrong. My poor mother used to admire it.

GERALD: Still, I don't suppose he ran your poor mother out in her nighty all over the shop.

RHODA: No, she was very happy with him.

GERALD: She wasn't, I suppose, cursed with this craving for wurts?

RHODA: She used to say he was what a man was really *meant* to be.

GERALD: That depends who meant it.

RHODA: Yes – *(Pause.)* – I suppose so.

*They both laugh with embarrassment.*

Well, what am I meant to do?

GERALD: Well, I'm not quite sure. You see *we* know what's happened, and we know it's true. But I ask you, would anyone else believe it?

RHODA: But where do you think I'd better go? *(Smiling.)*

GERALD: You'd better go to bed. I don't see where else you *can* go in those.

*(RHODA crosses L. to stairway. She is very shy and looks around twice as she crosses.)*

Wait a minute. What are we going to do if Mrs Twine comes back?

RHODA: Mrs Twine – she won't come here, will she?

GERALD: She may; my cousin's coming back anyway – he's all right – but she might come back too.

RHODA: Well, couldn't I lurk somewhere? *(Looks at door D.L.)* What's in there?

GERALD: The kitchen quarters. Perhaps you could lurk in there?

RHODA: *(Opens kitchen door.)* She wouldn't come in here, would she? *(Goes in.)*

GERALD: No, I don't think so.

RHODA: *(Off L.)* There are some back stairs here.

GERALD: Well, there you are. If she goes in there you could nip up the back stairs.

RHODA: *(Returning.)* Yes, that's quite safe.

*A knock at the front door. He turns. She speaks in a whisper.*

Is that your cousin?

GERALD: No, he'd come straight in.

RHODA: There you are then. *(Turns L.)* Kitchen, and back stairs if necessary. *(GERALD nods.)*

GERALD: You've only got one step-father I suppose? *(She goes quietly off L., closing the kitchen door.)*

*Picks up bottle as protector; crosses to front door and calls.*

Who is it?

*No reply is heard. He opens front door. It is TWINE.*

TWINE: *(Heartily.)* Hallo! *(Entering.)*

GERALD: No.

TWINE: Welcome to Chumpton.

GERALD: Who said so?

TWINE: Clave told us you were here.

GERALD: Where *is* Clave? *(Edging towards L. in front of table L.)*

TWINE: Behind with Gertrude.

GERALD: But I want to go to bed.

TWINE: *(Cross L.C. following GERALD.)* I'm sorry. Gertrude
    would come. She insisted.

GERALD: Go and meet her and tell her I'm just going to bed.
    *(At foot of stairs.)*

TWINE: Yes, but that's just it. She wants to come and see you –

GERALD: See me going to bed?

TWINE: No. To see you that you're all sort of –

GERALD: Sort of what?

TWINE: Well, sort of O.K.

GERALD: Then run quickly and meet her and tell her I am AI.

TWINE: *(Stubbornly.)* No, I don't –

GERALD: Well, I do. *(Up the stairs a little.)*

GERTRUDE: *(Off.)* Come along Clive!

CLIVE: *(Off.)* All right.

TWINE: Here she is. *(L. of table C.)*

GERALD: *(Turning back into hall.)* Curse!

    *GERTRUDE enters with CLIVE.*

    *Before looking at GERALD, GERTRUDE surveys the disorder of the
    hall with severity. CLIVE and GERALD interchange glances of protest
    and helplessness respectively. GERTRUDE catches them at it.*

GERTRUDE: *(Cross to above table C.)* Well, this is a nice time to
    arrive!

GERALD: Oh, don't apologize.

GERTRUDE: You seem to have made the place in a beautiful
    muddle.

GERALD: Yes, that's right. I did that so that I could clear it up.
    *(At foot of stairs.)*

45

GERTRUDE: So this is what happens directly you get away from Clara. *(Cross L.C. to GERALD.)*

GERALD: What do you mean? *(Anxiously.)*

GERTRUDE: All this mess. *(Indicating the mess in the hall.)* Is mother very seedy? Will she and Clara be coming soon?

GERALD: I hope not.

*TWINE at back of stage, looking over L. shoulder at CLIVE and GERTRUDE.*

GERTRUDE: What?

GERALD: I hope mother's not very seedy.

GERTRUDE: H'm! Which room are you going to? *(Looking up to balcony L.)* That double room?

GERALD: Yes, that's the one Mrs Lightfoot said.

*TWINE up L.C. looking over L. shoulder with back to audience.*

*CLIVE R.C., GERTRUDE L.C., GERALD D.L.*

GERTRUDE: I think that room had better be left. Clara may want to sleep with mother.

GERALD: Well, I don't mind.

GERTRUDE: I'd better just see. *(Going upstairs.)*

GERALD: Yes.

GERTRUDE: Come up with me, please.

GERALD: *(Following.)* But surely I can sleep in that room *tonight?*

GERTRUDE: That would only give trouble, moving your things about. *(Opens door of bedroom.)*

*(GERALD looks down at CLIVE, who is helping himself to another whisky R.C., and they exchange looks of sympathetic affliction.)*

Now let me see. What other rooms are there?

*She goes towards R., GERALD following.*

TWINE: Can I help at all, dear? *(Standing C., looking up at GERTRUDE.)*

GERTRUDE: *(Going off at R. end of landing.)* No – stay where you are.

46

GERALD: *(Leaning over banisters, to TWINE.)* You can move about a bit, you know.

*She goes off R. of landing, followed by GERALD.*

GERTRUDE: *(Off.)* Now this looks a good room. What's the matter with this?

GERALD: *(Off.)* I don't know. I haven't been in there yet.

*TWINE sits L., near kitchen door. CLIVE sits on table.*

CLIVE: *(With a sigh – after a slight pause.)* Go on, boy, now's your chance. Have a nibble at your straw hat.

TWINE: *(Who has turned his head towards kitchen door.)* Hush a moment.

CLIVE: What's the matter?

TWINE: I thought I heard something. *(Rising.)*

CLIVE: *(Unexcited.)* Heard – what?

TWINE: *(Cross L. to door D.L. and listening, looking at CLIVE.)* I thought I heard a sort of sound.

CLIVE: Don't be a fool, Harold.

TWINE: Oh, it's a cat.

CLIVE: Don't you let that cat out here.

TWINE: Poor thing – it's mewing.

CLIVE: Well, let it mew.

TWINE: Perhaps it's lost its milk.

CLIVE: What do you mean, lost its milk?

TWINE: Poor pussy! *(Opening kitchen door.)* Where are you? Come along. *(In practical tones.)* It's all right, come out.

RHODA: *(Voice off.)* Thank goodness!

*(TWINE falls back amazed. CLIVE leaps into a sitting attitude. RHODA sails out into the doorway.)*

I was getting cramp. *(She sees them, claps a hand to her mouth and hurries back again, closing the door.)*

*TWINE stands back L.C., open-mouthed. CLIVE leaps to his feet and crosses L. There is a crash in the kitchen.*

CLIVE: Ye Gods! Where did he find that?

TWINE: It's the girl from up the road.

CLIVE: Oh! Then me for up the road.

GERTRUDE: What was that noise?

*GERTRUDE and GERALD heard up R. CLIVE closes kitchen door, turn C.*

CLIVE: Not a word. On your honour, Twine. Leave it to me.

TWINE: All right.

*GERTRUDE and GERALD on balcony.*

*Table*

*Settee*

*TWINE C., CLIVE D.L.*

*GERALD, as he enters up R. and comes downstairs L., wildly alarmed.*

GERALD: Well, I don't know. Stay there and I'll see.

*GERTRUDE appears and follows GERALD down. CLIVE turns to them blandly.*

GERTRUDE: What was that noise?

CLIVE: It's all right. It's Harold.

GERALD: But that noise?

CLIVE: That's right. Harold.

*GERALD crosses to L. in front of settee.*

He went in the kitchen.

GERALD: *(Alarmed.)* In the kitchen? Why?

GERTRUDE: Did you make that noise, Harold? *(Coming down and crossing to C.)*

*Table*

*TWINE C., GERTRUDE L.C., GERALD L., CLIVE D.L.*

CLIVE: Yes, he did.

GERALD: *(To CLIVE.)* But why did he go in the kitchen?

CLIVE: Good job he did. Next time he wants to make a noise like that he'd better go in the garden.

GERTRUDE: What was it? Why did you go in there, and what happened?

GERALD: *(To CLIVE.)* Leave this to me. *(Cross to L.C.)*

GERTRUDE: *(To TWINE.)* Why did you go in the kitchen?

CLIVE: I told him to.

GERTRUDE: I'm asking *him. (To TWINE.)* Why did you?

TWINE: I heard a mew.

GERTRUDE: A what?

TWINE: A mew, dear. I heard mews.

CLIVE: Don't be stupid. A mew is a sort of sea-gull.

GERALD: Mews are stables.

TWINE: Well, then, a mi-ow. I heard a mi-ow.

CLIVE: Oh, don't be a baby. He heard the cat.

GERTRUDE: Did you hear the cat?

TWINE: Yes, dear.

CLIVE: He went to let the cat out.

GERALD: *(To CLIVE.)* And *did* he let the cat out?

CLIVE: *(Quickly to GERALD.)* Yes, a beauty.

GERALD: I see. He ran up against something?

CLIVE: He certainly did.

GERALD: Oh, I'd better have a look. *(Opens kitchen door and goes in saying as he goes.)* Look out!

GERTRUDE: *(Turning L.)* What do you mean – look out?

*CLIVE gets in front of GERTRUDE; they bump.*

GERALD: I mean, look out if you're coming here. There are saucepans all over the floor.

*CLIVE intentionally obstructs GERTRUDE from going into the kitchen by standing in front of the doorway looking in.*

CLIVE: *(To GERALD.)* Is it all right?

GERALD: Yes, old boy, it's all right now.

GERTRUDE: *(Pushes past CLIVE.)* Clear out of the way now. What a nuisance you are, Harold!

*Goes in. CLIVE cross C. to R. of TWINE.*

*GERALD returns and come hastily down to the other two.*

GERALD: You saw? *(Confidentially.)*

CLIVE: Yes, but not long enough.

GERALD: And you saw? *(Nervously to TWINE.)*

>   *GERALD takes TWINE's left arm and CLIVE his right.*

TWINE: Yes.

>   *Then the three cross R.C. arm-in-arm.*

GERALD: Listen, quick! It's on the level. She was driven from home. She had to come here. But don't tell Gertrude.

CLIVE: No, no.

TWINE: Oh, I say, but –

GERALD: But nothing. As man to man – swear not to say a word.

TWINE: Oh, but it's awful.

CLIVE: It isn't.

GERALD: It isn't. Come round early tomorrow and I'll tell you all. Till then, swear!

CLIVE: Go on. Swear, blast you!

TWINE: Oh!

GERALD: You're always in the vocative. Swear!

CLIVE: Hurry up! Swear!

TWINE: Oh, botheration!

CLIVE: Not that kind of swear, you fool! Promise.

TWINE: Well, I daren't tell Gertrude that that girl's here.

GERALD: Daren't? That's all right. That's a swear. And come round in the morning early.

TWINE: But the harm will be done by then.

GERALD: Harm? There's no harm, I tell you.

CLIVE: Of course not, you evil-minded little man.

>   *GERTRUDE appearing at kitchen door D.L.*

GERTRUDE: Harold!

>   *CLIVE and GERALD pretend to be having a joke with TWINE.*

GERALD: Harold's just told a beauty.

TWINE: Oh, what, dear?

GERTRUDE: Are you going to leave me to pick all these things up?

TWINE: *(Cross L. to her.)* No, dear.

GERTRUDE: I should hope not.

*They go, leaving kitchen door open.*

*CLIVE and GERALD cross C.*

CLIVE: *(To GERALD.)* Now then, you naughty boy. Explain this windfall.

GERALD: A perfectly innocent, sweet little girl driven from home.

CLIVE: Go on.

GERALD: True. You wait till you see her.

CLIVE: I'm going to. But Gertrude'll see her now.

GERALD: No, she won't. She's gone up the back stairs. But you must help.

CLIVE: With pleasure.

*Voices heard off.*

GERALD: She's got to stay here tonight. What shall I do? I can't stay here alone with her.

CLIVE: No, you oughtn't to.

GERALD: I know. You ought to stay here too. Can't you manage it?

CLIVE: I ought to.

GERALD: You must if you can.

CLIVE: Well, you ask Gertrude.

GERALD: No, you ask her.

CLIVE: It would seem better coming from you.

GERALD: No, but you lie better than I do.

CLIVE: Do I? All right. I'll have a pop.

GERTRUDE: *(Off.)* Leave things alone.

*Enter D.L.*

GERALD: Go on then. Now.

*GERTRUDE and TWINE reappear from kitchen. She is still upbraiding TWINE. Closes door.*

CLIVE: *(Cross to GERTRUDE.)* Oh, Gert – *(Stops to look back at GERALD, who prods him.)*

*Table*

*GERALD C., CLIVE C., GERTRUDE L.C., TWINE L.*

GERTRUDE: *(Coldly.)* Gert?

GERALD: *(Aside to CLIVE.)* That's a bad start, old boy.

CLIVE: No, Gertrude. Er – we thought it wouldn't be a bad idea if I stayed here, just for tonight, with Gerald.

GERTRUDE: Why?

CLIVE: *(To GERALD.)* Why?

GERALD: You know why, old boy, I told you.

GERTRUDE: Well? Why?

GERALD: *(Cross to GERTRUDE.)* You see – the daily woman isn't coming till eight-thirty; earlier than that she cannot be – and I oversleep – and he doesn't – do you?

CLIVE: Yes.

GERALD: Yes. And I want to be up early – because I want to have lunch before breakfast at seven – or half-past – well, a quarter to eight – and –

GERTRUDE: What are you talking about?

GERALD: Dinner. *(Crosses up L. of table to behind table C.)*

CLIVE: *(Cross to GERTRUDE.)* No – simply – I'd like to stay with him.

GERTRUDE: You're staying with me, aren't you?

CLIVE: Oh yes.

GERTRUDE: Very well then. Come along. I'm going now. *(Cross to door R.C.)* Harold!

TWINE: Yes, dear.

CLIVE: All right then. You go ahead, you two – I'm just coming.

GERTRUDE: *(To CLIVE.)* You can catch us up. I'm not going to hang about.

*Exit R.C.*

GERALD: *(Seizing TWINE as he is following.)* Remember, Twine – you've sworn.

TWINE: Oh, misery me!

GERALD: Haven't you?

TWINE: I'm not going to keep my mouth shut indefinitely.

CLIVE: You've sworn, until tomorrow.

TWINE: Oh-h!

GERALD: Haven't you?

TWINE: Very well. Yes.

GERTRUDE: *(Heard off.)* Harold!

CLIVE: Don't hang about. Go on.

GERALD: Go on. Get out.

*TWINE exits up R.C., leaving door open.*

*Door open.*

CLIVE: Well, you made a nice show of asking Gertrude.

GERALD: You said you'd ask her, and didn't.

CLIVE: How could I, when you were standing there blathering a lot of tripe about early lunch – seven-thirty – eight-fifteen?

GERALD: Well, don't blame me, and if you stay here long she may get suspicious and question Twine.

CLIVE: He won't tell.

GERALD: Don't give him the chance.

CLIVE: Dash it, he's bound to get the chance. He sleeps with her.

GERALD: Yes, poor devil!

CLIVE: Gerald, just let's have another *look*.

GERALD: All right – shut the door.

*CLIVE shuts the front door R.V. GERALD calls upstairs.*

Hi! Step!

*RHODA appears at L. end of landing. She is anxious again and penitent.*

RHODA: Is it all clear now?

GERALD: Yes, she's gone.

RHODA: *(Coming downstairs L., pointing to door.)* I thought Mr Twine was with you.

GERALD: Yes, but *Mrs* didn't see you.

RHODA: *Mr* did.

GERALD: That's all right. Don't worry. This is my cousin I told you about. Clive Popkiss – same name as me. I'm Gerald Popkiss.

CLIVE: How d'ye do?

GERALD: Very likely he'll help us tomorrow.

CLIVE: There's no very likely about it. He's going to.

RHODA: *(Who has come half-way downstairs.)* Thank you.

CLIVE: Oh, you wait until tomorrow.

GERTRUDE: *(Voice heard outside.)* Clive!

*General scurry. RHODA runs up to the landing, stands at back of balcony up L.*

CLIVE AND GERALD: Look out! Quick! Gertrude! *Etc.*

*GERTRUDE opens front door. RHODA is hidden from her by the floor of the landing jutting out into the hall, under which GERTRUDE stands.*

GERALD: What was that you said?

CLIVE: *(Cross R. referring to golf bag R.)* This is a nice top.

GERTRUDE: *(To CLIVE.)* Why have you shut this door again? Will you please come along at once? *(She turns indignantly and goes out again.)*

CLIVE: Oh, sorry, Gertrude. *(Going.)* Well, I'll have to go, old boy. *(Looks up smiling at RHODA.)* Good night, old boy.

GERALD: Good night, Clive, old boy.

*CLIVE goes, leaving door open.*

*CLIVE comes back to door, looks up at RHODA and smiles.*

CLIVE: Good night. *(To GERALD.)* Good night, Gerald.

GERALD: Good night, Clive, old boy.

CLIVE: Good night.

GERTRUDE: *(Heard off.)* Clive!

CLIVE: Blast!!

*Exits R.C. closes door.*

*GERALD is staring straight in front.*

*RHODA exits into bedroom L. GERALD sits on the sofa, preparatory to turning in.*

*CURTAIN*

# Act Two

*The hall next morning. Bright sunshine is seen through the open doorway. The hall has been cleared and the portmanteau and unpacking have disappeared.*

*GERALD and CLIVE in fresh, clean attire are talking things over.*

*CLIVE at door R.C., GERALD on settee L. up stage.*

GERALD: So that's the whole story of why she came here.

CLIVE: 'M.

GERALD: What do you think of it?

CLIVE: *(With a grimace.)* I believe it, of course. *(Cross to above table.)*

GERALD: But you don't think anyone else would?

CLIVE: Oh, I don't know. The marines *might*.

GERALD: I know it sounds unlikely. I told her so last night.

CLIVE: It sounds a great deal worse this morning. *(Crosses to above table.)*

GERALD: Why? I haven't seen her since last night.

CLIVE: I quite believe that too. But I wouldn't press that even on a marine.

GERALD: You don't think Clara would accuse me?

CLIVE: *(Shrugs, crosses behind to table L.C.)* I don't know. You see, you've been married such a short time.

GERALD: Yes. *(Smiling.)* That's an advantage.

CLIVE: Is it?

GERALD: *(His face falling.)* Isn't it?

CLIVE: Well, you can't have broken her in much in six weeks. *(Sits on table, L. corner up stage.)*

GERALD: Oh no, old boy. I'm sure she'll trust me.

CLIVE: Oh, good. I hope so, I'm sure.

GERALD: I'm certain she will. Our first night apart. *(Rising, cross D.L.)* Good Lord!

CLIVE: Well, that's all right then. You know her best.

GERALD: Yes. Oh, Clara won't suspect me for a moment.

CLIVE: Fine. There you are, then.

GERALD: I mean, of course, if she doesn't hear anything about it.

CLIVE: Oh, I thought you meant you'd tell her.

GERALD: Tell her? Oh, why? If we get this girl away there'll be nothing to tell. *(Cross R.C.)*

CLIVE: If Gertrude finds out – Clara will be told all right.

GERALD: She'll be told all wrong. If there's a chance of that I must tell Clara first.

CLIVE: Oh yes, old boy. I should tell her in any case. You know – airily, as if you had nothing on your conscience – I should say *(Acting.)* Ha! Rather funny thing happened the other night. A little girl drifted in here – pretty little thing she was – no, perhaps you hadn't better say that – driven from home.

GERALD: You think that sounds as if you've nothing on your conscience?

CLIVE: Well, it's difficult for me to say what a married man's conscience is like – me being single mine's rather elastic. *(Crosses R. to front of table.)*

GERALD: Much better get the girl some clothes and take her away.

CLIVE: Yes, you're quite right. *(An afterthought.)* What's the time?

GERALD: *(Looking at his watch.)* Oh, about a quarter-past.

CLIVE: A quarter-past eight?

GERALD: Yes.

CLIVE: *(Jumping up.)* Well, what about eight-thirty?

GERALD: What?

CLIVE: The daily woman, you fool.

GERALD: Good Lord, yes. Eight-thirty. Earlier than that she cannot be. *(Looks over at kitchen and crosses R. to CLIVE.)* What shall we do? She's got the back door key.

CLIVE: Stop her getting to the back door, that's all.

GERALD: What – you mean go and meet her?

CLIVE: Yes, and tell her not to come.

GERALD: *(Crossing to door R.C.)* You come *with* me. You can tackle her better than I can.

CLIVE: All right. You go to one gate. I'll go to the other. You never know which way she's coming; these fat women live in all directions.

*They exit R.C. CLIVE goes off R. GERALD is seen going off L., leaving door open.*

*RHODA comes out of bedroom L and looks out of the window C. of balcony; she stretches her arms as she looks out.*

*Then the kitchen door is opened and in comes MRS LEVERETT. Surprised to see the front door open, she crosses towards it and looks out. She has already removed her hat and left it in the kitchen. She stands beneath the canopy of jutting landing. By standing where she is MRS LEVERETT can see without being seen. Her expression becomes one of furious amazement as she hears RHODA call.*

RHODA: *(Comes to front of balcony and looks down into hall – calling softly.)* Mr Popkiss! Mr Popkiss!

*No reply. RHODA turns and goes back into the bedroom, again closing the door. MRS LEVERETT comes forth from her hiding-place as though in a sort of indignant trance. Then she rouses herself to action; hurries into the kitchen; hurries out again, putting on her hat as she does so and, after taking another look at the bedroom door, goes quickly away through the kitchen. Closes door.*

*Voices are heard outside R.C. The first person who appears is TWINE, who is in plus fours. He is speaking over his shoulder as he enters R.C. from R.*

TWINE: Well, now that I am here – *(Anxiously.)* come inside, please. *(Cross to R. of table.)*

CLIVE: *(Following.)* Why? *(Cross door R.C.)*

TWINE: I don't want to be seen.

CLIVE: Oh, I shouldn't worry. You look fairly all right.

TWINE: No, but I told Gertrude I'd go to the golf club. She asked where you were. I said I didn't know.

CLIVE: I see. And you came over here because of your last night's swear?

TWINE: I felt it my duty to come here.

CLIVE: And I don't believe you'd have come at all, if I hadn't caught you dithering at the gate.

TWINE: You don't seem to realize. I told Gertrude I was going straight up to the golf club. *(Turning away.)* I've told her a lie.

CLIVE: Oh, that's nothing. You'll do better than that.

TWINE: Oh, but, Clave –

CLIVE: What?

TWINE: *(With emotion.)* What is all this terrible affair? It must be *stopped. (Close to CLIVE's face.)*

CLIVE: Quite right, old boy; we'll stop it between us. All boys together.

TWINE: No, no; I won't be mixed up in it. I've already *lied* to Gertrude. I'm feeling very uncomfortable.

CLIVE: What, already? You *wait.*

*GERALD returns breathlessly from running past windows. Enters R.C., cross to L., looks in kitchen.*

GERALD: I've looked right down the road – there's no sign of that daily woman.

*CLIVE R., TWINE R.C.*

CLIVE: Well, if she comes, we'll get rid of her somehow. I was just telling Harold – now *he's* here to help us, we'll get on better.

GERALD: *(Crossing to R. of table, taking TWINE's hand.)* Indeed, yes. Thank you, Harold.

TWINE: Oh –

*CLIVE R., TWINE R.C., GERALD (front of table).*

CLIVE: No, no – stop that!

GERALD: Yes – from the start, Harold, that 'oh' business is out.

TWINE: I've lied to my wife.

GERALD: You have? Stout fellow! A very good beginning.

TWINE: Oh, don't, please! This is not the time for funning.

CLIVE: There you are. The very first comment he makes. Sound common sense. *(Slapping TWINE on the back.)*

GERALD: Yes. Bravo, Harold!

CLIVE: Now, first of all, you've got to believe, Harold, that that girl is a pure, nice, good, innocent little child.

GERALD: Absolutely. I know it's hard for you to believe, Harold because a man like you – a man of the world, who's knocked about with all sorts of wild women –

CLIVE: Yes, of course – when a man like this sees a girl in your house, naturally he leaps to conclusions.

GERALD: Leaps – why, he bounds!

CLIVE: Yes, the old scoundrel – he's been knee-deep in daisies many a time.

TWINE: Oh –

CLIVE: Ah!

GERALD: Another 'oh' and we shall have to swear you about it.

TWINE: The girl's got a very queer reputation, anyhow.

GERALD: Yes, and who queered it?

CLIVE: Now, look here, Twine. Experience may have made you a cynic about women. *(Crosses down R.)* Possibly you may have been stung once too often. *(Coming back R.C.)* But, believe me, old boy, there can still be such a thing as a good girl.

GERALD: Yes, Harold. Even in the same town as you.

TWINE: Then why should she be here – at night, in –

CLIVE: In what?

TWINE: *(Hesitating.)* Well, wearing those things –

GERALD: She was run out.

TWINE: What?

CLIVE: She had trouble at home. You know what trouble at home is, don't you?

TWINE: Yes.

CLIVE: Yes, none better.

GERALD: You'd better see her for yourself and judge. *(Crosses L.C.)*

TWINE: Why, good *heavens*, is she *still* here?

GERALD: Yes, of course she is – up in that bedroom. I'll introduce you. *(Turns to go upstairs L.)*

TWINE: *(Cross in front of table to L.C.)* No, no, no. I'm going to golf. *(Edging towards R.C. door.)*

CLIVE AND GERALD: *(Who pause incredulously on stairs.)* Golf?

TWINE: Yes, I'd rather go to golf.

CLIVE: You'd rather golf than see this girl?

TWINE: Much.

GERALD: You'd rather golf *much*? *(At top of stairs L.)*

TWINE: Yes. Not only that, I told Gertrude. Besides, I've got a match.

CLIVE: But dash it, man, noblesse oblige.

GERALD: Yes and honi soit – you stay there. *(Goes to bedroom door up L. and knocks.)*

RHODA: *(From inside bedroom.)* Come in.

GERALD: No, you come out.

*RHODA appears.*

RHODA: Good morning.

GERALD: Good morning.

RHODA: *(To CLIVE.)* Good morning.

CLIVE: *(Heartily.)* Good morning.

*GERALD goes down two or three stairs L. Introduction.*

GERALD: Here we are. Mr Harold Twine – Miss Rhoda Something.

RHODA: Good morning. Rhoda Marley, my name is.

CLIVE: *(To TWINE.)* Go on – How do you do?

TWINE: *(Unable to resist.)* How do you do?

CLIVE: Good! Well, now that you've how do you done, just look at that girl.

GERALD: *(Beaming at RHODA.)* Yes.

CLIVE: I mean, can you, Harold – can you possibly suspect?

TWINE: *(Feebly.)* N-n-no.

GERALD: No. Come on, heartily, Harold. *No.*

CLIVE: Perish the thought.

TWINE: Yes, certainly.

CLIVE: Go on then. Let's hear it.

TWINE: Perish the thought.

> *CLIVE cross R.*

> *GERALD brings RHODA downstairs L. to L.C.*

GERALD: And you admit that Gertrude was and is wrong in saying things about her?

TWINE: I don't know. *(Cross L.C.)*

GERALD: You *do* know, Harold.

TWINE: Oh dear, well – yes.

GERALD: So now it is your duty to make amends.

CLIVE: That's right. And to do what we tell you to help Miss Marley.

TWINE: I can't make any promise, but I'll tell you what I'll do. I'll tell Gertrude –

GERALD: What!

CLIVE: You blithering idiot!

TWINE: No, now Clave. *(To CLIVE.)* Gerald, I'll tell Gertrude I think she's made a mistake.

RHODA: *(Quickly – as CLIVE and GERALD protest.)* Please, Mr Twine!

TWINE: What?

RHODA: I'd rather you didn't tell Mrs Twine I'm here.

CLIVE: Of course he won't. Don't you worry.

TWINE: *(Obstinately.)* Then I'll take no part in it at all. And in any case I've got to go to golf now. *(Turns up R.)*

*GERALD crosses back to table to TWINE as he attempts to go; pushes him towards L. and goes to door. TWINE crosses R. to CLIVE as he speaks line 'I've arranged to play with Admiral Juddy'. GERALD comes down L. of TWINE.*

GERALD: Harold, if this is your attitude, you'll see the inside of no bunker today.

TWINE: But I must. I've arranged to play with Admiral Juddy.

GERALD: *(Crosses down L. of TWINE.)* But not yet.

TWINE: Yes, before nine. Because the course gets so congested at this time of year.

CLIVE: Well, you can't; that's all.

TWINE: *(In a panic.)* Oh, but I must. You don't know Admiral Juddy.

CLIVE: No, and I don't want to.

*All move down stage a little.*

TWINE: He's been years in China and he flies into rages and uses terrible expressions.

GERALD: That won't matter. You won't be there to hear them.

RHODA: Oh please, Mr Popkiss.

GERALD: Yes?

CLIVE: Yes? *(They both turn to her, softening quickly.)*

RHODA: I'm sure Mr Twine won't do or say anything to hurt me if I ask him nicely. Can't he go to his golf?

TWINE: Thank you. I won't say a word about you to anyone.

GERALD: And if you can help, you will?

TWINE: Yes. Willingly.

RHODA: *(Smiling sweetly at TWINE.)* That's right.

*Noise of door latch in kitchen D.L.*

GERALD: *(Crosses down L. front of table, listening, then speaking in a hoarse whisper.)* Look out! Listen! *(At noise in kitchen – .)*

63

TWINE *O, RHODA O, CLIVE O, GERALD O*

*(Then – )*

RHODA *O, CLIVE O, TWINE O, GERALD O*

THE OTHERS: *(Turning.)* What?

GERALD: *(As before.)* The back door. *(Crosses L.C.)* It's the d.w.

CLIVE: *(Crosses to front of table C.)* Damn it, she's come after all.

GERALD: What shall we do?

CLIVE: *(To RHODA and GERALD.)* You go up in that room. *(Indicates bedroom on L. of balcony.)*

TWINE: *(R.C. to CLIVE.)* Who is it?

CLIVE: The daily woman.

TWINE: *(Turning towards front door.)* Oh!

*CLIVE catches at his arm as he attempts to go. The subsequent scene is played in a subdued manner.*

CLIVE: Don't go now, you fool. She may see you and tell Gertrude. Then Gertrude will know that you've lied to her.

TWINE: Oh, my gracious!

CLIVE: You come up to that bedroom, too.

*GERALD crosses to stairs and goes up. RHODA follows. TWINE is following behind, being hustled by CLIVE.*

TWINE: *(Very scared.)* What, to the bedroom? No –

CLIVE: Yes. Shut up! *(Giving TWINE a lift with his knee.)* Now up you go, quick!

*RHODA exits into bedroom.*

TWINE: Oh!

CLIVE: Go in there. *(He turns.)*

*CLIVE and GERALD shove TWINE into bedroom after RHODA.*

*(Turns to GERALD.)* Gerald, you wait for her at the top of the stairs, and when you hear her coming upstairs, stand in the doorway and sack her.

GERALD: Good! You go in, old boy.

*CLIVE exits into bedroom.*

TWINE: *(Reappearing in doorway.)* Look here, I say –

*They bear him forcibly inside and close the bedroom door.*

*After a moment MRS LEVERETT comes very stealthily into the hall. She looks about her. GERTRUDE follows into the hall close on her heels.*

MRS LEVERETT: *(L.C., with her head thrown back. Whispering hoarsely.)* If she's still here she's in the bedroom.

*They both look up at bedroom L.*

And also he too has gone back in there himself as well, what's more.

GERTRUDE: *(L.C., whispering back.)* It seems incredible. You honestly promise me you saw her yourself with your own eyes?

MRS LEVERETT: Yes, by the Testament I saw her with me hand on me heart.

GERTRUDE: *(To herself, pensively.)* H'm. Six weeks. Well, I shall know what to do if it's true. I shall go straight to Bath and get his wife.

MRS LEVERETT: She ought to be told.

GERTRUDE: She will be told. She'll not only be told, she'll be brought here and shown.

MRS LEVERETT: When will you go for her, madam?

GERTRUDE: At once, if it's true.

MRS LEVERETT: Oh, it's true enough.

GERTRUDE: *(Looking up L.)* You'd better go up and knock and see what happens.

MRS LEVERETT: *(Crosses to foot of stairs L.)* Yes.

GERTRUDE: Don't appear to suspect anything.

MRS LEVERETT: No. *(Going upstairs.)*

GERTRUDE: I shall wait by the back door. *(Crosses to door D.L.)* You come out and tell me what happens.

MRS LEVERETT: Yes.

GERTRUDE: Very likely you'll find there's no one in the room at all.

MRS LEVERETT: *(Very certain.)* Oh! *(Goes up two or three stairs.)*

GERTRUDE: If so, go along there to the room I told him to sleep in and see if he's there.

MRS LEVERETT: Yes.

GERTRUDE: Go on then. You'd better not be wearing your hat. Give it to me.

*MRS LEVERETT hands it to her. Goes upstairs quietly and listens outside bedroom door. Then knocks. Immediately the bedroom door flies open. MRS LEVERETT falls back a step or two, as GERALD stands in a commanding attitude at the foot of the stairs, just inside the kitchen door L.*

GERALD: *(Loudly.)* What! At *this* hour?

MRS LEVERETT: I beg your pardon?

GERALD: *Not* granted.

MRS LEVERETT: Eh?

GERALD: How dare you do this? You're very late and very late.

*GERTRUDE exits D.L.*

If you can't come here at all, don't come here at the proper time.

MRS LEVERETT: I don't understand your meaning.

GERALD: Luckily for you. You – dare to come here like this, hours afterwards, crawling upstairs like a balloon –

MRS LEVERETT: Balloon!

GERALD: Yes, and me with no tea and early cot hold water – shave – you know – hot pot tea and shaving – go away with you – right away –

MRS LEVERETT: I'm not far be'ind me time. I have come here as promised. What more do you want me to do?

GERALD: There's only one thing for you to do, and that is your old friend, the quit.

*GERTRUDE exits into kitchen D.L.*

MRS LEVERETT: Oh, indeed! Very well, then.

GERALD: Yes, awfully well then.

MRS LEVERETT: You don't want me here?

GERALD: Not a bit of you.

MRS LEVERETT: Oh, in that case –

GERALD: Yes?

MRS LEVERETT: I say, in that case – I give you a week's notice.

GERALD: *(Taken aback.)* A week?

MRS LEVERETT: *(Turning to go downstairs.)* Yes. A week from now.

GERALD: Oh! *(Prompted evidently from the bedroom.)* What? Wait a minute! Oh, yes, I know. Here! You're going to be weighed –

MRS LEVERETT: What?

*Warning for door slam.*

GERALD: Paid – you're going to be paid off now. How much?

MRS LEVERETT: H'm – you seem in a great hurry to –

GERALD: Not a word. How much?

MRS LEVERETT: I'll take a pound –

GERALD: *(Over his shoulder.)* She'll take a pound. *(Correcting the impression that he was addressing anyone else by grinning at MRS LEVERETT, then correcting himself for grinning.)* You'll take a pound.

*GERALD turns to go into bedroom. MRS LEVERETT attempts to go into bedroom, but GERALD stops her.*

Stay there!

*She takes two steps upstairs; he goes in and shuts door. MRS LEVERETT nods to herself triumphantly and moves to bedroom door again.*

*He reappears. Nearly bumping her with the door.*

Take this and go. *(Hands her a pound note.)*

MRS LEVERETT: I did not like the looks of you from the start.

GERALD: And I don't like the look of you at the finish.

MRS LEVERETT: *(Coming downstairs.)* Very good then. I may say I'd *given* this *not* to work here.

GERALD: Why didn't you say that before?

*She goes out indignantly and shuts door D.L.*

*Short pause before door slam off L.*

*He runs down the stairs and listens. A door is heard to slam off L. He crosses to C. and calls to CLIVE and TWINE up L.*

*(Crosses D.L. to C.)* Come on; it's all right. She's gone.

*Clive comes downstairs, followed by Rhoda and Twine.*

CLIVE: I don't think you did that very well.

GERALD: Well, she's gone anyhow.

TWINE: Yes, and I must go now, please. *(Crosses to L.C.)*

GERALD: *(Detaining him.)* Is it all clear for Harold now?

CLIVE: Yes, let him go.

TWINE: I must, please. Admiral Juddy –

CLIVE: All right – go.

TWINE: Yes *(Starting up L.C.)*

*(All up stage.)*

*GERALD R.C., TWINE L.C., CLIVE L.C., RHODA L.*

Oh – well, all right. *(Goes towards door R.C.)*

GERALD: Stay there a moment – I'll see if it's all clear.

*He opens the door. GERTRUDE is standing on the threshold.*

Not to-day, thank you *(Closes door again and turns breathlessly.)* Gertrude!

TWINE: *(Letting himself go, below his breath.)* My God!

*Stands by door R.C. CLIVE steers RHODA across R. and opens door D.R., pushing her in; he then bundles TWINE in, closes door D.R.*

GERALD: *(Opening door R.C.)* Gertrude! – I beg your pardon, I thought it was the laundry.

GERTRUDE: *(Entering R.C., leaving door open – quite amiably.)* I thought you didn't see who it was. Oh, good morning, Clive.

CLIVE: Good morning. Gertrude.

GERTRUDE: You must have found your way over here very early this morning.

CLIVE: Yes, I thought poor old Gerald might want help.

GERALD: Yes. *(Above table.)*

GERTRUDE: Why, hasn't Mrs Leverett arrived? *(Crosses L. of table.)*

GERALD: Oh, most.

GERTRUDE: What?

GERALD: Most attractive – er – attentive.

GERTRUDE: And the room I chose for you was quite comfortable?

GERALD: Oh, more.

GERTRUDE: You slept well?

GERALD: More – er – most – er – quite.

GERTRUDE: Oh!

*CLIVE, with a frown at GERALD, strolls up near study door.*

Well *(Crosses to L. of table C.)*, my reason for coming over so early was that I've had a card from Clara.

GERALD: Oh, Clara! Yes, I remember. Oh yes, my wife – I mean – yes? Well, have you brought the postcard?

GERTRUDE: No, I left it at home. Apparently, mother is still very seedy.

GERALD: Really. That's very sad – and – terrible awful.

GERTRUDE: So I'm afraid it will be quite out of the question for Clara to come here to-day.

*GERALD and CLIVE exchange glances.*

GERALD: Oh!

GERTRUDE: She asked me to come and break it to you.

GERALD: Yes *(Assumes very saddened expression.)*

GERTRUDE: And to make matters worse *(Casually.)*, I'm afraid I've arranged to be away all day myself.

CLIVE: What a pity!

*GERTRUDE, tidying up cushions on settee L., takes a sly look at bedroom door on balcony L.*

GERALD: Oh! *(Assumes even more sadness.)*

GERTRUDE: So you two must keep each other company and get on as best you can.

GERALD: *(Looking at CLIVE.)* We'll do that.

GERTRUDE: Harold will be free later.

GERALD: Yes; he's gone up to the golf club.

*CLIVE digs GERALD with his knee. GERALD's knees give way through the shock, and he has to hold on to the corner of the table. GERTRUDE is looking on, so he turns it off by doing a few gymnastics; stands balancing on the same place.*

GERTRUDE: Why, have you seen him then?

GERALD: Yes. *(CLIVE digs him.)* No, he – he told me last night he was going early to play much golf – golf much – this morning – all the morning – early this morning.

GERTRUDE: I see. And what will you do with yourselves?

GERALD: Yes.

GERTRUDE: Just take it easy. I should.

CLIVE: I shall knit.

GERTRUDE: You've got a nice long time in front of you, with nothing to worry about. Then I'll say good-bye *(Crosses to door R.C.)* till this evening.

GERALD: Thank you very much.

GERTRUDE: What?

GERALD: I beg your pardon.

*GERTRUDE goes of R.C. to L.*

*TWINE enters cautiously from study, and he, CLIVE and GERALD exchange confidential grimaces.*

TWINE: Has she gone?

CLIVE: Yes.

GERALD: Yes.

*JUDDY is heard off L. talking to GERTRUDE.*

JUDDY: *(Off L.)* Day ter yah.

GERTRUDE: *(Off L.)* Good morning, Admiral Juddy.

*CLIVE, GERALD, and TWINE exclaim 'Juddy!' CLIVE and GERALD bundle TWINE back into the study. CLIVE closes the door as JUDDY appears at door R.C. with GERTRUDE.*

GERTRUDE: *(At door R.C.)* Harold has gone on a long time.

*Admiral JUDDY, a fierce and weather-beaten veteran with heavy eyebrows, pounds on to the scene. He is heated and annoyed. He has a habit of relieving his feelings in Chinese oaths below his breath.*

JUDDY: He has not.

GERTRUDE: What?

JUDDY: Not! *(Crosses to L. of table, glares at GERALD and curses in Chinese below his breath.)*

*GERALD and CLIVE stand close together R.*

GERTRUDE: But he left the house over half an hour ago.

CLIVE: I saw him go myself.

*CLIVE and GERALD are R., GERTRUDE R.C., JUDDY L.C.*

JUDDY: I didn't say he didn't leave the house. I said he didn't go to the b – to the b – to the golf club.

GERALD: *(To CLIVE.)* It's all right. Stand firm. Hearts of oak.

GERTRUDE: Where do you suppose he went?

JUDDY: I called at your house to see if he'd gone, and the maid told me she'd seen him coming over here.

GERTRUDE: *(Incredulously.)* Over here?

JUDDY: Yes, madam, over here.

GERTRUDE: He didn't come here, did he? *(To CLIVE.)*

GERALD: Not in the least.

JUDDY: Well, she said he had. Said he's probably come to see you. *(To GERALD.)* You're the tenant here, aren't you – his cousin or something?

GERTRUDE: He's waiting for you on the links. *(Going R.C.)* I'm going back now. I'll speak to the maid.

JUDDY: Well, I hope you'll punish her. I'm sick of these servants – gossiping and messing about instead of doing their work.

GERTRUDE: I *know* Harold was going straight to the club; because he told me so. So there. *(To GERALD.)* Well, till this evening, Gerald.

GERALD: Till – till –

*GERTRUDE exits R.C.*

CLIVE: *(Crosses to R. of table. To JUDDY.)* Well, sir, look here. I think the best thing will be for you to go to the golf club as quickly as possible –

JUDDY: I'm damned if I'm going to take orders from you, sir.

*GERALD crosses R.C. to CLIVE.*

CLIVE: *(Imitating business.)* No, please, don't misunderstand. I was going to suggest running you up there in my cousin's car.

JUDDY: Oh I see.

*GERALD protests.*

CLIVE: *(To GERALD.)* All right. We must get rid of the old blighter.

JUDDY: That's a different matter.

CLIVE: Good, then that's a bet. I'll get the car.

JUDDY: Thank yah.

*CLIVE ignores him.*

GERALD: *(To CLIVE.)* Clive, he said 'Thank yah'.

*CLIVE exits off R.C. hurriedly.*

*JUDDY approaches GERALD, who flinches again.*

JUDDY: Now, sir, this fellow Twine – *(Crosses to GERALD R.C.)* – he's an infernal nuisance.

GERALD: Yes. Oh, he's very troublesome.

JUDDY: Timid little ass. *(His manner is very fierce.)*

*GERALD changes his ground again.*

GERALD: *(As he moves away.)* Yes. I hate that sort of thing.

JUDDY: *(Going to him again.)* He's the same at everything. Golf – bridge – now, bridge. Yesterday at the club he was my partner. I dealt and called a brace of shovels. No – no – no.

Right. Two shovels it was. This feller here led something – I don't know – a small sparkler. Twine, if you please, lays down a hand stiff with bloodthumpers.

GERALD: Not really? Stiff?

JUDDY: Yes, stiff. And never a murmur! Don't you understand – he ought to have called!

GERALD: Called! He ought to have screamed!

JUDDY: Of course. There it was, I lost six tricks. He hadn't a trump in his hand – where were they?

GERALD: Up his sleeve?

JUDDY: Don't you play this game?

*CLIVE in car starts from off R. and pulls up outside door R.C.*

*JUDDY turns away up stage disgusted, swearing in Chinese.*

P'twee! Pong choo! *(To GERALD.)* Day to yer. Blast yeh!

CLIVE: *(Stopping at window in car.)* Come on, sir. The car's alongside.

JUDDY: Right away then. Don't keep me hanging about all day, *etc. etc.*

*Exit, raging, door up R.*

*JUDDY gets in car talking volubly, and while he is still standing the car starts, throwing him into seat, his hat flying off into the roadway as the car disappears off L.*

*GERALD: closes door R.C. and goes to study D.R., opens the door and brings RHODA on by the hand; she crosses L.C.*

GERALD: *(Looking into study.)* Twine, where are you? Come out from under that arm-chair. Old Jetty's gone.

*Enter TWINE D.R., closes door, GERALD crosses C. in front of table. TWINE R.C.*

RHODA: *(Cross C.)* I've told Mr Twine all about it.

GERALD: *(To RHODA.)* Right! *(Then to TWINE.)* Now the first thing to do is for one of us to go to her house and get her clothes from Putz.

TWINE: Yes, but who?

GERALD: One of us. I'd like to go myself, only if I go I shall have to leave you alone with Rhoda. *(TWINE smiles.)* But of course Gertrude would very likely come back.

TWINE: Oh! *(Face falls.)*

GERALD: So that's agreed; he'll get them all right. *(To RHODA.)* He's a man of great strength of character; he carries a lot of weight.

TWINE: *(Modestly.)* Oh no.

GERALD: Oh, you're a member of the Urban District Council.

TWINE: Yes.

GERALD: And – *(To RHODA.)* – he's President of the Girls' Friendly Society.

TWINE: No, not *this* year.

GERALD: Oh! Too friendly *last* year. *(Taking TWINE to door R.C.)* Well, all you have to do is to see Putz, get clothes – come back.

TWINE: I'd rather not.

GERALD: You'll find Putz an awfully nice chap.

TWINE: Shall I?

*GERALD opens door R.C.*

GERALD: Oh, awful.

*Exit TWINE R.C.*

*GERALD closes door after him.*

RHODA: I expect you want me out of the way soon, don't you?

GERALD: Yes. There's no great hurry. Mrs Twine's gone away for the day. *(To settee L; she sits up stage.)*

*GERALD sits on table facing her.*

RHODA: Well, I suppose – I don't know much about things, and I didn't realize at the time. But when I woke up here this morning, I thought it over and I saw what – what the world might think – isn't that the expression?

GERALD: *(Getting closer, crosses the settee, leans over back.)* Don't worry about the silly old world. There's plenty of other places besides that.

74

RHODA: I suppose it's because human nature is so cruel that people always think the worst.

GERALD: No, I think it's that the worst is the most likely.

RHODA: Whatever anybody thinks, you've been tremendously kind to me.

*Warning for dog.*

GERALD: Yes, haven't I? No, I mustn't say that. *(About to smooth her hair, but stops.)*

RHODA: I say it anyhow; you've been wonderful.

*He hold her hand for a moment and then lets it fall, then moves down stage behind settee.*

RHODA: *(In a more practical voice.)* Well, the thing now is to get away.

GERALD: Yes. My cousin's going to take you in the car. Where do you want to go?

RHODA: I've got friends in London. *(Moves down to GERALD on settee.)*

GERALD: *(Crosses to top of settee.)* Oh! Then you'd better go to London.

RHODA: The station will do.

GERALD: Well, we'll see. First of all, what about some breakfast?

RHODA: Is there any?

GERALD: Well, tea. There's surely tea.

RHODA: Shall I skirmish for tea?

GERALD: Right you are.

*Dog growl.*

*TWINE entering at door R.C. breathlessly.*

TWINE: Saved!

GERALD: *(Looking round at front door, then at RHODA.)* Here's another skirmish.

*He opens front door. CONRAD is heard in the distance. TWINE, very heated and breathless, appears at front door.*

You've been very quick, Harold.

TWINE: Yes, I – *(Out of breath.)* I had to be – oh, my goodness –

GERALD: Don't stand there sizzling. Tell me what happened.

*(Brings chair down to table.)*

RHODA: Did you see my step-father?

TWINE: *(Coming in, mopping his brow.)* I – I *saw* him.

GERALD: Did you go to the house?

TWINE: I didn't get as far as the house.

GERALD: Why not? Did you get stung by a butterfly or something?

TWINE: No, there was a dog.

RHODA: Oh! Was the dog *loose?*

TWINE: Yes, very.

GERALD: But a dog – good Lord! What's a dog? Do you think I'm afraid of a dog?

TWINE: *You* may not be. *(Cross D.R.)*

GERALD: I should think not. *(Crosses to door R.C., opens it.) You* go back.

RHODA: Wait a moment. You say you saw my step-father?

TWINE: Yes, he came to the gate and – er – leant –

GERALD: Lent what?

TWINE: Over.

RHODA: Did he seem more polite?

TWINE: No, he didn't.

RHODA: Oh! *(Very perturbed.)*

GERALD: What did he say?

TWINE: I told him what I wanted. He said something I didn't understand. Then he said something to the dog. I didn't understand that either.

GERALD: But the dog did.

TWINE: Yes. *(Quickly.)* It appeared to. *(Looks round at door R.C. furtively.)*

GERALD: *(To RHODA.)* You'll be here for breakfast.

*TWINE sits R. of table.*

RHODA: Yes. Skirmish for tea.

*She exits D.L.*

GERALD: *(Coming and sitting down beside TWINE on sofa.)* Well, I'm very glad you went over.

TWINE: Glad? *(Rising – GERALD puts him down.)*

GERALD: Yes. Now you can see the kind of man we're up against.

TWINE: Yes.

GERALD: I've got a little scheme. The situation may yet be saved.

TWINE: By me? *(Trying to rise again.)*

GERALD: *(Putting him down.)* Yes. Don't keep popping up and down like that, old boy. You're already hot. Now this is my great idea. This girl must get some attire.

TWINE: It's all very well to say that –

GERALD: Now don't interrupt. Gertrude has gone out for the day.

TWINE: Gertrude? No.

*TWINE is fidgeting with his trousers.*

GERALD: Yes. She said so herself. Don't fiddle about with your knickers, old boy. We must concentrate. As I say, this girl must have something to wear.

*TWINE, inquiring look.*

And Gertrude has gone out for the day.

TWINE: Well?

*GERALD taps his knee and speaks emphatically.*

GERALD: As I say, the girl must have some female garments – well, Gertrude has plenty. And she has gone out for the day.

*TWINE slowly turns a horrified expression of inquiry towards GERALD. The latter pulls out a cigarette case.*

Have a cigarette, old boy?

TWINE: No, thanks. D'you mean – ?

GERALD: Yes, by Jove! you're a marvel. I don't know anyone who would have seen it so quickly.

TWINE: *(Rising.)* You don't really seriously suggest that I should go and get some clothes of Gertrude's?

GERALD: *(Rising.)* Well, old boy, you had your chance of getting Rhoda's own clothes from Putz. You come back sizzling with your stocking half mast and say we can't get them. Well, we must get some.

*TWINE fiddles about.*

Keep still – do. I've told you that before. Have you got woollies on? Now listen – if you get some things of Gertrude's –

TWINE: *That* I positively will not do.

GERALD: *(Incredulously.)* You won't get them?

TWINE: Absolutely no.

GERALD: You – in fact – you don't agree with my idea?

TWINE: No. Certainly not.

GERALD: No. Well, well – it's a pity, but there you are. The best of friends must differ.

*CLIVE enters R.C. quietly and stands just inside door.*

TWINE: I abso –

GERALD: Now, old boy. No need to be pugnacious about it. I'm perfectly sure that I'm right, but you don't hear *me* saying I abso-

TWINE: Nothing will induce me.

*CLIVE stands inside doorway R.C.*

GERALD: Quite. Quite.

*GERALD looks at CLIVE.*

And mark you, you may be justified. I want to be quite fair. I say it's a good idea, you say no. Of course what one really wants in these cases is a third party – as referee.

TWINE: Nobody would persuade me.

GERALD: Now, there you lose sympathy. For my part I'd agree to abide by a third parties decision. Of course we must find somebody entirely disinterested – you agree to that *(Taking it for granted.)* – yes. *(Look at CLIVE.)* Now, who can we find? You don't know anyone, I suppose?

*TWINE stares vacantly.*

TWINE: No.

GERALD: Old boy, I've got it.

TWINE: What?

GERALD: Clive shall decide.

TWINE: *No. (Nervously.)*

GERALD: Oh, who better! He's neutral. We'll put it to him.

TWINE: Oh!

GERALD: Now personally I think you'll win.

*TWINE smiles broadly. CLIVE slams door R.*

CLIVE: Hallo, boys!

GERALD: Hallo, Clive!

CLIVE: What's up?

GERALD: Harold and I are just holding what might be called an extraordinary general meeting.

CLIVE: Oh? *(Surprised.)*

GERALD: We're at a deadlock about a certain proposition and need an arbitrator, and we thought of you.

CLIVE: Thank you very much, Harold – that's nice of you. What's the snag?

GERALD: This. *(Pacifying TWINE.)* No, I'll put it fairly. We can't get a rig-out from Putz. But a rig-out for this girl we must have.

CLIVE: There can't be any dispute about that.

GERALD: No. Oh no. But Gertrude having gone for the day –

CLIVE: Yes, I saw her go off in her car –

GERALD: Yes, I was telling Harold about that. Well, one of us says 'Get a rig-out from Gertrude's wardrobe'. The other says 'No'. That's all.

CLIVE: Oh, don't be a blithering idiot.

GERALD: You think I'm wrong?

CLIVE: Wrong? Of course you're wrong.

*TWINE is very pleased.*

GERALD: *(To TWINE.)* It's all right – you've won.

CLIVE: Here's a heaven-sent inspiration, and you turn it down. *(To TWINE.)* Congratulations, Harold.

*GERALD crosses to settee, sits L.*

TWINE: I beg your pardon?

CLIVE: I think it's a fine idea of yours. I unhesitatingly vote for it.

TWINE: But I'm against it.

CLIVE: Against it?

GERALD: Yes, old boy, I don't want to boast, but I'm the one who said 'Do it'.

CLIVE: It doesn't make any difference. My decision stands. It's the best idea of the whole morning, and, besides, Gertrude has got some very nice things.

GERALD: Well, then, I think – the sooner the better. What?

TWINE: *(Jumping up.)* Listen, you fellows –

CLIVE: No. *You* listen for a change. You've done nothing but yap, yap, yap all the morning. Just think what we've done for you. We hid you from Gertrude. We saved you when that Admiral came in here, breathing fire from his nostrils.

*CLIVE and GERALD exchange looks.*

TWINE: Yes, I dare say. Thanks.

CLIVE: We're not asking for gratitude. But something has got to be done quickly – poor old Gerald may get into trouble.

GERALD: Yes. That's the most important point.

CLIVE: And we must stand by him. We're in the same camp.

GERALD: Yes. And we must have loyalty in the camp.

CLIVE: Yes. And if necessary enforce it.

TWINE: *(Nervously.)* What?

CLIVE: The alternative is surrender. Make a clean breast of it all to Gertrude –

GERALD: And the Admiral –

CLIVE: Tell Gertrude the girl was in that study while she was in the hall –

GERALD: And you were in that study –

CLIVE: With the girl –

GERALD: Alone –

CLIVE: For a long time. *Or* – keep Gertrude from finding out –

GERALD: Ever –

CLIVE: By getting the girl some clothes.

*Pause. TWINE stands miserably. GERALD speaks dramatically into his ear.*

GERALD: So clothes –

CLIVE: Or Gertrude –

CLIVE AND GERALD: Choose!

*TWINE only moans. GERALD and CLIVE life TWINE by the arms and seat him on the table. GERALD turns to CLIVE practically.*

CLIVE: Carried.

GERALD: Now, what will she want?

CLIVE: We'd better ask Rhoda what she wants. Where is she?

*GERALD turns to the kitchen door D.L. TWINE attempts to go, but CLIVE holds him by the arm.*

GERALD: *(Speaking into kitchen.)* How are you getting on?

RHODA: *(Off L.)* Splendidly. I've found some tea.

GERALD: We want you here a minute.

RHODA: Yes?

*GERALD crosses L. RHODA enters L., crosses to L.C.*

GERALD: Mr Twine is just going to get some clothes.

CLIVE: Some of Mrs Twine's.

RHODA: Oh, but really –

CLIVE: Well?

RHODA: It's very kind of Mr Twine to think of it – but I couldn't wear hers.

TWINE: No. You see?

RHODA: I mean they'd be too old for me.

GERALD: Oh, but she's got some new ones.

CLIVE: *(To GERALD.)* No, you fool. *(Crossing to RHODA.)* It's simply to have an outfit here in case you can't get your own.

RHODA: Oh, I see.

CLIVE: Yes. Now what will you want? Will you just tick off the items with Mr Twine?

*TWINE attempts to go – CLIVE holds him by the arm.*

RHODA: Well, it's very kind of Mr Twine –

GERALD: Never mind that. Tick of the items.

RHODA: Well, just a frock and something to go under it.

GERALD: *(Severely to TWINE.)* Do you know what goes under it?

CLIVE: All right. *I* know. I'll tell him. *(To TWINE.)* A bodice.

GERALD: *(To TWINE.)* Has Gertrude got a bodice?

TWINE: *(Resignedly.)* Oh, I suppose so.

CLIVE: You mustn't suppose.

GERALD: No – you must know. You've been married for years. Get a bodice.

TWINE: All right. A bust one.

GERALD: *(In horror.)* Certainly not – a sound one.

CLIVE: *(To GERALD.)* That's all right.

GERALD: Is it?

CLIVE: Yes. Bust. You know. Be careful what you're saying!

GERALD: Oh, sorry. Harold began it.

CLIVE: Well, then, a frock and its underneath –

RHODA: And I suppose, some shoes and stockings –

CLIVE: *(To TWINE.)* Only with the stockings you'll want –
*(Trying to be tactful.)* – to arrange for them to keep up.

RHODA: *(To GERALD.)* And possibly a hat if he can manage it.

GERALD: Oh easily. *(To TWINE.)* Manage a hat. And choose
the things that Gertrude won't miss. Put'em all in a bag.

TWINE: *(With an air of one delivering an ultimatum.)* When I've
done this, I've finished with you.

GERALD: Then do it quickly.

CLIVE: You can take Gerald's car. Go on.

GERALD: *(Turns, crosses towards R.C.)* Steady on, old boy, it's
my car.

CLIVE: Yes, let him have the car.

GERALD: All right. *(To TWINE.)* Hurry up then. Hop in the car.
*(Taking TWINE's arm and leading him to front door.)* I'll see
you off.

TWINE: *(Trying to shake GERALD off.)* Oh, let me go!

GERALD: *(Turning to CLIVE as he takes TWINE out.)* There you
are. He *wants* to go.

*GERALD goes out with TWINE R.C.*

RHODA: *(To CLIVE.)* Oh, Mr Popkiss –

CLIVE: Yes?

RHODA: Do you mind if I ask you something? I want your
advice.

CLIVE: Do you? Come on then. *(Cross to table C.)* Sit down
here and tell me about it. *(Sitting on table.)*

*CLIVE R.C. RHODA L.C.*

RHODA: It's only – I couldn't help coming here. But isn't it my
duty now to give in and go home?

CLIVE: Your duty – who to? Me?

RHODA: No. I meant to your cousin.

CLIVE: Oh, old Gerald – but you needn't worry any more
about *him.* You're not going to stay here anyhow. You're
coming with me in the car, aren't you?

RHODA: Yes, if you – really – don't mind.

CLIVE: If *I* don't mind. You needn't let that worry you. But you like to come with me, don't you?

RHODA: Yes.

CLIVE: I'll take great care of you.

RHODA: I'm sure you will. I knew that directly I saw you.

CLIVE: Did you? That's fine, because, you know, directly I saw *you* I knew something too. When you came out of that room last night on to the landing and smiled that little smile of yours –

*She smiles.*

yes – that's the one – do you know what I knew then?

RHODA: No –

CLIVE: *(Seeing her embarrassment.)* Well – I – er – never mind – we've plenty of time for that. Anyhow, you're glad you're coming with me in the car, aren't you?

RHODA: Yes, very. But I want to go to friends in London. Can you go all that way?

CLIVE: Can I? You try and think of some friends in Scotland! *She smiles again.*

What a bit of luck that I'm here, isn't it? *(Taking her hand.)*

RHODA: *(Again embarrassed.)* Yes.

*CLIVE, hands bus.: CLIVE takes RHODA's right hand in his left, palm to palm, and with his right hand lifts his fingers, letting them drop back.*

CLIVE: I mean – of course, old Gerald would probably take you himself if I wasn't here. I say, isn't that funny? Do you see the way your fingers flop back, like a piano? He's married – and so on.

RHODA: Yes. I'm afraid I've done quite enough to compromise him already.

CLIVE: Yes – I didn't mean that – but what I meant was – it would be wasted on him.

RHODA: Oh, I see. Then – *you're not* married?

CLIVE: Me? No, I'm not married. Not – yet.

RHODA: Oh. Then you're going to be?

CLIVE: What? Well, I – I didn't think so; but if – I – *(Hums a few bars of a song.)*

*GERALD enters R.C., comes down R., and CLIVE sees him.*

RHODA: Oh, I think the kettle's boiling.

GERALD: Oh, is it? Good! *(Making no effort to go.)*

RHODA: I'd better see to it.

*Goes to kitchen.*

CLIVE: Yes, I'll come with you. *(Going after her.)*

GERALD: No, stay here, old boy.

CLIVE: Oh, but I haven't seen a kettle boil for years.

GERALD: *(Holding door D.L.)* This is no time for kettling. Quick now! What are we going to do? *(Cross R.C.)*

CLIVE: She's coming with me.

GERALD: In Gertrude's clothes? *(R.C.)*

CLIVE: Yes. Why not?

GERALD: This is desperate stuff.

CLIVE: I know, but every minute's delay is dangerous.

GERALD: But Gertrude's gone away.

CLIVE: Other people will see her.

GERALD: Who?

CLIVE: Tradesmen, you fool. Milkmen – gardeners – probably the vicar.

GERALD: Yes, all right, old boy. Don't be impulsive. It was I who said we must do something quickly.

CLIVE: Well, do it.

GERALD: But do you think she'll be all right in Gertrude's things?

CLIVE: Of course she will. She'd look lovely in anything.

GERALD: I don't mean that. You don't have to tell me that. I've known her a good deal longer than you have. I mean, oughtn't we to get her own if we can?

CLIVE: And let Putz know that we're trying to smuggle her away?

GERALD: What about an offensive on Putz? A combined offensive?

CLIVE: No. Cut Putz clean out of it.

*PUTZ appears silently R.C. and walks slowly down R., unnoticed.*

Unless, of course, we can *wangle* her things from Putz.

GERALD: Ah! By diplomacy with Putz?

CLIVE: Yes. But better ignore him completely.

GERALD: Simply don't see him at all.

CLIVE: No. Let sleeping dogs lie.

*PUTZ is now down R.C.*

GERALD: Quite right, old boy. *You're* right. *(Turns and sees PUTZ, assumes a false heartiness in his embarrassment.)* Hallo!

PUTZ: *(With challenge.)* Who shall go out from hereout in a motor? *(Pointing through window up L.)*

GERALD: He heard what we were saying.

PUTZ: Not only do I hear, I see him. Who shall go?

GERALD: Oh, you mean, who went?

PUTZ: Aller right. Who shall vent?

CLIVE: *(Crosses to PUTZ.)* You think that your step-daughter's gone. Well, allow me to tell you she's going, and you needn't think you're going to stop her. So you'd better not come and try any of you bluff on us, you damn great stiff. *(To GERALD.)* Introduce me, will you?

PUTZ: Speak. *(To CLIVE.)*

CLIVE: Well, what d'you think I'm doing – singing?

PUTZ: *(Crosses D.R., addressing GERALD. Aggressively.)* Who shall go presently already in the motor hereout? Also *that* I see and hear.

GERALD: *(To CLIVE.)* Diplomacy. Oh yes! Now look. Putty, old thing. *(Approaching PUTZ.)*

*CLIVE backs him up.*

Don't you worry about that car. That was just my brother-in-law – or, rather, not exactly my brother-in-law – because sisters and brothers have I none. But that man's father –

PUTZ: Speak!

GERALD: Yes; try not to say that, old boy. It's just one of those little things that irk.

PUTZ: I know of you.

*GERALD moves back.*

*(To GERALD.)* My howskeeper she know all of it of you. Die vife of der little man is die enemy of Rhoda. Und she is die sister of your vife. And if your vife shall come, und Rhoda remain herein der hows, it make for you some hell of a business. *Fürchterlichkeit. Sturm und Drang. (Pronounced: Fear-ster-lick-kite – Fearfulness. 'Sturm and Drang' – Thunder and lightning.)*

GERALD: Speak. *(Turns to CLIVE.)*

*CLIVE crosses to PUTZ.*

CLIVE: *(To PUTZ.)* Now, you. Quick. One way or the other. Are you going to give us her clothes or not?

PUTZ: I give.

CLIVE: What?

PUTZ: I give. I bring heah. Und I vait. Und she put on dis clode. Und she com back wit me to der hows.

CLIVE: No damn fear.

PUTZ: *(Flaring up.)* Zo. I also have no fear already. You shall try to send her from me, und, Herr Gott! I will make for you hot like hell.

GERALD: But you ran her out.

PUTZ: You t'ink you shall send her away also from hereout? Aller right. You shall try. Mit out die clode she cannot flee. Und I keep from her die closeys aller der time.

CLIVE: *(To GERALD.)* Oh, go on. Kick him out.

GERALD: *(To PUTZ.)* Get out.

PUTZ: You t'ink you can fight it mit me, ja?

GERALD: What *(To CLIVE.)* Tell him to go.

CLIVE: *(Cross R. to PUTZ.)* Get out.

PUTZ: *(Folding his arms.)* I go ven I vish.

GERALD: What can we do to make him wish? *(Crosses behind table to R.C.)*

*TWINE enters heatedly, carrying a bag. He has a lady's hat in his hand and shoes sticking out of his pockets.*

TWINE: Now look here, you chaps. I've brought these things, but I've determined –

*They signal to him violently to keep quiet.*

CLIVE: Shut up, you idiot!

PUTZ: *(Turning on them, suddenly seizing the bag from TWINE with an angry roar.)* Zo! You t'ink to give her die clode. You shall not it.

*Dialogue during struggle.*

GERALD: Hold him, Harold.

TWINE: Don't! Don't!

CLIVE: I've got him!

*These lines are repeated until PUTZ is heard at door R.C. ('I win,' etc.)*

*PUTZ snatches bag from TWINE and moves L.C. TWINE catches PUTZ by the leg and they both fall; GERALD throws himself on the top, catching hold of TWINE; then CLIVE comes round top of table to L. PUTZ wriggles out L. front with bag and crosses L. CLIVE intercepts PUTZ and tries to snatch the bag – they struggle. PUTZ hits CLIVE on the head with the bag. CLIVE sinks on to the settee dazed. PUTZ then crosses behind table to door R.C. and – with bag raised in his right hand – exclaims.*

PUTZ: *(At door up R.C.)* I vin – Deutschland über Alles!

*GERALD is still holding TWINE down C, but he is looking at CLIVE, who is just recovering from the knock on his head. RHODA appearing at kitchen door D.L. with tray of tea, etc. CLIVE looks at her and smiles broadly.*


*CURTAIN*

# Act Three

*Door R.C., closed.*

*The hall – about two and a half hours later.*

*The curtain rises on angry voices. CLIVE discovered seated on stairs; GERALD L.C.*

CLIVE: She didn't say it to you; she said it to me.

GERALD: Liar! That's all. Liar!

CLIVE: Are you calling me a liar?

GERALD: I said to her, 'He'll help us', and she said 'Thank you' to me for asking you to help.

CLIVE: You know as well as I do, I said, 'I'm going to help', and she, poor little soul, burst into a smile.

GERALD: That was simply because she saw your face for the first time. I did the same.

CLIVE: Ah, wait a minute. *(Crossing round back of settee to front.)* Don't you begin on faces. The enemy's well in your country if you do.

GERALD: *(Crossing to R.C. front of table.)* You're jealous because I found her first.

CLIVE: *(Crossing to L.C. front of table.)* And you're as wild as hell because she likes me best.

GERALD: Lies and muck!

CLIVE: And I like her far better than you can.

GERALD: And I like Harold better than I like you. Also Putz, Nutts, and Conrad.

CLIVE: You tried to keep her a secret from me. When you knew I was coming you bunged her in the kitchen along with that humming cat.

GERALD: That's another hideous lie. But I'd rather she met the cat than you.

CLIVE: I saved the whole situation from the start.

GERALD: What! Who started that drivelling idea for outing that woman?

CLIVE: What woman?

GERALD: The daily one – Mrs Thunderguts.

CLIVE: That'll do. Over the only nice thing that happens in this place you butt in and down me, or try to, you blighter.

GERALD: I butt in! I like that. I come in here and find you sitting on the table holding her poor little hand and trying to sing.

CLIVE: I sing a damn sight better than you do. I've heard you, thank you. Like the last bit of the bath running out.

GERALD: Anyhow, I don't want you to sing any more. I promised her decent treatment.

CLIVE: Yes, that's just it, and now you're sorry you promised her anything.

GERALD: Oh! The champion lie. That's yours.

CLIVE: I'll take it. You'd send her back to Putz if I let you.

GERALD: Clive, be careful, I warn you. Don't rouse me too much. I get like a lion.

CLIVE: You were a damn fine lion when Putz came in this morning.

GERALD: You made a bee-line for the door.

CLIVE: I went to the door to try to cut Putz off; and what did you do? – you sat on the floor to try and cut poor Harold off.

GERALD: For all the use you've been you'd better clear out.

CLIVE: I'm going to, and she's coming with me. *(Cross to L. of table.)* She told me herself she wanted me to take her.

GERALD: I told her to tell you so, and you know it, you dog's body.

CLIVE: *(Crossing to GERALD, threateningly.)* You – you –

*RHODA has appeared above from bedroom.*

RHODA: *(Shocked.)* Oh!

CLIVE: *(Seeing RHODA, starts to sing.)* – Ukelele lady.

RHODA: If you're going to quarrel about me, I'd better go home.

GERALD: *(To RHODA.)* We were only just wondering which of us was most anxious to help you.

RHODA: You're both most anxious. That's been proved.

*(Coming down L.)*

GERALD: I proved it first.

CLIVE: I'm going on proving it a long time after you are.

RHODA: Well, I think I'd better go home. *(Cross front of settee to L.C.)*

GERALD: No, no. That would be a pity.

CLIVE: Pity! You're not going back there.

RHODA: Oh, I don't want to. I only meant for his sake.

GERALD: There you are – for *my* sake.

CLIVE: It's for your sake she's willing to go, and for my sake she doesn't want to.

*RHODA moves away L.*

GERALD: Oh, do at least be fifty-fifty while she's here.

CLIVE: Yes, all right, old boy. Sorry!

GERALD: That's all right, old boy.

RHODA: *(Crossing to CLIVE R.C.)* Only it seems hopeless. I can't really get to London without my own things.

CLIVE: *(To GERALD.)* Are you sure there are no more of Clara's things among your luggage?

GERALD: Another pair of golf shoes and two more pairs of golf stockings – oh, and an umbrella!

*GERALD looks away.*

CLIVE: Oh! A string of beads and we're home. *(To RHODA.)* Anyway, couldn't you trick Putz somehow?

GERALD: Me? No, old boy, I don't think so.

CLIVE: I was talking to Rhoda.

RHODA: I wonder. Of course if I went over there dressed – I mean in any old dress –

CLIVE: Well?

RHODA: I could say, 'Here I am – all ready to go to London,' then he might give in.

GERALD: And hand over your own things?

RHODA: Yes. I know him. When he's winning he's a devil. But if he thought I'd beaten him, he might plead.

GERALD: You hear that? Just any old frock and we could get all her things from pleading Putz.

CLIVE: Yes. There's something in this. It's worth trying.

GERALD: Yes. I said so, old boy.

CLIVE: Well, we'll set about it. *(To RHODA.)* You'd better get back to that room. *(Indicating room up. L.)* There's always a chance you may be seen.

RHODA: Yes. *(Going upstairs L.)* Any kind of frock would do, and I believe I could fool him.

*CLIVE smiles at her as she goes into room up L. on balcony.*

GERALD: *(To RHODA.)* Good girl. *(To CLIVE.)* Isn't she?

CLIVE: *(With smile disappearing.)* All right. Don't start that again.

GERALD: *(With a very tolerant smile.)* Now don't start arguing.

CLIVE: What? I wasn't arguing.

GERALD: I didn't say you were. I said 'don't'.

CLIVE: That's the same thing as saying I was.

GERALD: Oh, is it?

CLIVE: Yes, it is it.

GERALD: Then I'm sorry.

CLIVE: That's quite all right.

GERALD: Not at all, old boy. Still, personally I don't think it is.

CLIVE: You don't think it is what?

GERALD: The same thing to say to a person 'don't' as to say 'you are'.

CLIVE: What the hell are you talking about?

GERALD: Well, old boy, you ought to know. You began it.

CLIVE: Began what? *(Raising his voice.)*

GERALD: I said 'don't', and you said –

CLIVE: Don't what?

GERALD: I forget now. Oh yes, I remember. I said 'don't let's argue'.

CLIVE: Well, anyhow, this frock – the shops will be open now.

GERALD: But I've told you. No shops are open today.

CLIVE: You went down before the shops were open, and that's why you found the shops were shut.

GERALD: I keep telling you there are no shops open in the place today; it's sort of a local regatta.

CLIVE: *(Crosses to settee and sits.)* I know you did.

GERALD: The man who keeps the milliner's shop is in the town band.

CLIVE: I don't care if he's in the fire brigade. Round him up.

GERALD: I can't. He's in the band on the front, shaking his exhaust out of the butt end of a cornet.

CLIVE: *(Crossing to L.C. above table.)* Well, there are other towns within reach – without regattas.

GERALD: I never said there weren't.

CLIVE: *(Cross to GERALD.)* No, but you never remembered there *were.*

GERALD: Well, go and find one if you're so clever.

CLIVE: I'm going to, and I'm going to take the car. *(Cross up L., GERALD R.C.)*

GERALD: There you go again. My car. *(Crosses to L.C. front of table.)*

CLIVE: *(R.C.)* Well, hell's delight, it's for your sake.

GERALD: You don't say 'May I take the car?' You say 'I'm going to take the car'. That's what gets my goat.

CLIVE: Anyway, I bet you I get in a shop here.

GERALD: I bet you. There! I've been and seen. The only things you can buy are flags and beer.

CLIVE: Then why didn't you get some beer?

GERALD: I did.

CLIVE: You *would.*

GERALD: Go on, Good-bye.

*CLIVE, going R.C., turns back and goes to kitchen door.*

CLIVE: Well, I hope you'll enjoy yourself. You'll have nice company.

GERALD: *(With a smile.)* Yes. Why are you going that way?

*JUDDY is seen through window R.C.*

CLIVE: Because old Admiral Bloodhead is coming up the drive.

*Exit D.L. to kitchen.*

GERALD: Oh, curse him! What does he want?

*Knock at door R.C.*

Come in.

*JUDDY enters as CLIVE goes.*

JUDDY: Hallo, yer young devil! *(Door R.C.)* I've heard about you. Where is she?

GERALD: Where's who?

JUDDY: That girl. Come on. I'm not one of the people who abuse that girl. I like her. Like her looks. Always have.

GERALD: Yes. I always have too.

JUDDY: Well, you needn't think I'm going to let her be kicked out of the house like this.

GERALD: Oh, it's not a question of her being kicked out at all.

JUDDY: It is. I'm going to make the devil of a row about it.

GERALD: But, Mr – Captain – she's not being kicked out.

JUDDY: She was kicked out by that swine, wasn't she?

GERALD: Oh, by Putz. Quite right.

JUDDY: How long is she going to be here?

GERALD: Well, the trouble is she's got no clothes.

JUDDY: Hasn't she? Oh! *(Cross L.)* I'd rather like to have a word with her. Where is she?

GERALD: No, I'll tell you what. Have you a wife?

JUDDY: It doesn't matter if I've got fifty wives.

GERALD: I refer to the one in this port.

JUDDY: Eh?

GERALD: I mean what size is she?

JUDDY: Mind yer own business.

GERALD: I was only thinking I might perhaps be allowed to look through her clothes.

JUDDY: What?

GERALD: No, no. All right. On second thoughts I won't.

JUDDY: I didn't come here for you to insult my wife for me.

GERALD: Didn't you? What did you come here for?

JUDDY: To take that girl away.

GERALD: Where?

JUDDY: To my house.

GERALD: *You'll* take her?

JUDDY: Certainly. I'll wait for her.

GERALD: She's just waiting for a frock.

JUDDY: Oh, well, I'll go and arrange for her to come. You bring her over.

GERALD: Ay, ay, sir. Very likely. Very quickly.

JUDDY: See yer do it then. *(Cross R.C.)* And show a leg. Bustle about.

GERALD: Oh, show a leg and a bustle.

JUDDY: *(Cross up R.C.)* And if yer don't I'll come back and fetch her myself. Day ter yer.

*Exit, shutting door R.U.*

*RHODA appears on balcony.*

GERALD: Ah! Day ter yer.

RHODA: Well, what did he say?

GERALD: Oh, a lot of nautical nonsense I didn't understand. I think the old rascal likes you rather.

RHODA: Yes, I think he does. *(Coming downstairs to behind settee L.)*

GERALD: Why, do you know him?

RHODA: No, but when I've passed him in the road he's been looky. You know – *(Bus.: looking coyly.)* – like that.

GERALD: Looky! If he's been looky like that it's off.

RHODA: What's off? *(Crosses in front of settee to GERALD L.C.)*

GERALD: There was an idea you might go there.

RHODA: Where? To Admiral Juddy's? *(At the bottom of the stairs.)*

GERALD: Yes, and Mrs Juddy's.

RHODA: And those horrible Juddy girls?

GERALD: Good Lord! Has he got young?

RHODA: Oh, please. I couldn't. Those two Miss Juddies would make an awful scandal.

GERALD: Well, you shan't go.

*RHODA sits on L. of settee.*

I don't want you to go at all – don't think that.

RHODA: No, I quite understand.

GERALD: *(Sitting on settee.)* Our little friendship mustn't end here.

RHODA: Your kind of friendship never ends.

GERALD: Oh, dear, dear, dear! No. Isn't that nice to think of?

RHODA: *(Looking into GERALD's eyes.)* And the same with your cousin.

GERALD: As a matter of fact, I'm very glad he's taking you. He's an awfully simple, soft-hearted chap. He's very fond of canaries. Oh, well, I'll go and tell old Juddy and say you're not coming. *(Leads RHODA across to stairs L.)* Will you be all right? *(Cross R. to door up R.)*

RHODA: Yes. I'll stay in the bedroom. But you don't think my stepfather will call again, do you?

GERALD: I hope not. You do like Clive, don't you?

RHODA: Yes, I think he's awfully nice.

GERALD: Yes – *(Pause.)* – and I'm a nice little chap too.

*Exit door R.C. to R. Close door.*

*RHODA up at window on balcony. MRS LEVERETT puts a stealthy head through the kitchen door. She catches sight of RHODA, who is waving to GERALD, who is going off round the drive. RHODA calls to GERALD 'Goodbye'. RHODA wheels round and they see each other. MRS LEVERETT L.C.*

RHODA: What are *you* doing here?

MRS LEVERETT: Same to you, *(At table C.)* only from last night onward.

RHODA: *(Anxiously, coming down L. behind settee.)* How do you know about that?

MRS LEVERETT: Oh, I've known about it from first thing this morning. And I'm not the only one that knows.

RHODA: No, in that case I don't suppose you are. *(Cross down stairs to L.)*

MRS LEVERETT: That'll do, miss. *(Turns to RHODA.)* Impertinence always goes with the other.

RHODA: *(Hurrying down.)* Come here, please. I want to speak to you.

MRS LEVERETT: *(Moving to RHODA, her temper rising.)* You'll get spoke to all right before long; I'll promise you that.

RHODA: *(Cross L.C. to MRS LEVERETT.)* But you weren't told to come back by Mr Popkiss.

MRS LEVERETT: Him! No. And he'll pop no more of his kisses after this.

RHODA: What d'you mean?

MRS LEVERETT: You wait and hear what his wife's got to say.

RHODA: *(Very alarmed.)* His wife?

MRS LEVERETT: Yes. Oh, you can't get away. *I* saw you, this morning. Out you comes on the landing – *(Putting on voice. Cross R.)* – 'Mr Popkiss! Mr Popkiss!' Yes. And back he went to the room, what's more.

RHODA: Why didn't you speak?

*Waiting for knock.*

MRS LEVERETT: Oh, I *did* speak.

RHODA: *(Horrified.)* I can guess. You sneaked to Mrs Twine.

MRS LEVERETT: *(With satisfaction.)* And will shortly be back.

RHODA: *(Greatly agitated.)* Oh, good heavens!

*Door knock.*

*There is a sharp knock at the front door. RHODA instinctively runs upstairs L. She pauses by bedroom door.*

See who that is.

MRS LEVERETT: *(Looking up at RHODA.)* You order such about as what is yours to order.

*RHODA is half hidden by standing close up to the wall. MRS LEVERETT opens front door.*

*POPPY DICKEY appears. She is a local maiden in a bright summer frock and carrying a tray of small flags. She laughs a little laugh in two notes, rather like the cry of the cuckoo.*

POPPY: *(Seeing MRS LEVERETT, she laughs.)* Flags for the Lifeboat?

MRS LEVERETT: No, thank you. My husband is on board.

POPPY: What about the gentleman who's come here? Has he got his little flag?

MRS LEVERETT: Out.

POPPY: Well, what about the one who's staying with Mrs Twine? They said *he* was here. *(Laugh – cuckoo laugh.)*

MRS LEVERETT: Oh, well, he's not here now, miss.

POPPY: Oh, how too crushing of him! No little flags at all? Well, good morning, P'r'aps I'll meet one of the gentlemen in the road.

*Exits R.C., and MRS LEVERETT closes the door.*

MRS LEVERETT: *(At door.)* P'r'aps you will. *(Cross to C. behind table and look towards door R.C.)* And it wouldn't be the first time you've done that!

*She returns to kitchen. Closes door.*

*RHODA immediately runs down to door R.C. She opens it and runs a few yards out in front drive.*

RHODA: *(Calling in a guarded voice.)* I say! I say! Come here! *(Cross D.R.C.)*

*POPPY reappears, looking extremely surprised and intrigued. RHODA beckons her in. POPPY enters wide-eyed. She crosses D.R..*

POPPY: *(Taking stock of her.)* Well, it takes a good deal to surprise me.

RHODA: I know you by sight. You live in Chumpton, don't you?

POPPY: That's right. My name's Poppy Dickey. I've heard about you too. But what's *this* little episode?

RHODA: Oh, do be kind and help me.

POPPY: But I'm selling flags for the Lifeboat. I'd love to know what *you're* doing!

RHODA: I simply *had* to come here. *(Close door R.C.)*

POPPY: Why? Did you know these boys before?

RHODA: No. But I came in here last night.

POPPY: What, and said, 'Oh, I simply had to come' – like that?

RHODA: No. Well – I came here because – there was nothing else to do.

POPPY: *(Breezily.)* Really? *(Cross to front of table.)* That's what I call a good reason but a bad excuse.

RHODA: Listen, please. *(Glances at kitchen door, then speaks intensely.)* I'm in great trouble.

POPPY: I'm not surprised. I've asked for a bit of trouble myself before now, but I've never chased it quite as hard as this.

RHODA: Let me tell you. I had a row at home. So I came here.

POPPY: Last night, this was?

RHODA: Yes.

POPPY: And you've stayed here?

RHODA: Yes, I've had to.

POPPY: Like you are now?

RHODA: Yes, more or less.

POPPY: All night and ever since?

RHODA: Yes.

POPPY: Think of that! And me selling flags!

RHODA: But I do want help. *(Very distressed.)*

POPPY: You don't strike me as wanting much help.

RHODA: I do. Terribly. Oh, stay and help me! There may be trouble. That's why I want your help.

POPPY: *(Crosses to settee.)* Well, I like that. If I didn't have a hand in the crime I don't see getting stung for the inquest. *(Sits on arm of settee down stage.)*

RHODA: *(Cross to settee, kneels.)* Listen. Lend me that frock for ten minutes and I shall be saved.

POPPY: Really? And what'll *I* be?

RHODA: Those two will be back directly. You wait in that bedroom and tell them.

POPPY: *(Rise.)* Me wait in that bedroom with no frock on for the two boys?

RHODA: Yes. Oh, it would be wonderful if you would!

*POPPY laughs.*

*(Imploringly – rising.)* You'll do it?

POPPY: Well, it's a bit out of the usual. But I can see you're in trouble.

*Warning for knock at door.*

*(Hesitating.)* Yes, but *(Cross to lower end of settee.)* – you're sure these boys will enter into the spirit of the thing?

RHODA: Of course. They're darlings. *(Laughs.)* You'll be doing *them* a good turn too.

POPPY: Yes, but it's me I'm thinking of.

RHODA: Well, you too. Because, you see, you can sell them flags for the Lifeboat.

POPPY: *(With her cuckoo laugh.)* Strikes me, I *am* the Lifeboat. *(She turns, goes upstairs, with RHODA following. Halts half-way up.)* But if I do this, you will bring back my frock?

RHODA: Yes, yes. I promise I will. Immediately.

POPPY: Righto. *(Cross upstairs L.)* You needn't overdo it. I dare say *fairly* quickly will do.

*A loud knock at the front door. RHODA hustles POPPY into bedroom L.*

RHODA: Look out. Come on. In here. Quick!

*She gets POPPY into bedroom MRS LEVERETT enters from kitchen. RHODA pretends to be looking out of bedroom.*

There's somebody at the front door.

MRS LEVERETT: You kindly keep your orders for such as is theirs to get. My name is not Nutts.

*RHODA goes into bedroom.*

*MRS LEVERETT goes and opens the front door. TWINE is waiting outside. He is startled to see MRS LEVERETT, and much embarrassed.*

TWINE: Oh!

*Steps inside.*

MRS LEVERETT: Well, sir?

TWINE: Well?

MRS LEVERETT: Well? *(Brief pause.)* Well?

TWINE: I – I didn't expect to see *you.*

MRS LEVERETT: Why not?

TWINE: I didn't think you were here.

MRS LEVERETT: Why shouldn't I be here, sir?

TWINE: Oh! For no reason I know of.

*During these lines TWINE moves down R., MRS LEVERETT follows.*

MRS LEVERETT: Then why didn't you expect to see me.

TWINE: I don't know exactly.

MRS LEVERETT: You knew I was working here, didn't you?

TWINE: Yes, dear.

MRS LEVERETT: What!

TWINE: I beg your pardon. I mean yes.

MRS LEVERETT: Well, then?

TWINE: Mr Popkiss told me you'd gone.

MRS LEVERETT: Oh! Then have *you* been here this morning?

TWINE: *(Cross to R.C.)* Oh! No – I – I met him out.

MRS LEVERETT: Ah! Just now when he went out? *(Cross to TWINE R.C.)*

TWINE: *(Gladly.)* Yes.

MRS LEVERETT: *(With triumph.)* Then if you met him just now, who did you come here expecting to see?

TWINE: Oh! I came – *(With an inspiration.)* – about a bag I lost.

MRS LEVERETT: Where?

TWINE: Here.

MRS LEVERETT: When?

TWINE: Oh! No, I didn't lose it. *(Crosses to C. front of table.)* He lost it. I want to know if it's come back.

MRS LEVERETT: Come back from where? *(Following Twine C.)*

TWINE: From wherever it went to.

MRS LEVERETT: You said it went here.

TWINE: Oh!

MRS LEVERETT: *(Peering at him suspiciously.)* Mr Twine!

TWINE: What?

MRS LEVERETT: Do you know anything?

TWINE: *(Very nervously.)* Know?

MRS LEVERETT: Yes – know.

TWINE: No.

MRS LEVERETT: No?

TWINE: Yes. No. Really. It's all right about the bag. Don't mention it. *(He turns tail and goes between table and Mrs Leverett.)*

*Exit R.C.*

*MRS LEVERETT follows him into porch and stands staring after him and shaking her head suspiciously.*

*RHODA in POPPY DICKEY's dress nips out of the bedroom – glances into the hall, then goes quickly down the stairs, having ascertained that MRS LEVERETT is in the porch; exit door down L.*

*As MRS LEVERETT returns to L. of table, TWINE again enters R.C. and comes down very stealthily to R. of table.*

MRS LEVERETT: –

MRS LEVERETT: *(Very startled.)* Oh, well, what now, sir?

TWINE: *(Moving towards her C. front of table.)* You said something about – did I know? Tell me, do you know something?

*(Very close to MRS LEVERETT.)*

MRS LEVERETT: Do I know what?

TWINE: Oh! I don't know – I'm sure I don't know.

MRS LEVERETT: Do I know what you don't know?

TWINE: *(Gladly.)* Yes.

MRS LEVERETT: Well, if you don't know what you know, how do I know if I know it?

TWINE: *(Turning R. towards door R.C.)* Oh, I think I'll get out. *(Turns R.)* Oh dear! – *(In fear.)* – here comes Mr Popkiss back.

MRS LEVERETT: Oh, does he! I've had enough of him today. I'm going back to my kitchen.

*Exit D.L.*

*TWINE tries to sneak out D.L. GERALD enters and stops him.*

GERALD: Hallo, Harold!

TWINE: Oh, blow!

GERALD: What's the meaning of this?

TWINE: Of what?

GERALD: Of this. This – this. You know what *this* means, don't you?

TWINE: Yes.

GERALD: Well, what's the meaning of this?

TWINE: I don't know.

GERALD: You told Admiral Thing!

TWINE: I had to.

GERALD: You swore you wouldn't.

TWINE: I couldn't help it.

GERALD: You broke a swear. That's one thing a gentleman never breaks.

TWINE: I don't think anything will matter now. *(Look over L.)* That woman's back in the kitchen.

GERALD: What! Why not say so? *(Crossing to door D.L. quickly and calling in.)* Where are you? No, not you, cat. *(To imaginary cat.)* The other one.

TWINE: Isn't she there?

GERALD: No. What's the meaning of this?

TWINE: *(Annoyed.)* Don't keep asking me *that*.

GERALD: I didn't say *that*; I said *this*.

TWINE: I don't even know what you mean by *this*.

GERALD: Come, come, Harold. That's what I was asking *you*.

*Enter CLIVE R.C. from L., running, with very small parcel, which he puts on the table.*

CLIVE: Here you are. I told you I'd get it.

GERALD: A frock?

CLIVE: Yes. And everything else.

TWINE: But what about Gertrude's bag?

GERALD: Well, go and get it back from Putz.

TWINE: I won't.

GERALD: You won't?

CLIVE: But you gave it to Putz.

GERALD: Well, get out of this, anyhow. We don't like your trousers or your face.

TWINE: Blow you both. *(Cross up R.)* I beg your pardon, but really you make me lose my temper.

*Goes off R.C. to L.*

CLIVE: I'll take these things up to Rhoda.

GERALD: No. *I* will. *(Taking parcel.)* I shall only go as far as the door. *(Going upstairs.)*

TWINE: *(Rushing back R.C.)* Quick! Look out! Something appalling.

GERALD: *(Halting on stairs.)* Then don't bring it in here.

CLIVE: What is it?

TWINE: Gertrude, Clara, and mother. And the daily woman at the gate.

GERALD: Clara! *(He comes downstairs again and throws away parcel.)*

CLIVE: Treason. Somebody's done the dirty.

GERALD: You swine of a Twine.

TWINE: No; it's Gertrude. But don't say I said so. Good-bye, you fellows. *(Hurries out through kitchen door L.)* Good-bye. *Exit.*

GERALD: Clive! What'll I do? What'll I say?

CLIVE: Show her the girl.

GERALD: But her mind's been poisoned by Gertrude.

CLIVE: Show her the girl. That's enough for anyone.

*Enter CLARA R.C., cross D.R.C.*

GERALD: Clara! Darling!

*MRS POSSETT, GERTRUDE, and MRS LEVERETT enter R.C. from L. They go to settee.*

CLARA: Oh, Gerald, if there were anything wrong, could you kiss me like that?

GERALD: Of course I could, darling.

CLIVE: Couldn't, you fool.

GERALD: Couldn't, you fool. Couldn't, darling. *(Turns.)* You needn't sit down all over the place. I want to speak to Clara.

CLIVE: Yes, alone.

GERTRUDE: Certainly not.

CLARA: Thank you, Gertrude. I prefer to speak to him alone. *(Cross L.C.)*

GERTRUDE: Mrs Leverett, is that girl still here?

MRS LEVERETT: She is. In the bedroom.

GERTRUDE: There.

CLARA: She *is* still here?

MRS POSSETT: I feel sick.

CLIVE: Oh, stop that. *(To MRS POSSETT.)* There's quite enough on hand without that.

GERTRUDE: Mrs Leverett, take my mother to the drawing-room.

GERALD: That'll be nice for the drawing-room.

MRS LEVERETT: *(Helping MRS POSSETT.)* I didn't come here for that.

CLIVE: No, but she *did.* Take her away.

MRS LEVERETT: I came here to say my say, and say my say I mean to do.

*Exit with MRS POSSETT R. to drawing-room.*

CLARA: *(To GERALD.)* Now, perhaps you'll tell me why that girl's still here.

CLIVE: Go on, the gong's gone.

GERALD: *(Cross to CLARA.)* Certainly. I'm very glad she is. *(To CLIVE.)* Am I?

CLIVE: Delighted!

GERALD: There you are. I'm delighted. She came here last night – poor little soul – alone in pyjamas. In pyjamas alone. Driven from home. Driven by Putz.

GERTRUDE: Rubbish! She's a notorious girl.

CLIVE: She's the sweetest little girl I've ever seen.

GERALD: She's certainly the sweetest *I've* ever seen – almost.

CLIVE: I tell you she's above suspicion.

GERALD: Yes. Like Potiphar's wife.

CLIVE: She radiates purity and innocence.

CLARA: Well, I haven't accused. I'll see her and judge.

CLIVE: Yes, go on. Call her out of that room.

GERALD: *(Boldly.)* Quite right. *(Calls.)* Little girl. Come out of that room.

*They all look up at bedroom, with their backs to audience.*

CLIVE: Now you shall see.

*POPPY DICKEY enters in cami-knickers from bedroom on balcony L.; crosses to the other end of balcony, singing and dancing.*

POPPY: 'Oh, sir, she's my baby –

Yes, sir, she's my baby;

Oh, sir, she's my baby now!'

*She turns to look over front of balcony; as she does so she calls out, 'Flags for the Lifeboat!' Realizing the situation, she gives a scream and rushes back into bedroom L. GERALD and CLIVE turn to each other, looking thunderstruck.*

GERTRUDE: What's the meaning of this?

GERALD: Don't ask me.

CLARA: Is *that* the girl?

GERALD: No, it isn't.

CLARA: Then who is it?

GERALD: *(To CLIVE.)* Who is it?

CLIVE: I didn't put it there.

GERALD: Some mistake. Darling.

CLARA: Rubbish! You said 'Come out', and out she came.

GERALD: Yes; but this wasn't the one we wanted to come out.

GERTRUDE: That's another local girl – she's one of the Dickeys.

GERALD: *(To CLIVE.)* You hear that! She's one of the Dickeys.

CLIVE: Yes, she looks it.

*POPPY re-enters from bedroom wearing RHODA's dressing gown.*

GERTRUDE: They've evidently been collecting all the fast girls of the place.

POPPY: *(Above.)* Don't you start on me, Mrs Twine.

GERTRUDE: *(Crosses stairs.)* Where's that girl from up the road? Is she there too?

POPPY: I don't know anything about any girl from up any road.

GERALD: *(To CLIVE.)* What happened?

CLIVE: Don't ask silly questions. I'm not a wizard.

GERALD: Somebody is.

GERTRUDE: Why did you come here?

POPPY: I came selling flags, and I went upstairs to mend my frock. I caught it on the gatepost.

GERALD: Is this friend or foe?

CLARA: It's all a pack of lies. I know that.

*GERTRUDE goes upstairs.*

GERALD: Oh, darling – not a whole pack.

POPPY: *(To GERTRUDE.)* Where are you going? That's *my* room.

*They exit into bedroom up L.*

CLARA: There you are. *Her* room.

CLIVE: Yes, but the other bedroom is elsewhere.

GERTRUDE: *(Off.)* Just as I thought.

POPPY: *(Off.)* Mind your own business.

GERTRUDE: *(Enters.)* There's not a sign of a frock in that room.

*POPPY enters from bedroom L. on balcony.*

CLARA: Then this is the one that was here all night.

GERALD: No, darling. I keep telling you. A much better one than that. The other one radiates purity. Nothing likes this Dickey thing at all.

POPPY: Well, you're a nice one to try and help.

GERALD: You think you're helping me?

CLIVE: Of course she is. A jolly fine effort. Well tried, Miss Flags.

POPPY: Thank you. I'm glad someone's got a glad hand.

GERTRUDE: It's quite clear. You were to stay here and tell lies while the other little wretch escaped. Go into that room. I'll tell your mother.

POPPY: You try. Mother's a sport, and she hates you like hell.

*Exit into bedroom on balcony L.*

CLARA: I see there are two of them.

*GERTRUDE crosses behind table.*

GERALD: That's right.

CLARA: One each.

GERALD: That's right. No, there aren't two. Well, yes, there are two – but – *(To CLIVE.)* Go on. Can't you say something?

CLARA: Why are there two?

GERALD: *(To CLIVE.)* Why are there two? That's you.

CLIVE: Now get this, Clara. For some reason, about which we're a trifle hazy, there are two – namely, radiates purity and Flags for the Lifeboat.

GERTRUDE: And one's as bad as the other.

GERALD: No; she's worse.

CLIVE: We've never set eyes on this Dickey thing – neither of us. I don't quite know why *I* haven't –

*GERALD digs CLIVE, drawing his attention to the fact that GERTRUDE is eyeing him suspiciously.*

– but there it is.

GERTRUDE: *(Crosses to R.C. from behind table.)* If it wasn't all some intrigue, why didn't you ask for my help last night?

CLIVE: I'll tell you that. Because you're a jealous, green-eyed, back biting woman.

GERALD: Thank you, Clive.

CLIVE: That's all right. She's got some more to come. *(Then to GERTRUDE.)* You're very fond of calling other people liars – but what about you, with your vile scandals and venomous libels and dirty little tattling tea-parties?

GERTRUDE: You'll gain nothing by rudeness.

CLIVE: I don't care whether I gain or not. It's well overdue to you. *(Turns to CLARA.)* And, Clara, don't you accuse Gerald. The girl he's defending is the victim of a wicked scandal. So long as Gertrude can find some mud to fling she doesn't care a damn whether it sticks.

GERALD: Quite right.

GERTRUDE: You needn't lose your temper. Just because you arranged for the girl to be here last night and then weren't allowed to stay here yourself too.

*Goes into drawing-room R.*

CLIVE: That woman's got a mind like a very ingenious sink.

*CLARA crosses R.C.*

GERALD: Clara darling. Don't go.

CLARA: Oh, I know it's true what she says. You're only trying to deceive me.

GERALD: No, I'm trying not to.

*CLARA exits up R.*

CLIVE: Look here – we must play our trump card, that's all.

GERALD: Have we got one?

CLIVE: Yes, I'm going along to that house.

GERALD: No, don't risk bringing Rhoda back. She's too pretty. She wouldn't go well. I know she wouldn't.

CLIVE: No, no, I don't mean her. I'm going to get Putz.

GERALD: Putz?

CLIVE: Yes. I'm going to get a big boulder and fling it in the pit of Putz's stomach and run like hell with him after me.

GERALD: Fine, Clive! – that's fine! That'll show Clara. Infuriate him. Don't throw stones, throw wurts.

CLIVE: *(Going.)* All right. Oh, if you can, Gerald, have that cat handy –

GERALD: Why?

CLIVE: Because with any luck I'll bring Conrad too.

*CLIVE goes hurriedly up R.C.*

*GERALD takes thought, then he picks up the parcel that CLIVE gave him with the dress, and makes for the stairs.*

*There are sounds of dissension in the drawing-room and CLARA returns. She speaks as she enters.*

CLARA: *(Entering from R. and saying as she enters.)* Quite enough to stand without that.

GERALD: *(Running down the stairs with the parcel behind him, hiding it from CLARA.)* What's the matter, darling?

CLARA: I wasn't speaking to you.

GERALD: Oh! You sounded so cross, I thought you were.

CLARA: It's Gertrude. You can't even misbehave yourself without Gertrude finding it out.

GERALD: No, I know I can't. Nobody can.

CLARA: Then you *did* misbehave yourself?

GERALD: You don't believe that, do you?

CLARA: I have to. But a girl coming in here with pyjamas on. *(Looking away.)*

GERALD: I know, dear. I didn't want her to have them on.

CLARA: What!

GERALD: I mean I'd rather she'd been wearing a hat.

CLARA: Oh, be honest with me. I'm trying to be loyal and loving.

GERALD: I know you are, darling, and I'm trying to explain it away – to explain, I mean – without the away.

CLARA: I don't think you need try to tell me any more.

GERALD: Thank you, darling. *(Attempting to embrace her.)*

CLARA: No. *(Pushing GERALD away gently.)* You admit to keeping the girl here all night?

GERALD: No, dear, letting her stay here all night. That's all the difference. Think of this poor little girl. She came here last night through the long and dewy grass. She was soused – I mean soaked.

CLARA: I don't care.

GERALD: But you must care – the poor little soul, she was cold. Her poor little toes were rattling like dominoes. Her trousers were wet up to the knee, so what did I do? I gave her mine.

CLARA: Your trousers?

GERALD: Yes, my spare bedwear pair. I couldn't turn her out again into the dark and dewy night.

CLARA: Why not?

GERALD: Why, I didn't want mine wet as well.

CLARA: Why did she leave home?

GERALD: Why, think of her home-life with only this man and Mrs Nutts. A great, big brute of a step-father stepping all over the place. A bully of a man cracking a whip, cracking her and cracking Nutts. Oh, think of it – a poor little child in distress, a life in peril. I said I must save her. Clara would wish it, so I saved her till this morning.

CLARA: It sounds a very unlikely story.

GERALD: Yes, that is what I told Clive.

*GERTRUDE entering from drawing-room.*

*GERALD cross L. of table to C.*

GERTRUDE: Clara, I must see you about a room for mother.

*CLIVE comes hurrying back R.C. Crosses L.C. to GERALD.*

CLIVE: One moment. Look out! *(To CLARA.)* There's someone here I want you to see.

GERALD: *(To CLIVE.)* Putz?

CLIVE: Yes.

GERALD: Is he all right?

CLIVE: *(With a nod.)* Livid with fury. *(To CLARA.)* Now, listen, Clara. You've got to be told about this man – the step-father.

GERTRUDE: He's not her step-father at all.

CLIVE: You shall judge that when you see him.

GERALD: Yes, and once you've seen him you won't want to see her.

CLIVE: No. You'd help to save any girl from a devil like that.

GERALD: He's a monster – a fiend in human shape.

CLIVE: A violent, savage swine.

GERALD: Without respect for God or man. You wait and see!

*PUTZ appears in the doorway; he knocks loudly, a double rap.*

*(Seeing PUTZ.)* This is the man.

*CLARA crosses D.L.*

Yes, come in.

*PUTZ comes down R.C.*

And say your worst.

PUTZ: *(Cross behind table, speaking very gently.)* Zee vorst? Ach, nein – I want to say you something nice. It is now aller right.

GERALD: It doesn't look all right to me.

CLIVE: *(Cross R. to PUTZ.)* No, certainly not. Look here! if you can't misbehave yourself properly you'd better get out of this.

GERTRUDE: *(To PUTZ.)* Will you kindly say what happened last night?

PUTZ: *(Crosses D.R.)* They try to take her from me. Aller der night she stay away from me. But I forgive her. Und I forgive you, my dear frent, absolute. *(Cross C. in front of table to GERALD.)*

CLIVE: *(To PUTZ.)* You liar! *(To GERALD.)* This is no good. *(Behind table R.C.)*

GERALD: No. Go on. Infuriate him – wurts!

CLIVE: *(Cross to PUTZ, who is R.C. in front of table.)* If you don't send her straight back here I'll come and fetch her. Come on. You come with me now.

PUTZ: Wait, please, I wish for peace. *(Goes up to chair.)*

CLARA: Is this the fiend in human shape?

GERALD: He's the wrong shape to-day.

PUTZ: *(Coming down R.C.)* Look, please. The trunk and the hud.

GERTRUDE: *(Seizing hat.)* What's the meaning of this outrage?

CLIVE: *(Cross L.C. in front of table.)* Clara! You mustn't believe this lying German humbug.

CLARA: I believe my own eyes and ears.

GERALD: Yes, but you can't believe his nose and mouth.

CLARA: He's the quietest man I've ever seen.

GERALD: Don't go, Clara!

CLARA: No. One hour apart from me and back you go.

GERALD: Back where?

CLARA: Back to your old life with Clive.

GERALD: It's Bognor again.

*Enter RHODA, cross down R.*

CLIVE: Look out! Here she is!

*RHODA is in her own clothes – outdoor costume.*

CLARA: Is this the girl?

GERALD: Yes. But don't be misled. She doesn't look nearly so nice in pyjamas.

CLARA: She certainly doesn't look what Gertrude says.

RHODA: I'm not. But your husband's been tremendously kind to me all the same.

GERALD: Oh, not tremendously – just kind.

*Enter MRS LEVERETT R.*

MRS LEVERETT: Well, I've finished this job.

CLIVE: *(To GERALD.)* Hold on. I see a ray. *(Cross to R. MRS LEVERETT.)* You, Mrs Flanagan – that was a deliberate untruth you told me last night!

MRS LEVERETT: Me? How dare you! And what do you mean?

CLIVE: *(Pointing to PUTZ.)* You told me this little girl and this man Putz were living in sin.

PUTZ: *(Changing his manner quickly.)* Was it das? *(Fiercely.)* What you make?

*GERALD crosses up L. of table R.C.*

GERALD: That's an awful thing to say.

PUTZ: Who shall say of her?

CLIVE: *(Bringing MRS LEVERETT forward.)* Come on. Ask *her.*

PUTZ: *(Cross R. furiously to MRS LEVERETT.)* You are who?

MRS LEVERETT: I only said I'd always heard. *(Cross to other side of Putz L.)*

PUTZ: You are who to say of her and Rhoda –

MRS LEVERETT: Mrs Twine told me –

GERALD: *(Pushes MRS TWINE forward to PUTZ – L. of PUTZ.)* This is Mrs Twine.

GERTRUDE: Gerald, how dare you?

PUTZ: *(Wheeling on GERTRUDE.)* Herr Gott! You shall say of my step-daughter that she is not *so* gut. *Allerferdampter – Schwein – verfluchter Cammail!*

*During this speech he forces MRS TWINE and MRS LEVERETT over and backwards L. GERALD and CLIVE follow behind Putz to L.C. Finally, he picks up the bag of clothes and flings it to the ground, and with a final roar of anger –*

*Exits R.C.*

Kreuz! Himmel! Donnerwetter!

*Pronounced: Croyts, Himmel, Donner-vetter.*

*(Cross, Heaven, Thunder-weather.)*

*At PUTZ's outburst CLARA has instinctively gone to GERALD for protection and RHODA to CLIVE.*

*RHODA is in CLIVE's arms and CLARA in GERALD's. Unseen, CLIVE and GERALD, who are standing back to back, shake hands, CLIVE's L. hand and GERALD's R., with their eyes still on RHODA and CLARA.*


*CURTAIN*

THARK

# Characters

*(In order of appearance)*

HOOK

WARNER

CHERRY BUCK

LIONEL FRUSH

MRS. FRUSH

SIR HECTOR BENBOW, BART., M.F.H.

RONALD GAMBLE

LADY BENBOW

KITTY STRATTON

JONES

WHITTLE

SCENES:

ACT I.
Sir Hector Benbow's library in his flat in Mayfair.
An Autumn evening.

ACT II.
The same. Next morning.

ACT III.
SCENE I. The dining room at Thark. A week later after dinner.
SCENE II. Ronny's room at Thark. 3 A. M. the following morning.

*Thark* was first produced on 4 July 1927 at the Aldwych
Theatre, London, with the following cast:

| | |
|---|---|
| HOOK | J. Robertson Hare. |
| WARNER | Ann Furrell. |
| CHERRY BUCK | Ena Mason. |
| LIONEL FRUSH | Kenneth Kove. |
| MRS. FRUSH | Mary Brough. |
| SIR HECTOR BENBOW, BART., M.F.H | Tom Walls |
| RONALD GAMBLE | Ralph Lynn. |
| LADY BENBOW | Ethel Coleridge |
| KITTY STRATTON | Winifred Shotter. |
| JONES | Gordon James. |
| WHITTLE | Hastings Lynn. |

# Act One

*SCENE: The library of SIR HECTOR BENBOW's flat in Mayfair, on an October evening. The room is described as the library, but really it is the large room in the flat which is apportioned to the husband, as contrasted with the wife's drawing-room It is the room of a man of ample means, out-of-door and sporting tastes, rather than indoor and bookish; and really more at home in the country than in the West End. It is a sumptuous room with oak-panelling, a fine ceiling and with an ample degree of comfort in its furniture. A door in the C. background leads from the passage, the front door of the flat being just outside this room, which is the first room one comes to in the flat, as it were. The front door is not necessarily seen outside. There is another door in the R. wall, also an opening up L. The windows are up in the R.C. corner in a bow, and the fireplace down L., with the fire burning. The furniture is Japanese blue and gold lacquer upholstered grey. There is a settee R. A round table up R.C. A small armchair L. of the table, another down L., four other chairs, one L. of the cabinet, one R. front of the cabinet, one down R. below door., one R. of centre of door. An electric chandelier hanging from ceiling C., also four two-light brackets, one up R. on wall, one on back wall and two on L. wall. A standard lamp up R. above settee. What pictures – and such decorations – there are, relate almost entirely to sporting tastes, whether hunting, shooting or the turf. There may be relics of big-game shooting expeditions. There is a table up L. of the door. On this is a telephone. Between the door and the windows up R.C. there are two foxes' brushes hanging and a huntsman's horn underneath.*

*HOOK, a middle-aged and rather careworn man-servant, with a manner which is the result of years of bullying, discovered talking on the telephone, when the curtain rises. He is R. of writing-table.*

HOOK: *(On 'phone.)* Yes?… *(More keenly.)* Yes. It's me speaking… *(Surprised.)* Is that you, mother?… 'Ere, what are you doing, telephoning me 'ere?… Had to? Why?… *What?* You mean it's *happened?* It's all over?… Well, what is it?… A girl? Oh, jest a girl? I mean, that's *all?*…

*(Relieved.)* Ah! 'Ow's Florrie – keepin' *up?*... She is – all right, I'll come round as quick as I can. The boss isn't in, but I told 'im it was on the cards. I'll leave word.

*During the last few words, WARNER, a smart maidservant, has put her head in from the opening up L. As HOOK hangs up the receiver she comes down excitedly.*

WARNER: Oh, Mr. Hook, has it happened?

HOOK: *(Agitated.)* All right, all right. *(Cross to table R., picks up letters and moves D.C.)* Now, don't you worry me. I've got to get along there.

WARNER: *(Moves to HOOK.)* A little girl, is it? Dear little thing! Oh, Mr. Hook, aren't you *proud* of it?

HOOK: I haven't seen it yet. Now look here *(Crosses down to WARNER.)*, if the master returns before I do, just attend to this.

WARNER: Me? What?

HOOK: *(Picks up telegram from table C.)* There's a telegram for him – see?

*WARNER notes it.*

It came this morning and *(Cross to table.)* there's his letters – that's all. Oh! no, there's another thing. *(Cross D.C.)*

WARNER: What?

HOOK: He's expecting a lady to call in. She hasn't yet. But if she does, she's to be asked to come back. He's taking her out to dinner.

WARNER: *(Coming down.)* What lady?

*Warning door bell.*

HOOK: He didn't say.

WARNER: Well, but how am I to know? What sort of lady? Is it business or pleasure?

HOOK: Is it for you to ask? Simply, if a lady calls by appointment, you say, 'Oh, it will give Sir 'Ector much pleasure if you will dine with him, calling here at seven-fifteen.'

WARNER: All right. *(Moves L.)*

HOOK: That's all. *(Puts telegram on desk up L.)* Now I'll get along.

*Bell heard outside. He is agitated.*

Oh Lawd! There's someone there now.

WARNER: I'll see to it, if you like.

HOOK: *(Going up C.)* No, no. If I'm here, I'd better.

WARNER: Oh, very good then.

*WARNER goes off L.*

*HOOK goes out at C., leaving door open.*

*CHERRY's voice is heard off just afterwards.*

CHERRY: *(Off R.)* Sir Hector Benbow in?

HOOK: *(Off.)* Not yet, madam.

CHERRY: *(Off, cross D.L.) Ah!* Then will you kindly step this way, please, madam?

*He reappears followed by CHERRY BUCK. She is about twenty-five, smart and confident.*

CHERRY: I thought he'd be here. *(C.)*

HOOK: You were the lady Sir 'Ector was expecting? *(Cross. L.C.)*

CHERRY: *(Cross D.C.)* Well, Sir Hector said something about – what about a little dinner?

HOOK: That's quite correct, madam. It will give Sir 'Ector much pleasure if you will dine with him, calling here at seven-fifteen.

CHERRY: Oh, strong! When will he be in though?

*HOOK is restless and trying to get away.*

HOOK: *(Coming down C.)* I hardly know, madam. He went to the races this morning with his nephew and hasn't got back yet. Lady Benbow is away from 'ome, you know.

CHERRY: I didn't know, but I guessed. What nephew is it then?

HOOK: *(Trying to go.)* Oh, there is only one, madam. Mr. Gamble – Mr. Ronald Gamble.

CHERRY: Oh! Is that the Mr. Ronald Gamble who's engaged to Miss Stratton?

*Warning door bell.*

HOOK: Yes, yes, that's quite right, madam.

CHERRY: Yes, I saw her picture in the *Mirror*.

HOOK: Yes. But she's also out of town. In fact, she's with Lady Benbow. *(Moves away a little.)*

CHERRY: I see. *(Watching HOOK's movements.)* Are you anxious to get away or something?

HOOK: Well, yes, please. I want to get 'ome. I've – er – had news from 'ome, you see. *(Coming down a little.)*

CHERRY: Not bad news, I hope?

HOOK: Well, I dunno. Half and 'alf, I suppose. The fact is, madam, I've just had a baby!

CHERRY: *(With a short shrill laugh.)* Sounds as if you ought to have *left* home. Well, I'll trot away and get dressed. *(Moving up stage.)*

HOOK: Very good, madam.

*Door bell rings.*

Oh dear!

CHERRY: Is that Sir Hector?

HOOK: No, madam, it can't be – er – he's got his key with him. I'll see. *(Cross L., calls to WARNER.)* Warner, attend to the door.

CHERRY: Well, p'r'aps I'd better not be seen around in here.

HOOK: Well, madam, that's hardly for me to say. But I shall be going down be the servants' stairs if – you'd care to be shown the way.

CHERRY: Oh, strong! That is, if someone's coming in. Shall I come with you now?

HOOK: Just half a jiffy, while I get me 'at.

*He goes up to L.*

*CHERRY looks door C. and listens, opening door a little. MRS. FRUSH's voice is heard. Then her son's.*

MRS. FRUSH: Oh, but it's by appointment.

LIONEL: Well, never mind, mother –

*CHERRY moves D.L.*

WARNER: If you'd come in, please, I'll see.

*WARNER shows LIONEL on and – exits C.*

*WARNER immediately opens door and shows in LIONEL, but does not herself enter. LIONEL is a boy of twenty or so – very feeble but affable and with a keen eye for the ladies. He eyes the MAID as he comes down R., then seeing CHERRY he bows half inquiringly.*

LIONEL: *(Little laugh.)* Oh, I beg pardon. *(To CHERRY.)*

CHERRY: *(Also slightly self-consciously.)* That's quite all right, thanks.

LIONEL: I didn't know there was anyone here. I came to see Sir Hector.

CHERRY: Yes. So did I, as a matter of fact.

LIONEL: Oh, perhaps I'd better call later.

CHERRY: I'm just going. *(To C.)*

LIONEL: Don't go on my account.

*CHERRY laughs softly. He laughs in response. Brief pause.*

Nice evening.

CHERRY: *(Nodding.)* Not bad for London.

LIONEL: I'm a stranger to London. I've just taken a place in the country.

CHERRY: Lucky you. I do love the country.

LIONEL: London's all right for a change, but I get awfully lonely, when I'm alone.

CHERRY: I never go out with strangers.

LIONEL: My word! I wish I could find somebody like you who does! *(Cross R.C.)*

*HOOK reappears L. carrying a coat and a bowler hat. He does not notice LIONEL.*

HOOK: *(To CHERRY.)* If you're ready, madam?

CHERRY: *(Airily.)* Oh – no hurry.

*LIONEL coughs. HOOK turns away and faces LIONEL.*

LIONEL: Oh, are you the butler? *(Looking him up and down.)*

HOOK: Yes, sir.

LIONEL: I'm Mr. Frush. I called to see Sir Hector. Did the maid tell you?

HOOK: No, sir. I haven't seen the maid. Sir 'Ector shouldn't be long, sir.

CHERRY: *(To LIONEL, indicating HOOK.)* He wants to go off home.

LIONEL: Oh, righto! I'll wait here, if I may.

HOOK: Certainly, sir. *(To CHERRY.)* It's this way, madam.

CHERRY: *(To HOOK.)* Thanks.

*He shows CHERRY way out L. She, as she goes, nods to LIONEL.*

*(To LIONEL, smilingly.)* Good evening.

LIONEL: *(Smiling, following her to exit up L.)* Good evening.

*CHERRY and HOOK go off.*

*Immediately afterwards WARNER re-renters at door C.*

WARNER: Oh, excuse me, sir – was that the butler, sir?

LIONEL: Yes. It's all right. I've seen him. I'm going to wait.

WARNER: Oh, very good sir. *(Cross D.R.)*

LIONEL: *(Going up to doorway.)* Mother! Mother!

MRS. FRUSH: *(Off. L.)* All right. I'm just having a look round.

*Entering C. from L.*

*(To WARNER.)* Isn't there anyone at home?

*MRS. FRUSH is an elderly dame of middle-class, a new-rich caricature, a woman who has lost her natural homeliness under the influence of money and ambition. She is a shade over-dressed, but not grotesquely so.*

WARNER: I'm afraid not, madam.

*WARNER R.C., MRS FRUSH C., LIONEL L.*

MRS. FRUSH: Well, I may tell you I've come all the way from Norfolk to keep this appointment. *(Takes out a letter from her handbag.)* Here's the letter if you don't believe me.

WARNER: Certainly I believe you, madam.

LIONEL: *(Always on tenterhooks when his mother is about.)* Of course she does. Hush, mother!

MRS. FRUSH: *(With vigour.)* Hush yourself! *(Takes letter from bag. Reads:.)* 'Please call here on your arrival from Norfolk and I will make an appointment with you.' There!

WARNER: *(Brightening up.)* Oh, well, I see. Then I was to say that if the lady Sir Hector Bowen expected called in, would she please dine with him, calling back here at seven-fifteen?

MRS. FRUSH: Ah, that's better. Yes, with pleasure.

LIONEL: *(Cross to MRS. FRUSH.)* Well, there you are then.

MRS. FRUSH: Yes, that's very nice. But what about you, though? I don't think I mentioned you were coming?

LIONEL: Oh, that's all right. You dine alone with him. If you can be trusted.

MRS. FRUSH: *(With lorgnettes.)* What d'you mean, Lionel?

LIONEL: *(To WARNER.)* Well, I mean, perhaps – if I might just have a word with my mother alone?

WARNER: I beg pardon, sir.

*Exit up L.*

LIONEL: *(After seeing her go.)* Now, look here, mother dear – you must be more careful what you do and say here.

MRS. FRUSH: *(Moves D.R.)* I don't care. I'm as good as he is even if he is a Bart.

LIONEL: *(Cross to MRS. FRUSH.)* Do, please, be tactful. I mean – for instance, you ought to have come straight in here just now, instead of nosing about in the hall.

MRS. FRUSH: Nonsense! I like to see how such people furnish. And Lionel – *(moves up to him.)* – you need never have bought an umbrella-stand. They don't have one here. They've got one of them 'igh Chinese vaises.

LIONEL: Well, don't comment on things. Anyhow, they're not vaises – they're varses.

MRS. FRUSH: To those as likes to call them varses they're varses. And to such as prefer to call them vaises they're vaises.

LIONEL: Well, whatever you do, don't start complaining about Thark to-night.

MRS. FRUSH: Why not? That's why we're here. He's sold us the place and it's non-inhabitable.

LIONEL: But leave all that till to-morrow. Besides, it wasn't Sir Hector's house. It was Miss Stratton's house. He was acting for her, that's all.

MRS. FRUSH: I don't care. I'm here to complain, and complain I'll see I do. If you buy a house that size you expect to find it all right.

LIONEL: I always told you the house was much too big.

MRS. FRUSH: But it isn't too big! You can't find a house too big for me. But all *right* it is *not*, and he knows it. *(Turning away.)*

LIONEL: Well, don't discuss it to-night. You can't accept a man's invitation to dinner and then accuse him of sharp practice while you're eating it.

*Warning door bang.*

MRS. FRUSH: Oh, I suppose that's some of your usual college 'how-to-behave' talk. Still, never mind. I'm not going to refuse his dinner. Come on, I must go and get into my best evening.

LIONEL: No, you go on. *(Cross D.L.)* And I'll wait and make a business appointment –

*MRS. FRUSH is going up C.*

for to-morrow. *(As MRS. FRUSH is going up.)* One moment, mother. You must let the maid show you out.

MRS. FRUSH: All right, all right! I know.

*As WARNER appears up L.*

Show me out, please.

*WARNER cross up C.*

*MRS. FRUSH goes off C.*

*After a moment, WARNER opens door C.*

LIONEL: I'm waiting a little while longer. I'm Mr. Frush.

WARNER: *(Vaguely.)* Oh – yes, sir? *(C.)*

LIONEL: *We* bought Thark.

*Warning door bang.*

WARNER: I beg your pardon, sir?

LIONEL: I say – *(Moves to her.)* – *we* bought *Thark.* The house in Norfolk that belonged to Miss Stratton.

WARNER: Oh, yes, sir.

LIONEL: And, of course Sir Hector's her guardian and does all that sort of thing for her so – that's what it is.

WARNER: Yes, sir.

LIONEL: *(Rather nervously.)* I suppose it's all right my waiting here? I mean – it won't upset Sir Hector? I know he gets rather easily – upset. *(Gives a little nervous laugh.)*

WARNER: *(With the housemaid's slow wriggle of embarrassment.)* Well, it's not for me to say, sir –

LIONEL: Still, I think we'll risk that, shall we?

*Door bang.*

*The voice of SIR HECTOR BENBOW heard off in a loud summons. LIONEL crosses D.L.*

BENBOW: *(Off.)* HOOK!

WARNER: *(Turning quickly.)* Excuse me, sir! *(C.)*

*BENBOW appears in the doorway. LIONEL is L. BENBOW is a middle-aged very-well-turned-out man of the Master of Hounds type. He is dressed for racing with field glasses, etc. There is a good deal of ginger in his character. He has grey military moustaches and grey hair.*

BENBOW: *(As he enters.)* Hook! *(To WARNER.)* Where's Hook? Where's Hook? *(He hands her his coat, hat, stick and race glasses.)*

WARNER: If you please, sir, he had to go home.

BENBOW: Why?

*She dithers in silence.*

Why?

129

WARNER: *(In subdued tones.)* Oh, sir – he had a domestic event.

BENBOW: Oh, yes, of course! *(Who has now seen LIONEL, who smiles uncomfortably.)* Hallo! Oh, yes – I forgot about you.

WARNER: There's a telegram, sir, and also –

BENBOW: *(To WARNER.)* All right, girl. You can go – needn't wait.

*WARNER goes out L.*

*(Then to LIONEL.)* Yes, your mother wrote to me. What is it? Anything about Thark?

LIONEL: Yes, I'm afraid it is.

BENBOW: 'Smatter?

LIONEL: I beg pardon?

BENBOW: *(Loudly.)* Stand up! – 'Smatter?

LIONEL: Oh – well – *(Crosses to SIR HECTOR.)* – it's rather a difficult subject to embark on.

BENBOW: Well, don't – *(Glasses on.)* – embark on it now I've got to dress for dinner.

LIONEL: Yes, yes, I know. My mother's coming along.

BENBOW: Yes, confound it, I forgot about her too. *(Crosses to table, picks up letter.)* But I think we'll deal with Thark to-morrow. See you in the morning. Good-night to yer.

LIONEL: That's exactly what I wanted.

BENBOW: Well, you've got what you wanted, and I'll see yah in the morning. Good-night to yer.

LIONEL: Oh, good-night, sir. *(Pausing as he goes.)* Only, don't let my mother start telling you her troubles.

BENBOW: It's no good trying to stop a woman talking once she gets started. We mustn't let her begin, that's all.

LIONEL: Good! As long as you won't let her begin.

BENBOW: Well, I'll do my best not to, and I'll see you in the morning. *(Waving him away.)* Good-night to yer.

LIONEL: But, sir, how do I get down?

BENBOW: *(Edging up C.)* You can go down the stairs or take the lift…

*LIONEL disappears.*

*BENBOW closes the door, returns, places letters on table C.*

Or fall over the banisters and break your bloody neck. *(He turns to the writing-table and picks up a letter. As he tears it open – .)*

*HOOK enters at door C.*

HOOK: *(Out of breath.)* Oh, I was just – on my way home, Sir 'Ector.

BENBOW: Yes –

HOOK: And I saw your car – so I thought I'd best come back – in case you wanted me, sir.

BENBOW: Why, what's the trouble at home consist of?

HOOK: It's a girl, sir. Thank you very much.

BENBOW: A girl – eh? Clever boy! Oh, that reminds me. Has anyone called to see me?

HOOK: Yes, sir. The lady says she'll be please to dine, calling here at seven-fifteen.

BENBOW: Good. What's the time now?

HOOK: Gone half-past six, sir.

BENBOW: Then put my bath on.

HOOK: Yes, sir. *(Crosses L.)*

BENBOW: And Hook –

HOOK: Sir! *(Stopping.)*

BENBOW: Fetch me some cigarettes.

HOOK: Yes, sir. *(Crosses R.)*

BENBOW: And Hook!

HOOK: Sir! *(Stopping.)*

BENBOW: Get me a whisky and soda.

HOOK: *(Going.)* Yes, sir. *(Crosses up L.)*

BENBOW: Stand still when I'm talking to you, can't you? Mr. Ronny's in the car down below. He can take it on to his place and send it straight back here. Go and tell him.

*HOOK moves again up stage, fidgeting about.*

*(Halting him.)* Now!

HOOK: *(Halting rigidly.)* Sorry, sir.

BENBOW: Get me the whisky first.

HOOK: *(Remaining stationary.)* Yes, sir.

BENBOW: Well, go on!

*HOOK vanishes L.*

Don't stand there like a small-sized lamp-post – with no light on top!

*He follows HOOK up stage and sees telegram on desk. He picks it up and opens it. He consults telegram – singing to himself – gives an exclamation of surprised dismay and goes to door and calls:*

HOOK!

HOOK: *(Off L.)* Sir!

BENBOW: Her ladyship's coming home to-night. Did *you* know that?

HOOK: No, sir.

BENBOW: Well, she is. Arriving Paddington six-thirty.

*HOOK reappearing with a drink on a tray.*

HOOK: Very good, sir. *(Follows BENBOW about with the whisky at a respectful distance.)*

BENBOW: Very good be damned! *(Crosses D.R.)* It's very bad! She'll be here by seven-fifteen.

HOOK: Oh, before that, sir.

BENBOW: She'll be here *at* seven-fifteen, I tell you, that's the point. And that lady's coming here to be taken out to dinner.

HOOK: Can't she be put off, sir?

BENBOW: Well, if you're so clever, ring her up and put her off.

HOOK: Yes, sir. *(In a tone of polite inquiry.)* I'm afraid I don't know the lady's name, sir.

BENBOW: No, and neither do I, you damn fool, that's just the trouble.

*A short, perplexed pause, and he picks up hunting horn which is hanging on wall L. of window, goes to window up stage R.C. and sounds it. He then calls:*

Hi! Ronny! Come up here! *(Turns to HOOK.)* Did he hear?

HOOK: I don't know, sir.

BENBOW: Go and find out then. Don't stand there holding that damned thing. *(Waving him off.)* Go on, go on, go on!

*HOOK places drink tray on table.*

HOOK: *(Hurrying off up C.)* Yes, sir.

*HOOK goes hurriedly C., leaving door open.*

*BENBOW calls through the opening C.*

BENBOW: Hi! you – girl – whatever your name is! – Warnah! Her ladyship is coming home to-night. Did you know that? Well, she is. You'd better light the fire in her room. (*Crosses down L.*) And you'll want another one in the drawing-room. What the hell am I going to do? I don't know!

*He goes off stage L.*

*The library is empty for a moment.*

*RONALD GAMBLE strolls in C. He is a man of thirty or so, and like his uncle is very well dressed for his race-meeting. Seeing a whisky and soda on the table he has an imaginary conversation as though trying to refuse it, pushing his head forward with his left hand and takes the drink with his right. He drinks the whisky and soda. Just as he has finished it, BENBOW re-renters L.*

Hey! That's my drink!

RONNY: *(Handing him the empty glass.)* Oh, sorry! Where's mine?

BENBOW: Ah –

*BENBOW goes to door L. and RONNY marches three steps with him, halting just behind him in the doorway. They both raise their voices together.*

BENBOW and RONNY: HOOK!

HOOK: *(Heard off.)* Sir!

BENBOW: Bring the whisky in here.

RONNY: I'll only have one if *you're* going to have another.

BENBOW: Thank you, I enjoyed that one immensely. Don't you run away with the idea that I called you here to drink.

RONNY: Then what did you call me up for?

BENBOW: I've had some very awkward news, my boy. Your aunt's coming back to-night.

RONNY: What? And Kitty?

BENBOW: No. Just your aunt – that's enough, ain't it?

RONNY: I say, why is auntie coming home? Has she heard something about you?

BENBOW: What d'yer mean? There's nothing to hear about me.

RONNY: I know. That's why I asked in that surprised way –

*HOOK enters with tray with drinks. He substitutes this for the other tray on table C., shuts door C., and crosses L., behind BENBOW and RONNY.*

BENBOW: There's nothing to hear, I tell you. *(Hands glass to RONNY.)*

RONNY: I know – that's just what I say. And very glad I am of it.

BENBOW: Glad of what?

RONNY: Glad that she heard nothing – because she can't have, because there's nothing to hear. *(Hands glass to BENBOW.)*

BENBOW: I can think of nothing that could have brought her home.

RONNY: Well, naturally *I* can think of nothing.

HOOK: *(Coming down L. of BENBOW.)* Excuse me, Sir 'Ector.

*BENBOW puts glass of tray.*

RONNY: *(To HOOK.)* Why, can *you* think of something?

HOOK: *(To BENBOW, ignoring RONNY.)* After her ladyship's arrived, would it be convenient if I popped round home, sir?

BENBOW: Hell do you mean? – popped!

HOOK: *(With an embarrassed smile.)* I feel I must do my duty to my wife, sir.

BENBOW: Oh – you appear to have done that. Go on, then.

*Exit HOOK up L.*

RONNY: I say, uncle, what's the matter with Hook?

BENBOW: He's got a little girl.

RONNY: Oh, really, I thought he said he was going to see his wife. *(Crosses to table C., pause – bus.: pouring drinks.)* But now auntie's coming home, Kitty will be left all alone in Bath.

BENBOW: That's all right, she's old enough to look after herself. *(He crosses to fireplace, looks at telegram.)*

RONNY: I know, and that's just when girls begin to get looked after. You know, uncle, Bath's a very dangerous place. *(Gets drink.)* Full of Beaux – you know – Beau Somethings.

BENBOW: Not now. Only old people with gout.

RONNY: Oh, I see, bow legs.

BENBOW: *(Crosses to RONNY.)* They only go there to drink water.

RONNY: *(Takes a drink to BENBOW.)* Oh, really? I'm surprised you've ever heard of the place. Well, good luck, uncle! *(Drinks.)*

BENBOW: Thank yer – but I don't think there's much good luck coming my way to-night.

RONNY: Why not?

BENBOW: Yer aunt'll be here in five minutes. Is *that* good luck?

RONNY: Oh, well – *fairly* good luck. *(Raising glass, drinking.)*

BENBOW: Now listen, Ronny. At seven-fifteen a lady who thinks she's being taken out to dinner by me – will arrive here for that purpose.

RONNY: Who is she?

BENBOW: That's the trouble. I don't know.

RONNY: You don't know? What do you mean? Have you won her in a raffle, or something?

BENBOW: Now listen, my boy. I want you to help me.

*RONNY looks suspiciously.*

No, no, it's all right. Now there are one or two things I'm a pretty good judge of. I'm a pretty good judge of a horse –

RONNY: Good Lord! You're not going to have dinner with a horse, are you?

BENBOW: *(Ignoring this.)* You can't tell me anything about a terrier –

RONNY: I wasn't going to.

BENBOW: I know a good glass o' port as soon as I *smell* it.

RONNY: That's very funny. That's just how I know the terrier.

BENBOW: And I've never had occasion to mistrust my judgement of a pair of ankles. Now listen. *(He crosses L., puts his glass on mantelpiece, and sits on club fender.)*

RONNY: Ankles – I will listen. *(Brings chair down L. and sits, after putting glass on mantelpiece.)*

BENBOW: I was walking down South Molton Street yesterday morning. You know those women's shops there – little places with nothing in the windows except a hat on one peg and frock on another, and a damned stuffed cat in the corner, and that's all.

RONNY: A cat now! Why do you keep on being zoological! What exactly is your trouble, uncle? Tell me.

BENBOW: I'm telling you, ain't I?

RONNY: As I interrupted, sorry; yes?

BENBOW: As I passed by there was something else in the window.

RONNY: Not one of the girls who work in the shop?

BENBOW: Why not?

RONNY: Well, you said you passed by.

BENBOW: I didn't hurry by. I just strolled by – anyway, there she was – fiddling about – you know – arranging something.

RONNY: Yes. I bet she's arranged it very well.

BENBOW: She was a good looker, my boy.

RONNY: Yes. I bet you were, too.

BENBOW: I had a good look at her through the glass –

RONNY: Through the glass?

BENBOW: Well, there was glass in the window, wasn't there?

RONNY: Oh, I'm sorry, I thought you meant you brought out a telescope.

BENBOW: I stood and looked at her through the glass. And when she went out of the window, I slipped into the shop, gave her my card, and said, 'You come and have some dinner with me to-morrow night, my girl.' She began the usual way – *you* know how they do – 'Oh, I never go out with strangers.' *(Laughing.)* They always begin like that –

RONNY: *(Laughing.)* Oh, rather! *(Checking himself.)* Do they?

BENBOW: *(Hastily.)* Well, anyway, this one did. Then along comes the old woman who runs the place – you know, one of those old prize pouters –

RONNY: *(Alarmed for himself.)* And you had to ask her as well? No, thank you. I'm not taking that on. *(Rising crosses C.)*

*BENBOW crosses C. to RONNY.*

BENBOW: No! Don't be silly! Point is, I only had time to say to the girl, 'Call at my address and say whether you're coming.'

RONNY: And has she called?

BENBOW: She has.

RONNY: And is she coming?

BENBOW: She is. *(Looking at telegram.)* At seven-fifteen. That's why I called you up, my boy.

RONNY: *What's* why?

BENBOW: Now then, don't be dense. I can't have girls coming here to be taken out to dinner with your aunt looking.

RONNY: Oh, I see. You want me to take auntie out to dinner to keep her out of the way.

BENBOW: That's a good idea, I never thought of that! But no – I think on the whole the little girl from the shop had better be *your* friend. It'll be safer.

RONNY: Safer for who?

*Warning door bell.*

BENBOW: Well, ain't you pleased? You will be when you see her. Only we don't want her coming up here, so I'll tell the hall-porter to keep her down below. *(Looks to opening L. and calls.)*

HOOK!

RONNY: I say, uncle, what about Kitty? She gets so frightfully jealous.

BENBOW: *(Scornfully.)* That's all right. She can't possibly find out. Where's that Hook?

*Bell.*

*As HOOK appeared L. the bell is heard off. HOOK is in a nervous state. They put glasses on the table C.*

HOOK: Oh, sir, it's her ladyship.

BENBOW: Well, why should *you* worry? *(Crosses to RONNY R.)* Now look here. You'll have to see the hall-porter about keeping her down below. I leave it all to you.

RONNY: Right you are, uncle. I don't mind doing you a good turn.

BENBOW: You're not doing yourself a bad one. You wait and see. Well, what do you want? *(To HOOK.)* Well, move, can't you? You know how to open a door!

*HOOK disappears C.*

Now look here, you'll have to see the little girl, and tell her it'll have to be another time instead.

RONNY: You mean, as well.

BENBOW: That's right – another time as well, instead.

RONNY: You another time as well, instead of *me*, as well as me this time…

HOOK: *(Off stage.)* Good evening, my lady.

LADY BENBOW: *(Off.)* Good evening, Hook.

BENBOW: *(Listening.)* Look out! Shut up!

RONNY: I'll tell her –

*HOOK opens door C.*

*LADY BENBOW appears from C.*

*HOOK exits C.*

LADY BENBOW: Oh, here you are! *(Crosses D.C.)*

*LADY BENBOW is a fashionable, shrewd and rather sarcastic lady – a nice character. She wears a becoming travelling costume. BENBOW and RONNY welcome her in a self-conscious and effusive manner.*

BENBOW: Oh, welcome home – home, my love. Glad to see you. *(Kisses her.)*

RONNY: We both are. How are you, auntie dear? What a good thing you've come back!

*BENBOW gives RONNY a look, than at LADY BENBOW.*

LADY BENBOW: But why, Ronny?

RONNY: I mean – he's missed you so much. Uncle's missed you frightfully. Why, only the other day out shooting he said to me, 'Ronny, I've missed her.'

LADY BENBOW: *(Crosses L., sits on club fender.)* What do you want to see the hall-porter about? Some guilty secret?

*BENBOW crosses to table C., takes a drink.*

RONNY: Oh no, auntie. Knowing you were home, I ordered a few flowers to be sent in for you and I thought I'd go and see whether they'd arrived.

LADY BENBOW: Flowers?

RONNY: *(Making shapes with his hands.)* Yes, you know, large at the top and peter off to nothing. They smell like nothing on earth.

LADY BENBOW: Oh, RONNY! *(Pleased.)* How nice of you. What made you think of that?

RONNY: Oh, don't know, auntie, I can generally think of something. *(Passes this faux pas off as best he can.)*

*Exits C. with an expressive look at SIR HECTOR.*

BENBOW*: (Hastily changing the subject.)* Well, what brings you home, my love? *(Crosses to LADY BENBOW.)*

LADY BENBOW: Kitty, of course!

BENBOW: Kitty? What? Is Kitty here, too?

LADY BENBOW: She insisted on coming to town –

*BENBOW looks anxiously towards door C., he is thinking of RONNY.*

to see you about this trouble at Thark.

BENBOW: Well, that's my trouble, not Kitty's.

LADY BENBOW: I know. She's never even seen the Frushes. But they wrote to her. They seem to think they've been swindled or something.

BENBOW: *(Incredulously.)* Oh, do they? Where's Kitty now?

LADY BENBOW: I brought on her boxes. She went on to Ronny's rooms. Thought he'd be there. She'll be here in a minute.

BENBOW: What the devil did you want to bring Kitty back here for?

LADY BENBOW: Well – why not?

BENBOW: What?

LADY BENBOW: *Why not?*

BENBOW: What?…Oh, well, it doesn't matter a damn. *(Sits by her L.)* Have you had a nice time, my love?

LADY BENBOW: Very! I said we should probably go back there again.

BENBOW: Oh good! Splendid! – When?

LADY BENBOW: And how have you been getting on?

BENBOW: Oh – I don't think there's much I can tell you about myself.

LADY BENBOW: Well, we'd better dress and dine out somewhere.

BENBOW: Quite right. Quickly! *(Rising and helping LADY BENBOW up.)* You must be hungry. We'll aim for dinner at seven.

LADY BENBOW: It's close on seven now.

BENBOW: Is it? My God! *(Takes watch out.)* Then we must hurry.

LADY BENBOW: My dear, I'm not in the least hungry.

BENBOW: No? – well I am, and you ought to be. Come on, get a move on!

LADY BENBOW: Hector, what's the matter with you?

BENBOW: I don't know, but I've got a nasty faint feeling coming all over me.

*They both exeunt L as –*

*HOOK enters hurriedly C. He wears his great-coat and carries his bowler. BENBOW hustles LADY BENBOW out and HOOK just fails to catch him. He turns. RONNY re-enters C. He is just about to take a drink, but puts it down quickly as HOOK speaks.*

HOOK: *(As BENBOW goes.)* Sir Hector – Sir Hector – *(Then turning to RONNY.)* Oh, Mr. Ronald!

RONNY: What's the matter now?

HOOK: I haven't told the master yet, sir, but I'm afraid there's been an awful mess-up.

RONNY: Mess-up? What are you talking about, Hook?

HOOK: I mean about the lady who's coming here to dinner, sir.

RONNY: Well, that's all right. I'm dealing with her, aren't I?

HOOK: Yes, sir; but Warner's gone and told another one to come.

*RONNY looks straight into HOOK's eyes.*

RONNY: Instead?

HOOK: No, sir – as well!

RONNY: What, *two* of them? Good Lord! Tell me about it.

HOOK: *(Groaning.)* It's all through this trouble of mine at home. Warner saw one I *didn't* see and told her, as well as the one I *did* see and told.

RONNY: Yes, that's quite clear. *(Earnestly.)* But who is the other one – Warner's pick? Who is she?

HOOK: The lady who's bought Thark, sir.

RONNY: Oh, well. There needn't be any secret about her, surely?

HOOK: Not that I know of, sir.

*Warning bell.*

RONNY: I daresay I can manage somehow. Oh, Hook, are you going out?

HOOK: I was, sir. Just to see the wife.

RONNY: Ah! That's very nice. Well, as you go, if you find a shop open, buy a few flowers, will you? *(Hands HOOK a ten-shilling note.)*

HOOK: Oh, thank you very much indeed, sir.

RONNY: And bring them back here.

*Door bell rings.*

Look out! There's someone here already.

HOOK: I'll take my coat off. Would you mind helping me?

*HOOK pauses in doorway C. to divest himself of his coat. In his hurry he gets tied up and RONNY trying to help him only makes matters worse.*

*BENBOW enters L. very apprehensively in his shirt-sleeves and slippers.*

BENBOW: Look out! Did you see the hall-porter?

RONNY: *(Struggling with HOOK.)* Of course I did.

*HOOK is still trying to get his coat off.*

BENBOW: *(Furiously.)* Hook! Will you stop that Houdini business and go and answer the door?

*RONNY helps HOOK to struggle out of his coat and –*

*HOOK goes off closing door C.*

RONNY: *(Holding the coat and hat.)* Look here, there's been a muddle up. *(Crosses D. R.)*

BENBOW: I know, my boy. I'm awfully sorry, I didn't know she was in town.

*RONNY and BENBOW work down R.*

RONNY: You must have known. You asked her to dinner.

*MRS. BENBOW entering suddenly L.*

LADY BENBOW: Asked who to dinner?

*They look at each other hesitating.*

*Before they can answer KITTY STRATTON hurries in C. She is a young, pretty girl dressed for travelling, rather put out at the moment.*

KITTY: *(As she enters.)* A nice sort of way to be treated!

RONNY: *(Then completely taken aback, hands coat to BENBOW and unconsciously puts hat on, crosses to KITTY, and realising mistake hands it to BENBOW, who is very annoyed.)* Kitty! Hallo! Good Lord! Good-bye! Why didn't you come yesterday?

KITTY: Why yesterday?

RONNY: *(To BENBOW.)* Why yesterday? *(To KITTY.)* Well, because it would have been a day sooner. I'd have seen more of you. But, darling, I'm delighted to see even this much of you.

KITTY: Yes; what was the idea in tying to stop me from coming up?

*RONNY R.C., BENBOW R.C., KITTY L. C. , LADY BENBOW L.*

LADY BENBOW: What do you mean?

KITTY: Well, the hall-porter said he'd had orders from Ronny.

BENBOW: *(To RONNY.)* That's right. Muck it up!

RONNY: That's quite right, darling. I said to the hall-porter – I simply said: 'Now look here, hall-porter' – I know his name, he had it on his hat – 'don't let the lady come up to the flat.' I didn't mean you, darling. I meant the lady.

LADY BENBOW: What lady?

RONNY: Uncle's lady!

BENBOW: Now then, don't be a B.F.! *(To RONNY.)*

143

RONNY: It's all right. You see, uncle has a lady coming here to dine this evening.

*BENBOW trying to control himself performs contortions at RONNY.*

LADY BENBOW: What for?

RONNY: For to eat. And when you see her you won't blame him.

BENBOW: *(Trying to stop RONNY.)* Oh yes, she will!

*Lights check.*

RONNY: Oh, no, she won't – oh, you won't. When you see who it really is.

LADY BENBOW: Why, who is it?

RONNY: *(Triumphantly.)* It's the lady who's bought Thark.

*BENBOW opens his eyes wide, realising it is a way out.*

LADY BENBOW: Oh, is that who it is?

*BENBOW drops hat and coat on settee R.*

RONNY: Not only who it is, auntie – but who it was – and who we hope it to be… *(Looks at BENBOW.)* We hope!

*KITTY embraces RONNY with relief.*

BENBOW: *(To LADY BENBOW.)* Yes, quite right. You know you're very suspicious, Maud. Soon as I saw her I said: 'Come to dinner' instinctively.

RONNY: As any gentleman would. But knowing you were coming home, uncle said to me: 'Ronny you take it on –

*BENBOW and RONNY exchange looks.*

you take her to dinner,' because he wants to be alone with you for once –

*LADY BENBOW looks.*

Not for once, just alone with you for once again. That's twice.

*He fusses her, putting her coat straight and finishes up by pulling the ends of a waistcoat she is wearing.*

KITTY: Oh, but that's splendid! Ronny, I'll come and dine with you as well!

RONNY: Yes –

*BENBOW signals him not to.*

Oh, will you? – Oh! – *(Crosses to R. of KITTY.)* Oh, no, you won't.

KITTY: Oh, but why not?

RONNY: *(To BENBOW.)* Why not? Have you anything for that? Because I haven't. *(Crosses to settee, sits.)*

BENBOW: *(Crosses to KITTY.)* Now look here, Kitty, I won't have you see this woman.

KITTY: But I've come all the way to town to see her. She wrote and asked me to.

*Warning lights.*

BENBOW: I don't care. You're not going to see her before I do. Whatever her troubles are, they're for me to deal with, not you.

KITTY: *(Submissively.)* Oh, very well, then. No need to make a scene about it. I'll dine with *you. (To LADY BENBOW.)*

*She crosses to LADY BENBOW, L., sits.*

RONNY: *(Rising, crossing. To BENBOW.)* I've been thinking.

BENBOW: Careful!

RONNY: Now that it's the lady from Thark –

*Enter WARNER C., switches on lights, draws curtains, takes tray from table.*

BENBOW: Now?

RONNY: Now that the lady from Thark *is* –

BENBOW: What are you trying to say?

RONNY: Wouldn't it be better for all of us – I mean for all of me – to dine with Kitty and for you to take Mrs Thark?

BENBOW: *(To RONNY.)* Now don't spoil it, you fool!

LADY BENBOW: *(Rising to WARNER who is going up L.)* Warner, a lady's coming. Tell the hall porter she's to be shown straight up.

WARNER: Yes, my lady.

145

*Exit L.*

LADY BENBOW: Hector – Hector!

BENBOW: Yes, my love?

LADY BENBOW: Come and get dressed.

BENBOW: I will. I love dressing. I'll be there, don't you worry.

LADY BENBOW: *(To KITTY.)* You'd better go and dress too, dear.

KITTY: All right. In a minute.

*LADY BENBOW goes towards door L. KITTY follows, has a word with LADY BENBOW and crosses to back of stage to behind table C. She takes her hat off and takes her small mirror from bag and arranges her hair. BENBOW managed to get a word in with RONNY.*

RONNY: Look here, there's some mistake – there are two.

LADY BENBOW: *(Coming down C.)* What are you whispering about?

RONNY: Hello, auntie, there you are again! No, I wasn't whispering – I was just telling uncle about a little chorus.

LADY BENBOW: Oh, I don't think you can tell your uncle anything about chorus!

RONNY: Oh, yes – the chorus of a song. It goes like this – *(To BENBOW.)* The words: *(Sings to BENBOW.)*

This girl is not the only girl,

Not the only girl for you;

There's another one – coming afterwards –

You've gone and made a date with two!

*(Pointedly.)*

– You! –

BENBOW: Yes, that's what I should call a very pretty ditty, but what the hell are you getting at?

LADY BENBOW: Hector! *(Pulling him up the arm by L.)* – Come and get dressed. You said you were starving.

RONNY: *(Crossing to BENBOW, holding him by the other arm.)* But there's another verse.

LADY BENBOW: Oh, hurry up!

RONNY: *(Still trying to detain him.)* It's about two birds.

BENBOW: Yes, I've got to go and moult. I'll see you later.

*BENBOW goes out R. with LADY BENBOW.*

KITTY: *(Coming to RONNY.)* I say, Ronny – Ronny, this is a shame. Ronny, I was looking forward so much to being with you this evening.

RONNY: And you know, darling, how much I want to be with *you.* If I'd known you were coming, wild horses wouldn't have dragged me from you. Unless, of course, there'd been a lot of them.

KITTY: I'm sure of it, Ronny, so don't worry any more about it.

RONNY: I *won't* worry.

KITTY: What?

RONNY: I mean I won't *not* worry. But, darling, will you believe me when I tell you that – all the time I am with her this evening at dinner – every bite I take I shall wish it were you!

KITTY: Well, I am quite happy as long as I know that you really love me.

RONNY: Really love you! Darling, don't say that. Of course I do. Why, if anyone came up to me – it wouldn't matter how big he was – *(Bus.: gestures a very small man then quickly changes to tall one.)* – and said 'Ronny' – or Ronald, if he didn't know me very well – 'you don't love her' – I – I wouldn't believe him – honestly!

KITTY: No – and if it was a lady who said so, you wouldn't believe her either, would you?

RONNY: Lady? No lady would ever talk to me!

*KITTY protests.*

Kitty, darling, you don't know how I hate the idea of dining with this female to-night – she's practically a robber –

*KITTY look surprised.*

147

she's robbing *me* of the happiness of being with you. *(Crosses to chair R.C.)* Kitty darling, I want to be with you.

*KITTY is kneeling on the chair by the side of the table C. RONNY holds her hands.*

KITTY: No, never mind, it's all been fixed now. Besides, I want Mrs. Frush to be treated nicely.

RONNY: Of course, darling. She bought the house.

KITTY: Yes. But you get rid of her as soon as you can and meet me for supper.

RONNY: And lunch to-morrow.

*BENBOW, a stage more undressed in a dressing-gown, looks in fiercely L. He is lathering his face; as he enters he catches RONNY's eye and indicates with lathering brush thee door. RONNY does not get it, and he absentmindedly rubs KITTY's chin as with a lathering brush.*

BENBOW: Why aren't you downstairs in the hall?

RONNY: *(Rising, crosses to C.)* Oh, yes. Quite right; I forgot.

KITTY: Why should he go to the hall?

BENBOW: Because there's a – there's a little parcel coming for me. Go on, go on! *(He grimaces at RONNY and – exits L.)*

*Throughout the next scene RONNY is trying to get away.*

KITTY: *(Rising, crosses to RONNY.)* Ronny, why can't the parcel be sent up here?

RONNY: Well, darling, it's hardly a little parcel, you see. It's more of a large bundle. *(Runs to go to door C.)*

KITTY: Yes, Ronny. What's the hurry?

RONNY: Well, darling, I mustn't keep the parcel waiting.

KITTY: *(Crosses up stage.)* Well, one moment, Ronny. We *will* meet for supper?

RONNY: *(Bringing her down stage.)* Meet for supper, darling! Of course we will, darling! *(Returning.)* Oh, supper with you – in some shady – night-club – with nothing between us but the table and knives and forks, of course – and flowers on the table, and waiters – waiters on the floor; with you by my side – by my front – good-bye! *(Kisses her. Crosses up stage.)* Till that – *(Trying to go.)*

*At door he misses the handle of the door, absentmindedly picks up tall brass vase and puts it down again.*

KITTY: *(Holding him up again.)* But, Ronny, where are we going to meet? And when?

RONNY: *(Bringing her back again.)* Meet – and when? Lucky you called me back again. Meet – and when? Leave it entirely to me. As soon as I'm free, I'll phone you.

*Warning bell – door.*

KITTY: Yes, but where shall I be?

RONNY: Darling, I don't care where you go. Wherever you are, I'll 'phone you. Darling, you do trust me, don't you?

KITTY: Of course, Ronny.

RONNY: Well, kiss me. *(Kissing her.)*

*Door bell – the bell is heard off.*

Good Lord! *(Rather in a panic, crosses up L.)*

KITTY: There's Mrs Frush.

RONNY: Yes, or –

KITTY: Or what?

RONNY: Or not.

KITTY: What do you mean 'or not'?

RONNY: Well, if it isn't her, it's not.

KITTY: Who's not?

RONNY: *(Abstractedly, listening.)* What not?

*BENBOW appears R. He is in another stage of dressing and purple with anxiety. He has managed to get into his dress shirt and trousers and is fastening his collar.*

BENBOW: Look out – there you are, you fool! Too late!

*KITTY and BENBOW look at each other.*

Go and meet her in the doorway. *(Twice.)*

RONNY: What?

BENBOW: Go and meet her in the doorway.

KITTY: But Mrs. Frush can come in here, can't she?

BENBOW: No. She can't. I don't want you to see her.

*He moves KITTY over R.*

*RONNY goes to door C., opens it and voices are heard outside.*

WARNER: *(Off.)* I know, madam, but there's some mistake.

CHERRY: *(Off.)* There can't be! I was told at quarter past seven.

*KITTY and BENBOW both over at R.C.*

RONNY: She's being brought in here anyway.

BENBOW: Blast! *(Pushing KITTY off R.)* Then, Kitty, you go in the drawing-room.

KITTY: But why shouldn't I meet her?

BENBOW: Because I say not. Go on.

*Sends KITTY off R., shuts door.*

Get rid of her quickly, boy!

RONNY: Supposing it's the other?

BENBOW: Hell d'yer mean – the other?

*KITTY reappears R.*

KITTY: I really fail to see why I shouldn't meet the lady.

BENBOW: No, yer don't!

*Pushes her off R., crosses up L.*

RONNY: *(As BENBOW goes up L.)* She may not be the right one.

BENBOW: Not the right one be damned! – Did you ever know me to pick a wrong 'un.

*Exit L.*

*WARNER enters C.*

WARNER: The lady, sir. *(With an anxious glance she goes, closing the door.)*

*Exit.*

*RONNY crosses and sits on club fender, L.*

*CHERRY is boldly dressed for the occasion with an evening cloak over her dress. She had her left white suede glove on and carrier her other glove and her evening bag. She greets RONNY, then sees her mistake.*

CHERRY: Hallo! Oh, my mistake! Wrong one!

RONNY: *(D.L intensely and confidentially.)* Are you Mrs. Frush?

CHERRY: Me? No. My name's Cherry Buck.

RONNY: Stuffed cat!

CHERRY: I've called to see Sir Hector…You're his nephew, I s'pose?

RONNY: *(Indicating door C.)* Yes. That's right. *Quick*! Come outside – come on!

CHERRY: What?

RONNY: Come *out* with me. *(Opening door up C., trying to entice her out.)*

CHERRY: Oh, but perhaps I don't want to! *(Becoming rather coy.)*

RONNY: Well, you needn't come far. Just come outside. Come on. Come to dinner.

*Goes through door C. and coyly beckons her to come out.*

CHERRY: *(Move down R.)* I never go out with strangers.

RONNY: I know that's a very good idea of yours, but you must not be seen here.

CHERRY: But I was asked here!

RONNY: Oh, but you can't stay here.

CHERRY: Who says so?

RONNY: I'm sorry – I say so.

CHERRY: Really? Well, if you don't like the look of me, others do.

RONNY: I do. Very much. That's just the trouble. You look marvellous *(Very extravagantly.)* Oh, you're marvellous! Oh, do please come with me out on to the staircase!

CHERRY: You *fresh thing!*

RONNY: I *must* see you.

CHERRY: Well, here I am. You can *see* me, can't you?

RONNY: Not properly. I want to see you elsewhere.

CHERRY: I *beg* your pardon!

RONNY: I want you to let me see you outside. Don't you understand? I want to see you without. *(Crosses up to opening L., looks off, returns to CHERRY.)*

CHERRY: Huh! I daresay you do.

RONNY: Too late! Somebody coming. Stay there. Look here – be a sport for my sake and uncle's will you? You're Mrs. Frush – you've taken Thark.

CHERRY: I should love to know what *you've* taken.

*RONNY is trying to explain to CHERRY by making shapes near the floor with his hands.*

*LADY BENBOW enters L. in evening dress and an evening cloak. She is very surprised at the appearance of CHERRY. She comes down to the left of RONNY – he catches sight of her and starts to limp up to the table, holding his knee as if in pain – he pours some whisky out on to his hand and rubs his knee, looking as though in agony at LADY BENBOW. He then moves down stage and explains to LADY BENBOW by pantomiming a swing as if playing golf.*

RONNY: I've been playing golf and I've got golfer's knee. *(Then pulling himself together.)* Oh, allow me, auntie – this is Mrs. Frush – er – my aunt Lady Benbow.

CHERRY: *(To RONNY.)* Lady Benbow –

RONNY: *(Bus.: – .)* Yes. The wife of –

LADY BENBOW: Oh, how do you do?

CHERRY: *(Taken aback at finding LADY BENBOW at home.)* How do *you* do?

RONNY: Do what?

LADY BENBOW: I understand my husband was taking you out to dinner?

*CHERRY O, RONNY O, LADY BENBOW O*

CHERRY: *(Uncertain what to say, looking at RONNY.)* Well – I –

RONNY: Oh, yes, he was – but not now. I'm taking her instead.

LADY BENBOW: I'm afraid he put you off because of me. I'm sure he would have loved to have taken *you* out. You have met my husband, haven't you?

CHERRY: Well, I – I –

RONNY: *(Quickly, seeing CHERRY hesitate as before.)* Oh, rather – yes – she's met your husband and she goes on further to say – I mean if she hadn't met uncle she'd never have taken Thark. Would you, you rascal? *(Slapping her playfully.)*

*CHERRY resents this.*

LADY BENBOW: I'm so sorry to hear you don't like Thark.

CHERRY: *(Exchanges look to RONNY, who signals her to take care.)* No, I'm afraid I don't – but I suppose it's *got* to be taken.

LADY BENBOW: Doesn't it agree with you?

CHERRY: Well, the doctor seemed to think it was the best thing. But – it's not very pleasant.

RONNY: You see, auntie, that's the Norfolk air. *(To LADY BENBOW.)* You'll be all right. You're doing very well. Now – *(Taking CHERRY up stage.)* Come to dinner.

LADY BENBOW: There's no particular hurry.

RONNY: Oh, isn't there?

LADY BENBOW: No, she'd like to see your uncle.

RONNY: No, she wouldn't.

CHERRY: Yes, she would. Go and see if he's dressed. *(Takes cloak off, puts it on chair L.)*

RONNY: *(Starting to go, but stops.)* No, he isn't. I know he isn't dressed, because he was in here just now and he was undressed then. *(To CHERRY.)* Wasn't he?

*CHERRY gives RONNY an angry look.*

*Enter KITTY R.*

LADY BENBOW: Kitty! What are you doing in there?

KITTY: Ohm, I stayed in there so as not to meet Mrs. Frush.

LADY BENBOW: Oh, nonsense! Come in. *(Bringing KITTY to CHERRY.)* This is Mrs. Frush – Miss Stratton, my husband's ward.

KITTY: *(Obviously surprised at CHERRY's appearance.)* Oh! I'm sorry. Good evening.

CHERRY: Pleased to meet you.

*RONNY bus.: keeping them apart.*

RONNY: She's delighted. *(Crosses to KITTY.)*

*BENBOW enters up L. and takes in the situation.*

KITTY: Yes. I've been told not to talk to you about Thark.

CHERRY: *(Losing her control.)* Thank God for that!

LADY BENBOW: *(As BENBOW is about to sneak off again.)* Hector!

BENBOW: *(Coming down, plausibly.)* Yes, my love.

LADY BENBOW: Come in. Here's Mrs. Frush.

*Warning door bell.*

BENBOW: *(Trying to evade it.)* Oh! When? – *(Then seeing CHERRY.)* Oh, Mrs. Frush – yes – How'd you do? *(With a sickly smile.)*

RONNY: Yes, here she is. Good old Mrs. Frush. Dear old thing! *(Slapping her playfully on back.)*

*KITTY D.R., RONNY R., CHERRY C., BENBOW Up L.C., LADY BENBOW D.L.*

*CHERRY looks at BENBOW and makes a little face.*

CHERRY: *(Overcome by her position and showing sudden resentment.)* Now look here! Whatever you people are up to, I don't see why I should be made a fool of.

RONNY: *(Quickly, amid general consternation.)* Spanish! Now, now! Whatever your troubles are at Thark, you mustn't begin fighting here.

CHERRY: Then take me to dinner.

*Door bell rings.*

*Makes another little face at BENBOW. Turns to say good-bye to KITTY and sees her looking very disdainfully. CHERRY is looking at BENBOW with anger.*

RONNY: *(Appeals to KITTY, who ignores him.)* Kitty!

*RONNY does wing-flapping bus.: as he crosses up to C.*

*WARNER, still looking very scared, opens the door C.*

*RONNY up R.C., WARNER up C., CHERRY up L.C., KITTY R.C., BENBOW L., LADY BENBOW D.L.*

*As WARNER opens the door – MRS. FRUSH, wonderfully got up for the occasion, advances into the room.*

*WARNER disappears.*

*MRS. FRUSH at door C. – to RONNY.*

MRS. FRUSH: *(To RONNY.)* I *hope* I'm not too late. How d'ye do *? (Then crosses to BENBOW.)*

*CHERRY has a word with RONNY and crosses to R.C.*

How d'ye do? *(Then to LADY BENBOW, who is watching BENBOW and RONNY D.L.)* How d'ye do? *(She pauses, then notices KITTY over R. She crosses to her and says:.)* Miss Stratton, I think? How d'ye do?

*MRS. FRUSH R.C., RONNY C., CHERRY L.C., BENBOW L., LADY BENBOW D.C., KITTY R.*

KITTY: How d'you do? *(Looks over at LADY BENBOW, surprised.)* Who is this lady?

MRS. FRUSH: Why – I'm expected. I'm Mrs. Frush!

KITTY: *(To RONNY.)* You beast! *(Then crosses to LADY BENBOW.)*

*Another slight pause – LADY BENBOW watches the shrunken figure of BENBOW – CHERRY turns her head away.*

RONNY: *(Anxiously to BENBOW.)* D'you hear what I am? Well, can't you say something?

BENBOW: I could, but, my God, you'd be sorry if I started!

*RONNY turns away from him to discover –*

*HOOK, who has just come back L. with a bunch of flowers – offering him the flowers.*

*RONNY takes the flowers absent-mindedly whilst arguing with BENBOW, looks at them, and pushes them back into HOOK's arms.*

*CURTAIN.*

# Act Two

*The same room next morning.*

*Bright daylight.*

*WARNER, in a neat print costume, is putting final touches to the morning's work on the room.*

*HOOK arranging papers on table R.C.*

HOOK: You're talking nonsense, Warner, that's what you're talking.

WARNER: No, I'm not.

HOOK: Yes, you are. How do you know Miss Kitty's thrown him over?

WARNER: If she hasn't, why is she going back to Bath?

HOOK: Well, it's very 'ard. Because it wasn't his fault.

WARNER: *(Crosses up C.)* If you ask me, what really put the lid on it was you walking in with a bunch of flowers. *(Opens door up C.)*

HOOK: That'll do. You attend to your business.

*WARNER exits centre, goes left.*

*Almost immediately RONNY hurries in C. from R. with troubled, inquiring air. He puts hat on table C.*

RONNY: Good morning, Warner. I'm glad you're here. You've got to help me, you two. *(To HOOK, who shows signs of quitting.)* You, too.

WARNER: Oh, Mr. Ronny, anything we can do for you, we'll do gladly.

*HOOK R., RONNY C., WARNER L.*

RONNY: That's fine! *(To HOOK.)* And you? Gladly too?

HOOK: I don't see I can do much, sir.

RONNY: Not so gladly.

HOOK: But, Mr. Ronald, my first duty is to remember my place.

RONNY: Your first duty is to remember a place I'm going to tell you in South Molton Street.

HOOK: *(Startled.)* What, sir?

RONNY: Don't say 'what.' Waste of time. I want you to jump in a taxi and bring back Miss Cherry Buck.

HOOK: Oh, I wouldn't do this if I were you, sir.

RONNY: I'm not going to. You are. You see, Miss Warner… Miss Kitty won't listen to me. So I'm getting Miss Buck to come and explain.

WARNER: Miss Kitty's going back to Bath this morning, sir.

RONNY: What! Good Lord! *(To HOOK.)* There! You see?… You must hurry. The address is 13A South Molton Street – bring her back at once. Here's your taxi fare. *(Hands HOOK money and pushes him away.)*

HOOK: *(As he takes the money.)* Oh, I don't like doing this, sir.

RONNY: *(Pushing him to the door C.)* Not at all. It's only fair that I should pay for the taxi.

*HOOK unwillingly exits C.*

*(Crosses to WARNER.)* Now, Warner. Where are they all?

WARNER: Still in their rooms, sir. They've breakfasted here.

RONNY: Oh, I see.

WARNER: Sir Hector's now in his bath.

RONNY: Oh, is that what it is? I thought it was a gramophone.

WARNER: And Mrs. Frush and her son are calling here early, sir.

RONNY: I don't like the mother, and I've never met the son. I don't care. Now I'm going to pop out and get a few flowers… *(Crosses up C.)*…for Miss Kitty, and I'll give them to her with a few words. *(Hands his hat as imaginary bouquet to WARNER, with emotion.)* I've brought you these flowers because I love you.

*WARNER looks down coyly.*

Not you, Warner, what are you thinking about. Give them back. *(Snatching his hat away again.)*

*BENBOW's voice is heard off.*

BENBOW: *(Off up C.)* HOOK!

RONNY: *(As WARNER takes a step up L.)* No. *(Going up towards door L.)* Don't go to him.

WARNER: But, I think he's still in his bath.

RONNY: Well – let him get out by himself.

*RONNY hurries out C.*

*WARNER stands irresolute for a moment. Then BENBOW is heard again. WARNER looks scared. Makes up her mind to go out but has only just got to the door when –*

*BENBOW enters L. in bath gown, drying his ears.*

BENBOW: Here, you!

*WARNER returns.*

Where's Hook?

WARNER: I – think he's gone out, sir.

BENBOW: Why? He hasn't had another baby, has he?

WARNER: No, sir…I – I don't think so.

BENBOW: Where's he gone?

*WARNER wriggles her shoulders apprehensively.*

Ah, stop that. We don't want any of that Salome business. Where's HOOK?

WARNER: *(Crosses D.C.)* He took a message for Mr. Ronny, sir.

BENBOW: Where to?

WARNER: Oh! *(Moves down stage centre nervously.)*

BENBOW: Now then, come on my girl. I'm not going to eat you.

WARNER: The message was to a lady, sir.

BENBOW: What, at this time of the morning? What lady?

WARNER: The lady who was here last night.

BENBOW: *(Impatiently.)* Last night the house was stiff with ladies. Which one?

WARNER: Miss Buck, sir.

BENBOW: Well, then say so. What was it about?

*As WARNER hesitates.*

*Warning door bell.*

Now then, come on my girl – I'm not going to be angry with you.

WARNER: He sent Hook to bring Miss Buck here, sir.

BENBOW: *(Flaring up.)* Wha-at! Here? How? Is he mad?

WARNER: No, sir. I think he only wants Miss Buck to tell the truth.

BENBOW: The truth? My God, I'll see she doesn't tell the truth about *me.*

WARNER: He only wants Miss Buck to say that he wasn't the guilty party, sir.

BENBOW: Well, isn't that the same thing as telling the truth about me?

WARNER: I don't know, sir.

*Door bell is heard off.*

BENBOW: *(Goes up to opening L.)* Bell! That can't be her already.

WARNER: I'll see, sir.

*Exit up C. Disappears for a moment.*

*BENBOW moves up L. anxiously.*

*WARNER returns.*

No, sir, it's Mr. Frush.

BENBOW: Oh, it don't matter about him, he can wait. You can ask him in here and tell him to wait. Pop on your hat and go and stop Miss Buck from coming. *(Softening a little.)* And you don't know anything about me. Mind you don't.

WARNER: *(Stiffening rather.)* Yes, I will, sir.

BENBOW: *(Gently.)* No, no; I didn't mean you'd better not for your own sake, that's all right – I meant – don't know anything about me if you're asked.

WARNER: Oh – yes, sir.

BENBOW: That's right. Not that I've done anything wrong, mind you.

WARNER: No, sir…I'm sure I don't think that.

BENBOW: No, I don't suppose you do. Because you're a very good girl. I know I speak rather sharply to you at times, but you're a good girl… *(Holding her chin.)* I suppose. Are you a good girl?

WARNER: Yes, sir.

BENBOW: *(Severely.)* Then don't waste me time. Pop on your hat.

*BENBOW goes out L. drying his ear.*

*WARNER exits C.*

WARNER: *(At C. doorway – crosses R.)* Will you step this way, sir?

LIONEL: *(As he enters, crosses L.)* Thanks. Topping morning, isn't it?

WARNER: Yes, sir. *(Anxious to get away.)*

LIONEL: Do *you* get much time *off?*

WARNER: No, sir. Excuse me, I must hurry away.

*Exit C.*

LIONEL: *(Turns R. as she goes.)* Oh, sorry. *(He completes his turn as – .)*

*KITTY enters up L. in a pretty morning frock.*

KITTY: Oh – did you want to see Sir Hector?

LIONEL: Yes – I'm Lionel Frush, you know.

KITTY: Oh, I'm Kitty Stratton. How do you do? *(Shakes his hand.)*

*He is impressed.*

LIONEL: How do you do?

KITTY: Is your mother here?

LIONEL: *(Rather coldly.)* Not yet. She's coming. Are you going to be in town for long?

KITTY: *(Cross D.R.)* No, I'm going away again.

LIONEL: *(Crosses R.)* Oh! Pity – I – I find it awfully lonely here alone. I don't know another girl. I swear I don't.

KITTY: We must try and find you a little friend.

*RONNY enters C. with flowers, puts them on table C.*

LIONEL: *(L.)* I don't want another girl. I want *you.*

KITTY: *(Laughing frankly.)* Oh, thank you very much. You don't waste much time, do you?

RONNY: *(After watching with distaste, coming down.)* Hallo!

*LIONEL turns and shakes hands instinctively.*

How are you? Not at all. Good-bye. *(Takes him up L. Taking his hand and placing it on arm of chair L.)* Just hook on to that a minute. *(Crosses to KITTY.)* Who and what?

KITTY: *(With disdain, to RONNY coldly.)* This is Mr. Lionel Frush. *(She moves away.)*

RONNY: Oh – that's Lionel Frush, is it? The son of the larger Frush. *(Looking at LIONEL.)* Seems very attractive.

KITTY: Oh, yes, yes, quite charming.

RONNY: Yes. He's got a flashing eye. Sort of Ben-Hur type. More Hur than Ben.

KITTY: Quite.

RONNY: *(Still going after her.)* Oh, you think so? I thought so too, the moment I saw him. Yes. Quite. *(Turns to LIONEL.)* Good morning.

*LIONEL offers his hand to shake.*

Oh, you can keep that, that's yours. Isn't she charming?

*KITTY moves up to table C, looking at papers.*

LIONEL: Quite.

RONNY: Oh, you little chatterbox! She's so easy to talk to.

LIONEL: Oh, rather. We get on awfully well together.

RONNY: Oh, do we really? *(Forcing him over the chair.)* You like talking to her?

LIONEL: She's so topping and friendly. Do you know I could talk to her for hours and hours.

RONNY: Yes, will you make it seconds and seconds?

KITTY: Are you going to be in town long?

LIONEL: Well, my mother's going back at once. But I shall be here for some time.

RONNY: Oh, that's fine. I hope that we shall see – nothing of you.

LIONEL: I'm waiting for a car. It'll be about a week.

RONNY: Oh, nonsense, my dear fellow, don't be absurd. *(Going up stage, calling out of window:.)* Hi! Taxi! Taxi!

LIONEL: But it's a new car.

KITTY: You're going to drive it to Thark?

LIONEL: Yes. That was the idea.

RONNY: *(Leading him over C.)* And a very good idea, too.

LIONEL: *(Breaking away and crossing to KITTY.)* Well, perhaps I'd better see you later.

KITTY: *(Cross D.R.)* Oh, but I thought you were waiting for your mother.

LIONEL: Oh yes, of course, but I think I'd like to go and buy a few flowers.

RONNY: *(With challenge.)* Who for?

LIONEL: *(Suddenly getting to a fury.)* I suppose I can buy flowers if I want to, can't I? If I'm so disposed…

RONNY: *(Moving away, feigning fear, then going back.)* Did that come out of you? You'll be indisposed if you do.

*LIONEL drops his stick and stoops to pick it up.*

Don't bend down like that, you look like a prawn. Go away.

*He hustles LIONEL out C. and closes the door.*

*He picks up brass vase, right of door, places it in front of door C. and strikes up an attitude leaning on vase. Picks up flowers from table C. He holds them behind him in his L. hand; as he crosses to KITTY she turns and is about to cross L. RONNY stops her by moving towards her with his right hand raised, he then brings his L. hand from behind him and in a grand manner offers KITTY the empty paper (the flowers having dropped on the floor behind him.) He looks down, and seeing what has happened, he quickly picks them up and puts them in the paper holder and again offers them. He then recites:*

Kitty darling, I bring you these few fresh fragrant flowers because I love you. *(Rustling the paper they are wrapped in.)* Look, look, look, look!

Each one has a separate meaning. *(Taking one bloom.)*

This one means devotion – *(Taking another.)*

This one means emotion – *(Then pushing aside another.)*

This one means – love and laughter. *(Laughing audibly.)*

I won't tell you what that one means.

KITTY: What about those flowers last night? You didn't buy those for me? *(Ignores flowers.)*

*RONNY puts flowers on table C.*

RONNY: *(Crosses to KITTY.)* We hadn't quarrelled then – don't be angry about last night. I know I did wrong.

KITTY: *(Keenly.)* Oh, did you?

RONNY: No, nothing wrong actually. But it wasn't my fault.

KITTY: I see. You tried to? *(Turning to him.)*

RONNY: No, Kitty, listen. I was entrapped – and just as I was walking out, you walked in.

KITTY: It's no good making excuses. Ronny, I'm terribly upset.

*RONNY bus. Goes to chairs and mantelpiece.*

RONNY: I know – I'm always upsetting someone or something. I upset a basin this morning. That's a terrible thing to do. Nothing's worse than a basin when it's upset. It either breaks into small pieces or else runs round the room on the bias.

KITTY: No, Ronny, no, you've hurt me very much. *(Crosses to settee – sits R.)*

RONNY: *(Crossing to her.)* I'm sorry, Kitty darling – Kitty – Kitty –

*She ignores him.*

Kitty – it's Ronny speaking. Will you forgive me? I ask you in so many words – *(Counting them mentally.)* – four words. Darling, I think of you by day as well as night; lat last night when I was going home I was saying to myself: 'Kitty – Kitty – Kitty – Kitty – Kitty – Kitty, Kitty, Kitty…' and when I got to my gate there were fourteen cats behind me. *(Then sincerely.)* Kitty, there's no one in the world means anything to me but you. *(Sitting holding her hand.)*

*HOOK in a state of nervous enthusiasm, opens the door C. quickly and ushers in CHERRY in a neat morning costume with fur coat.*

*(To CHERRY.)* What do you want?

CHERRY: *(C.)* Well, you sent for me.

RONNY: *(Blankly looks at KITTY.)* Did I?

HOOK: *(In self defence.)* Yes, sir *(D.L.C.)*

RONNY: *(Rising to HOOK.)* I wasn't talking to you. *(HOOK moves L.)*

CHERRY: He said you couldn't get along without me.

*KITTY is furious.*

HOOK: That's right, sir. As per your instructions.

*RONNY R.C., CHERRY L.C., KITTY R., HOOK L.*

*Warning door slam.*

RONNY: *(To HOOK, in a surprised voice.)* Don't be audible. *(To KITTY.)* And do you know why I couldn't get along without her?

KITTY: *(Rising.)* Yes. I may be very young, but I'm old enough to know that.

*She goes out, crossing between CHERRY and HOOK.*

*RONNY is about to follow her when HOOK gets in his way.*

RONNY: *(To KITTY as she disappears.)* Not quite, Kitty. *(Cross to HOOK.)* What do you want?

HOOK: Your change from the taxi, sir. *(Has it in L. hand.)*

RONNY: *(Taking it.)* Well, you can't have it. *(Cross to L., looks.)* Kitty, Kitty! Kit…ty!

*Door slams off L.*

She's slammed the door in my face – *(Then back to CHERRY.)* Just as I got everything straightened up you came in and bent it.

CHERRY: Well, I never!

RONNY: I sent for you so that you could tell her –

CHERRY: *(Interrupting.)* All right – I had quite enough of that in the taxi.

RONNY: *(To HOOK.)* Why, what had you been doing in the taxi *? (Walks round him and repeats:.)* What have you been doing in the taxi?

CHERRY: He kept yapping at me all the way telling me what to do as if I were some baby.

RONNY: *(Severely at HOOK.)* Hook! So you think this lady is some baby?

*HOOK looks helpless.*

You've ruined everything. How dare you? You – you butler! There's no one can help me now. Except uncle. Hook, tell him I've something to show him.

HOOK: Thank you, sir.

*HOOK exits L.*

CHERRY: Fancy her being so jealous of me.

RONNY: *(Going on innocently.)* Oh, but – you know what young girls are. You just cast you mind back – to the days when you were young –

CHERRY: Well! I've never been so insulted for *years. (Going up.)* I'm going back to the shop.

RONNY: *(All over R.)* No, no – you can't do that. *(Holding her by the arms.)*

*CHERRY sees KITTY L.*

I want you to tell Kitty the truth. I want you here. I do really – I want you.

*He puts his hands on her shoulders. KITTY enters L. She hears the last words. RONNY pretends to be dusting CHERRY's coat. He turns to KITTY embarrassed.*

Hallo! What am I doing? I'll tell you. No. She'll tell you. *(Breaking away from KITTY.)*

CHERRY: Very well, then.

KITTY: Yes, I expect you've got quite the story ready by now.

RONNY: Yes. It goes like this. Two mornings ago…

CHERRY: Am I going to tell her, or you?

RONNY: Oh, sorry.

CHERRY: *(To KITTY.)* Two mornings ago I was in the shop where I work – in the window –

RONNY: She doesn't always work in the window. *(Catching CHERRY's eye.)* Oh, sorry…

KITTY: I won't listen to a lot of lies. *(Cross D.L.)*

CHERRY: Well, while I was there, along came a gentleman.

KITTY: What gentleman?

*BENBOW enters L. dressed. He speaks as he enters.*

BENBOW: Look here, Ronny, what d'you want to send… *(Seeing CHERRY.)* Good lor'! She's here!

*CHERRY R., RONNY UP R.C., BENBOW UP L.C., KITTY L.*

RONNY: *(To KITTY.)* This gentleman. *(To BENBOW.)*

BENBOW: Why is this little girl here again?

RONNY: To tell Kitty the truth about you.

BENBOW: Yes, that's what I expected. *(To RONNY.)* You go and mess up the whole business and then you blame it on me.

RONNY: *(Taking BENBOW aside.)* It's up to you, as a sporting man, to clear me.

BENBOW: But I can't tell this to a young girl. She's my ward. She respects me.

RONNY: *(Soothingly.)* No, she doesn't.

BENBOW: Besides, she'll tell your aunt.

RONNY: No, she won't.

BENBOW: You don't think she would?

RONNY: No.

*KITTY crosses to BENBOW.*

BENBOW: *(To KITTY.)* Well – we – Kitty, I hesitate to tell you this –

RONNY: Then I will. Two mornings ago this girl was in her shop window when uncle was coming down the street

166

*– (Imitating BENBOW's walk, broadly twirling an imaginary moustache.)*

BENBOW: *(Annoyed.)* Now – that'll do, that'll do, that'll do, that'll do. That's quite enough of your version. Thank you. I'll tell me own tale. *(Pushing RONNY aside.)* Now, Kitty, this is roughly – pretty roughly, I admit – what occurred. I was on my way to see old Dobbie – *(To RONNY.)* You know old Dobbie – ?

RONNY: Yes – young Dobbie's old father.

BENBOW: Yes, old Davey Dobbie! Why, he was Master o' Hounds before me. Finer fellow never breathed.

RONNY: Never mind about his breath, go on with the story.

BENBOW: Will you shut up and not interrupt? Well, as I say, I was on my way to old Dobbie's flat – he's a great friend of mine. By Gad, that feller can shift port. Oh, a hell of a sportsman – married his cook. You ought to see him on a horse. He's got a wonderful seat – *(To RONNY.)* – hasn't he?

RONNY: Oh, enormous, but get on with the story.

BENBOW: Well, as I say, I was on my way to Dobbie's – I was going – past the shops – when I noticed someone.

*LADY BENBOW appears up L. BENBOW perceives LADY BENBOW and pauses.*

Who was it? Why, old Dobbie. *(Sees LADY BENBOW.)* Oh, good morning, my love. Nice morning.

RONNY: Oh, a beauty.

*BENBOW gives RONNY a look and moves up C.*

LADY BENBOW: Why is this lady here again?

KITTY: *(Excitedly.)* To put me off the scent.

*KITTY sits D.L.*

CHERRY: That's all rats, what she's saying. Sorry, but really it is.

LADY BENBOW: Yes. Will you sit down, please?

*CHERRY brings chair up from down R., sits R.*

RONNY: Oh, good morning, auntie.

LADY BENBOW: Sit down.

*RONNY brings chair from L. of table and sits in front of it C. BENBOW is up stage C., studying a picture which is hanging on the back wall. He is obviously trying to dodge the situation.*

Hector!

*BENBOW pretends not to hear.*

Hector!

BENBOW: *(Turning round unconcerned.)* Yes, my love?

LADY BENBOW: You sit down, too.

BENBOW: Oh –

LADY BENBOW: *(She turns to CHERRY.)* Now, to begin with –

BENBOW: *(As he brings chair from back of table C., to RONNY on his L.)* This is going to be awkward.

*They are all sitting obediently, after inter-changing glances.*

LADY BENBOW: Whom did you really come here last night to see?

RONNY: *(To BENBOW.)* Stand up.

BENBOW: *(Rising.)* Really, Maud darling, I don't wish you to be lugged into this business.

*CHERRY R., RONNY R.C., BENBOW R.C., LADY BENBOW L., KITTY D.L.*

*LADY BENBOW ignoring BENBOW. BENBOW looks at RONNY in despair – sits.*

LADY BENBOW: *(To CHERRY.)* Who did ask you out to dinner?

CHERRY: You really want to know?

LADY BENBOW: Yes, of course I do.

*Anxiety from BENBOW and RONNY.*

CHERRY: All right then, Mr. Hook.

KITTY: *(Scornfully.)* Oh, rubbish!

RONNY: All right then, ask Hook. *(To BENBOW.)* Can we rely on Hook?

BENBOW: Yes. *(Definitely.)*

*RONNY rises, crosses C. LADY BENBOW protests.*

LADY BENBOW: *(Intervening.)* No, Ronny! I won't have Hook brought in here to give your uncle away.

BENBOW: Give me away! My gad, he'd better not. Besides, I'm absolutely blameless.

RONNY: Me, too. I'll prove it to you now and then – here and now. Hook! *(Crosses up L., calls off L.)* Hook! Yes, you too, Warner! Come here. Come in here. *(Crosses to his chair.)*

*HOOK and WARNER follow him, standing up stage L. looking sheepish.*

*(To WARNER and HOOK.)*

Closer, closer.

*(They move down.)*

Halt! *(Placing his foot on chair L.C.)* Now then, Hook, I understand that you are of American origin, are you not?

HOOK: Yes, sir.

RONNY: Don't say, 'Yes, sir' – say 'Yeah bo.' Are you of American origin?

HOOK: Yes, bo-sir.

RONNY: Right, then I know I'll get the truth. I believe that. Now then – *(Indicating CHERRY BUCK.)* Did this lady come here last night to see me?

HOOK: *(Looking at LADY BENBOW, then to BENBOW.)* Er – no, sir, I hardly think that.

RONNY: There you are – hardly. That's rather indefinite. Did she come here to see your master, Sir Hector?

HOOK: What, sir? *(Looks at BENBOW.)* Oh, good Lord, no!

RONNY: Then I put it to you – *(Pointing at HOOK with L. hand.)* – she must have come to see you. *(Putting his R. hand in his pocket, rattles his money suggestively.)* You acknowledge that?

HOOK: Oh, no, sir.

BENBOW: *(To HOOK.)* Oh, yes, sir.

RONNY: Why can't you tell the truth like everyone else? *(Indicating BENBOW.)*

LADY BENBOW: That'll do, Ronny. I won't have the servants questioned.

*WARNER and HOOK move to go, but RONNY stops them by saying;*

RONNY: One moment. In fairness to me. Warner! Now then, Warner, your name's Warner, isn't it?

WARNER: Yes, sir.

RONNY: I warn you, Warner, I want you to tell the truth, the whole truth, or something like the truth. You are a maid of the establishment of Benbow, are you not? *(Then looking from SIR HECTOR to LADY BENBOW.)* You are a maid of some sort or another – kitchen maid look after the kitchens – parlour maid look after the parlours – chamber-maid to look after the other things. It was you who asked Mrs. Frush?

WARNER: Yes, sir. I didn't know Mr. Hook had too.

BENBOW: He didn't ask her. He asked *her. (Pointing to CHERRY.)* Didn't you?

HOOK: No, sir, I didn't!

BENBOW: What?

HOOK: Yes, sir, I did.

RONNY: You see, auntie, it's all perfectly clear.

KITTY: *(Jumping up.)* Well, I don't care. You dined with her.

CHERRY: *(Jumping up.)* Well, why the devil shouldn't he?

RONNY: Oh, hush, not in this department. *(Sits.)*

LADY BENBOW: *(Rising. To HOOK and WARNER.)* Leave the room at once.

HOOK: Thank you, my lady.

*They turn inwards – exeunt L.*

LADY BENBOW: *(To BENBOW.)* Hector!

BENBOW: Yes, my love.

LADY BENBOW: You knew she wasn't Mrs. Frush.

BENBOW: Yes, but I didn't want to give Ronny away.

RONNY: Oh! – you – you wicked uncle.

CHERRY: *(To BENBOW.)* Give him away? Did you think I wasn't respectable?

BENBOW: Well, I – I never had the chance to find out.

*RONNY moves and KITTY faces him.*

KITTY: Well, I don't care. *(To RONNY.)* And you can go to lunch with her. I'm going to Bath.

*She goes out L. in a temper.*

*RONNY is following, LADY BENBOW stops him.*

RONNY: *(Rising.)* Oh, Kitty, don't bath. She shan't blame me like this. *(Brokenly.)*

LADY BENBOW: Leave her alone.

RONNY: But if you only knew what happened.

LADY BENBOW: Of course I know what happened. Do you think that I was married yesterday?

*Exit L.*

BENBOW: *(Rising, to RONNY.)* Now then, look here, Ronny, I won't have you telling Kitty things about my character.

RONNY: *(At the door L.)* It wouldn't matter. Sooner or later she's bound to learn the disgusting side of life. *(Broken-heartedly.)*

*Exit L.*

BENBOW: *(Cross down L.C.)* Well, I'm awfully sorry about all this, my dear.

CHERRY: *(Cross L. to him.)* So I should hope.

BENBOW: *(Putting his hand in hi breast pocket.)* If there's any little compensation that I can make by way of – what shall we say – half a dozen pairs of silk stockings –

CHERRY: No, thanks. Take a girl's character away and then offer her presents, is that it?

BENBOW: No, it's generally the other way about. I mean – quite the contrary.

CHERRY: Well them, we'd better say good-bye.

BENBOW: What, not good-bye forever?

CHERRY: We'd better not meet again.

BENBOW: Oh, good Lord, why not? You needn't be frightened –

LADY BENBOW: *(Heard off L.)* Hector!!

BENBOW: Curse! *(Taking CHERRY up stage.)* All right then, my dear. Under the circumstances, if you really wish it, what more can I say? Good-bye forever. But don't you worry. I'll be able to see you again next week – they're going away again.

*Exit BENBOW L.*

*As CHERRY turns R.C. LIONEL FRUSH enters box of flowers C., closes door.*

LIONEL: *(Seeing CHERRY with interest.)* Oh, good morning. I saw you here last night, of course.

CHERRY: Oh, yes. *(Moves up a little.)* Excuse me, I must go.

LIONEL: Oh, you're always just going out when I come in. *(Cross D.L.)* I say – *(Offering her box of flowers.)* – just a moment. Would you care for these flowers?

CHERRY: But you didn't get them for me.

LIONEL: I've got no one else to give them to. You have them. *(Gives her flowers.)*

CHERRY: Well, that's very kind, I'm sure.

LIONEL: That's all right. Where are you going to lunch?

CHERRY: *(Definitely.)* Oh, really I mustn't. *(Fiddling with ribbon on box.)* What time?

LIONEL: One o'clock – at the Berkeley.

CHERRY: I don't think I ought to.

LIONEL: I say, do. *(Moves to her.)* I'm terribly on my own. I don't know another girl. I swear I don't. Or I wouldn't ask you.

CHERRY: You funny boy.

LIONEL: You will meet me, won't you?

CHERRY: *(Pausing – taking stock of him.)* Now look here. You seem a nice boy, and I'm looking for a bit of real friendship myself. Will you come out on the level?

LIONEL: Yes, rather.

CHERRY: All right then. I'll meet you just outside the Berkeley at one o'clock. 'Bye.

LIONEL: Good-bye. *(He runs up C. in time to open door for her.)*

*Bell warning.*

*She goes out C.*

*He stands and raises his eyebrows.*

*KITTY enters L., crossing R. with RONNY following her. She speaks to him in a petulant ton as they enter.*

KITTY: Oh, don't follow me all over the flat.

RONNY: I'd follow you all over the sticks. *(Sees LIONEL.)* Is that the same one? Good Lor'! Are you still here? I didn't think you'd keep.

*Pause – Bell – Door bell.*

LIONEL: *(To KITTY.)* That'll be my mother, I expect.

KITTY: Oh, well, now we are going to talk about Thark.

RONNY: *(To KITTY.)* Not you.

KITTY: Why not?

RONNY: Uncle said that *he* was going to talk to Mrs. Frush.

KITTY: Oh! Then I'll talk to *Mr.* Frush. *(Turning her back.)*

LIONEL: *(To RONNY.)* Yes, if you don't mind, it's awfully private.

RONNY: Yes, and whether you mind or not, you're privately awful.

*HOOK enters C.*

HOOK: Mrs. Frush.

*MRS. FRUSH enters. She is in quite an affable mood at the start.*

MRS. FRUSH: Oh, you've got there, Lionel. *(To KITTY.)* Good morning.

KITTY: Good morning.

MRS. FRUSH: *(To RONNY.)* Nice day! *(Crosses L.)*

RONNY: Who for? *(Cross L. to MRS. FRUSH.)*

*HOOK exits C. closing door.*

MRS. FRUSH: I'm afraid I should have been here sooner.

RONNY: Oh, don't be afraid of that.

*LIONEL R. C., KITTY R., RONNY L. C., MRS. FRUSH L. C.*

MRS. FRUSH: The traffic always seems worse when you've got a bit behind. *(Moves D. L.)*

RONNY: *(Scrutinising her figure – .)* Yes –

*BENBOW enters L.*

BENBOW: *(Coming down L.C.)* Good morning!

MR. FRUSH: *Good* morning.

BENBOW: Oh! There he is! *(To LIONEL.)* Good morning to you.

LIONEL: *(Rising.)* Good morning, sir.

RONNY: *(To LIONEL.)* Sit down, you'll smash.

*LIONEL sits.*

*(The to BENBOW.)* Good morning, uncle.

BENBOW: *(To RONNY.)* You get out. You're not wanted.

RONNY: No. Only when you want helping out of trouble. I suppose you don't anticipate getting into trouble with *that*!

*He indicated MRS. FRUSH, who hears and gives a little exclamation.*

*(He crosses to her.)* What's the matter? Has something happened to you?

MRS. FRUSH: No, it has not.

*KITTY and LIONEL are sitting R.C.*

RONNY: Oh, I thought I heard you give way.

*RONNY crosses to LIONEL and KITTY and tries to join in their conversation – then turns to BENBOW.*

BENBOW: *(To RONNY.)* Will you get out when you're told?

RONNY: All right! I'm going. *(Crosses L.C.)* – And remember, I'll never call you Uncle again. *(Crosses up L. – at door.)* Good-bye, mother's brother.

*Exits L.*

BENBOW: *(To MRS. FRUSH.)* St down, madam. *(Indicates chair D.L . – she sits next to him.)*

MRS. FRUSH: Thank you.

BENBOW: *(Sitting L.)* Now, madam, come on, put your hounds in. Let's hear something.

MRS. FRUSH: Have you ever been to Thark?

BENBOW: I've seen some very good photos of it.

KITTY: I've been there. *(Crosses to L.C.)*

*LIONEL follows.*

It belonged to my family. Well, to *me*.

BENBOW: And I sold it for you. *(To MRS. FRUSH.)* And you bought it. We all know that. Now, what's wrong with Thark?

MRS. FRUSH: I'm going to speak my mind.

LIONEL: Careful, mother.

MRS. FRUSH: Careful yourself! *(To BENBOW.)* Oh, I know you've been very polite and gave me a nice dinner and all that, but it shall not make me shrink!

BENBOW: No, I didn't expect it would.

KITTY: Well, what's wrong with Thark, anyway?

MRS FRUSH: *(To BENBOW.)* You know well enough without being told.

BENBOW: It's a magnificent house, madam! It would do for a Dook.

MRS. FRUSH: It would do for anyone.

BENBOW: Why? Come on, let's have it. Why?

MRS. FRUSH: I'll tell you why. *(Dramatically dropping her voice.)* 'Aunted!

BENBOW: *(Blinking densely.)* Oughtn't it? *(Looks vaguely at LIONEL and KITTY – then to MRS. FRUSH.)* Oughtn't it to *what*?

LIONEL: *(Cross to BENBOW.)* Well, sir, my mother thinks, sir, that Thark is haunted.

MRS. FRUSH: I don't *think*.

BENBOW: Haunted? Preposterous!

MRS. FRUSH: It's unliveable in.

BENBOW: Haunted, my – *(Mildly.)* – foot! You don't like the place so you're trying to repudiate the deal.

KITTY: *(To BENBOW.)* Well, of course – there always *was* some sort of a *legend* about Thark.

BENBOW: Legend! Bunkum! And what *d'you* want to say so for?

KITTY: Well, it's only honest to say so.

BENBOW: I don't say don't be honest, I say don't be silly. Legend – my hat! What is the trouble – have you investigated?

*KITTY moves away R.C.*

LIONEL: *(Crosses to BENBOW.)* Well, sir, how would *you* care to go down and investigate something funny that goes on in one of the bedrooms?

BENBOW: I mightn't mind. Whose bedroom is it? It's probably rats.

MRS. FRUSH: It is not rats. There's more goes on there than was caused by any rat *you* ever saw.

BENBOW: Oh, thanks for the compliment!

MRS. FRUSH: The butler went to have a look one night, and he came back trembling in every pore.

*BENBOW frowns at her.*

BENBOW: *(To MRS. FRUSH.)* I know what your trouble is. When you've had a couple, you fancy things.

MRS. FRUSH: Well, I don't fancy ghosts. *(Rising boldly.)* So what are you going to do about it?

BENBOW: Ah! *(Rising.)* Here we have it, this is what I've been waiting for. You're going to ask me to cancel the sale.

MRS. FRUSH: I don't ask you to – I'm telling you to.

BENBOW: Oh, thank you, I am not going to try and sell that house again. I've had enough trouble to get rid of it once.

LIONEL: Yes, sir, quite, sir; but –

BENBOW: Down sir! No, madam. Certainly not. Business is business.

*LIONEL L. C., KITTY L. C., BENBOW L., MRS. FRUSH L.*

LIONEL: *(To MRS. FRUSH.)* I *told* you what it would be.

KITTY: *(To MRS. FRUSH.)* Don't be afraid. I'll see you're *properly* treated.

MRS. FRUSH: Thank you. *(To BENBOW.)* There speaks at least a lady.

BENBOW: *(To KITTY.)* I wish you'd mind your own business, my child.

KITTY: It looks as if I shall have to. *(Crosses R.)*

LIONEL: *(Cross to BENBOW.)* Don't be offended by my mother.

BENBOW: Go to hell! Get out of it!

*LIONEL cross R.C.*

MRS. FRUSH: It's all very well for you – *(Cross to LIONEL.)* You stay gadding about here in London waiting for your motor, while I have to go back to Thark and sleep there alone for six nights with a butler and a bogey.

*She exits C. followed by LIONEL.*

*KITTY turns with animation to BENBOW, who is chuckling.*

KITTY: *(Cross L. C.)* You're not treating that old woman properly.

BENBOW: *(Cross R.)* Oh, nonsense! I've treated her all right. She understands it.

KITTY: It's my house – or was. And it's quite true. It was always supposed to be haunted. *(Cross L.C. following BENBOW.)*

BENBOW: *(Sharply.)* Haunted! Tripe!

KITTY: I don't care. If you won't go, I'll jolly well go myself.

BENBOW: What? Go to Thark?

KITTY: Yes. I'll write to Mrs. Frush and arrange to go down there next week. If you won't look into it, I will.

*HOOK enters L.*

BENBOW: Now then, don't talk to me like that.

*BENBOW turns up R., picks up morning paper. From table.*

HOOK: *(Up L.C. to KITTY.)* Excuse me miss, Warner's done your packing for Bath. Would you see whether she's put in all you require?

KITTY: Yes, I'll go in a minute. Oh, Hook, your wife was my aunt Mary's parlour maid at Thark, wasn't she?

HOOK: *(Apprehensively.)* Yes, miss.

KITTY: Did she ever say anything about Thark being haunted?

HOOK: Oh – *(With dread.)* – frequent, miss.

*(KITTY exchanges looks with BENBOW.)*

I should be very sorry to go near the house myself.

KITTY: Thank you.

HOOK: Thank you, miss.

BENBOW: Get out!

HOOK: Yes, sir.

*HOOK goes out L.*

KITTY: And you mean to say you never heard?

BENBOW: *(D.R.)* Never! And I don't want to now. It's a great mistake to encourage people like these Frushes.

RONNY: *(Entering L.)* Quite right, sir. I'm very glad to hear you say so.

BENBOW: *(Ignoring RONNY.)* If you go to Thark, further advances will only be made.

RONNY: Advances? *(To KITTY.)* You're not going to Thark?

KITTY: Yes, I am.

BENBOW: What for? To be taken around at night by young Frush and made to listen to a lot of rats?

RONNY: I won't have you go ratting with young Frush.

KITTY: *(To BENBOW.)* I tell you I am going.

BENBOW: *(Roused.)* Very well. Go and manage your own affairs. *(Going up L.)*

KITTY: I must go. It's only fair and friendly.

BENBOW: Friendly? What the devil do you want to be friendly with an old woman like that for? By gad! She looks like a female froth-blower.

*Exit L.*

RONNY: Kitty! You're trying to make me jealous. Yes, you are – of this nasty new friend of yours – this Leopold Thark, that nasty little fellow with Chippendale shoulders and Adam's legs.

KITTY: He wouldn't go about with Cherry Buck, anyhow.

RONNY: Nor would I, Kitty, on purpose. She was thrust upon me when I wasn't thinking. I couldn't be unkind to her, could I?

KITTY: *(With meaning.)* No.

RONNY: *(Noticing her tone.)* No, of course not. Kitty, let's be friends – you know I'm a friendly little chap.

KITTY: *(Pointedly.)* Yes, you are.

RONNY: Don't say it like that – say, yes, you are; not *yes, you are.* You're fond of me, aren't you?

KITTY: Oh, yes. In a way.

RONNY: *(Trying to embrace her.)* Well, how far away?

KITTY: *(Turning to him – they embrace.)* Well, Ronny, you do promise not to see this girl again?

RONNY: Well, what about you and this boy – this nasty little filleted sheik?

KITTY: Don't be so absurd. I've only met him for five minutes.

RONNY: Well, that's long enough, isn't it?

KITTY: I don't want to see him, but I can't help it if I go to Thark.

RONNY: You're not going to Thark.

*HOOK enters L. and droops down by RONNY's L.*

KITTY: You don't understand. There's something at Thark that's got to be done. Your uncle won't do it, so I must.

RONNY: But what is it? *(To HOOK.)* What is it?

HOOK: Excuse me, miss – it's nearly time you went –

RONNY: No, it isn't. Don't come and say things like that when I'm getting on so well. I had both her hands in mine before you came in, and now I haven't got one. I shan't tip you now. I wasn't going to anyway. *(Goes up to table C. – takes up paper and puts it on chair in front of table C.)*

HOOK: Warner wants to show you what she's packed, miss.

KITTY: *(Cross in front of RONNY and HOOK.)* Oh very well. I'll go and see.

RONNY: I say, Kitty, don't be long. I want to talk to you.

*She goes out L.*

*HOOK starts to go up L. and stops.*

HOOK: May I just say, Mr. Ronald, I'm sorry, sir, about that slight 'itch this morning?

RONNY: What hitch?

HOOK: Bringing the lady in at the wrong time, sir.

RONNY: Oh, that! Yes. Oh, very bad that – oh, it's terrible – that was terrible! I don't know what's the matter with you. You're a mass of hitches. I suppose it must be this baby. You'd better not have any more.

HOOK: Very good, sir.

RONNY: *(Relenting, patting his shoulder.)* All right, Hook. You can if you like.

HOOK: *(Smiling.)* Thank you, sir.

*HOOK goes out L. as –*

*LADY BENBOW enters busily L. followed by BENBOW. She is dressed for travelling.*

LADY BENBOW: *(To RONNY, who is at the table C. looking at a paper.)* Where's Kitty?

RONNY: She's just gone out there –

BENBOW: It's no use trying to stop her, the headstrong little devil. *(Cross to table C.)*

*RONNY resents this.*

LADY BENBOW: *(To RONNY.)* I won't have her go to Thark and do this business.

*BENBOW takes paper from table C., cross down L., sits.*

RONNY: *(With sudden determination.)* Look here, if Kitty wants anything done, it shall be done. *I'll* do it.

LADY BENBOW: Very well, then – you'd better. But it won't be very pleasant –

RONNY: I'd do the nastiest job in the world to please her. I'll even examine the drains for her sake.

BENBOW: It isn't the drains, you ass! *(Cross L., sits.)*

RONNY: I don't care what it is. *(Cross to BENBOW.)* I'll do it. *(With less defiance.)* What is it?

*KITTY returns L., crosses R. C.*

*KITTY L.C., LADY BENBOW R., RONNY L.C., BENBOW L.*

LADY BENBOW: *(D.R. to KITTY.)* Oh, Kitty, is it true what Hector tells me, that you're going to Thark?

KITTY: Yes.

LADY BENBOW: Then I shall come with you. And so shall he.

KITTY: Oh, you needn't – either of you.

LADY BENBOW: My dear, do you think I'd let you go and tackle a job like that alone?

*RONNY listens with increasing interest.*

KITTY: Well, somebody's got to do it.

BENBOW: Well, Ronny says *he* will. So there you are.

KITTY: *(Joyfully.)* Oh, Ronny! Will you? Really?

RONNY: Yes, dear, of course.

KITTY: Oh, how brave of you!

RONNY: What?

KITTY: *(Holding his arm.)* How splendid of you!

RONNY: Oh, darling, it's all right, it's nothing. *(To BENBOW.)* Is it?

BENBOW: No. Of course it isn't.

KITTY: Oh, isn't it? Well, I'm very proud of him – and I shall be very pleased if he comes out of it safely.

*HOOK enters C.*

HOOK: The car is here, my lady.

LADY BENBOW: *(Busily.)* Oh, Kitty, I'm not quite ready, are you?

KITTY: Not quite, but there's heaps of time.

*They exeunt L.*

*HOOK at door C., BENBOW is R. with his paper.*

BENBOW: Hook!

HOOK: Sir? *(Closes door, comes down to BENBOW.)*

BENBOW: You'd better arrange with your wife. I shall be going out of town in a few days, and I shall want you to come with me.

HOOK: Very good, sir. Excuse me, sir. Might I inquire – where shall we be going?

BENBOW: Thark!

HOOK: *(In an involuntary exclamation.)* Thark! *(Turning to RONNY, aghast.)* Oh, my God!

*Exit C.*

RONNY: *(After watching him off, cross L. to BENBOW, his knees shaking.)* I say, uncle, what's all this about won't be safe, worse than drains, and Hook's looks?

BENBOW: Why, what's the matter? You're not frightened, are you?

RONNY: *(Trying to be brave.)* Frightened, no! I'm not frightened, but it sounded strange for the moment.

BENBOW: Well, you know a lot of women – you know what they are – they're all scaremongers.

RONNY: Yes. They do get excited.

BENBOW: Yes – you buck up. Don't you worry.

*RONNY crosses R., picks up the 'Tatler' and sits, crossing his legs.*

RONNY: I shan't worry. I've got nothing to worry about.

BENBOW: *(Still unconcerned, looking at his paper.)* No, of course not. Personally, I don't think anything will happen to you at all.

*RONNY looks across at BENBOW suspiciously.*

*CURTAIN.*

*PICTURE: CURTAIN.*

*BENBOW L. is looking over his glasses at RONNY, who is sitting over R. looking very uncertain, with a sickly smile.*

# Act Three

*SCENE: The dining-room at Thark, after dinner on a night a week later; it is a fine old room. There is a door to the hall C. back, another door down R. Fireplace D.L. Windows up L. in back wall. Staircase shown up L. leading to the bedrooms in the left wing. There is another entrance at the back of stairs left which leads to the front door, which is not shown. Three massive columns each side of the room, and three Venetian lamps in miniature showing an amber light are dotted about – one each side of the stairs and one on the landing up L. – there are two large candelabra on the dining table, which is set upon the oblique down L.C. The candles are burning and casting shadows, giving the room a sombre and eerie effect. The furniture is all antique. There is a monk's stool on lower landing stairs, an oak cabinet above door R., three armchairs, tapestries, one at the foot of the middle column R., the other two at the foot of the back columns. A three-seat cane settle set above opening R. An oak cabinet up stage R. There are two leather-backed armchairs at dining-table, one on R. and the other at the back. Curtains excepting one left of door up C. There is a bell pull right, just below opening R.*

*RONNY and BENBOW are sitting alone over their port and dessert at dining-table R.C. BENBOW back of table, RONNY R. They are wearing dinner jackets. BENBOW has dined well and is quite pleased with things in general, enjoying his cigar, but RONNY is doing his best to disguise extreme dislike for the business on hand. It is a wild night, and at the opening of the act and at frequent intervals the wind can be heard.*

*Wind is heard loudly as curtain rises.*

BENBOW: *(Sitting behind table near RONNY – as the storm is heard outside.)* Wind's up.

RONNY: *(Sitting R of table – with challenge.)* What's that?

BENBOW: All right – I was only referring to the elements. *(Pause.)* I think it's working up for a nasty night.

RONNY: What do you mean 'working up' for one? It's one now, isn't it?

BENBOW: Well, I don't care. I'm not sorry we came. The old woman put up a very good dinner.

RONNY: Yes, the lamb was particularly good. I didn't care for the butler. He eyes me eating.

BENBOW: M'yes. Perhaps he didn't like the idea of you sleeping in the haunted room.

RONNY: He's got a fat lot to worry about, hasn't he?

BENBOW: Yes, he's like Pickwick's fat boy, he likes to make his own flesh creep.

RONNY: Besides, the room isn't haunted. Ridiculous.

BENBOW: Well, of course not.

RONNY: Then why did you say it was?

BENBOW: I didn't.

RONNY: Yes, you did. You said just now, 'the haunted room.'

BENBOW: You seem very sensitive about it.

RONNY: You needn't think I'm afraid.

BENBOW: Nothing to be afraid of.

RONNY: I shouldn't be afraid if there was, I don't suppose.

BENBOW: No, of course not. Ghosts – bunkum. Have you ever met anyone who's seen a ghost?

*Warning for wind.*

RONNY: No; but I've never met anyone who hasn't met someone who *has*.

BENBOW: Go on. *(Passing decanter.)* Have some more port. You'd better have plenty.

RONNY: *(With challenge again.)* Why?

BENBOW: Oh – because it's surprisingly good port, that's all.

RONNY: Oh, in that case I will. *(He is obviously very nervy and shakes as he helps himself, rattling the glass with the decanter.)*

BENBOW: It's no good your trying to tell me. You're scared of this place.

RONNY: You said yourself just now there's nothing to be scared of.

BENBOW: I say so, yes.

RONNY: And so do I.

*Wind is heard only.*

I ought to know

*Warning for lightning.*

I dressed in the room.

BENBOW: Yes, and almost before you started you had yer head stuck out of the door shouting Hook! I believe you'd lost yer nerve.

RONNY: Nothing of the kind. I'd lost my braces.

*The wind suddenly gains force. An outer door is heard to bang, followed by flashes of lightning, which light up the room and catch JONES' face as he enters C. Distant thunder is heard, lasting till JONES is down stage. JONES is MRS. FRUSH's butler, a very sinister-looking man, who walks with a measured, gliding step, slightly on his toes. He carries a little silver tray with a letter on it. He fixes RONNY with his eyes as he comes down stage, keeping dead centre, and stands on his R. RONNY is keenly aware of this.*

What are you looking at me like that for? What's the joke?

JONES: *(Fixing him with his eye, crosses to RONNY.)* It's no joke, sir.

RONNY: What isn't?

JONES: *(Looking straight in front.)* This night's work.

BENBOW: Why, nothing's happened to you, and you've been alone in the house.

JONES: No one is ever alone in this house, sir.

BENBOW: Oh, I heard that none of the other servants would sleep here, and that all the maids went home at night.

JONES: *(To BENBOW.)* Yes, sir. *(To RONNY.)* And maybe it's lucky for them they do.

BENBOW: Is this feller trying to be personal?

RONNY: *(To JONES.)* Now look here. You've been alone in this room at night – you know what I mean – this – my little room? *(Indicates room up L.)*

JONES: *(Eyeing him and nodding.)* Yes, sir. *(Suddenly.)* And don't you! *(Forcibly.)* Don't you!

RONNY: Why shouldn't I, if – if I'm keen on it? *(Drinks.)*

JONES: It isn't only that room, sir. *(Looking L.)* It's all down that wing. It's there. It's there. *(Looking straight in front.)*

RONNY: Yes, I know it's there all right, but what is it that is there?

JONES: *(Slowly.)* Maybe *you'll* know, sir, better, even than I.

BENBOW: Well, he won't know much if he don't.

JONES: *(Looking straight ahead.)* It may not give him time to learn much, sir. *(Turns R.)*

RONNY: Hi, you! Yes, but – here – *(He comes back.)* What's your name again?

JONES: My name, sir? Well, here in this house they only call me Jones – that's all.

*Warning for thunder.*

BENBOW: Oh, is it? Well, you wait till I've been here a bit longer.

RONNY: They *call* you Jones? I see. A sort of pet name?

JONES: Mrs. Frush wouldn't call me by my real name. So she called me Jones. *(Straight in front.)*

RONNY: Why, what's your real name Jones?

JONES: My real name, sir?

RONNY: Yes.

JONES: Death.

*RONNY is about to crack a nut. He does so involuntarily as JONES speaks.*

RONNY: *(To BENBOW.)* Death!

*As RONNY speaks, lightning flashes fiercely into the room, followed immediately by heavy thunder, which goes on for some seconds.*

*It is obviously getting on their nerves. RONNY is particularly nervy, twitching and twisting the nut crackers round and round. BENBOW shows more annoyance than fear; he tests his cigar with his fingers, then smells it, trying to appear unconcerned. After the thunder has died away he carries on with the conversation.*

BENBOW: Ah, well, that's nothing; I don't care a damn. I used to know a chap named Death. Major Death, he was in the Blues.

RONNY: I'm not a bit surprised.

*BENBOW lights a cigar.*

JONES: *(To RONNY.)* If you really mean to sleep in that room, sir, would you care for me to come along to you there to-night?

RONNY: No thanks, Death! It's quite all right.

JONES: Oh, very well, as you please, sir. *(Turns L. a little.)*

BENBOW: I say, what is it you've got there? Is that something for me?

JONES: No, sir. *(Looking at RONNY apprehensively.)* It's only the last post.

*Wind strong.*

*Exit up R.*

RONNY: Nice quiet sort of fellow, isn't he? Makes one feel so restful. The last post!

BENBOW: Yes, that reminds me. *(Cross in front.)*

*Wind drops to nothing.*

*(Cross in front of table L.C. Taking a letter from his pocket.)* I was going to ask you about this.

RONNY: What is it?

BENBOW: I thought I hadn't seen much of you lately.

RONNY: No, I haven't been about much.

BENBOW: This is from Cherry Buck.

RONNY: What? That's not my affair.

BENBOW: Oh! Isn't it? We'll see. Listen to this. *(Reads.)* 'Thanks for the invitation.'

RONNY: Invitation? *(Rises.)*

BENBOW: *(Airily.)* Oh, that's nothing. I didn't mean to read that. That's another part of the letter altogether. I thought it only fair to ask her out again.

RONNY: *(Excitedly.)* What? Good Heavens! When I've lugged you out of trouble once –

BENBOW: Never mind about that, listen to this. *(Reads.)* 'The truth is I'm cutting that stuff right out. I've never met the boy who is really it.'

RONNY: You don't think I'm the boy who is it – do you?

BENBOW: No. Well, what about this then – 'You can console yourself by knowing it was through you I met him. Happy days – Cherry Buck.'

RONNY: Well, who has she met through you?

BENBOW: Only you.

RONNY: Me?

BENBOW: Have you been seeing her again?

RONNY: *(Hesitating up R.)* Well, I – I just met her by accident.

BENBOW: Oh, then let me tell you I consider it to be rotten bad form – in a chap who's just going to be married. *(Pouring out port.)* Why can't yer wait?

RONNY: *(Coming down.)* But I tell you I just met her in the street.

BENBOW: Did you stop and talk?

RONNY: Certainly not. I just halted and spoke a few words.

*KITTY enters up R.*

BENBOW: *(Offering letter to RONNY. Who crosses D.R.)* Well, there you are. You can read it yourself.

*As RONNY takes the letter, KITTY enters up R. in a pretty evening dress. BENBOW turns aside with a nonchalant air. RONNY holds the letter out of sight in his left hand.*

*BENBOW cross D.L. and sits.*

KITTY: *(To RONNY.)* Hello! Have you had a letter too?

RONNY: No, darling. Something of uncle's. A business thing. *(He holds it in his hand while talking.)*

KITTY: Well, Mrs. Frush has just heard from her son. He's coming back.

RONNY: I don't care. Do you care, Kitty?

KITTY: *(To BENBOW.)* But Hecky's got his room.

RONNY: Well, that's fine, he can have my room. *(Moves front of table L. to BENBOW.)*

*MRS. FRUSH and LADY BENBOW enter up R. Both are in evening dress. MRS FRUSH carries a letter.*

MRS. FRUSH: *(As she enters.)* Well, I must see what had best be done.

LADY BENBOW: *(Looks at BENBOW, who has crossed to L.)* My husband won't mind. He's not very particular where he sleeps.

BENBOW: *(Sitting – D.L.)* Oh, isn't he, thank yah.

*Wind softly.*

RONNY: *(Crosses back of table – to MRS. FRUSH.)* Does your son know that I'm here?

MRS. FRUSH: No, he doesn't know anyone's here. You can see what he says. *(She hands the letter to RONNY.)*

BENBOW: I suppose you didn't expect him home? That's why you put me in his room, eh?

MRS. FRUSH: Yes. You see, we haven't furnished many of the bedrooms.

*RONNY has now both letters in his hand. Still retaining both letters, RONNY turns aside and talks to KITTY.*

*LADY BENBOW R., MRS. FRUSH R., RONNY C., KITTY L.C., BENBOW L.*

BENBOW: *(Rising.)* Well, if he wants his room, where am I to go? What other rooms have you got?

MRS. FRUSH: Well, the only other bedroom we've got furnished is the room in the East Wing *(Dropping her voice significantly.)* next door – to his.

*Wind loud.*

*Indicates RONNY, who has gone up with KITTY and is still talking to her eagerly aside.*

LADY BENBOW: I won't have him sleep there.

RONNY: You won't get him to sleep there either.

BENBOW: Oh, I'm not afraid. I'll show you. I'll tell Hook to move my things into the room next door to you. *(He goes up to door C.)*

*KITTY crosses front of table to fireplace L.*

MRS. FRUSH: Allow me, I'll give the orders proper.

*She crosses up R., pulls bell-pull which is hanging on the wall just below extreme R.*

*BENBOW goes up to door C.*

LADY BENBOW: When is your son coming? What does it say in his letter?

*MRS. FRUSH goes down to KITTY.*

MRS. FRUSH: *(Indicating RONNY.)* He's got it.

BENBOW: *(At door C. calling.)* Hook!

*MRS. FRUSH crosses back of table to KITTY R., and sits.*

LADY BENBOW: *(Going to RONNY, who hands her CHERRY BUCK's letter.)* Let me have a look at that.

RONNY: *(Distracted from his talk to KITTY.)* Certainly, auntie, you have it.

*BENBOW comes down from door.*

*LADY BENBOW stands L.C. and looks at the letter. Her expression changes. RONNY sees LADY BENBOW's expression. He glances at the letter in his hand – he realises that she has got CHERRY's letter.*

*Leaving MRS. FRUSH with KITTY, he comes across L. and as BENBOW comes down, RONNY attracts his attention to the appalling mistake he has made. Horrified dumb-show takes place. LADY BENBOW, looking up, catches them at it, and they assume their respective forms of innocent carelessness. Finally LADY BENBOW tears the letter into small pieces, and puts them on a plate on the table L.C. corner. BENBOW looks at RONNY furiously.*

KITTY: Darling – *(With respect for MRS. FRUSH.)* Why have you torn up Mrs. Frush's letter?

RONNY: *(Quickly.)* No, that's not it. This is it. You needn't worry about that. *You* needn't. *(Looks towards BENBOW.)*

MRS. FRUSH: *(Rising.)* Well, let us return to the drawing-room. The atmosphere there is more vivacious.

*JONES is seen coming down C. from the distance.*

KITTY: *(Still a little puzzled about the letter.)* Are you coming, Ronny?

RONNY: In two two's, darling. Less. One two.

MRS. FRUSH: Well, come along all of you, and we'll have a nice rubber of Poker.

*Exit R.*

*KITTY follows.*

*RONNY signs to BENBOW, turns to LADY BENBOW.*

*JONES stands just above LADY BENBOW – R.*

RONNY: Look here, auntie – *(Seeing JONES.)* What do you want?

JONES: This bell rang. Did you ring it, sir?

RONNY: *(Back of table.)* No, I did not.

JONES: *(Mysteriously.)* Queer!

LADY BENBOW: Mrs. Frush rang. She is in the drawing-room.

JONES: Oh, thank you, my lady. *(To BENBOW.)* Still, it were *this* bell that rang. *(To RONNY.)* Queer, very queer.

*RONNY glances up towards left wing.*

*JONES exits R.*

*HOOK enters, comes down and stands looking at him. JONES stops, looks at him and exits R.*

RONNY: *(After looking at BENBOW, to LADY BENBOW.)* Look here, auntie, about that letter. *(He breaks off again.)*

*HOOK has entered C. standing C.R. of LADY BENBOW.*

*(To HOOK.)* Well, what do you want? Can't I be allowed to speak at all. First of all – *(Imitating JONES' voice.)* – Queer,

192

very queer and now you. Go away – *(Cross to HOOK, waving him back, then turns to LADY BENBOW.)* That letter didn't refer to me. So don't tell KITTY!

KITTY: *(Reappearing R.)* Don't tell Kitty what?

RONNY: *(Assuming a very light-hearted manner.)* Ah – h! you mustn't be told that one. Oh, that was a beauty – *(To BENBOW.)* Wasn't it, uncle?

BENBOW: Yes, a little too near the knuckle for my liking.

RONNY: On the knuckle. That was one of auntie's best. You rascal.

*Goes off with KITTY up R.*

BENBOW: You just trot along to the drawing-room, my love, I'll give Hook orders about moving my things into this other room.

LADY BENBOW: Hook, just wait outside a moment.

HOOK: Yes, my lady.

*Exit C.*

*BENBOW realises he's for it, tries to appear unconcerned.*

LADY BENBOW: Well, Hector?

BENBOW: *(Heavily.)* Oh, I know you think the worst. But let me tell you I wrote to that little girl to come and see me about a frock I ordered for you, and she must have misunderstood what I wanted her for.

LADY BENBOW: I think that extremely unlikely. Besides, she said in her letter that she's cutting that stuff right out.

BENBOW: Yes, that's what I say – she's cutting out the stuff for the frock

LADY BENBOW: Oh, *no*, Hector.

BENBOW: *(Lamely.)* No?

LADY BENBOW: *(Firmly.)* No.

BENBOW: Nothing doing?

LADY BENBOW: Nothing at all.

*Warning for crash.*

BENBOW: Well, all I can say is, it's a great pity. Still, I had to say something. You can't stand there like a damn fool when you've been bowled out.

LADY BENBOW: *(Rising very suspiciously.)* Who does she mean in this letter that she's met through you? It can't be Ronny.

BENBOW: *(Cross to LADY BENBOW.)* Why not?

LADY BENBOW: Well, is it likely? Ronny things of no one but Kitty, otherwise he wouldn't be down here sleeping in that room.

BENBOW: *(Cross to table.)* Why – you're not frightened, are you?

LADY BENBOW: Yes, I am. This house gives me the creeps. Doesn't it you?

BENBOW: *(Cross to table, pours out a glass of port.)* No, I don't let it.

LADY BENBOW: I wish I'd never come here.

*A tray crash heard off up C. She runs and clasps him – BOTH are very startled.*

My goodness, what was that? *(Falls into BENBOW's arms for protection.)*

*HOOK appears. He comes down centre agitated and in a hurry.*

HOOK: I beg your pardon, my lady. I just knocked over a brass tray in the 'all.

BENBOW: Well, you stop knocking things about or I'll knock you about. *(He kisses LADY BENBOW's hand affectionately.)*

HOOK: I'm very sorry, my lady. *(Down C.)*

LADY BENBOW: Never mind, I think we're all a little bit jumpy to-night.

*Exits R. into drawing room R.*

*Wind rises.*

BENBOW: Hook – *(Rather confidentially.)*

HOOK: Yes, Sir 'Ector.

BENBOW: You know this room they call the haunted room? *(Picking up glass of port.)*

HOOK: I've heard, sir.

BENBOW: Yes. Well, there's a room next door to it. I want you to go up there. *(Drinks a little port.)*

HOOK: Me, sir?

BENBOW: Yes. I hope you'll find it all right. If you don't, you can come back and let me know. *(Drinks half a glass of port.)*

HOOK: Oh, but you – you don't wish me to sleep here, sir?

BENBOW: Oh, I don't; that's the last thing I wish. I'm going to sleep there myself. I want you to move my things there.

HOOK: Oh, very good, sir.

*RONNY returns up R., comes down R. HOOK moves up C.*

RONNY: *(Eagerly to BENBOW.)* I say, uncle, did you tell auntie that wasn't me – in that letter?

BENBOW: Yes, I did. *(Cross to RONNY.)* What the hell did you want to give it to her for?

RONNY: I didn't give it to her at all; she grabbed is from me.

BENBOW: Grabbed it! – rot! *(Turning away.)* What next will you say? *(To HOOK, who is still standing centre.)* Well, go on, move, can't you?

*Wind gently.*

HOOK: *(Going up L.)* Oh, you – ah – wish me to go now, sir?

BENBOW: I'm telling you now, ain't I?

HOOK: *(Dithering.)* Yes, sir; I – ah – I'm not quite sure of the way. I suppose I shall find it all right.

RONNY: *(Crosses up to HOOK, who is on the stairs.)* Yes, and while you're up there, go and look in my room next door. You stay up there for a long time. Then if something happens to *you*, I shan't have to go up there at all.

HOOK: Oh! *(Turns miserably towards stairs L.)*

BENBOW: *(In a sharp, altered tone.)* Hook!

HOOK: *(Halting.)* Sir?

BENBOW: *(As before.)* What are you frightened of?

HOOK: *(Up three stairs.)* I'm not frightened, sir. Just slightly uncomfortable.

BENBOW: Why?

HOOK: It's this butler, sir. I don't take to the man.

RONNY: No, I don't take to him either.

HOOK: I think he's morbid.

RONNY: I think he's putrid. But I say, Hook, you haven't heard sounds or anything coming from my room, have you?

HOOK: No, sir – I haven't listened yet.

RONNY: Well, go and listen now. *(Cross D.L.)*

*JONES enters C. and comes down C.*

*Wind heard loudly.*

HOOK: Oh, yes, sir.

BENBOW: And Hook.

*RONNY crosses D.L.*

*Wind goes down a bit.*

*Warning for bell.*

HOOK: *(Halting.)* Sir?

BENBOW: In young Mr. Frush's room you'll find a duck gun and some ammunition.

*Wind softly.*

Take 'em along with you.

HOOK: Oh, no, thank you, sir.

BENBOW: You do as you're damn well told. I want the gun beside my bed.

HOOK: Oh, I beg your pardon, sir. Certainly. *(Turns again.)*

*RONNY crosses to front of table L.C.*

*As HOOK is going, JONES moves to him.*

JONES: *(To HOOK.)* I'll come with you up there.

HOOK: No, no, I'd rather go alone.

*Bell.*

*Bell heard off. THEY ALL come to attention – HOOK is up the stairs. JONES moves down a stage a few steps.*

JONES: What was that?

BENBOW: *(Rudely to JONES.)* Hell, what did you think it was? –
A cornet?

JONES: No one here rang, sir. *(Point R.)* And it weren't that
bell. I know the sound.

RONNY: *(D.L. uneasily.)* Queer. *(Looks at BENBOW.)* Very queer.

JONES: *(With an exclamation that makes RONNY jump.)* Ah! The
front door bell. Young Mr. Frush maybe.

RONNY: *(With relief.)* Oh, not queer. *(To BENBOW.)*

JONES: *(Going – to HOOK.)* You go on up. I'll come after you
with the sheets.

HOOK: Don't you come after me with no sheets. I won't have
it.

*Exits up the stairs hurriedly.*

*JONES exits behind stairs L.*

BENBOW: Well, I think we'd better join the ladies.

RONNY: No, uncle, I want to talk to Kitty. D'you mind telling
her I'm here?

BENBOW: Yes, I'll tell her. *(Crossing to RONNY.)* Well, you'll be
all right now, my boy, with me next door to you with a
duck gun.

RONNY: Personally I don't think this trouble is caused by
ducks.

*They both drink.*

BENBOW: Nothing had better trouble me. You don't walk in
your sleep, do you?

RONNY: I don't know. If one's asleep, how does one know if
one's walking?

BENBOW: Well, don't walk into me, that's all. Or I'll walk
into you. Like a feller I knew – old Dasher Pink. His kid's
governess used to walk in her sleep. Nice-looking girl she
was, too.

RONNY: Well, I don't care.

BENBOW: No, but old Dasher did. She walked into *his* bedroom one night. He though *she* was a ghost. He must have been a bit tight at the time, I should think.

RONNY: Why, what did he do?

BENBOW: Nothing. He thought she was a ghost.

*He goes off R.*

*RONNY is about to take some port – JONES appears L. followed by WHITTLE, who comes down R.C.*

JONES: *(Indicating RONNY.)* Ah! Here's the very gentleman you want.

*WHITTLE is a man in the thirties, voluble and pushing; he wears a leather coat and carries a cap. WHITTLE comes quickly down to RONNY. He shows signs of a journey. JONES stands up stage C.*

WHITTLE: *(To JONES.)* Thank you. *(Then to RONNY – offering his hand.)* How are you, sir, by Jove?

RONNY: *(Shaking hands.)* Oh, I'm pretty well, great Scott! Who are you?

WHITTLE: My name's Whittle.

RONNY: Why? *(Signals to JONES to go.)*

*JONES looks furtively up L. and –*

*Exits up C.*

WHITTLE: I've come from Norwich. I heard about this. Just at the right time. What a bit of luck!

RONNY: *(Feebly.)* Luck? Who for?

WHITTLE: For me. I say, can I be in this?

RONNY: In what?

WHITTLE: Why in this stunt. In that room. Can I be in *that?*

RONNY: *(Keenly interested taking his arm.)* You want to be in that room?

WHITTLE: Rather, if I may.

RONNY: To-night?

WHITTLE: You bet. I'm awfully keen.

RONNY: *(Pleased.)* Come inside.

WHITTLE: Thanks. *(Crosses to table, helps himself to port.)* You see, I'm a reporter.

RONNY: *(Indicating port.)* That's fine, then report.

WHITTLE: *(Helping himself to another port.)* I'm a free lance.

RONNY: Good! Make yourself at home. Have plenty of port – a couple of oranges – etc.

WHITTLE: Oh, thanks most awfully, I say.

RONNY: Not in the least. You mean you want to sleep in that room to-night stead of me?

WHITTLE: No, no sir, I don't want to do *you* out of it.

RONNY: That's all right, don't worry about that, sir, I shan't.

WHITTLE: *(In confidence.)* What I really want is – when you go to bed – I want to come up and sit and watch.

*RONNY slides up and down the carpet, self-consciously.*

RONNY: Well, I'm afraid I don't think I look very nice in bed. But –

*KITTY enters from R.*

I'll do what I can.

*KITTY has moved over to RONNY. She touched his arm: he turns to her startled: he is obviously very nervy.*

WHITTLE: That's fine.

KITTY: *(Coming down R.C.)* You wanted me, Ronny?

RONNY: A gentleman from Norwich, darling. You've heard of Norwich?

KITTY: Yes.

RONNY: Well, this is the gentleman. He's a long way from home, he can't get home, nowhere near home – can you – no – and it's very late and Norwich is shut. He's very wet and my room's very dry. I thought it was a good idea to put him in my room and air him.

KITTY: *(To WHITTLE.)* Are you a friend of Mrs. Frush's?

WHITTLE: Thanks very much. I'd like to meet her.

RONNY: You shall meet her, sir. You couldn't miss her.

*BENBOW enters up R. speaking as he does so.*

BENBOW: I'll see who it is. *(Confronting WHITTLE.)* Who is it?

WHITTLE: *(Cross to BENBOW.)* Good evening, sir. You're Mr. Frush, I fancy.

BENBOW: Oh, thank yer. I don't very much fancy that myself.

RONNY: Oh, uncle, this is Mr. Lance of Norwich.

BENBOW: *(Suspiciously.)* Eh?

RONNY: He's looking for rooms and I find I'm not so very tired so thought he might have my room.

WHITTLE: I'm very keen to make a report –

BENBOW: Oh, I see, you're a newspaper man, are you?

WHITTLE: Yes, sir.

BENBOW: Well, I'll make a report at you with a duck gun, if you don't get out.

WHITTLE: I'd give anything to be allowed to stay.

BENBOW: *(Losing his temper.)* Get out, I tell you!

WHITTLE: Oh, sir. The chance of a lifetime!

RONNY: Let the gentleman chance his lifetime.

BENBOW: Get out, I say. And don't you dare to mention a word of this in your pestilent papers.

*Walking him off L.*

WHITTLE: It's a wonderful opportunity thrown away.

RONNY: Yes, don't throw it away, sir, please.

WHITTLE: Sir, I won't mention any names.

BENBOW: No. Well, I'll mention one or two in a minute, if you don't get out. *(Following him up stage.)* Get out, you saucy monkey, coming into other people's houses without being invited.

*He goes off L. behind stairs.*

*BENBOW goes D.R.C. very angry.*

And you're making quite big enough fool of yerself without putting it in the papers.

KITTY: *(Indignantly.)* He isn't.

BENBOW: Yes, he is. And so are you.

RONNY: *(Firing up.)* Well, do the job yourself. *(Cross to BENBOW.)* I'm doing it for Kitty, not you.

BENBOW: Yes. *(Going up to door R.)* If she's stupid enough to credit such stuff. Crass bunkum. It's wrong. Worse. It's next door to immoral.

*Exit up R.*

RONNY: *(Calling off up R.)* Yes, I've heard you're sleeping next door.

*KITTY goes after them, watching from up R.*

*JONES enters, crosses L. putting tray on table. WHITTLE peers in again, then, making sure he isn't seen, he creeps off in the direction of the East Wing up the stairs. JONES starts to put things on his tray. RONNY and KITTY cross down to R.*

Listen, Kitty.

*KITTY is annoyed at RONNY's rudeness to BENBOW.*

You have heard what he said. *(He sees JONES.)* What do you want?

JONES: *(Behind table.)* You don't mind if I clear, sir?

*Wind softly.*

RONNY: No. I *want* you to clear.

KITTY: Ronny, if you don't like this business, don't do it, will you?

RONNY: *(Eyeing JONES, who is messing about at the table.)* But you want it done.

KITTY: Yes, darling, I thought you were keen to do it. You never said you minded until now.

RONNY: I know, but – as night approaches –

*JONES makes a strange groaning noise – 'Ah!' and looks at RONNY.*

– and people come and look at you with the evil eye –

KITTY: My dear, if you can't face it, I wouldn't dream of letting you. We'll tell them. *(Turns to go.)*

RONNY: *(Stopping her.)* Oh, no. You're disappointed in me, I'll do it.

*JONES hisses and exits C., having cleared the table except a plate in the corner with torn letter on it and fruit-dish, cigar-box and ash-tray centre.*

*KITTY cross to table watching JONES off.*

KITTY: Oh, that man's so weird.

RONNY: I know, dear, but don't worry about him. He probably used to be in the siphon business.

KITTY: I'd do it myself like a shot if they'd let me.

RONNY: I know you would, darling – you're a brave little girl.

KITTY: After all, if anything happened you could make some loud noise.

*She has picked up a piece of the letter from the plate and is toying with it.*

I mean, as a signal. *I* know. Take the gong.

RONNY: The gong?

KITTY: The dinner-gong. Then if anything happens you can beat it.

RONNY: I shall probably beat it in any case.

*KITTY has picked up a piece of the torn letter – she looks at it absently. RONNY turns and sees a shadow on the wall R., this scares him a bit until he, after a few movements, sees that it's his own reflection – he turns to KITTY.*

KITTY: *(Reading.)* Cherry? *(Looking down at plate.)* Ronny, what was this letter?

RONNY: Oh, something of uncle's. Why?

KITTY: *(Examining the scrap.)* Cherry!

*RONNY moves away R.*

That's that odious girl.

RONNY: Yes. Horrible! Uncle's been writing to her.

KITTY: *(Crosses to RONNY.)* Ronny!

RONNY: What? You don't think that I've been seeing her again?

KITTY: I should hope not. You promised me you wouldn't.

RONNY: I know I did. That's why I haven't.

KITTY: *(Rather sharply.)* Oh, is *that* they only reason?

RONNY: Darling, don't I always do what I promise? Aren't I sleeping in that – haunted room – with nothing to beat but a gong – just because you want me to?

*HOOK heard off from the balcony up L. screaming.*

*(Turns quickly.)* Good Lord, what's that?

*HOOK hurries on. He is yelling and in a dire state of funk. He is seen to run past on the balcony round the stairs and down to RONNY and KITTY.*

HOOK: Oh, Heaven! Oh, sir!

KITTY: What's happened?

RONNY: What? What? Speak, can't you?

HOOK: Hardly, sir.

RONNY: Well, make signs or something.

*BENBOW, LADY BENBOW, and MRS. FRUSH enter R.C. JONES enters up C.*

*BENBOW down L.C. MRS. FRUSH down R. LADY BENBOW down L.C. left of BENBOW, JONES down L.*

BENBOW: What's the matter? What's up? What's happened? *(Cross D.L.C.)* What's he done? What is it?

KITTY: *(Indicating HOOK.)* It's him. He's just come downstairs.

RONNY: Why did you fall downstairs? Come on.

HOOK: Oh, sir, it's happened to me.

JONES: *(Standing L. of table.)* Ah! *(In a terrifying tone.)*

*This startles the others, making them all lose their balance. MRS. FRUSH, who is on the right, gets the full force of the bump.*

MRS. FRUSH: *(Terrified.)* Ah!

*HOOK C., KITTY R.C., BENBOW L.C., RONNY R.C., LADY BENBOW L.C., MRS. FRUSH R., JONES L. of table.*

*Close together in a semicircle.*

RONNY: *(To MRS. FRUSH.)* Quiet, please. *What's* happened?

HOOK: *(Addressing BENBOW.)* I was in your room, sir – I'd just done your bed and that –

RONNY: And that? And what?

HOOK: And that, sir.

RONNY: And *what?*

BENBOW: Stop that that-ing. Go on. And what else?

HOOK: Well, your bed and so on, sir.

BENBOW: Stop that, I say. What occurred?

RONNY: Come on, let's have it.

MRS. FRUSH: *(To RONNY.)* Don't flurry him. It isn't easy to say what you've seen when all you know is you've seen something you don't know what it is.

BENBOW: Will you let the man speak?

KITTY: Go on, Hook!

HOOK: Suddenly, the door opened –

RONNY: And then?

*A brief moment's pause – ALL listening intently.*

HOOK: It shut again.

KITTY: Who opened it?

HOOK: I don't know. Before I could look it was shut.

MRS. FRUSH: That's right. The doors *do* open and shut.

LADY BENBOW: Well, so I suppose.

MRS. FRUSH: *(Quickly.)* But automatic.

RONNY: No one could have opened it. We were all down here.

BENBOW: Go on, will you? What did you do?

HOOK: For the moment I stood as if rooted.

BENBOW: Why?

RONNY: *(To BENBOW.)* Be reasonable. This is enough to root anyone.

HOOK: Then I looked out, sir, and saw – nothing exactly I can tell of. Something –

BENBOW: Nothing-something.

HOOK: Something – as it were a figure – flit.

JONES: Ahh!...

> *They ALL look at JONES in anger and fury. MRS. FRUSH and RONNY bump back to back.*

BENBOW: *(To JONES.)* Will you shut up there?

HOOK: It was worse than what it sounds.

RONNY: *(To KITTY.)* It doesn't *sound* any too good to me.

BENBOW: Go on! What did you do? Did you follow it?

HOOK: Oh, it disappeared somewhere – *(Looks at RONNY.)* – by the 'aunted room, sir.

> *RONNY grips MRS. FRUSH's throat unknowingly, making her shout 'Oh!' as he nearly chokes her.*

BENBOW: Never mind that. Did you follow it?

HOOK: No, I did not, sir. I 'urried down here, sir.

MRS. FRUSH: *(To BENBOW.)* There, one of your own party has had a taste of it. What more d'you want?

RONNY: *(Cross to BENBOW.)* I don't think we want any more, do we?

> *KITTY and MRS. FRUSH cross to steps R.*

BENBOW: Nonsense! *(To HOOK.)* Go on! Go back and have another look, Hook.

HOOK: Oh, sir!

LADY BENBOW: No, Hector. *(To HOOK.)* You can go to your own room, Hook.

HOOK: Thank you, my lady. *(Goes with alacrity C.)*

> *JONES follows him to the door and watches him off, then listens to the conversation at door up C.*

LADY BENBOW: *(To SIR HECTOR.)* And, Hector, you don't sleep alone in that room to-night.

BENBOW: Why not? *(Pointing to RONNY, who is standing with KITTY R.C.)* My room's all right – it's his room that's haunted.

RONNY: And jolly glad you are of it.

BENBOW: What? You don't suppose I'm afraid of a draught blowing a door open, do you? *(Cross to RONNY.)* I know what you'd like. You'd like me to sleep in the room instead of you.

RONNY: Not in the least.

BENBOW: *(Readily.)* Oh! That's all right then. *(Turns aside again.)*

RONNY: *(On second thoughts.)* All the same – I dare you to.

BENBOW: That's about all the daring you're capable of. *(Turning away.)*

RONNY: *(With a satirical laugh, in an undertone.)* Funk.

BENBOW: *(Cross to him.)* Don't you call me a funk while all the time you're doing your best to back out of it.

RONNY: And all the time you're doing your best not to back into it.

KITTY: Look here! Ronny's is a double bed. *(To BENBOW.)* Why don't you sleep there too?

LADY BENBOW: Now *that* I wouldn't mind.

RONNY: *(To her.)* Thanks, she didn't mean you.

MRS. FRUSH: There's safety in numbers.

*Warning for thunder.*

RONNY: I refuse to have numbers. *(To MRS. FRUSH.)* You stay in your own room.

KITTY: *(To BENBOW.)* Come on. You're so scornful and fearless. Will you sleep there with him?

BENBOW: *(Goaded.)* Yes, I don't care. *(To RONNY – to LADY BENBOW.)* And I bet you I sleep like a top.

RONNY: Yes, a humming-top.

BENBOW: All right, then, that's a bet.

RONNY: We sleep together.

*JONES, who has been listening at the stairs, comes down.*

BENBOW: We'll split the bed.

RONNY: And sleep on the floor. *(Sees JONES, who has come down centre and stands just above RONNY and BENBOW.)* Death!

JONES: What time would you like your call?

*Wind, lightning and thunder.*

*QUICK CURTAIN.*

## SCENE II

*SCENE: RONNY's room at Thark. There is only one door, which is in the back wall R.C. Windows to the ground in the L. wall. Curtains hang over them. A fireplace R. with a fire, the glow of which lights up the bed. Dressing-table up in L.C. corner. A chair near the fire D.R. A smaller chair near the door L.C. The bed runs down the centre. It is a large double bed of Jacobean type, with a canopy, but no foot-rail. By the side of the bed, L. a small table against which is leaning the duck gun. By the R. side of the bed another small table on which is the gong and gong-stick. On the table L. stands a decanter, also glasses and a siphon. There is a chest of drawers up L. above fireplace – on this are some dress clothes – those that RONNY has taken off – his dressing-gown, a silk one, is dangling over the foot of the bed. BENBOW's clothes are on a chair up L. corner. His dressing-gown – a velvet one – is lying on a cabinet down L. His slippers are just by bed, L. side. It is not a dismal room, and there are some pictures, including one of the ancestral type, which hangs on the wall R. It is a portrait of considerable size, with a massive frame. Four electric light brackets – one R., one L., two back wall.*

*The room, however, is in darkness when the curtain rises. Only the light given by the fire flickers feebly. A clock in the distance strikes three. Another, not quite so distant, strikes immediately afterwards. Then a stable clock, heard off L. strikes with a light, cracked note. Silence follows.*

*A light shows in the passage behind, as the door is silently and slowly opened. The figure of LIONEL FRUSH can be seen, lighted by the illumination in the background. He is wearing a leather motor coat over his ordinary clothes. He peers into the room. Then the figure of CHERRY joins him and peers in too.*

LIONEL: *(In a hoarse whisper.)* They're *both* here.

CHERRY: *(Also sotto voce.)* Well, where am *I* to go?

LIONEL: I don't know. Mother left that note, but she didn't say
who was sleeping where. You'd better try the little room
next door.

*THEY disappear. The door is closed with a slight click and –*

*RONNY's voice is heard from the bed.*

RONNY: What's that? *(He reaches out for switches on R. post of bed and turns on light.)*

*Lights on.*

*Both are in pyjamas. RONNY creeps from the bed, puts slippers on and listens. BENBOW wakes up. RONNY does not notice him. RONNY makes as if to open the door, then, thinks better of it. BENBOW quietly helps himself to whisky. BENBOW's siphon is one of those which make a loud, hissing noise. This startled RONNY, who is still at the door listening.*

*(Swinging round.)* I wish you wouldn't do that.

BENBOW: I wish you'd stay in bed, and not keep fiddling about the room all night. I haven't slept a wink.

RONNY: If you don't know you've been asleep, you're the only one who doesn't.

BENBOW: What d'yer mean?

RONNY: Why, you've been giving a nasal organ recital.

*RONNY slips his slippers off R. of bed.*

BENBOW: Well, that's no reason for you to keep hopping in and out of bed. You made me dream I was trying to mate canaries.

RONNY: Uncle, the door opened, and then shut again.

BENBOW: Get back into bed!

*As RONNY gets back, he looks furtively at the door.*

Door opened! You're worse than Hook. My God, I'd rather sleep with Hook.

RONNY: I'd rather sleep between Hook and Death.

BENBOW: Lie down. Put the light out. *(Reaches out to put down his tumbler – lies down.)*

*RONNY turns to switch the lights off; he notices the door opening and starts to waken BENBOW terror-stricken.*

*As BENBOW is about to protest, the door opens slowly. LIONEL appears but is not seen by BENBOW or RONNY as they sit side by side and watch it. It shuts slowly. RONNY throws his arms round BENBOW's neck, his nerve giving way. BENBOW shouts and throws him off.*

RONNY: It's your turn.

BENBOW: *(Getting out of bed and taking up the gun.)* By gad! I'll teach someone to play monkey tricks with me. *(Comes down, round the bed, and to the door.)*

*RONNY climbs out quickly R. to intercept him.*

RONNY: Hi! Hi! *(Struggling with him, trying to get the gun from him.)*

BENBOW: Let go of it.

RONNY: Don't shoot in here. Shoot out of the window.

BENBOW: What the hell's the good of shooting out of the window at something at the door?

*RONNY puts his hand over the muzzle of the gun – BENBOW knocks it away.*

Now – you open that door when I give the word.

RONNY: What word?

BENBOW: It doesn't matter a damn what word.

RONNY: *(Trying to gain time.)* Yes, it does.

BENBOW: Open the door.

RONNY: I won't.

BENBOW: *(Rushing forward.)* I'll open the door myself.

RONNY: *(Obtaining the gun.)* All right. I'll hold the revolver.

BENBOW: *(Throwing open the door.)* Hands up!

*The light is on outside, but no one is there. RONNY puts his hands up – he is still holding the gun.*

That's very odd.

*BENBOW leaves the door slightly ajar.*

RONNY: I told you. We're up against the supernatural.

BENBOW: You go and have a look in the passage.

RONNY: Why?

BENBOW: To see if there's anything there.

RONNY: *(Advances very cautiously, then turns back.)* If there was something there, what would you do?

BENBOW: I'd hunt it.

RONNY: Well, I wouldn't. So you go!

BENBOW: Go on. Have some guts. I'll foller.

RONNY: *(Holds gun as a walking-stick and limps up to door – speaking through doorway.)* Be very careful, will you, please. I'm coming. *(Opens door.)*

*As he takes a step, LIONEL appears – RONNY steps back, startled.*

*BENBOW steps back towards bed.*

*RONNY points gun at LIONEL, who has both hands up.*

LIONEL: *(Cheerfully, dropping his hands at his sides.)* Hallo!

*RONNY, looking at LIONEL, unconsciously points gun at BENBOW's stomach.*

BENBOW: Hi! Hi! Hi! Mind what you're doing with that thing. *(Points to his stomach in horror.)* D'ye see what you're doing, pointing it right there. *(Indicating stomach.)*

*RONNY points gun into fireplace.*

*(With sarcasm, to LIONEL.)* How are you? What do you want?

LIONEL: Oh, well, I'm sorry! I didn't mean to disturb you.

BENBOW: Go on out of it. *(Returning L. and pouring another whisky.)* I like your idea of not disturbing people – jackassing about with their doors in the middle of the night.

LIONEL: Oh, yes, I've only just blown in!

RONNY: Well, blow out again! *(Pointing to BENBOW, who is standing with his back to the audience, head thrown back, finishing his drink.)* Can't you see he's trying to get some sleep?

LIONEL: Yes, but I never got my car till late.

RONNY: Go away now. Your own room's unoccupied. *(Indicating BENBOW.)* He unoccupied it on purpose.

LIONEL: *(Well R.D.)* Oh! But what about the room next door?

RONNY: I don't know anything about that.

LIONEL: There are somebody's things there.

BENBOW: *(Getting back into bed.)* Yes, they're mine. You leave 'em alone.

*He attempts to climb into bed, but as he puts his foot on the bed it slips off, making him overbalance and fall flat face downwards on the bed.*

*(Very annoyed – to LIONEL.)* Get out of it! *(Climbs into bed.)*

LIONEL: Oh, right ho! There's no one sleeping there. That's fine. Well, good-night. I hope you won't be disturbed at all.

*Goes out up R., closing door.*

BENBOW: Well, what d'you think of that?

*RONNY puts gun at foot of bed L.*

*(Getting back into bed.)* There's impertinence, if you like.

RONNY: Yes. Lucky I didn't shoot. I nearly shot. *(Shoes off.)*

BENBOW: Well, there's that ghost for you anyway.

*BENBOW is in the centre of the bed, with very little room left for RONNY, who kneels on his own side, measuring the amount of room BENBOW has taken. BENBOW is very comfortable and is obviously nursing a hot water bottle under the clothes. RONNY gets in and there is a lot of shuffling for position – each trying desperately to get even a chance to lie comfortable, both are elbowing each other.*

BENBOW: Keep on your side.

RONNY: *(Trying to make room for himself.)* I'll keep it when I get it.

BENBOW: *(As RONNY takes a handful of bedclothes.)* Now.

*He pulls clothes furiously, there is a struggle for bedclothes. RONNY at last gives in.*

RONNY: You're awful in bed. From the very start you pinched both the hot water bottles.

BENBOW: *(Taking most of the bedclothes and settling himself.)* What does a young man like you want with a hot water bottle?

RONNY: What does an old man like you want with two?

BENBOW: I like one on my stomach as well.

RONNY: *(Sitting up, trying to get some clothes.)* Am I to have nothing on my stomach? Look at me! Not one piece of blanket have I got.

*Warning light out.*

*RONNY shuffling in bed.*

BENBOW: Keep still, will you? *(Heaves, pushing RONNY nearly out.)*

*RONNY's leg shoots out of bed, which saves him from falling out completely – he rests his elbow on the table right of bed.*

RONNY: Look out! You nearly pushed my elbow into my gong!

BENBOW: Oh, my God, what a night! *(As he turns over, facing RONNY's back.)* Go on, put the light out. I want to drop off.

RONNY: I am dropping off.

*Light out.*

*(Very fed up.)* Take your knees out of my back – they're like rock-cakes.

*A short silence. Suddenly there is a sharp rapping on the window D.L.*

*(Sitting up.)* Uncle!

*Warning lights up.*

BENBOW: *(Well under bedclothes.)* What's the matter now?

RONNY: Something rapping at the window.

BENBOW: What's rapping?

RONNY: Spirit rapping.

*Window rapping is heard again.*

BENBOW: Spirit rapped be damned. Put the light up! It' that infernal boy again.

*Lights up.*

RONNY: *(Turning on the lights.)* How can he get outside the window?

BENBOW: There's a balcony runs all down the wing.

*Knocking repeated.*

Well, don't sit here.

*RONNY lies down again.*

Go on.

RONNY: Me?

BENBOW: Yes. It's your turn.

RONNY: Oh, is it?

*RONNY, very unwillingly, gets out of bed. He wastes time with his slippers, and then advances towards the window. As he does so, the rapping is repeated, and he makes a dive for the bed. BENBOW, sitting up in bed, keeps him out.*

BENBOW: Go on! Pull the curtains aside and have a look.

RONNY: *(Pulling the curtain gingerly and peering.)* Great Scott!

BENBOW: What?

RONNY: It's a woman!

BENBOW: *(Excitedly.)* Open the window – quick! *(Scrambles from bed, puts his slippers on.)*

*Wind is heard rising.*

*RONNY opens the window – CHERRY rushes in. She is obviously very cold. She is clad in pyjamas.*

CHERRY: *(Clinging to RONNY.)* Oh, help me!

BENBOW: Good Lord! It's Cherry Buck!

CHERRY: Oh, I've been frightened stiff!

*Wind drops.*

BENBOW: How on earth did you come here, my child?

CHERRY: I came with Lionel. We've got engaged. I told you in my letter.

RONNY: There you are! Lionel Frush!

BENBOW: I don't care! *(To CHERRY.)* Well, what happened?

CHERRY: He put me in the room next door here, and there's someone there.

RONNY: Good lord! Human or otherwise?

CHERRY: I went in there and undressed – and just as I was getting into bed, I saw the curtain of the cupboard move. And then I saw a foot.

RONNY: How long? A foot? What shape?

CHERRY: Well, a shoe.

BENBOW: Well, that's nothing. Hook put my shoe there.

CHERRY: But it moved. Oh, I was scared. I daren't go past it to the door. So I got out on the balcony.

BENBOW: Who the blazes can this be, I wonder?

RONNY: *(To BENBOW.)* It's your turn.

BENBOW: I don't care. Who's afraid?

RONNY: No one's afraid at all, but it's your turn.

BENBOW: Whoever's found a way in here had better find a way out again. *(Going L. takes gun, crosses L. to window.)*

CHERRY: You'll have to go by the balcony. I locked the door from the inside.

BENBOW: *(Going to window.)* I'll soon settle somebody's hash. *(Putting on dressing-gown.)*

RONNY: *(Nervous at being left with CHERRY, crosses to BENBOW as he is going out.)* I say, uncle, hadn't I better come along as well?

BENBOW: *(Pausing at window.)* No, you stay here with her.

RONNY: Oh, but I don't want to stay in here with her alone.

BENBOW: You don't? Here, you take the gun!

*RONNY pushes him out.*

RONNY: *(To CHERRY.)* Look here – this is rather awkward. You go over there by the fire – I'm going to bed.

*Taking his slippers off and climbing into bed from L., he drops slippers on floor R. of bed.*

CHERRY: It's jolly cold. *(Crosses R. to fireplace, warming her hands.)*

RONNY: Yes, that's why I'm getting into bed.

CHERRY: I'll be you're not as cold as I am.

RONNY: Oh, yes, I am; you've got more on than I have.

CHERRY: I haven't. Look at me!

RONNY: No, thanks. I'd rather not.

*BENBOW enters hurriedly through door. RONNY seeing door open, screams with nerves.*

Oh, no, no, no! Oh, no!

BENBOW: It's all right. There's no one there. The door was open.

CHERRY: Well, there you are. There *was* someone there.

RONNY: There isn't now. So you can go back.

BENBOW: *(To CHERRY.)* No, you stay here. Someone's up to mischief. I'm going to round him up.

RONNY: Well, don't make a row about it.

BENBOW: Row! When I catch him, I'll make a hell of a row about it.

*Exit, closing door.*

RONNY: I hope he doesn't catch him.

CHERRY: I hope he does. I want to get into bed.

RONNY: Well, you can't get into it here.

CHERRY: I could if you got out. I don't see why you shouldn't.

RONNY: You'd better try and find out why, because I'm not going to.

CHERRY: *(Coming to bed R.)* Oh, be a sport. I'm absolutely freezing.

RONNY: *(Sitting up, alarmed.)* Go away. You're too close.

CHERRY: All right then. I'll jolly well make you get out.

*Makes as though to get into bed – RONNY gives a cry and prevents her.*

RONNY: Stop that, you forward girl. *(In his hurry, he bashes into table R. The gong falls, making a resounding crash – he jumps out of bed. CHERRY runs down R.)*

*(Picking up the gong.)* Now see what you've done.

CHERRY: I didn't do it.

RONNY: That was the signal. We've roused the whole house. *(Replacing the gong on stand.)*

CHERRY: It's all right. Lock the door.

RONNY: Yes. *(At door.)* There's no key.

CHERRY: On the outside.

RONNY: Oh! Yes. *(Opens door, listens.)* No, too late. *(Shuts door hastily.)* Someone's coming. *(Turning to her.)* Get back on that balcony.

CHERRY: I won't.

RONNY: You must.

KITTY'S VOICE: *(Off.)* Ronny!

*CHERRY runs towards window.*

RONNY: Go on. *(Picking up dressing-gown.)*

CHERRY: Your dressing-gown.

RONNY: *(Handing it.)* Take it. Go on. Quick!

*Enter KITTY.*

KITTY: What is it?

RONNY: Nothing, darling.

*RONNY is helping CHERRY on with dressing-gown, standing behind her, and half-embraces her as KITTY runs on down stage.*

KITTY: *(Seeing CHERRY.)* What?

RONNY: I don't want you.

KITTY: You here?

RONNY: It's all right. She was *just* going.

KITTY: So you've got to bring her even down here?

RONNY: No; she came after me – after I did. I didn't know she was here.

KITTY: Didn't know she was here? When I find you holding her in your arms.

RONNY: Directly she came there, I beat the gong for *you.* *(To CHERRY.)* That's true, isn't it?

CHERRY: Well, *you* knocked it over, I didn't.

RONNY: Don't spoil it.

*LIONEL enters quickly – he is in pyjamas.*

LIONEL: What are you doing? She's my girl.

RONNY: *(Taking his dressing-gown off CHERRY.)* Oh, well, give me my dressing-gown.

LIONEL: *(Crossing to CHERRY and putting his own dressing-gown on her shoulders.)* I didn't bring her up here for you.

RONNY: Very well then, take her away, and bring her up properly.

CHERRY: Oh, Lionel, I had to come here, I was frightened out of that room.

LIONEL: Never mind, my darling. You shall have mine.

CHERRY: *(To RONNY as they cross R.)* You're a fine gentleman to protect a girl, aren't you?

LIONEL: *(Taking her off R. turns to RONNY and speaks very sternly.)* Don't you touch her again or, my word, I'll touch you! *(To CHERRY.)* Come on, darling.

*Exit LIONEL with CHERRY, shutting door up R.C.*

RONNY: There's a bully for you. *(Shot.)*

KITTY: Did that girl come here with Lionel Frush?

RONNY: Of course she did, Kitty. And don't you keep accusing me of things. You stop it. Or you'll never find yourself alone with me in a bedroom again.

KITTY: I don't care. I don't want to. *(Going to door.)*

RONNY: The girl came through that window – *(Indicating window D.L.)* – and I –

*Turns to find KITTY going out.*

*(Following her.)* Kitty, but you must listen.

*During the following lines, WHITTLE enters from balcony. Tries to get through room, finds way barred by KITTY and RONNY in doorway, and sneaks under bed from L. side. He is limping badly and obviously in pain.*

KITTY: *(Off stage R.)* She was here with you. That's enough.

RONNY: *(At door looking off R.)* It isn't enough. You heard the reason.

*WHITTLE enters.*

KITTY: But who could have frightened her?

RONNY: Uncle's gone to find out. Come back here. I'm not going to talk to you in the draught.

*WHITTLE is now under the bed. KITTY and RONNY come down C.*

KITTY: Well, Ronny, any girl would have suspected who saw what I saw.

RONNY: Why – what did you see?

*BENBOW enters from balcony L., leaves window open.*

*Wind is heard and curtains blow.*

BENBOW: Where's he gone? I believe I winged him. I know I've winged him. I'll get him.

*Exit up R., shutting door.*

*RONNY closes window L. Wind drops.*

RONNY: *(On his dignity.)* There you are, you saw what happened – now what have you got to say? – I'll give you a hearing.

KITTY: Well, I see now. I was wrong, Ronny.

RONNY: I should think you *were* wrong. Making all this fuss over one single girl in my bedroom. Remember I'm spending the night in this awful room – I'm liable to see quite strange things without you coming in. *(Pause.)*

KITTY: Oh, but listen Ronny!

RONNY: No – *you* do the listening. I'm the master here. I can't help my room having a girl in it, can I? And more than that bed can help having an uncle in it.

KITTY: Yes, I know I was wrong to be angry.

RONNY: You were very wrong – *(Cross R.)* – a girl in my bedroom – that's nothing. *(Puts his hand toward fire.)* Besides, she was quite decently clad.

KITTY: I'm very sorry.

RONNY: So was I – so am I. I should hate to have a suspicious little wife for a wife.

KITTY: *(Crossing to RONNY.)* Oh, but you're not.

RONNY: Oh, I am. At least we'll see. I've a jolly good mind not to have a wife at all.

KITTY: Ronny!

RONNY: Don't think I can't do without one. I've done without one before now – up to now.

KITTY: Oh, Ronny – you will marry me, won't you?

RONNY: Only if you're not jealous when you see me looking at another girl. That's always the trouble with wives – they accuse their poor innocent husbands even before they've had time to do anything.

KITTY: Oh, please, don't go on at me, Ronny. You make me feel ashamed. *(Almost crying.)*

RONNY: *(Not looking at her.)* I'm telling you now because I might forget in the morning. *(He looks at her and sees that KITTY is crying; he at once relents, he rests her head on his shoulder.)* Now don't cry, I can't stand anyone crying. We Gambles never could. I'm sorry. When we're married and go about together – sometimes – don't inquire too deeply what I'm doing or you may be ashamed again. Remember, I look on girls in a very peculiar way. Come on now, stop crying, dry your eyes. Haven't you got a hanky? Never mind, here's one.

*KITTY is crying – RONNY dries her eyes on his handkerchief and places it at her nose.*

Come on, blow – blow that little bit of putty.

KITTY: Well, I'll try to understand, I promise you.

RONNY: That's right. *(Cross L.)* Just look on me as a very attractive man who can't help himself –

*BENBOW enters through door.*

BENBOW: Missed him – confound it, I missed him. *(Throws gun on bed – to KITTY.)* Hi! And what are you doing here? – wandering about the house in the middle of the night, looking like a stick of Brighton rock. You go back to your bedroom.

KITTY: Ronny, kiss me and forgive me.

RONNY: Yes. But don't let it occur again.

BENBOW: No. It had better not.

*RONNY kisses KITTY.*

And stop that! Quite enough time for that during decent hours.

RONNY: Good-night, darling – *(Kisses her.)* – till decent hours.

KITTY: Good-night, Ronny. *(To BENBOW.)* Good-night, Hecky.

BENBOW: Good-night, you little monkey. *(He kisses her and slaps her playfully as she goes.)*

*Exit KITTY C., closing door.*

*BENBOW crosses L., peeps through window D.L., holding the curtains apart a little. RONNY sees BENBOW taking his dressing-gown off – at once slips his own off and his slippers and gets into the centre of the bed before BENBOW sees him. BENBOW turns towards the bed and sees RONNY, who is looking quite comfortable and unconcerned; he givers a little grunt, takes the gun from the bed and puts it by the table close to the bed.*

BENBOW: *(Pouring out whisky at table R.)* Are you going to have one just to rock you off? You'd better.

RONNY: All right, then. A good stiff one. My nerves are shredded and tattered.

BENBOW: *(After handing RONNY a drink.)* Let me tell you something. *I'm* not going to be disturbed any more to-night if you are.

RONNY: I've got a sort of feeling I shall be.

*Wind is heard and distant thunder.*

That's the confounded storm coming back.

BENBOW: *(Getting into bed.)* That only goes to show yer that all this talk of haunted places is absolute tosh.

*BENBOW again falls face on the bed.*

Everything that's happened in this house to-night has been accounted for. *(Drinks.)*

RONNY: Oh, has it?

*Wind is heard rising and falling till the end of the act.*

BENBOW: Yes, it has.

RONNY: Then who was it frightened Cherry Buck?

BENBOW: Why, that tick of a newspaper man.

RONNY: Good Lord! Did *he* stay here?

BENBOW: Not quite long enough. But I think I dusted his trousers for him, all the same.

RONNY: Oh, I thought Cherry Buck had seen the ghost.

*Thunder louder and wind.*

BENBOW: Seen the ghost? Nobody's ever seen a ghost – or smelled a ghost – of heard a ghost.

*Wind rising and falling.*

*WHITTLE starts to come out from under the foot of the bed; his head and shoulders appear, but the pain of his leg makes him groan and he gets back.*

What was that? Was that you?

*Warning light on.*

RONNY: Somebody moaned.

BENBOW: Oh, nonsense, only the wind.

RONNY: Well – I don't know the cause of their suffering. But somebody moaned.

BENBOW: Go on. Drink that up – *(Lies down.)* – put the light out.

*Light out.*

I want to get my beauty sleep.

RONNY: You certainly do.

*During the next few lines WHITTLE is seen dimly to come from under the bed and exit through window L.*

BENBOW: Now then, keep your elbow down.

RONNY: You lift yours even in your sleep.

BENBOW: Ah, well, good-night to yer.

RONNY: And a filthy night to yer.

*By this time WHITTLE is at the window; as he pulls the curtain aside the lightning flashes through, lighting up his face – he disappears through the window, leaving them open; the wind is howling furiously, blowing the curtains across the room – an enormous clap of thunder is heard, blankets and quilt are blown nearly off the bed.*

*RONNY puts the light up and BENBOW gets his gun and is pointing it towards the window – at that moment the force of the storm blows the brass candlesticks from the mantelpiece R., also the huge picture falls from above the fireplace – which makes BENBOW turn quickly and point the gun that way. RONNY jumps out of bed and starts to beat the gong as the*

*CURTAIN FALLS. (FIRST CURTAIN.)*

*TABLEAUX CURTAIN.*

*MRS. FRUSH, LADY BENBOW, and KITTY rush into the room followed by JONES and HOOK, who stands at the door – a huge branch of tree has fallen through the window – they are all scared. RONNY is still hitting the gong while BENBOW is on the bed pointing the gun round the room from the window to the door.*

*CURTAIN*

PLUNDER

*Plunder* was first produced on 26 June 1928 at the Aldwych Theatre, London, with the following cast:

| | |
|---|---|
| OSWALD VEAL | J. Robertson Hare |
| PRUDENCE MALONE | Ena Mason |
| MRS HEWLETT | Mary Brough |
| SIMON VEAL | Gordon James |
| FREDDY MALONE | Tom Walls |
| MABEL | Ann Furrell |
| JOAN HEWLETT | Winifred Shotter |
| SIR GEORGE CHUDLEIGH | Ralph Lynn |
| LADY CHUDLEIGH | Nancy Nielson |
| HARRY KENWARD | John Charlton |
| RUTH BENNETT | Enid Maby |
| WILLIAM | Robert Adam |
| BUCKLEY | Fred Morgan |
| MRS ORLOCK | Ethel Coleridge |
| CHIEF CONSTABLE GRIERSON | Philip Carlton |
| CHIEF DETECTIVE INSPECTOR SIBLEY | Herbert Waring |
| POLICE CONSTABLE DAVIS | Alfred Watson |
| DETECTIVE SERGEANT MARCHANT | Arthur Williams |
| DETECTIVE SERGEANT BRYANT | Fred Cavell |

The cast of the revival in January 1976 at the National Theatre was:

| | |
|---|---|
| OSWALD VEAL | Trevor Ray |
| PRUDENCE MALONE | Diana Quick |
| MRS HEWLETT | Dandy Nichols |

| | |
|---|---|
| SIMON VEAL | Paul Dawkins |
| FREDDY MALONE | Frank Finlay |
| MABEL | Catherine Harding |
| JOAN HEWLETT | Polly Adams |
| D'ARCY TUCK | Dinsdale Landen |
| SIR GEORGE CHUDLEIGH | Michael Beint |
| LADY CHUDLEIGH | Brenda Kaye |
| HARRY KENWARD | Michael Keating |
| RUTH BENNETT | Carol Frazer |
| WILLIAM | Desmond Adams |
| BUCKLEY | Michael Stroud |
| MRS ORLOCK | Barbara Keogh |
| CHIEF CONSTABLE GRIERSON | Daniel Thorndike |
| CHIEF DETECTIVE INSPECTOR SIBLEY | Derek Newark |
| POLICE CONSTABLE DAVIS | Patrick Monckton |
| DETECTIVE SERGEANT MARCHANT | Glyn Grain |
| DETECTIVE SERGEANT BRYANT | Andrew Hilton |
| PLAIN CLOTHES DETECTIVE | Peter Rocca |
| COOK | Rose Power |
| MAIDS | Jeananne Crowley |
| | Brenda Crowley |
| | Brenda Blethyn |
| | Nora Connolly |
| | Rynagh O'Grady |
| | |
| DIRECTOR | Michael Blakemore |

## SCENES:

### ACT I
The library at Marvin Court, near Horsham

### ACT II
Scene I Hall of Freddy Malone's House, The Gables, Walton
Heath

Scene 2 A room at The Gables

Scene 3 Same as Scene 1

### ACT III
Scene 1 Chief Constable Grierson's Office at Scotland Yard

Scene 2 Hall at The Gables

# Act One

*Marvin Court, near Horsham, The Library.*

*A February afternoon.*

*A well-furnished library. Door from the hall L. of back wall. Another door leading off L. French windows up R. These are practical French windows used as an entrance to the garden. L.C. a fireplace with a fire burning and a club fender. Some pictures, but not modern ones. Bookshelves with some uniform editions and a bust or two. A writing-table near entrance with a swing chair. An armchair close at hand to the R. of writing-table L. C. The furniture is all good stuff and in good order, but belongs to a former generation.*

*PRUDENCE is sitting on the club fender. She is holding her hands to the fire, but her attention is really given to OSWALD, who is standing indecisively over by the windows. PRUDENCE is well dressed in excellent taste, in a country outdoor costume and hat. OSWALD is thirty-five or so. He wears a rather emphatic country outfit. He suggests what he is – a modest clerk promoted in the social scale and having rather a struggle to maintain the dignity of the position. He is essentially an underling. He glances round, then away, his lips moving nervously.*

*PRUDENCE takes a glance at him, then away and smiles. Then with an effort he rounds on her; advances centre and grips a chair.*

OSWALD: *(Pacing up and down, crosses to PRUDENCE.)* I love you.

    *PRUDENCE gives a quick nervous laugh.*

    Oh, I say; don't laugh at me.

PRUDENCE: I'm not. It's only nervousness.

OSWALD: You must have known I was going to say something.

PRUDENCE: Oh, but don't think I encouraged you, Mr Veal.

OSWALD: Please, please don't call me Mr Veal.

PRUDENCE: Well – Ozzy.

OSWALD: Oh, please, not Ozzy either. That's mother's dreadful name for me.

PRUDENCE: All right – Oswald then.

OSWALD: I don't mind your calling me Wal. May I call you Pru?

PRUDENCE: You seem frightfully fussy about we're going to call each other. I mean – there's something to be done before that.

OSWALD: *(Offering to embrace her.)* You mean – this!

PRUDENCE: No, no. *(He pauses, taken aback.)* Oh, I hope I haven't been too responsive. I do like you and all that.

OSWALD: You mean – you won't marry me?

PRUDENCE: I don't know. That's what I mean, I don't know.

OSWALD: I suppose the fact is, when you first met me and Mother out at Monte Carlo, you thought we were better class people than what we really are.

PRUDENCE: Oh, rot! Of course I didn't.

OSWALD: I made no secret of it, did I? I mean about Mother being old Mr Hewlett's 'ousekeeper before he married 'er.

PRUDENCE: If I were in love with a man it wouldn't matter to me what his mother was. You must let me think it over.

OSWALD: Oh – how long for?

PRUDENCE: I don't know. But I'll begin right away.

*She smiles at him and playfully tugs the lapels of his coat and exits.*

*MRS HEWLETT puts her head in through the other doorway up L. C.*

MRS HEWLETT: *(Coming down C. to OSWALD.)* Well?

OSWALD: She wants to think it over.

MRS HEWLETT: Oh – you and your love-making. I don't know where you get your passions.

OSWALD: Well, Mother, it's all been too hurried, I think.

MRS HEWLETT: We can't have you spooning all over the house now. There'll be trouble enough for us without that. You know Joan Hewlett's arriving here today from New Zealand.

OSWALD: That's why I wanted to bring Pru to a head.

MRS HEWLETT: Why?

OSWALD: Because when Miss Hewlett arrives there's bound to be a row.

MRS HEWLETT: Yes. She must have heard somehow that her grandfather had died. But she doesn't know that he married me before doing so.

OSWALD: How do you know she doesn't know?

MRS HEWLETT: Because if she'd known she'd have addressed her telegram *(Moving away.)* to me as Mrs Hewlett and not as Mrs Veal.

OSWALD: Well, don't get rattled, Mother. *(Following her.)*

MRS HEWLETT: *(Turning on him.)* Who's rattled? I'm ready for her.

OSWALD: But she'll come here thinking all the place belongs to her.

MRS HEWLETT: Then she'll very soon go away knowing it doesn't.

OSWALD: Look out! Here's Uncle Simon.

*SIMON VEAL appears at French windows and enters.*

SIMON: What time's this girl coming?

MRS HEWLETT: She didn't mention. She just said, 'Arriving this afternoon with a friend.'

SIMON: 'Oos the friend? *(Throws his hat on settee.)*

MRS HEWLETT: Oh, goodness knows who she is.

SIMON: *(To OSWALD.)* Well, your Prudence Malone and her brother stand to hear a pretty story when she *does* arrive.

OSWALD: They know Mother was Mrs Hewlett's house-keeper before he married her.

SIMON: Before she married him. *(Look from MRS HEWLETT.)*, you mean. What about all the girl's letters you kept from the old man? And his to her that you never posted? She'll have something to say about *that*.

MRS HEWLETT: I shall answer her quite straightforward. I shall tell her he got them all and made no reply.

SIMON: *(Crosses to MRS HEWLETT.)* And this is what she'll say. He was old and sick and silly, and you got 'old of him and married him – and *that's* the truth.

MRS HEWLETT: You're a nice one to turn saint. Here was the chance waiting to be picked up. So I picked it.

SIMON: Oh, I'm not blaming you Margery.

MRS HEWLETT: I should hope not. You haven't done yourself a bad turn out of it.

SIMON: Maybe. But if Miss Malone and her brother hear the story a fine chance Ozzy will stand.

OSWALD: Why are you so against me marrying Pru?

SIMON: You can marry 'oo you like when I've got my share of this property.

OSWALD: It's Mother's money to do with as she likes.

SIMON: Oh no it's not. It's hers to do with as *I* like. I may want more than I'm getting now. *(He crosses towards door R.)*

*MRS HEWLETT and OSWALD exchange a helpless glance. After a pause SIMON turns to OSWALD.*

And I'll have none of your smart young women and their clever brothers wanting to know why I get it. *(Moves toward windows.)*

MRS HEWLETT: Don't aggravate him, Ozzy.

SIMON: *(Turning.)* You do my bidding. You know what I could tell if I choose. *(Takes another step towards windows.)*

MRS HEWLETT: Hush, Simon. That's never to be spoken of.

SIMON: *(Turning to have a last word.)* Well, if it's not to be spoken of it's got to be paid for. Don't you forget it.

*He goes out.*

OSWALD: This makes it very awkward now I've asked Pru. She may come back and say yes.

MRS HEWLETT: Don't let him frighten you. If he started telling secrets they'd recoil on him as much as on us.

OSWALD: I don't know. He can always threaten.

MRS HEWLETT: That's all he can do.

OSWALD: Well, look here, Mother. Get the Malones and tell them Miss Hewlett is coming. It may save unpleasantness.

MRS HEWLETT: All right. All right. I know what's best to be done. Go and get the Malones.

OSWALD: *(Going up L. open door.)* All right, I think it's safer, and we ought to play for safety. On, here's Pru, now, coming downstairs. *(Speaking off.)* I say, come in here to Mother, will you? *(Stands up C.)*

*PRUDENCE enters.*

PRUDENCE: Has Oswald been telling you things?

MRS HEWLETT: Yes, dear. And I've no doubt you mean to make him happy. Look at him. Isn't he a dear boy?

PRUDENCE: I wonder.

MRS HEWLETT: I'm sure your brother would be delighted. *(To OSWALD.)* Go and get him.

OSWALD: I don't know where he is.

MRS HEWLETT: *(Pointing through French windows.)* Well, use your eyes. There he is on the lawn. Practising hits with his golf-stick. *(Sits.)*

PRUDENCE: *(Crosses to French windows, calling.)* I'll get him. Freddy!

FREDDY: *(Heard off.)* Hallo?

PRUDENCE: Here! *(Returning, leaving French windows open.)* It doesn't matter what *he* says, you know.

OSWALD: I expect he'll say that you ought to find someone better.

MRS HEWLETT: *(Severely to OSWALD.)* Don't keep picking holes in yourself.

*FREDDY Malone enters at French windows. He is in the thirties, very calm and polished. He carries a mashie.*

FREDDY: Picking holes in yourself, Ozzy? What's the matter with you?

PRUDENCE: Well, Oswald's – *(To OSWALD.)* You tell him.

OSWALD: No, no – please – you.

MRS HEWLETT: *I'll* tell him. *(To FREDDY.)* He's popped it.

FREDDY: What! He's picking holes in himself and he's popped it?

PRUDENCE: He's asked me to marry him.

FREDDY: *(To OSWALD.)* You've asked *her* – to marry *you*? *(Prods him with golf club.)*

OSWALD: Well, I – I shouldn't ask her to marry anyone else should I?

FREDDY: *(Making a pass at OSWALD with the mashie.)* I would if I were you.

PRUDENCE: But, Freddy, I haven't said yes. And I haven't said no. I don't know *yet* what to say.

FREDDY: Well, it isn't for me to say, is it? *(To OSWALD.)* It's a jolly good job for you it isn't.

*Makes another pass at him with the mashie – OSWALD ducks.*

OSWALD: Yes, I say – don't keep doing that, please. D'you mind?

FREDDY: Well, you must be patient, Ozzy. You know what girls are.

OSWALD: No, I don't. I haven't mixed with them much.

FREDDY: Oh nonsense! You can find out a thing like that without mixing. You must give Pru time to think. *(To MRS HEWLETT.)* You always took a bit of time to think, didn't you?

MRS HEWLETT: Well, in my days it was thought ladylike to get the flutters.

FREDDY: *(To OSWALD.)* Oh, was it, well then you leave Pru to me. I'll try and find out what's really behind the flutters.

OSWALD: All right, thanks.

FREDDY: That's it. Then you trot off.

*He takes OSWALD to door.*

OSWALD: I may have come out with it a bit previous; but my intentions –

FREDDY: *(Following OSWALD.)* Go on, hop it. I know all about that.

*OSWALD goes out.*

MRS HEWLETT: *(To FREDDY.)* Mind you, I'm not surprised. I always had a very big inkling.

FREDDY: Yes, I thought you looked as if you had. Well, I'll talk it over with Pru.

MRS HEWLETT: Ah! But there's something I want to tell you.

FREDDY: Come on then, tell us.

MRS HEWLETT: There's a girl calling here this afternoon.

FREDDY: A girl? Oh, but your news is good.

MRS HEWLETT: Well, two of them. She's bringing a friend. I don't know who the friend is, but the girl's Joan Hewlett.

FREDDY: Joan Hewlett? Who's she?

MRS HEWLETT: You won't have heard of her. She's my late husband's grand-daughter.

FREDDY: Oh? So Mr Hewlett had a grand-daughter, had he?

MRS HEWLETT: Yes, but she's no claim to any of this. He left it all to me.

FREDDY: But does she pretend she has any claim?

MRS HEWLETT: She can't. And serve her right. *(With feeling.)* She left her grandfather. His only relative she was. And she deserted him and went abroad.

PRUDENCE: How very short-sighted of her.

MRS HEWLETT: It was wicked of her. If I hadn't been here to look after the poor gentleman, I don't know what he'd have done.

FREDDY: No, indeed. Even as it was he died.

MRS HEWLETT: Yes, but me being here with him he died 'appy.

FREDDY: I suppose he was tickled to death.

PRUDENCE: But why's this girl coming back?

MRS HEWLETT: Oh, to try and make a scene about it, I suppose. But if she tries to argue the matter with me, she'll get a rude shock.

FREDDY: I should think there might be a bit of rudeness all round.

MRS HEWLETT: If it comes to a rudeness match I'm afraid of no one.

*She goes out.*

*FREDDY closes the door after her.*

*The manner of both entirely change. They become absolutely practical and rather like a business man and his secretary.*

PRUDENCE: Is that all right?

FREDDY: Well, I didn't expect him to propose just yet. Don't you go and accept him. She'd pop it in the papers.

PRUDENCE: No need to accept him. He'll keep.

FREDDY: Then it's easy. But that's the danger. It's too easy. Now's the time we've got to go very, very carefully.

PRUDENCE: It's all right so far. None of your friends know we're staying here.

FREDDY: My God, they mustn't!

PRUDENCE: If Arthur Mills knew he'd be rabid.

FREDDY: Never mind about his being rabid. He'd be inquisitive – that's the point.

PRUDENCE: Yes. Of course no sane girl would turn down Arthur and dally with Ozzy.

FREDDY: Exactly. So what are we up to? That's what they'd ask. And the answer is something odd. Well, my strong suit is never to be up to anything odd.

PRUDENCE: I know that. But you're going to invite these people to your house.

FREDDY: I shall be jolly careful who they meet – don't you worry. This is the whole point. We *must* associate with them for a few weeks longer. And nobody that matters must find out.

PRUDENCE: If anyone did find out – you'd have to drop it.

FREDDY: By gad. I'd take a big risk before I dropped this. It's much too good to drop.

PRUDENCE: Well, can't you get through with it quickly?

FREDDY: I'm going to. *(Crosses the stage, rings.)* I'll spring this invitation to Walton right away. You must keep Ozzy well in the strings.

PRUDENCE: Oh, I've got him like that. *(Under the thumb.)* He's sloppy with it.

*MABEL, the maid, opens door.*

FREDDY: *(Raising his voice.)* Yes, but it's double the horse-power of your two-seater.

*MABEL enters as he speaks.*

MABEL: Did you ring, sir?

FREDDY: Oh, Mabel, I want to speak to Mrs Hewlett, and young Mr Veal. Here, please.

MABEL: Yes, sir.

*She goes out.*

FREDDY: I think you'd better be taking it a little to heart, you know.

PRUDENCE: Shall I cry? I can easily cry if you like.

FREDDY: No. I think just a little nose business with the handkerchief.

PRUDENCE: I know. *(Prepares to be a bit upset.)*

FREDDY: That's it. There's not much I can teach you in that line.

PRUDENCE: *(Smiling with reserve, like a secretary being praised.)* Thank you.

MRS HEWLETT: *(Heard off L.)* Well then, you shouldn't have.

FREDDY: *(Raising his voice again.)* Now, don't go and upset yourself. They'll understand.

*MRS HEWLETT and OSWALD enter.*

*(To OSWALD.)* You'll understand, won't you? You'd understand anything?

OSWALD: Yes, but what?

FREDDY: Pru's a bit distressed and uncertain.

OSWALD: Well, I hope – I may hope?

FREDDY: That's right. That's a good idea. You hope. *(To MRS HEWLETT.)* Now look here. We're leaving here tomorrow. But suppose you two come to us in a few day's time?

MRS HEWLETT: To stay with you?

FREDDY: Yes. At Walton. Pru will know her mind better by that time.

PRUDENCE: Freddy, don't forget that we've asked the Chudleighs and Lady Kilkenny on the tenth.

FREDDY: I know, why not? There's plenty of room.

MRS HEWLETT: Lady Kilkenny! I should like to meet *her.*

FREDDY: Yes. Smart woman. Oh, and she'll meet a smart woman too, if you're looking your best.

MRS HEWLETT: *(Delighted.)* Oh, come off it. I can hold my own all right.

FREDDY: I'll bet you can. You'll be a regular little handful.

PRUDENCE: Well, Freddy – if they come on the tenth –

FREDDY: The tenth? Right! *(Crosses to OSWALD.)* That's a fixture. *(To OSWALD.)* Cheer up. You're as good as home.

*MABEL enters.*

MRS HEWLETT: *(To MABEL.)* What's the matter with *you*?

MABEL: Miss Hewlett, 'm. She's just driven up in a car.

FREDDY: *(Picking up the mashie.)* Oh, perhaps we'd better leave you. Come on, Pru. *(Handing OSWALD the mashie.)* Here, do something with that.

*FREDDY goes off with PRUDENCE.*

MRS HEWLETT: Very well. Show her in here.

*As MABEL turns.*

But Mabel! Mind what I told you. Don't you answer any questions.

MABEL: No'm. *(Going.)* It isn't a lady with her, it's a gentleman.

*Goes off.*

OSWALD: *(Crosses to MRS HEWLETT.)* A gentleman! Then p'raps she's heard of the marriage. It may be her solicitor.

MRS HEWLETT: *(Showing signs of excitement.)* Well, who cares? I'm going up to get myself together. And my proofs and that.

OSWALD: She'd better not see me. She'd want to know who I was.

MRS HEWLETT: No, and don't let her see Simon either. If he comes in here, you must come and get him out again.

OSWALD: All right, I will.

MRS HEWLETT: I must get up to my bedroom. Me marriage lines are in my ottoman.

*Bustles off.*

*OSWALD looks across R., hears JOAN, then quickly puts down the mashie and – follows her off.*

*JOAN's voice is heard off.*

JOAN: Oh, I've left my bag in the car.

*MABEL, looking rather uncomfortable, shows in JOAN Hewlett. JOAN, who wears a becoming motor-coat and hat, is elated at seeing Marvin Court again, regarding it as her own property.*

Oh, it all looks just the same.

MABEL: Yes, Miss Joan.

JOAN: But where's Mrs. Veal?

MABEL: I don't know, Miss Joan.

JOAN: I thought she was here. You'd better find her.

MABEL: Yes, Miss Joan. She said, if you'd wait here –

JOAN: *(Not unkindly.)* Well, good gracious me, I shall wait where I like. I want to show Mr Tuck all over the house. He's the gentleman I'm engaged to, Mabel.

MABEL: Really! Oh – I hadn't heard, Miss.

JOAN: No, I only met him on the boat coming home; well, go and find Mrs Veal.

MABEL: *(After a second's hesitation.)* Yes, Miss Joan.

*MABEL hesitates as though to speak and goes out. JOAN is going up to door when her eyes fall on the mashie. She picks it up and frowns puzzled. Then she puts it down and opens door and calls.*

JOAN: *(Calling through door.)* D'Arcy! Come in here. This is the library.

*D'ARCY Tuck comes in, parks her bag. He is in every-day London clothes, with a motor-coat and carrying a cap. He is looking around eagerly at the house.*

D'ARCY: So it is.

JOAN: Well, are you pleased with the place?

D'ARCY: Can this be possible? It all belongs to you.

JOAN: Of course. And it's going to belong to you, too.

D'ARCY: I love to hear you say that. But Joan, remember, I loved you before I ever knew you had this house and property and money. I suppose there's some money, isn't there?

JOAN: Oh, yes. I don't know how much yet, but there's bound to be heaps.

D'ARCY: Yes, there's got to be. I mean with a place this size it stands to reason. But I love you quite apart from this.

JOAN: This is nothing. This is only the library.

D'ARCY: I don't care. I should love you just as much in any other of the rooms – drawing-room, dining-room, bath-room – I'm the same all over the house.

JOAN: Well, the place is all mine now for my very own. For ours, darling – together

D'ARCY: For ours, darling, together. Isn't that wonderful! All this lovely house, this delightful library, these nice books – look at this one. *(Pulls out a book and reads title.)* 'Thoughts before sleeping' – can it really be true?

JOAN: Of course. My dear old grandfather always said it was for me. And now he's gone.

D'ARCY: RIP. One of the best.

JOAN: As soon as we get back to town, we'll find his lawyers and see exactly all about the money and stuff.

D'ARCY: Yes. We'll take it out of their hands.

JOAN: Only I had to bring you here directly we landed to show you the house.

D'ARCY: Yes. Let's go on seeing it.

JOAN: Wait a minute. I want to see Mrs Veal. I'm going to give her notice.

D'ARCY: Why?

JOAN: I'm very annoyed with her. It was only quite by chance that I heard about my grandfather dying. She might have let me know.

D'ARCY: Yes.

JOAN: Besides we shan't want a housekeeper now.

D'ARCY: No, we'll do our own housekeeping now. I'll keep you when we're married, and you'll keep me – well – figuratively speaking. Never mind about Mrs Veal. Let's talk of jollier things – love and furniture.

JOAN: Oh, darling! Be quick and marry me.

D'ARCY: Darling, I'm quick already – and I will.

*D'ARCY kisses her.*

*As they embrace SIMON looks in through the French windows. He stands looking in. JOAN suddenly moves away, neither of them see SIMON.*

JOAN: *(In a changed tone.)* But you know, D'Arcy, all the same – *(Looking over her shoulder.)* there's –

D'ARCY: What's the matter, darling?

JOAN: I don't know. There's something rather queer –

D'ARCY: What d'you mean?

JOAN: Well, that maid – Mabel. I know her well enough. But she seemed sort of scared of me.

D'ARCY: P'raps she's expecting the sack too.

JOAN: And Mrs Veal – *(Looking round the room.)* why isn't she here? Why all this sort of silence and mystery.

D'ARCY: Oh, my darling, if there's anything mysterious about we'll soon find it out.

*SIMON opens the windows and enters, causing them both to start violently. JOAN catches hold of D'ARCY. SIMON gives them a grim bow and comes down.*

JOAN: Who is it?

D'ARCY: Don't you know?

JOAN: No. Ask him.

D'ARCY: *(To SIMON.)* Who is it?

SIMON: Ah, then you don't know yet. You'll find out before long.

JOAN: What are you doing here, please? D'Arcy, make him say.

D'ARCY: It's all right, darling. I think someone's let the house to Dracula.

JOAN: I'm Miss Hewlett, the owner of this house.

SIMON: Oh, are you?

D'ARCY: *(To JOAN.)* I'll do it. *(More boldly, to SIMON.)* Why do you walk in here like this and – and why?

SIMON: I just came in because I laid a pipe down here somewhere.

D'ARCY: *(Crossing to JOAN.)* It's all right. It's only the gasfitter.

*OSWALD makes a nervous appearance at the window, trying to attract SIMON.*

OSWALD: *(Clipping his fingers at SIMON.)* Wh't! Wh't!

*He sees JOAN looking at him and attempts to go.*

JOAN: Look! Somebody else.

D'ARCY: *(Going up to OSWALD.)* Here! Come in here, will you? Now – whoever you are – who are you?

OSWALD: I'm very, very sorry. I want to see my uncle.

D'ARCY: I don't care if you want to see your aunt. This is Miss Hewlett's house; and this is Miss Hewlett. How dare you come and want to see your uncle in the library?

OSWALD: *(To SIMON.)* I say. Do come out. *(Standing close to SIMON.)*

SIMON: Why isn't she here?

OSWALD: She went upstairs.

JOAN: Who did?

D'ARCY: *(To OSWALD.)* Listen, will you? Miss Hewlett arrives here and finds the place full of odd-looking people.

OSWALD: Yes, but please don't be put out.

D'ARCY: I'm very put out. You may not think you're odd-looking, but you are.

OSWALD: You ought to have seen my mother.

D'ARCY: Never mind who's to blame.

JOAN: Oh, I think I see. Your mother is Mrs Veal?

SIMON: Ha! She's not.

OSWALD: Yes, yes, yes. She is. At least – yes.

D'ARCY: Well, good Lord! Aren't you sure about it?

JOAN: If you're Mrs Veal's relations, why not say so?

OSWALD: *(To SIMON.)* Oh, go and tell her to come down.

SIMON: I'll tell her. *(Crosses in front of JOAN and D'ARCY, turn at door to OSWALD.)* Don't you get talking.

OSWALD: No, no. I'll come with you. *(Is about to cross in front of JOAN and D'ARCY but on second thoughts goes behind them.)* I'm really sorry.

*Exit.*

JOAN: Did you ever know such nerve? Fancy keeping those people here. That settles it. She goes at once.

D'ARCY: She's afraid to see you. Don't worry, darling, I'll fix all this. *(He goes to door and opens it, then stands back in amazement.)* Good Lord!

JOAN: What is it?

FREDDY: D'Arcy Tuck!

*Enters.*

But you're in Australia.

D'ARCY: Am I? I've just got back today. This is Miss Hewlett. We met on the boat. *(To JOAN.)* A friend of mine, darling – Freddy Malone. We were at school together.

FREDDY: *(With approval, to JOAN. Shaking hands.)* How d'you do?

D'ARCY: *(Parting them.)* Yes, very. But what on earth are you doing here?

FREDDY: Oh, I'm just staying here.

JOAN: But who with?

FREDDY: With my sister.

JOAN: Your sister doesn't live here?

FREDDY: No. I mean we're visiting.

D'ARCY: *You*? Visiting these people?

FREDDY: Yes. Why not?

D'ARCY: You don't mean to tell me that you're staying with this thing? *(Indicates where OSWALD stood.)*

FREDDY: What thing?

D'ARCY: Well, it's gone now, but it *was* here. *(Indicates OSWALD's exit.)* The thing that went round behind. An awful sort of thing, like an egg.

FREDDY: Certainly. We ran across him and his mother the other day out at Monte Carlo.

JOAN: At Monte Carlo, Mrs Veal?

FREDDY: The old lady, Mrs Hewlett.

JOAN: What do you mean?

D'ARCY: Don't be an ass, old boy, Mrs Veal.

FREDDY: *(Puzzled.)* No, Mrs Hewlett.

*At this moment MRS HEWLETT enters. She has documents in either hand.*

MRS HEWLETT: Yes, I'm here.

242

JOAN: *(To her, with indignation.)* Now look here, Mrs Veal –

MRS HEWLETT: *(Holds up paper in left hand.)* My marriage certificate. *(Holds up document in right hand.)* Your grandfather's will.

*A pause.*

*JOAN and D'ARCY stare at her.*

JOAN: *(Crosses to MRS HEWLETT.)* Are you trying to play some joke on me?

MRS HEWLETT: *(Handing her the paper.)* That'll show you. *(Indicating D'ARCY.)* Who's this?

D'ARCY: *(Going right up to her, with hostility.)* My name, I may tell you, is D'Arcy Tuck.

MRS HEWLETT: Well, keep it to yourself.

D'ARCY: I'm not going to. I'm going to give it to *her*. So I'm in this and you look out. There's been some dirty work here. *(To JOAN inquiringly.)* Hasn't there?

JOAN: *(Handing back paper.)* My grandfather married you?

MRS HEWLETT: *(Loftily – taking it.)* He did.

JOAN: He must have been mad.

D'ARCY: He must have been blind.

FREDDY: Look here; I don't want to butt in on this. I'll see you later.

D'ARCY: No. You'd better stay and hear the kind of woman you're paying visits to.

MRS HEWLETT: *He* knows I'm all right, anyhow. Don't you?

FREDDY: I know the marriage was all quite in order. I've also heard about the will.

MRS HEWLETT: *(To JOAN.)* Yes, you can see the will, too.

JOAN: I don't want to see it.

D'ARCY: Nor do I. *(To FREDDY.)* What does it say?

FREDDY: Don't ask *me*. She'll tell you.

MRS HEWLETT: Yes, I will tell you. It leaves me everything absolutely.

JOAN: *(Quickly.)* Give it to me. *(Takes the will and looks at it.)*
   *D'ARCY glances at it over her shoulder.*

D'ARCY: *(To FREDDY.)* Everything to her?

MRS HEWLETT: Absolutely. For life and after.

D'ARCY: *(Looking up from will – to FREDDY.)* The house – the
   – the money?-

FREDDY: Everything he'd got, I understand.

JOAN: It's all some intrigue. He was out of his mind.

MRS HEWLETT: The will was witnessed by his doctor.

JOAN: So this was your plot. Directly you got me abroad.

MRS HEWLETT: *(Boldly.)* You left him. Did he want you to go?
   You went gadding off to your friends. He never forgave
   you for that.

JOAN: Oh, that was your version? *(Crosses to her.)* That's how
   you worked it?

D'ARCY: I shall take action.

MRS HEWLETT: *(Fiercely.)* Then get out of my house and take
   it.

FREDDY: Now, now. *(To D'ARCY.)* It's no good trying to kick up
   the dust. You've got no dust to kick.

D'ARCY: Mind your own business.

FREDDY: I'm afraid you've got to face the facts.

JOAN: He's quite right, D'Arcy. Yes, I see it now. I never knew
   you were so wicked. Or so clever.

MRS HEWLETT: Don't you speak like that. He was grateful for
   all I did for him.

D'ARCY: You did for him, yes. When did he die? Next
   morning?

FREDDY: Steady, D'Arcy. I hear he was happy to die.

D'ARCY: What are *you* doing here, anyway?

FREDDY: Oh, very well. Perhaps I'd better retire.

MRS HEWLETT: *(To FREDDY, as he goes.)* I'm sure I can trust *you*
   not to harbour any improper thoughts about me.

FREDDY: That, at least, is a certainty.

*He goes into the garden.*

JOAN: *(To MRS HEWLETT.)* Well, I'm not going to wrangle with
you –

MRS HEWLETT: You'd better not try.

*D'ARCY watches FREDDY off.*

JOAN: I know now why I never heard from him. I can guess all
you did. *(Crosses to MRS HEWLETT.)* You're a vile and sordid
old woman.

D'ARCY: *(Crosses to MRS HEWLETT.)* And now me –

MRS HEWLETT: I want nothing from you.

D'ARCY: But you're going to get it – nothing.

MRS HEWLETT: *(To JOAN.)* And as for you, miss, it's always the
cornered cat that spits.

D'ARCY: *(Crosses to MRS HEWLETT.)* Stop that! How dare you
tell my fiancée dirty proverbs?

JOAN: There are some things of mine here, anyhow. In my
own room.

MRS HEWLETT: Your former room, you mean. Oh, you can go
and get them if you wish. *(Turns away, ignoring them.)*

JOAN: *(To D'ARCY.)* Come with me.

D'ARCY: Oh, but we can't take this like this.

JOAN: We must if we've got to. I've finished with her.

D'ARCY: Well, I haven't.

JOAN: It's terrible, but there it is. It's all proved. I've nothing
for you at all.

D'ARCY: Darling, I told before all this happened. The money
means nothing at all to me. It's just you.

JOAN: That's wonderful of you.

D'ARCY: Yes, dear. All the same, this ought to be looked into.

JOAN: Well, I'll leave it all to you.

*Exit.*

D'ARCY: *(After seeing JOAN off returns – assuming a very business-like manner to MRS HEWLETT.)* Now I'm going thoroughly into this. Take a seat.

MRS HEWLETT: Thank you. I take my own seat when I choose.

D'ARCY: Yes, and where you choose. But I want to raise some questions.

MRS HEWLETT: You're quite ad lib.

D'ARCY: Firstly, how did you get the old man to marry you?

MRS HEWLETT: What d'you mean – 'the old man'? Do you refer to my late husband?

D'ARCY: Well, if he was your husband, he was your old man, wasn't he? How did you get him?

MRS HEWLETT: He turned to me because he was in need of someone to lean on.

D'ARCY: And you leant back on him. And there he was… flattened out.

MRS HEWLETT: I married him to nurse him. To nurse him proper.

D'ARCY: Ridiculous! You don't have to be married to be a nurse. If a nurse nurses me is she improper?

MRS HEWLETT: I shouldn't be surprised.

D'ARCY: Now, it's no good quarrelling. Let me put it in a nice, friendly way. You married this poor imbecile old man and got his money. Never mind how. I want to keep this all quite pleasant. So never mind what lies or dirty work you used.

MRS HEWLETT: Well, his grand-daughter's got you, anyhow. That ought to make up for a lot.

D'ARCY: Yes. And she wanted to show me this house of hers. She'd been looking forward to that for a long, long time. Ever since we met on this voyage – the whole boat.

MRS HEWLETT: I expect it's a bit of a disappointment for *you*.

D'ARCY: Not for *me* at all. I don't care whether it's hers, or yours – not a scrap. Except, of course, I'd much rather it was hers.

MRS HEWLETT: She was always nasty to me. Now she can pay for it.

D'ARCY: Oh rats. That girl couldn't be nasty to a worm.

MRS HEWLETT: She always said nasty things behind my back.

D'ARCY: *(Turning to her.)* That's because there was very little room in the front.

*JOAN re-enters. She is more overcome.*

JOAN: Some of my things are locked up. I want the keys.

MRS HEWLETT: I'll hand them to you. The sooner I've finished with you the better. *(To D'ARCY.)* And with you, I'd finished before I began.

D'ARCY: *(Attempts to follow.)* What!

*She goes out.*

JOAN: Don't argue with her. I wouldn't take a thing from her now even if I could.

*Follows MRS HEWLETT out in anger.*

D'ARCY: I would. I'd take anything. I'd take her clothes when she was bathing. *(Shouting, at door.)* And sell them to a man who makes circus tents! *(Goes to French windows and calls.)* Freddy! Here.

*FREDDY re-enters from garden.*

FREDDY: Oh, you're alone? I say, D'Arcy, congratulations. What a charming little girl!

D'ARCY: Don't you speak to me. Not a syllable. Hardly a word. You knew about it all. Did you? Speak up!

FREDDY: I never heard of that girl till just now.

D'ARCY: What are you doing here, anyway? Staying here with these – vile Veals?

FREDDY: I don't require you to regulate my social activities.

D'ARCY: But a fellow in your position.

FREDDY: I like to mix it a bit on the quiet.

D'ARCY: You go about rubbing shoulders with duchesses. Look whose shoulders you're rubbing now!

FREDDY: These are democratic days. Look at young Pevensey. His mother-in-law was a professional remover of the guts of fish.

D'ARCY: An honest one, anyhow. She didn't remove other people's fishes' guts. Do you believe my little girl's story?

FREDDY: Yes. Oh, yes.

D'ARCY: Well then. That's enough for you. You'll cut the robbers clean out.

*OSWALD enters rather timidly.*

Won't you?

FREDDY: Of course, old boy, of course, there's nothing for you to be concerned about.

OSWALD: Oh, excuse me.

FREDDY: What do you want?

OSWALD: Oh – ah nothing in particular.

FREDDY: I see. Just dropped in to be matey.

D'ARCY: Well, drop out.

OSWALD: Steady, I say, please. This is more my house than what it is yours, so half time with that. *(To FREDDY.)* It's only Mother asked me to look in here and – ah – cast an eye.

D'ARCY: Then look out again or you'll cast a tooth.

FREDDY: Cast any eye? What at?

OSWALD: Mother thought you might be getting some wrong ideas.

D'ARCY: He's got the right one. He's through with you.

OSWALD: What! *(To FREDDY, anxiously.)* That's not true is it?

FREDDY: I'll see you later. Run along now, there's a good fellow.

OSWALD: Oh, but – me and Pru? It's O.K. surely?

D'ARCY: Pru! *(To FREDDY.)* Isn't that your sister?

FREDDY: *(Ignoring D'ARCY, to OSWALD.)* Here, I'll come and see your mother myself.

D'ARCY: Freddy! Your sister and *this*?

OSWALD: *(Boldly, to D'ARCY.)* 'Ere, half time with that, too.

FREDDY: Don't bicker, Ozzy. Come with me.

D'ARCY: I'll come too.

FREDDY: No, thank you. *(Bundling OSWALD to door.)* Go and tell your mother she needn't worry.

OSWALD: Oh, good egg! Then it *is* all right about me and Pru?

FREDDY: Get out!

OSWALD: All right, all right. Sorry, thank you. I beg pardon.

*He goes out.*

D'ARCY: Freddy! What the devil are you up to? You'd never let your sister marry that rat?

FREDDY: D'you know my sister?

D'ARCY: No. And if those are her tastes I don't want to.

FREDDY: I didn't pick him for her. Sisters are very peculiar things.

D'ARCY: Yours must be. Why, good Lord, she's engaged to Arthur Mills.

FREDDY: Is that your concern?

D'ARCY: I saw Arthur Mills this morning, and some others at the club. They said you were in Paris.

FREDDY: They just guessed that. Very likely guess, too.

D'ARCY: Rats! You're ashamed of being here. And no wonder – What's the idea – about your sister and this whelk?

FREDDY: Nothing. It's only a passing fancy in him.

D'ARCY: Well, it's passed. Because you're through with this old woman now. And your sister with her son.

FREDDY: Of course. I've told you so.

D'ARCY: Good! And *I'll* tell the old woman so. That's *something* I can get back at her.

FREDDY: *(As D'ARCY goes towards door.)* Here! *I'll* do that.

D'ARCY: *(Calling through door.)* Woman!

FREDDY: Stop it! I'll tell her myself.

D'ARCY: No, let me, old boy. I want to be unpleasant to her. *(Calls.)* Woman! *(Picking up mashie.)*

FREDDY: I tell you I'll manage my own affairs.

D'ARCY: Oh, don't be a kill-joy.

*MRS HEWLETT enters.*

MRS HEWLETT: Who are you calling 'woman'? I'm not a 'woman'.

D'ARCY: *(With mashie.)* I don't want to inquire into that at all. I want to warn you, that's all. I'm going to get my own back on you. *(Flourishing the mashie.)*

FREDDY: Put that down.

MRS HEWLETT: Pooh! I'm not afraid of him.

FREDDY: *(Takes mashie.)* No, but it's my best mashie.

MRS HEWLETT: *(To D'ARCY.)* And what do you think you can do?

D'ARCY: I don't know and I shan't tell you. But I'll do it. I'll take any means. Fair or foul.

MRS HEWLETT: Ah! Here we have the disappointed fortune hunter.

D'ARCY: What!

FREDDY: She jabbed you in the jaw that time.

D'ARCY: It's a lie. It's worse. It isn't even true. Now I'll make things even nastier for you.

MRS HEWLETT: *(To FREDDY.)* I wonder that any friend of yours can be so ungentlemanly.

D'ARCY: Well, *he's* finished with you now. And his sister – with your nasty son, Nozzle or something.

MRS HEWLETT: Rubbish!

D'ARCY: Is it rubbish? *(To FREDDY.)* Go on. Tell her so yourself.

FREDDY: I tell *you* – I won't have you butting in.

D'ARCY: *(Reacting.)* Oh! So you're going back on it, are you?

FREDDY: I will not be dictated by you, that's all.

MRS HEWLETT: I should hope not. *(To FREDDY.)* Thank you. Now I'm going to see what the young woman's taking away.

D'ARCY: You leave her alone.

MRS HEWLETT: One thing I don't mind her taking away is you.

*She goes off.*

D'ARCY: *(Angrily; to FREDDY.)* Skunk!

FREDDY: Oh, you're not worth getting annoyed over.

D'ARCY: Aren't I? I'll tell the world about this. Talk of young Pevensey and his fish. His name will be Eau-de-Cologne compared with yours.

FREDDY: And have everyone say what she said –

D'ARCY: What?

FREDDY: The disappointed fortune-hunter.

D'ARCY: You know as well as I do that's a lie.

FREDDY: Then why make it out to be true? Only fools advertise their failures.

D'ARCY: Well, Arthur Mills shall hear about this. I'll tell him. I'll tell them all.

FREDDY: *(Very strongly, holding him by the wrist.)* You'll tell nobody. Stop your dammed interference. D'you hear?

D'ARCY: I'm going to know the truth. What are you doing here with this people?

FREDDY: Well, listen. You're out to do that old woman down. Aren't you?

D'ARCY: Well, haven't you been listening? Of course I am.

FREDDY: So am I, you fool.

D'ARCY: *You* are? In what way?

FREDDY: I can see I shall have to take a hell of a risk with you. I'm going to let you into something.

D'ARCY: Let me into something?

FREDDY: Hold on. We'll have this in writing. *(Sits at table and prepares to write.)*

D'ARCY: Why? Who are you going to write to?

FREDDY: I'll put it in your own words. 'We agree to get level with Mrs Hewlett by any means, fair or foul. Freddy Malone.' *(Handing the pen to D'ARCY)* Go on. 'D'Arcy Tuck.' You sign it too.

D'ARCY: Good Lord! But even so, why write it? I don't like writing things. It's a bit of a risk.

FREDDY: It's nothing to the risk I'm taking with you. Go on.

D'ARCY: *(Puzzled, hesitating.)* All right. Still – I don't think I'm very keen on – on this pen. *(Signs.)* There you are. *(About to blot it.)*

FREDDY: *(Quickly.)* Don't blot it.

*FREDDY pockets paper.*

D'ARCY: But why should *you* take it?

FREDDY: To stop your silly tongue.

*Crosses to window, closes it, comes back.*

I've got to take a big chance with you. Either that or lose a very good thing.

D'ARCY: What thing?

FREDDY: What I'm going to tell you will be a bit of a shock. You'll find it difficult to believe. D'you remember at school we had an oath? There was an old stinks master with a beard – Allah we called him.

D'ARCY: Yes. We used to swear by the beard of Allah.

FREDDY: Yes, and it held. You and I have been all over the world since then and broken every commandment in turn. But did you ever break that oath – by the beard of Allah?

D'ARCY: No. No one ever broke that. It was sacred.

FREDDY: Right. You're going to swear it now.

D'ARCY: Swear what?

FREDDY: That what I'm about to tell you you'll never repeat.

D'ARCY: Good Lord! Is it as bad as that?

FREDDY: It's vital. Come on. Asleep or awake – sober or tight – you'll never tell a soul. Swear that.

D'ARCY: I swear by the beard of Allah.

FREDDY: Sit down.

*D'ARCY sits.*

*FREDDY sits on his right.*

Now I'll tell you what I'm here for.

D'ARCY: Well? What are you here for?

FREDDY: Plunder.

D'ARCY: Plunder? What do you mean?

FREDDY: That's what I do. That's how I live. That's my profession.

D'ARCY: Do you mean you're a cr…

*FREDDY gestures with his hand to stop him.*

FREDDY: Only one other man knows it and he's a foreigner n Marseilles. And one woman. My accomplice. Passes as my sister.

D'ARCY: She's *not* your sister. Why do you say she is?

FREDDY: Purely for business purposes.

D'ARCY: But you! Your friends! The people you know!

FREDDY: Yes, rather. All the topnotchers. I'm Freddy to them all, aren't I? Quite a lad. Yachtsman – big game shot, anything you like. Oh yes – I do it on very high-class lines.

D'ARCY: But what is it – that you do?

FREDDY: Steal.

D'ARCY: What?

FREDDY: Steal.

D'ARCY: Steal? But, good Lord, man, why?

FREDDY: I like it.

D'ARCY: You like it?

FREDDY: I love it.

D'ARCY: I don't believe it. *(Feels for his watch-chain – he can't find it for a second and gets a shock.)* What! Wait a minute! *(Finds it.)* No, I don't believe you.

FREDDY: Don't worry. I'm not that sort of thief.

D'ARCY: What do you thieve?

FREDDY: Jewels, for choice, from big houses

D'ARCY: What? A house-lifter!

FREDDY: That's why I'm here. Hers are worth a packet.

D'ARCY: You're going to take them?

FREDDY: I am. All of them. She hasn't got them all here. Some are in the bank.

D'ARCY: You're not going to break into the bank?

FREDDY: No. She's coming to stay at my house. She'll have them all with her then. I've seen to that.

D'ARCY: But if you were caught?

FREDDY: I'm not. I make that one of my strictest rules.

D'ARCY: This is all a lie. Society crooks are only in books.

*FREDDY rings.*

FREDDY: Oh, very well.

D'ARCY: What are you doing?

FREDDY: If there's time, I'll prove it to you.

D'ARCY: How long – do you pretend – you've been like this?

FREDDY: Always. D'you remember that half mile challenge cup that got lifted at school? That was me.

D'ARCY: Good Lord! And I *won* it.

FREDDY: One of my earliest recollections is my father catching me cheating at cards. He caught me taking an ace from my shirt.

D'ARCY: Good Lord! Then he ought to have lifted your shirt and flogged it.

FREDDY: He did. And after the flogging he showed me how to pull out the ace without being caught.

D'ARCY: Appalling! *(Pause.)* How do you pull out the ace?

FREDDY: I'd show you, only I don't happen to have an ace in my shirt at the moment.

*To MABEL, who enters.*

Find Miss Malone and ask her to come here, will you?

MABEL: Yes, sir.

*Goes out.*

D'ARCY: Tell me this. Where did you run across this old woman?

FREDDY: A few days ago at Monte Carlo. She'd come in for this money and she was flashing the jewels all over her stomach.

D'ARCY: *(Bitterly.)* Our money – Joan's and mine – and our jewels.

FREDDY: Yes, old boy, but her stomach. I couldn't take them then. I'd just pulled off another job and the police were on a false scent so I let them stay there.

D'ARCY: Oh, so that's why you're friends with them? That's why your sister's encouraging this – this growth?

FREDDY: That's it. And they're coming to stay with us on the tenth. And so's the jewellery.

*PRUDENCE enters.*

PRUDENCE: You want me, Freddy?

FREDDY: Yes. This is D'Arcy Tuck.

PRUDENCE: Oh, really. How do you do? I've herd a little bit about you. *(Offering her hand.)*

D'ARCY: *(Taking it nervously.)* And I've heard a great chunk about you.

FREDDY: Don't let this worry you. I've just told him about us.

PRUDENCE: You've *told*? Him!

FREDDY: Only just now I was saying to you I'd face a big danger for this. Well, he's the big danger.

D'ARCY: Yes. I can be a bit of a thunder-cloud.

PRUDENCE: *(To FREDDY.)* It's madness. What on earth's come over you?

FREDDY: He'll be all right. Treat him as a friend.

PRUDENCE: *(To D'ARCY.)* Well, what do you think of it?

D'ARCY: I don't know. I've never met a crook girl before.

PRUDENCE: I'll bet you have. *(To FREDDY.)* Why have you done this? He doesn't look dangerous.

FREDDY: I had to, that's all. You can trust me, can't you?

PRUDENCE: Of course. You know that.

FREDDY: Then you can trust him, too. *(To PRUDENCE.)* Run along now. I'll tell you all about it later on.

PRUDENCE: *(To FREDDY, before she goes.)* You've got him – ? *(She clenches her fist.)* You're sure?

FREDDY: Leave it to me.

*She exits.*

*(To D'ARCY)* There you are.

D'ARCY: Yes, but look here – Freddy – or should I say, Malone?

FREDDY: What?

D'ARCY: Look here! You've planned to pinch this stuff and I've just realised it's my little girl's. It's hers by rights.

FREDDY: I'm not going to take it by rights.

D'ARCY: *(Excitedly.)* You can't take that jewellery. Listen, you thief, you can't as a decent man!

FREDDY: What do you suggest I do? Pinch the stuff and make her a present of it?

D'ARCY: That would be the only really honest thing to do. How much is it worth?

FREDDY: Roughly round about forty thousand pounds.

D'ARCY: Forty thousand! Look here! Suppose it's sold?

FREDDY: Oh, it's going to be sold. That's what the gentleman at Marseilles comes in.

D'ARCY: Well, if Joan got it back that way – in money - coming from me, I could say it was part of a marriage settlement. What d'you think of that?

FREDDY: Something rather unrefined.

D'ARCY: But it's hers. Can't you be a sportsman?

FREDDY: *(With challenge.)* Who isn't a sportsman?

D'ARCY: Well, I'm sorry, but I think you – rather aren't.

FREDDY: Right. Now then. You shall be in this with me. We'll go fifty-fifty in the risk and fifty-fifty in the plunder.

D'ARCY: Me? Steal? No thanks, I don't think I care to be in it.

FREDDY: I see. So much for your 'any means, fair or foul'?

D'ARCY: And I meant it. At least, in spirit.

FREDDY: Oh! A man of spirit! Very well. I've made you a sporting offer. I don't want you.

D'ARCY: *(After a pause, going to FREDDY, waveringly.)* Freddy!

FREDDY: M'm?

D'ARCY: Regarding this risk – is there much of it?

FREDDY: A hundred to one on success, but if *you* came into it – *ten* to one.

D'ARCY: Ten to one. What's fifty-fifty of that? All right. You think I'm afraid. I don't think I am. I'll *(With determination.)* very likely do it.

*JOAN re-enters. She is now very red-eyed and overcome.*

JOAN: We'd better get back to town.

D'ARCY: All right, darling.

JOAN: All right! It's all wrong. *(Nearly weeping.)*

FREDDY: All right, indeed! She's had the biggest shock of her life. *(To JOAN.)* I can't say how sorry I am for you.

JOAN: *(With spirit.)* Well, if these people are your friends I'm sorry for you!

D'ARCY: Good! A very apt retort.

JOAN: Come on. *(Turns up stage.)*

*D'ARCY goes up stage with her.*

I'll see if they've put my things in the car.

*She goes off.*

FREDDY: Well are you coming to me on the tenth?

D'ARCY: Well – I should have to tell Joan, you know.

FREDDY: You'll tell nobody. Tell her you're going somewhere else.

D'ARCY: Tell her lies?

FREDDY: Only one. Besides, you've got to begin sometime.

D'ARCY: No. I've vowed a vow I'll never deceive her. I simply couldn't do it. You've no idea how cute she is. If it means lying to her it's off. Do the job yourself.

FREDDY: Oh, I can see there's only one way of trusting you and that's to incriminate you.

D'ARCY: You needn't be afraid. I won't say a word about *you*.

FREDDY: I'll see you don't. *(Producing paper.)* What about this? If I'm caught this'll fix you anyway.

D'ARCY: Oh, so you're going to hold that over me?

*FREDDY draws it away as D'ARCY snatches at it.*

FREDDY: I don't go to work that way. But I'm going to use this to compel you to keep silent.

D'ARCY: How?

FREDDY: Like this. *(He tears the paper up and puts the pieces in the fire.)* That's the sort of feller you're dealing with.

D'ARCY: Thanks, Freddy. But I won't take any further part in it.

FREDDY: All right, then. Don't blame me if I stick to the proceeds.

*JOAN returns. MRS HEWLETT follows as though chasing her. JOAN is crying.*

JOAN: Come on, D'Arcy, hurry up.

MRS HEWLETT: Yes, you've been here quite long enough. A short visit, though, compared with what you expected.

JOAN: Take me away quickly. Don't speak to her again.

MRS HEWLETT: He can't say anything that'll hurt me. It's only spite. Spite does me no harm.

JOAN: D'Arcy!

*She hurries out in tears.*

MRS HEWLETT: *(Pursuing her and shouting.)* Came here in fine feather, didn't you? *(To D'ARCY.)* Well, it's moulted!

*She follows JOAN off slamming door.*

D'ARCY: *(Closing door and turning, very worked up.)* Did you hear that? I'll ruin that woman. I'll spoil her. Yes, and every bit of jewellery she's got I'll pinch. Are you in this? I make you a sporting offer. Fifty-fifty.

FREDDY: Once and for all. Am I boss?

D'ARCY: Yes, anything you like.

FREDDY: You'll do what I tell you, when I tell you and how I tell you?

D'ARCY: Anything! After the way she's treated Joan.

FREDDY: Right! That's final, you come to me on the tenth.

D'ARCY: Any number you like. Tenth, eleventh, twelfth.

FREDDY: No, the tenth is the date I've fixed for the job.

D'ARCY: I've a good mind to start the job now. *(He picks up a silver cigarette box.)*

FREDDY: Put that down.

D'ARCY: Why? Is it yours?

FREDDY: NO. It's hers.

D'ARCY: Hers, right! Then here goes.

*He opens the box, takes out two cigarettes and hurries to the door.*

That shows you.

*Goes out.*


*CURTAIN*

# Act Two

*The Hall of FREDDY Malone's house at Walton Heath. A roulette party is in progress.*

*PRUDENCE is acting as Bank. FREDDY is standing over her, and near him D'ARCY. Round the table are seated MRS HEWLETT, OSWALD and four other guests, SIR GEORGE and LADY CHUDLEIGH, HARRY KENWARD and RUTH BENNETT. As the curtain rises the roulette is spinning. D'ARCY takes FREDDY by the arm and speaks confidentially.*

FREDDY: Don't spin it so hard, Pru, we'll have to wait all night for the damn thing to stop.

LADY CHUDLEIGH: I don't mind. I think it's the most exciting part of the game.

OSWALD: *(To MRS HEWLETT.)* Haven't you put on more than you meant?

MRS HEWLETT: Don't you interfere with me; you bet your own bets.

HARRY: *(To SIR GEORGE.)* Can you give me eight half-crowns for a quid?

PRUDENCE: Twenty-six. Black.

*SIR GEORGE hands HARRY the money.*

*FREDDY moves to D'ARCY who is signing to him.*

D'ARCY: Is this going on all night?

FREDDY: Don't keep fussing.

HARRY: Whose is that ten bob?

MRS HEWLETT: Mine.

RUTH: My lucky number, too.

D'ARCY: But when do we start?

*General buzz of conversation.*

SIR GEORGE: *(Rising.)* I'm through, Freddy. Golf tomorrow.

D'ARCY: Are you going to bed?

SIR GEORGE: Yes.

D'ARCY: Good.

FREDDY: Well, one more spin, then we'll all go to bed. No limit this time. Look out, Pru. Come on. I'll take the bank. No black or red – numbers only.

*PRUDENCE has risen; FREDDY takes her place.*

MRS HEWLETT: I'm going to have a plunge.

D'ARCY: Oh, why not wait till the morning.

*They all laugh.*

PRUDENCE: Last hand, Ozzy. Are you going to back your fancy?

OSWALD: Yes, thanks.

PRUDENCE: Well, what are you going to do?

D'ARCY: He's going to sit it out.

SIR GEORGE: Can I have a fiver on?

FREDDY: Yes, a pony if you like.

LADY CHUDLEIGH: Lend me ten bob, George.

FREDDY: Come on. Have you all done?

HARRY: Yes.

MRS HEWLETT: I'm ready.           } *Together.*

PRUDENCE: Hurry up, Ozzy.

FREDDY: Right. Well, here she goes. *(Spins.)* Fricasseé de Mouton!

D'ARCY: *(To MRS HEWLETT.)* How much have you lost, I hope?

MRS HEWLETT: I've got something to say about finding you here.

PRUDENCE: *(Earnestly looking at roulette wheel running.)* Go on! Go on! – don't stop! Don't stop!!

LADY CHUDLEIGH: George, let's see.

SIR GEORGE: You'll see soon enough – there goes my fiver!

FREDDY: Zero! That clears the board.

OSWALD: I wish I'd known.

MRS HEWLETT: *(To OSWALD.)* What does Zero mean?

D'ARCY: *(Butting in, to MRS HEWLETT.)* To you, nothing.

FREDDY: Fancy me doing that again. I hate taking your money this way.

SIR GEORGE: That settles it. I'm off to bed. What time's that foursome in the morning?

*LADY CHUDLEIGH follows her husband.*

FREDDY: *(To SIR GEORGE.)* We leave here at nine.

*The party breaks up. MRS HEWLETT stands apart with OSWALD.*
*The others prepare to go upstairs.*

RUTH: *(To SIR GEORGE.)* Well, you've got to be my partner, Sir George.

SIR GEORGE: Rather!

LADY CHUDLEIGH: *(To FREDDY.)* Goodnight, Freddy.

FREDDY: Goodnight, Kathleen. We're together, remember.

LADY CHUDLEIGH: Are we?

FREDDY: Yes. But not till the morning, I fear.

LADY CHUDLEIGH: Oh, shame.

RUTH: *(At top of stairs.)* Goodnight, Mr Tuck.

D'ARCY: I hope you'll have a very nice dream.

HARRY: Goodnight, Freddy.

FREDDY: Goodnight, everyone.

*LADY CHUDLEIGH and RUTH, followed by SIR GEORGE and HARRY, go upstairs, talking as they go.*

MRS HEWLETT: Now, Mr Malone – you know I had no wish to meet Mr Tuck, after what happened the other day.

FREDDY: He wants to make up for what happened the other day. *(To D'ARCY.)* Don't you?

OSWALD: It's well meant, Mother.

MRS HEWLETT: Yes, and I know well enough it's well meant who towards.

PRUDENCE: Oh, I think he's behaved very nicely to you all the evening.

D'ARCY: Absolutely. Didn't I pass you the mustard at dinner? Even before you asked for it?

MRS HEWLETT: Yes. With the fish.

D'ARCY: I don't complain about meeting *you*.

OSWALD: I don't either. Not about meeting *you*.

D'ARCY: Well, I should hope not.

OSWALD: That's quite right – I say, I don't,

FREDDY: *(Severely, to MRS HEWLETT.)* Will you stop quarrelling in my house?

MRS HEWLETT: But I am not going to melt.

FREDDY: I hope not. If you started to melt, naturally I should keep well out of it. *(Crosses away from her to OSWALD.)* Where's your Uncle Simon?

OSWALD: He's in the library.

MRS HEWLETT: Well, I'm going to bed.

FREDDY: I hope you'll have a very good night.

D'ARCY: Goodnight, fair damsel.

MRS HEWLETT: Oh, really? You'll have to go a long way to get round me.

*She goes upstairs.*

D'ARCY: Yes, you're quite right. I'd have to take a taxi.

OSWALD: *(To PRUDENCE.)* I say. Can I have a word with you alone?

PRUDENCE: Where?

OSWALD: In the drawing-room. I haven't seen you alone all night.

FREDDY: You can't expect to see her alone all night just yet.

PRUDENCE: Oh, Freddy! *(Laughs.)* Very well; Ozzy, but it can't be for long. I promised to see your mother before she gets into bed.

D'ARCY: Yes. Better before than after.

PRUDENCE: Oh, Mr Tuck, I'm surprised at you.

*PRUDENCE and OSWALD go into the drawing-room.*

FREDDY: Now look here. What do you want to row with the old woman for? It only makes for danger.

D'ARCY: Danger? All very well for you. You're an expert. It found it hard enough to get here at all. I had to lie to Joan.

FREDDY: Yes. By the way – what did you tell her?

D'ARCY: I told her I was going to sleep at my solicitor's in Yorkshire.

FREDDY: That's a pretty feeble effort. What do you want with a solicitor in Yorkshire? And who the hell wants to sleep with a solicitor in any case?

D'ARCY: It's all right. She trusts me, the little darling. She knows I wouldn't tell her a lie. But when are we going to do the deed?

FREDDY: Tonight, of course. Pru is going to the old dame's room to see to a few details and report.

D'ARCY: Why do it at night?

FREDDY: Because she wears a lot of the best stuff all *day*. You don't suppose I'm going to hold her down on a couch while you go all over her neck and chest.

D'ARCY: I hope not. I dislike mountaineering. I would be much safer in the daytime –

*Enter the FOOTMAN, with a syphon, followed by the BUTLER.*

*(Noticing FOOTMAN.)* Wouldn't it?

FOOTMAN: *(Puzzled.)* Sir?

D'ARCY: What have you got there? Oh, one of those things! Yes, I know them. *(Tests syphon.)* No, thanks.

*FOOTMAN puts syphon on table and exits.*

FREDDY: Anything you want, Buckley?

BUCKLEY: Yes, sir. Miss Orlock from the Lodge is here, sir. She's been waiting to see you for a long time.

FREDDY: What about?

BUCKLEY: You know, sir, Orlock went to Beckhampton for you this evening.

FREDDY: Well?

BUCKLEY: He sent a message, sir, to say he can't get back till the morning.

FREDDY: Well, why worry me about it?

BUCKLEY: I don't know, sir; but the woman seems very put out.

FREDDY: Oh, I'll see her in a minute.

BUCKLEY: Yes, sir. *(Turns to go.)*

D'ARCY: *(Up at the windows.)* Wait a moment. Here's a car. He's probably come back

FREDDY: *(To BUCKLEY.)* Go and see who it is.

BUCKLEY: Yes, sir. *(Goes up to front door.)*

*D'ARCY comes down to FREDDY.*

D'ARCY: *(To FREDDY.)* You may find this awkward.

FREDDY: What d'you mean?

D'ARCY: It may be someone for you.

FREDDY: Why should it be someone for me?

*BUCKLEY opens door. JOAN's voice is heard off.*

D'ARCY: Well, you never know.

JOAN: *(Outside.)* It's all right. You needn't wait.

D'ARCY: It's someone for me.

FREDDY: Blast.

*JOAN enters and sees D'ARCY.*

JOAN: Hallo, darling!

D'ARCY: *(Embarrassed.)* Oh – I – don't think so.

JOAN: *(To FREDDY.)* Good evening.

FREDDY: Good evening. *(Offering his hand.)* All right, Buckley.

*BUCKLEY closes front door and goes off.*

D'ARCY: But darling – why have you come here and because of what?

JOAN: I called at your rooms tonight – just in case you got back.

D'ARCY: Tomorrow, dear –

JOAN: And I saw a letter your man had re-addressed to you here.

D'ARCY: What an ass that man is. I changed my mind at the last moment. I was absolutely in the Yorkshire train when I changed it.

FREDDY: But why mustn't he come to my house?

JOAN: Because you're trying to keep in with the Veals. And *she's* here, too.

D'ARCY: Is *she* here?

JOAN: Yes. I telephoned to Marvin Court and found that out. Oh, I guessed what you were up to.

D'ARCY: Guessed! But you ought to have warned me you could guess like that.

JOAN: I won't have it. You shan't be nice to that woman.

D'ARCY: Oh, but I wasn't going to be very nice.

FREDDY: *(To JOAN.)* I see. You don't agree to letting us try to get the right side of her.

JOAN: No. I hired a car and came straight down to stop it. I wouldn't accept a penny from her.

D'ARCY: But she's not likely to give you one.

JOAN: That's all right then, and now you'd better take me back in your car.

FREDDY: Oh, nonsense! You're not going home tonight.

JOAN: But I can't stay here.

D'ARCY: No, we don't want her – *(Looks at FREDDY.)* – to stay here against her will, do we?

FREDDY: *(With a quick frown at D'ARCY, which the latter accepts with a resigned agreement.)* I'll get you fixed up right away. *(Turns towards door.)*

JOAN: But I haven't any things for the night.

FREDDY: My sister will see to that.

JOAN: But *Mrs Veal's* here.

FREDDY: You needn't see her. You can pop off in the morning before she's up. She's a late sleeper. I don't suppose she begins to unglue till about lunch.

*He goes off into the drawing-room.*

JOAN: I never meant to stay here.

D'ARCY: Well, darling, you shouldn't have come so late.

JOAN: I don't care. I'm not going to have you making advances to that woman. Come on; let's get in the car and go back.

D'ARCY: I can't do that. I must remain.

JOAN: Why?

D'ARCY: I've sworn to Freddy I'd do this.

JOAN: What?

D'ARCY: Why this – remaining?

JOAN: That doesn't matter. You came to see Mrs Veal. You're not going to see any more of her. Are you?

D'ARCY: Very little, I hope.

JOAN: Why did you do this? Does the money mean so much to you?

D'ARCY: You know it doesn't. But it's yours. She wronged you, and I vowed I'd get it back by hook or – that other thing.

JOAN: You silly old thing. I know you were trying to help me. But never do this sort of thing again. Will you? Even for me?

D'ARCY: Not likely.

*FREDDY enters from drawing-room with PRUDENCE.*

FREDDY: *(As he enters.)* Here she is. Come on – *(Speaking to OSWALD in drawing-room.)* Not you. You stay there. *(Shuts door.)* Here you are – my sister.

JOAN: How d'you do. I'm sorry if I've caused you any trouble.

PRUDENCE: Not in the least. I've a room for you and everything you want.

D'ARCY: She can have my room.

FREDDY: *(Crosses to D'ARCY behind PRUDENCE.)* I'll see to this. I'm sure you must be very hungry after your journey – take Miss Hewlett to the dining-room and give her something to eat.

*(Confidentially.)*

D'ARCY: Oh! Come on and eat.

JOAN: But I had a very good dinner.

D'ARCY: Well, I *didn't*.

*Goes off with JOAN.*

PRUDENCE: Why do you want her here?

FREDDY: I don't. But if she goes, D'Arcy'll go. I must keep him here.

PRUDENCE: You'd be a lot safer without him.

FREDDY: Not when it's over. If he's going to be partly guilty, he's going to be entirely quiet.

PRUDENCE: That's true. You're going to tell the old woman that the girl's here?

FREDDY: Most certainly. You tell her.

PRUDENCE: All right. What room had the girl better have? We're full up.

FREDDY: *(Going up.)* That's easy. I'll send Simon Veal to the Lodge. *(Rings bell.)* You go in there too. I think D'Arcy's safer under observation. I'll come along in a minute.

*BUCKLEY enters.*

Is Mrs Orlock still there?

BUCKLEY: Yes, sir.

FREDDY: I want her.

BUCKLEY: Yes, sir.

PRUDENCE: And Buckley – tell Brown to look out some pyjamas and dressing-gown, and put them in Mr Simon Veal's bedroom.

*Goes off into dining-room.*

FREDDY: It's all right, Buckley, Mr Veal's going to the Lodge.

BUCKLEY: Oh, I see, sir.

FREDDY: Have his things packed and taken there.

BUCKLEY: Yes, sir. *(Opens door.)* Mrs Orlock. The master'll see you now.

*He admits MRS ORLOCK and goes out.*

FREDDY: Good evening. I'm sorry to hear about Orlock.

MRS ORLOCK: What about me, pray? I've been waiting to see you for hours!

FREDDY: What about?

MRS ORLOCK: Well, about my husband. I don't like him stopping away all night.

FREDDY: It wasn't my fault.

MRS ORLOCK: Then whose fault was it, sir? You sent him.

FREDDY: Don't you speak to me like that or *you'll* get sent somewhere.

MRS ORLOCK: *And* I mightn't mind.

FREDDY: That'll do. Now listen to me. I'm sending one of the gentleman from here to the Lodge.

MRS ORLOCK: What for, sir?

FREDDY: For the night. You've got a spare room there.

MRS ORLOCK: No, thank you. I prefer not.

FREDDY: You don't understand. I'm telling you what I *wish*.

MRS ORLOCK: My husband isn't there. I shan't feel comfortable with a strange gentleman in the spare room.

FREDDY: Oh, nonsense! You flatter yourself. You'll be safe enough. Go and do what you're told.

MRS ORLOCK: I can't do it, sir. The sheets aren't aired.

FREDDY: That doesn't matter. He won't know until afterwards.

MRS ORLOCK: There's always something happening here what I don't like.

FREDDY: What do you mean by that?

MRS ORLOCK: What I say. Always comings and goings and strange events.

FREDDY: Strange events? – explain yourself.

MRS ORLOCK: Well, look at what I've put up with these last few days. The Lodge all higgledy-piggledy – workmen here, workmen there – nothing but pails and buckets. I hate the place!

FREDDY: That's enough – that's your finish. Now you'll go.

MRS ORLOCK: Go?

FREDDY: Go, yes – you can take a month's notice and leave.

MRS ORLOCK: Leave the Lodge?

FREDDY: Leave my service.

MRS ORLOCK: But what about Bert?

FREDDY: Take Bert with you. I'm sorry for him, but he's either got to lose his job – or lose his wife.

MRS ORLOCK: So this is justice!

FREDDY: That'll do. For the month you're here, you'll do as you're told – beginning from now.

MRS ORLOCK: It's foul treatment.

FREDDY: Control yourself. If you're nervous tonight I'll send Cook over to sleep with you.

MRS ORLOCK: Cook! My God, no, thank you!

*MRS ORLOCK goes out very angry.*

*MAID and FOOTMAN enter on landing. FOOTMAN walks round to bedroom door, opens it, switches on light and MAID exits through bedroom, and FOOTMAN follows her, closing door.*

FREDDY: Well, that's *your* funeral, anyhow.

*SIMON enters.*

FREDDY: Ah! You're the man I want. I hope you won't mind but I've had to move you to the Lodge tonight.

SIMON: Oh, indeed. And why?

FREDDY: Miss Hewlett's arrived, and we've had to give her your room.

SIMON: And who asked *her* here?

FREDDY: Well, who asked you, if it isn't a rude question, or even if it is! And furthermore, I regret to say that after tonight there'll be no room for you even at the Lodge.

*He goes off.*

*SIMON remains on stage moodily. The drawing-room door opens.*

*OSWALD peers out, then seeing SIMON, closes the door, which makes a slight noise.*

*SIMON hears in close and opens it again.*

SIMON: *(Seeing OSWALD.)* Oh, it's you, is it? Come out.

OSWALD: Oh! Goodnight.

SIMON: *(Follows him, stops him.)* Where's your mother?

OSWALD: Gone to her room. *(Following as SIMON makes for the stairs.)* No, no. Don't go up after her.

SIMON: I warned her. Before you got engaged. I want that cheque.

OSWALD: But I'm not engaged that I know of.

SIMON: No. Not till she's got me kicked out of the place tomorrow. And sent to the Lodge tonight.

OSWALD: She'll settle it when we get home.

SIMON: She'll settle it tonight – or I tell. Now then!

OSWALD: No, no, no! Don't keep harping on that. You wouldn't do yourself any good by telling.

SIMON: Yes, that's always her cry. It isn't only a threat.

OSWALD: Isn't it? I'd like to know what it is then.

SIMON: Hold your tongue! I'll call back here later. You get that cheque from her and meet me with it here.

OSWALD: When?

SIMON: When they're all asleep. Three o'clock.

OSWALD: Oh, I don't think I'd better.

SIMON: I think you had.

OSWALD: Oh! *(Going up stairs.)*

*He goes out.*

*OSWALD remains for a moment, then hearing others coming – exits upstairs.*

*MAID followed by FOOTMAN, carrying a bag, re-enter from bedroom. They exit slowly off landing.*

*Enter D'ARCY and JOAN from dining-room.*

D'ARCY: Here we are, darling. Here are the stairs. Now I'm sure you're ready for bed.

JOAN: But I don't know where it is.

D'ARCY: Well, the bed's in your room. I'm not quite sure where the room is, but we can easily find out.

*Goes to ring and – meets SIMON, who enters.*

D'ARCY: Hallo, I want to find out where this young lady's bedroom is – you ought to know, you've been in it.

SIMON: Yes. *(To JOAN, who is standing at foot of stairs.)* I'm much obliged to you. I'm sure.

D'ARCY: Well, where is it?

SIMON: There. First room at the top of the stairs. *(Indicates door up the stairs.)* Goodnight.

*Exit.*

D'ARCY: Yes. *(Then to JOAN.)* And goodnight to *you*, darling.

JOAN: You seem in an awful hurry to send me to bed. I'd like to sit up and talk a while.

D'ARCY: I mustn't talk tonight. I've got work to do.

JOAN: Work, you! What sort of work?

D'ARCY: Oh, about transferring some property. It's to do with a deed.

JOAN: Oh, nothing to do with me?

D'ARCY: No. You go to bed.

JOAN: All right. Goodnight, darling. *(Kisses him.)*

D'ARCY: That's it.

*And she goes upstairs.*

Oh, your coat. *(Handing it to her.)* And I hope you won't wake up till tea. I mean early tea. *(He stands kissing his hand to her.)*

*FREDDY and PRUDENCE re-enter.*

FREDDY: What are you doing?

D'ARCY: I'm goodnight-ing

FREDDY: Well, have we got rid of them all?

PRUDENCE: Yes. Ozzy's gone. *(Puts out light in drawing-room.)*

FREDDY: Now we must start business.

D'ARCY: Well – I'm ready.

FREDDY: Good! Now, Pru. There's the old lady to see to.

PRUDENCE: Yes. I'll see her settled down nice and comfy.

*(Goes to staircase.)*

D'ARCY: *(To her.)* Well, goodnight.

PRUDENCE: Don't you worry, I'm coming back.

*Goes upstairs.*

*BUCKLEY appears on stairs.*

D'ARCY: Now look here, Freddy –

PRUDENCE: *(From stairs.)* Goodnight, Buckley.

BUCKLEY: Goodnight, Miss. *(Comes down.)*

FREDDY: Buckley, you needn't wait up. I'll lock up. Were Mr Simon Veal's things taken to the Lodge?

BUCKLEY: Yes, sir. William took them. He's back, sir. The gentleman didn't have very much. Goodnight, sir.

FREDDY: Goodnight to you.

D'ARCY: And to you. *(To BUCKLEY.)*

*BUCKLEY goes off.*

FREDDY: *(To D'ARCY.)* Now, what were you going to say?

D'ARCY: Just that it makes it a bit difficult Joan being so trusting. Isn't she a darling?

FREDDY: Yes. The more I see of her the more I feel I may have been wrong in dragging you into it.

D'ARCY: But you haven't. I walked into it.

FREDDY: Now look here, D'Arcy. If you think you'll have any regrets, now's you're time to chuck it.

D'ARCY: Chuck it? I'm going through with it, for her sake. She might think it's wrong, but I know it's right. I'm in it up to the – shins.

FREDDY: Good boy! I'll see you don't suffer for it, whatever happens.

D'ARCY: Good!

FREDDY: Then now for it.

D'ARCY: Yes. Splendid.

FREDDY: You can have one more drink if you like.

D'ARCY: No. I don't want drinks. I've got no fear.

FREDDY: Haven't you? Then get some. That's where everyone falls down sooner or later at this game. They think it's easy.

D'ARCY: What? But you said this *would* be easy?

FREDDY: That's just why you've got to be afraid. Afraid of the tiniest slip. One footprint might do it – one finger-mark.

D'ARCY: I'll wear gloves. They always wear gloves.

FREDDY: Some people think the police are easily fooled. *Are* they?

D'ARCY: Well, you've fooled them before now.

FREDDY: Never. What I've done is never let 'em suspect I've got a very high opinion of Scotland Yard.

D'ARCY: Scotland Yard? But no one from Scotland Yard will come here?

FREDDY: Of course, they'll come tomorrow.

D'ARCY: Why?

FREDDY: Why? We're not going to scrump apples. Do you know what we could get for this?

D'ARCY: No.

FREDDY: Ten years.

D'ARCY: Ten! I didn't think it would be as much as that. You didn't make this very clear to me.

*PRUDENCE comes downstairs quietly.*

FREDDY: Of course I made it clear.

*D'ARCY looks over towards PRUDENCE. FREDDY sees her and stops talking.*

PRUDENCE: She's locked them all in that jewel-case. The key's under the pillow.

D'ARCY: That's done it. You can't get the key from under her pillow.

FREDDY: Oh, keep quiet. I've been making friends with that jewel-case. I shan't require the key.

PRUDENCE: *(To D'ARCY.)* He just says 'Open up, please,' and it does. You'll see. It's awfully cute.

D'ARCY: But you're not going to open it in her room, with a loud click?

FREDDY: It'll click all right, but not loud. *(To PRUDENCE.)* Where's she put it?

PRUDENCE: She's left it on her dressing-table.

FREDDY: Oh, dear. Is *that* all? She's not doing me justice.

PRUDENCE: And she's going to bolt her door. I didn't suggest it, of course. She told me.

D'ARCY: What! You've left a bolt on her door? Now you can't get in.

FREDDY: That's fine. That's just what I hoped she'd do. *(To PRUDENCE.)* Well, off you go. You know what you've got to do.

PRUDENCE: Yes. One moment. Here's Exhibit 'A.'

*Hands FREDDY a Chubb key.*

FREDDY: Yes. *(To D'ARCY, handing him key.)* You'll want that.

D'ARCY: *(Taking it with diffidence.)* Me? What for?

FREDDY: The key of the garage. I'll tell you about it.

PRUDENCE: *(Giving FREDDY a small glass bottle.)* And this.

FREDDY: Right. *(To D'ARCY.)* You may want this, too. But I hope not.

D'ARCY: So do I. What is it?

FREDDY: Just a little bottle.

D'ARCY: Scent?

FREDDY: No. Don't be inquisitive.

PRUDENCE: I'll go now. *(Turning to stairs.)* Bye-bye. *(To D'ARCY.)* Good luck!

*She goes upstairs.*

D'ARCY: *(To PRUDENCE.)* Yes, thanks – so do I, I'm sure. But how are you going to get into the room?

FREDDY: How I always meant to. From the conservatory roof.

D'ARCY: What, you're going in through the window?

FREDDY: Yes, up a ladder. I shall go first.

D'ARCY: Oh! and then – anyone?

FREDDY: I'll tell you. First of all, you meet me down here.

D'ARCY: When?

FREDDY: A quarter to three. Sharp! You'll be wearing pyjamas, dressing gown, soft slippers and a pair of gloves.

D'ARCY: Yes, all right. I know about the gloves.

FREDDY: When we get in her room –

D'ARCY: She may not be asleep.

FREDDY: I'll take care of that.

D'ARCY: She may wake up.

FREDDY: You'll take care she doesn't.

D'ARCY: Oh, you think *I'd* better do that. Yes?

FREDDY: When I've got the stuff I shall hand it to you and unbolt the door, let you out and bolt it again. You bring the stuff down here – out to the garage and hide it in your car.

D'ARCY: Oh, *I* do. In *my* car? Is that a very good idea?

FREDDY: Very. Put it somewhere safe: in the tool-box or under the cushions. Lock the garage and bring me back the key.

D'ARCY: But why in *my* car?

FREDDY: I shall get out down the ladder – and leave it there. Then, when we've finished, Pru will give the alarm.

D'ARCY: Alarm? Is there going to be any alarm.

FREDDY: Yes. She's going to say she saw a man running down the drive. The old woman will wake up – miss her stuff and raise hell. I shall take charge – round up the whole house. The telephone will have been put out of order.

D'ARCY: Who by?

FREDDY: By the burglar. I'll see to that.

D'ARCY: Yes.

FREDDY: So I shall send you for the police – *in your car.*

D'ARCY: But the stuff will be in the car. You want me to bring back a fat policeman in my car with the stuff?

FREDDY: Yes. The last place he'd expect to find it.

D'ARCY: I won't put it under the cushions. He may have a sensitive seat.

FREDDY: As soon as I get the chance I'll take it off you. I know what to do with it.

D'ARCY: But they may search the car.

FREDDY: What these local bobbies will search is the country-side for the burglar. I'll just see to that burglar right away.

*(Takes gloves from his pocket.)*

D'ARCY: Ah, there are the good old gloves. This is fine. I feel like a real crook.

FREDDY: You *are* a real crook, and don't you forget it. Now the telephone.

*Takes a pair of pliers from his pocket and cuts the telephone line.*

*D'ARCY goes into the room. And comes back with a pair of gloves, putting them on.*

Now the window.

D'ARCY: What about the window?

*During the next few lines FREDDY opens the window by the front door, removes a diamond of glass which he leaves lying on the floor, tests opening the window by reaching his hand through the hole, and leaves the window open.*

FREDDY: This window. The burglar's got to come in this way.

*D'ARCY breaks the glass and puts it down, puts his heel through it. FREDDY locks front door.*

D'ARCY: *(Watching eagerly.)* By Jove, yes, this work is pleasanter than I thought. *(Pulling on gloves tightly.)*

FREDDY: If they cop you, my God, your enthusiasm will wane. Well, there you are. Now you'd better go to your room.

D'ARCY: Yes, but Freddy, there's something else. This little bottle. What is it?

FREDDY: Oh, that? That is for you, just in case she gets wakeful.

D'ARCY: Why, what do I do with it?

FREDDY: Douse her with it.

D'ARCY: Oh, douse! All right, if she looks like waking, I'll just pour some on my handkerchief and douse. Then I'll gag her with it.

FREDDY: Your handkerchief, your name on it. That's damn brainy. And be convicted of robbery with violence. That's Dartmoor and the 'cat'.

D'ARCY: And the cat!

FREDDY: Go on. A quarter to three.

D'ARCY: *(Going upstairs.)* You may have to call me.

FREDDY: By Gad! I'll call you something if I do!

*D'ARCY goes upstairs, he waits halfway up, watching FREDDY.*

*FREDDY switches out the standard lamp and crosses to D'ARCY. They are seen going upstairs.*

*CURTAIN*

## SCENE 2

*MRS HEWLETT's room, a comfortable and well-furnished room with a fire still burning brightly enough to throw some illumination. It reveals MRS HEWLETT asleep in bed L. The door is L. The window in the back wall has curtains over it which reach to the ground. Other usual bedroom furniture is about the room, including the chest of drawers on which rests the jewel-case.*

*MRS HEWLETT who is wearing a boudoir cap, is facing the light, sound asleep and covered with a mass of bedclothes including a quilt. Only her face can be seen, her deep, regular breathing heard. The window curtains are cautiously parted and FREDDY appears. He peers towards the bed, then silently enter. He takes a step or two to the bed and scrutinizes her; then turns again to the window and signals. D'ARCY arrives on the scene. They are both wearing dressing-gowns over pyjamas and their hands are gloved.*

*FREDDY indicates the bed and D'ARCY crosses towards it and takes guard over MRS HEWLETT, while FREDDY immediately goes to the jewel-case. He brings it to the firelight. D'ARCY, engrossed in FREDDY's actions, forgets to watch MRS HEWLETT, who suddenly heaves restlessly and speaks in her sleep.*

MRS HEWLETT: Where?

*FREDDY turns quickly and for a moment or two watches intently.*

*D'ARCY produces the bottle and whispers to FREDDY.*

D'ARCY: Douse?

FREDDY: *(Whispering.)* Be prepared to.

*D'ARCY takes out his handkerchief, then remembering, holds it doubtfully. FREDDY, without apparently taking notice, puts out a hand and whips it away from him. D'ARCY crosses to the towel-horse and gets a face towel, which he brings back to the bed. He sniffs at the bottle and is almost over-powered himself by the effects. He falls on the bed, half-unconscious. FREDDY raises him to his feet. FREDDY, who has been operating on the jewel-case with a small instrument, has now got it open. He puts it on a chair, takes a thin silk petticoat of MRS HEWLETT's which is hanging over the back of the chair, and quickly wraps the petticoat round the jewellery. A distant sound is heard, like that of a chair being overturned on a parquet floor. FREDDY stands motionless, listening. D'ARCY makes questioning gestures. Then comes a more definite sound of movement outside the window. FREDDY turns, signs to D'ARCY to conceal himself, and himself quickly crosses the room to the window curtain, snatching a large batch of towels from the towel-horse as he passes.*

*After a moment the window curtains are parted. In the moonlight appears the face of SIMON Veal peering in.*

SIMON: *(In a subdued voice but with challenge.)* Margery!

*Silence. D'ARCY stands half-hidden by curtain. SIMON, holding to the sill with both hands, leans a trifle farther into the room. With a lightening movement FREDDY flings the bath towel over SIMON's head, and putting one hand to SIMON's mouth through the towel, twists the towel tightly and signals to D'ARCY who joins him. MRS HEWLETT gives a heave in bed and again groans loudly in her sleep.*

*FREDDY leaves the struggling SIMON to D'ARCY and hurries to the bed. FREDDY takes a glance at MRS HEWLETT; then unbolts the door and opens it. D'ARCY is struggling with SIMON, who makes muffled sounds through the towel. FREDDY returns and grapples with him, indicating to D'ARCY to go. D'ARCY makes for the door, forgetting the jewels. FREDDY lets go with one hand to snap his fingers, which recalls D'ARCY who catches up the petticoat and – darts from the room, shutting the door.*

*But SIMON has managed to release himself. He strikes out blindly, over-balances and falls back with a cry. There is a crash of glass and a thud. FREDDY darts towards the door and just as he bolted it MRS HEWLETT wakes with an exclamation.*

MRS HEWLETT: What's that?

*FREDDY throws the bedclothes over her head as puts up her beside light. There is a great upheaval of the bedclothes. FREDDY flies to the window and as she flings off the bedclothes slips behind the window curtain. MRS HEWLETT sees the empty jewel-case. She screams, and hugging the quilt round her, gets out of bed. She looks at the open window, then hurries to the door, unbolts it and – runs out screaming.*

Help! Help! Thieves and burglars! My joolry! Help! Help! Help! *(Her voice grows more distant.)*

FREDDY: *(Heard in the passage.)* Hallo! What's up? Who is it? What's the matter?


*CURTAIN*

# SCENE 3

*The hall is in darkness, expect for the moonlight shining through the row of windows running along the back wall.*

*OSWALD comes downstairs stealthily with a lighted candle and emerges into this moonlight. He is in his pyjamas, dressing-gown and bed-slippers. He holds a cheque in his hand and as he advances he makes the mistake of looking back guiltily over his shoulder, with the result that he knocks over a brass tray with a crash.*

OSWALD: Oh my God!

*He puts it into place again, then listens for a moment and goes to the front door, which he opens. He looks out expectantly.*

JOAN: *(Heard from the staircase – enters from bedroom.)* What's that down there?

*OSWALD blows out candle, quickly and quietly closes the front door and slinks back – JOAN coming downstairs.*

Who is it?

*OSWALD gains the archway as JOAN appears – he sneaks through this archway and off.*

*JOAN comes boldly down into the hall, crosses and switches on the lights. As she does so D'ARCY comes on landing, bolts downstairs, and runs right into her, he is still wearing his gloves and carrying the petticoat containing the jewellery.*

D'Arcy!

D'ARCY: Good Lord!

JOAN: What are you doing?

D'ARCY: Let me go. I must get out.

JOAN: Where are you going?

D'ARCY: To the post.

JOAN: What?

D'ARCY: Parcel post.

JOAN: What d'you mean? What have you got there?

D'ARCY: The parcel.

JOAN: Come here. What is this? *(Tries to get at the bundle.)*

D'ARCY: Don't! Dash! *(He drops a bracelet from the bundle.)*

JOAN: What's this mean?

D'ARCY: I've dropped it.

JOAN: D'Arcy! You've taken it.

D'ARCY: Yes. For you.

JOAN: Good heavens! All her jewellery. You've *robbed* it.

D'ARCY: Oh, darling, not that hard word.

JOAN: Well, what *have* you done?

D'ARCY: I've removed.

JOAN: You mad fool! Take it all back.

D'ARCY: I can't now. Even if I could, I couldn't.

JOAN: You must.

*MRS HEWLETT's voice heard exactly as at end of Scene 2.*

MRS HEWLETT: *(Off.)* Help! Help! Help! Thieves and burglars! My joolry! Help! Help!

D'ARCY: Listen. Quick. I must get out. Good-bye.

*Hurries out.*

FREDDY: *(Heard off.)* Hallo! What's up? Who is it? What's the matter?

SIR GEORGE: *(Heard off.)* Hallo, Freddy, what is it, what's the matter?

FREDDY: *(Off.)* Here! George! Harry! D'Arcy! Everyone! Quick.

SIR GEORGE: *(Off.)* Someone's been burgled.

MRS HEWLETT: Yes. I have.

*She comes downstairs.*

*JOAN quickly slips the bracelet up her arm, under her sleeve.*

FREDDY: *(Heard off.)* Buckley! Everyone! Get up! Come out, damn it!

*MRS HEWLETT coming downstairs.*

MRS HEWLETT: All my joolry. I've been thieved.

JOAN: Did you see anyone?

MRS HEWLETT: No. He stifled me with me quilt.

*FREDDY, SIR GEORGE and HARRY come hurrying downstairs.*

FREDDY: *(Coming downstairs – to MRS HEWLETT.)* Calm now. Did you see him?

MRS HEWLETT: No, he got away out of the window.

FREDDY: How do you know that, if you didn't see him?

MRS HEWLETT: Because my door was still bolted on the inside.

FREDDY: *(To the two guests.)* Run round quick and have a look.

*SIR GEORGE and HARRY go out.*

*A FOOTMAN and two scared MAIDS in overcoats over their night-dresses enter. LADY CHUDLEIGH runs downstairs. The two male guests go to front door.*

*(To servants.)* Come on, you! Everyone! Where's Buckley? *(Shouting.)* Buckley!

SIR GEORGE: *(Just inside – at front door.)* This door was unlocked.

*MRS HEWLETT sits in a state of collapse.*

JOAN: D'Arcy opened it.

FREDDY: D'Arcy?

JOAN: Yes. When the row started he ran down and dashed out.

*RUTH comes downstairs – stands at foot. BUCKLEY enters with Maids.*

BUCKLEY: Yes, sir?

FREDDY: *(To BUCKLEY.)* Come on! I want everyone. The whole lot.

*BUCKLEY goes out.*

*MRS HEWLETT sits on a chair and another FOOTMAN, tow more MAIDS and a COOK are brought in by BUCKLEY.*

LADY CHUDLEIGH: *(To JOAN.)* Hallo, who are you? When did *you* come here?

JOAN: Late tonight. I'm D'Arcy Tuck's fiancée.

LADY CHUDLEIGH: Oh, I see.

FREDDY: *(Interrupting.)* Yes. Don't interfere please. Sorry.

*FREDDY switches on lights. SIR GEORGE and HARRY run in from front door. OSWALD slinks in unnoticed – cross back of table to MRS HEWLETT.*

SIR GEORGE: It's old Veal.

FREDDY: What?

HARRY: There's a ladder up to the window. He's fallen through the conservatory.

MRS HEWLETT: Simon?

SIR GEORGE: He's knocked out. Unconscious.

MRS HEWLETT: But my joolry?

HARRY: No sign of that. Only a towel.

FREDDY: A towel?

*PRUDENCE appearing hurriedly on the stairs.*

PRUDENCE: Freddy! Freddy! A man! I saw a man!

FREDDY: You did? Where? Quick!

PRUDENCE: Running down the drive. I saw him from the landing window.

FREDDY: When?

PRUDENCE: Just now. He went past the lodge and out of the gate.

SIR GEORGE: It may be Tuck.

*D'ARCY enters at front door, still wearing gloves, which he takes off behind his back.*

D'ARCY: No, it isn't me.

FREDDY: Where've *you* been?

*PRUDENCE comes downstairs stands at foot.*

D'ARCY: To the gar-rounds.

HARRY: Did you see him too?

D'ARCY: See who?

PRUDENCE: A man! I saw a man escaping.

D'ARCY: No. That's why I went out. To look. But I didn't.

FREDDY: Well, it's too late now. Quick! Telephone the police.

D'ARCY: Yes. Good idea. *(Goes to telephone.)*

FREDDY: *(Turning to servants.)* Everybody here?

BUCKLEY: Yes, sir. All my lot.

D'ARCY: Hallo! Hallo!

FREDDY: Did any of you see anything? Come on. Speak up.

D'ARCY: Hallo! Hallo!

FREDDY: Here! Let me do it.

D'ARCY: Al right. I can phone. I've done it before. *(Suddenly holding the 'phone up.)* Hallo! Here! Look!

SIR GEORGE: The wire's cut.

FREDDY: By Gad! Then he got in her room.

HARRY: This window's open.

FREDDY: *(Cross to window.)* Where? Yes, and broken.

D'ARCY: Yes. Into pieces.

FREDDY: Here! You! D'Arcy! Don't stand looking like that! Go for the police. In a car! Quick! Take any car!

D'ARCY: Oh, I'd better take mine, hadn't I?

FREDDY: Well, go on, take it. Hurry up. Wait a moment. *(Crosses to sideboard.)* The garage key.

D'ARCY: I don't want that, do I?

FREDDY: *(At drawer of table.)* Yes. Here. Take it. *(Hands D'ARCY key.)*

D'ARCY: That'll do splendidly. Yes. Where's the police station? Oh, never mind. That doesn't matter.

*He goes out of front door.*

FREDDY: *(To FOOTMAN.)* You, William. Go with Mr Tuck. Show him the way.

WILLIAM: Yes, sir.

*FOOTMAN hurries out after D'ARCY.*

FREDDY: And Harry. You take another car for the doctor. Doctor Turner – you know where he lives.

HARRY: Yes, right, Freddy.

*Exit.*

MRS HEWLETT: What about Simon?

FREDDY: We'll see to him. You go and wait in the dining-room. Pru, take her there.

*PRUDENCE crosses to MRS HEWLETT and – takes her off.*

MRS HEWLETT: I want my dressing-gown.

FREDDY: Then you'd better stick to your quilt.

*PRUDENCE and MRS HEWLETT exeunt.*

LADY CHUDLEIGH: Shall we go with them?

FREDDY: Yes, you two go.

*The two ladies go.*

*JOAN is about to follow.*

Not you for a minute, please. Now, Buckley, go to Mr Veal. You, *(To OSWALD.)* you go too. You're his cousin or nephew or some damn thing. You, *(To a MAID.)* Brown, open the French window into the billiard room. Carry him in there, Buckley.

*MAID (Brown.) exits.*

BUCKLEY: Yes, sir.

*Goes with OSWALD out by front door.*

FREDDY: *(To the other MAIDS.)* You go in the kitchen and wait there till the police come. Go on, Cook, not the first time you've done it.

*Only FREDDY, JOAN and SIR GEORGE remain. FREDDY turns to JOAN, who is at foot of stairs.*

You were the first down here, it seems?

JOAN: Yes, the man was here when I came down.

FREDDY: *(Keenly.)* Who, the burglar?

JOAN: Yes. He knocked something over. That's what disturbed me. He got away just as I came own.

SIR GEORGE: You've got some nerve.

JOAN: Yes, p'raps I have. Anyhow, I turned on the light –

FREDDY: Then the row started, and you say D'Arcy came running down?

JOAN: That's right. He dashed out.

FREDDY: Did he say anything?

JOAN: Well, simply – 'Did you see anyone?' or 'It's a burglar' or something – I forget what he said now.

FREDDY: *(To SIR GEORGE.)* Well, the fellow can only have just got away.

*BUCKLEY returns at front door.*

BUCKLEY: Sir!

FREDDY: Well?

BUCKLEY: Here's Mrs Orlock, sir. Wants to see you.

FREDDY: Well, what the Hell does she want?

*BUCKLEY disappears.*

*MRS ORLOCK enters at front door. She is in day clothes but evidently hastily thrown on. She is without a hat and her hair is dishevelled.*

MRS ORLOCK: I saw it happen. I saw.

FREDDY: *What* did you see? From the start. Let's have it.

MRS ORLOCK: The gentleman sleeping in the Lodge came and knocked at my door. 'Get up,' he says, and 'and come out.'

FREDDY: What time was that?

MRS ORLOCK: Just before three. I went out to him. He had all his clothes on.

FREDDY: Never mind what he had on. What did he say?

MRS ORLOCK: He says, 'I've seen a ladder,' he says, 'up against a winder at the house,' he says. 'I'm going to see what it is,' he says. 'You foller in case you're wanted,' he says. With that he made off.

FREDDY: And did you follow?

MRS ORLOCK: I 'ad to put on some shoes and a coat. Then I did. Sure enough I saw the ladder and him on top. He was strugglin' with a man in the winder. He 'ad a sheet over 'is head.

SIR GEORGE: Who had? The man inside?

MRS ORLOCK: No, my gentleman.

FREDDY: What did the man inside look like?

MRS ORLOCK: I couldn't see. 'E was in the dark, in the room. I was over there by the bend of the drive.

FREDDY: Well – go on.

MRS ORLOCK: Suddenly he waved his arms, like as if he got a blow, and crashed through the conservatory roof.

FREDDY: He was knocked down. You're sure of that?

MRS ORLOCK: Positive. He was flung down. I screamed out. I watched for a minute then I went back into the Lodge.

FREDDY: Why?

MRS ORLOCK: What else could I do, like I was? I put on what clothes I could and came up 'ere.

*D'ARCY hurries in at front door.*

D'ARCY: We got a Bobby, just up the road.

FREDDY: What's the good of *one*?

D'ARCY: It's all right. He sent the footman for another.

FREDDY: What have you done with him?

D'ARCY: He's here. He's gone to see the accident.

FREDDY: I'll see him. Come on, George. *(To MRS ORLOCK.)* You'd better come too.

*FREDDY goes off with SIR GEORGE.*

*MRS ORLOCK remains for a moment, looking at D'ARCY, who dislikes it. Then she turns and – also goes out.*

D'ARCY: *(Looks round to see the coast is clear, coming to JOAN, who has turned from him.)* Joan – darling –

JOAN: *(Facing him, almost with anger.)* Do you understand what you've done?

D'ARCY: Do you understand why I did?

JOAN: Yes, I think I do. Is *that* what you really wanted?

D'ARCY: No, but this was my idea of how to get it back.

JOAN: You came here on purpose to do this. You planned it all – all this – this window – telephone – everything you did.

D'ARCY: Yes. I did it all on my own. It was your property, that's why. It was for you.

JOAN: For me! You know I'd never touch it even if I got it. You were never going to tell me.

D'ARCY: P'raps not. But I was going to give it to you.

JOAN: Yes. How much of it?

D'ARCY: Well, half.

JOAN: That's candid, anyhow. It was that you wanted, not me.

D'ARCY: You'll be sorry you said that – when you think of me doing 'time' – a long sentence, I expect. Dartmoor and the 'cat'.

JOAN: All our happiness ruined just for this beastly money.

D'ARCY: If you've finished with me I may as well be in gaol – But – one day – you'll realize – it was all done for your sake. Honestly. *(Taking her by the arm.)* Joan!

JOAN: Oh, don't. *(She steps away. Almost cries.)*

D'ARCY: Well, what are you going to do?

JOAN: If I speak now you'll be arrested.

D'ARCY: But you *can't* speak, you can't. Because you still love me.

JOAN: *(After a struggle with her emotion – turning away.)* Yes, but don't you see how terrible this is for me. *(Crying.)*

*She turns quickly to the stairs as –*

*FREDDY busily re-enters. He hurries down to the servants' door and speaks into the kitchen quarters.*

FREDDY: *(To D'ARCY.)* The Inspector's here. Now, please, in the dining-room – all of you.

*The four servants enter and go off with BUCKLEY.*

Keep them standing by, Buckley, till the Inspector's done with them.

*MRS ORLOCK has entered and they pass her. About to speak to JOAN when he sees MRS ORLOCK.*

What do you want now?

MRS ORLOCK: There's something I haven't mentioned. Maybe I should have done.

FREDDY: Well, mention it now.

MRS ORLOCK: Before I went back into the Lodge, I saw the lights in this hall go up.

FREDDY: Quite right. This young lady put them up.

MRS ORLOCK: Then I saw someone run out. That gentleman, if I'm not mistaken.

D'ARCY: No, no. No, you're not.

FREDDY: We know all about that.

MRS ORLOCK: Yes, sir, but I know *this*. Between the time Mr Veal was knocked down and the time these lights went up –

FREDDY: Well?

MRS ORLOCK: Nobody else got down the ladder. That I *do* know.

D'ARCY: Well Freddy – he may have – hidden somewhere –

FREDDY: In that case he must have hidden before he ran down the drive.

MRS ORLOCK: But that's not correct, sir. Nobody *did* run down the drive. I'd have seen him.

D'ARCY: But he might have slipped by you. While you were dressing.

MRS ORLOCK: No, I kept a sharp look-out. Nobody don't slip by *me* as easy as all that.

*SIR GEORGE enters.*

SIR GEORGE: Freddy! Where are you?

FREDDY: I'm here.

SIR GEORGE: Can I speak to you a moment?

FREDDY: Yes. *(To MRS ORLOCK.)* You can go through there to the others.

*She goes.*

*(Turns to JOAN.)* I'm sorry, but the Inspector wants everyone there – to hear all they know.

JOAN: I've told *you* all I now. I know nothing else – nothing whatever.

FREDDY: Well, you might go and tell the Inspector that, will you?

JOAN: Certainly.

*She goes off.*

FREDDY: D'Arcy, you, too.

D'ARCY: Yes. *(To SIR GEORGE. Turns to FREDDY.)* Oh, what a thing for someone to have done.

FREDDY: *(To SIR GEORGE.)* Well, what is it?

*D'ARCY goes out.*

SIR GEORGE: I say, old man. This is serious.

FREDDY: Well, I know that.

SIR GEORGE: Yes, but now it's dammed serious.

FREDDY: Why?

SIR GEORGE: That man – old Veal –

FREDDY: What about him?

SIR GEORGE: He's dead.

FREDDY: He's dead. Are you sure?

*D'ARCY appears at door and is coming in but steps back when he sees that FREDDY is not alone.*

SIR GEORGE: Yes.

FREDDY: All right. I'll come.

*SIR GEORGE goes off.*

*FREDDY is at the same moment going. Closes door.*

*D'ARCY enters at front door.*

D'ARCY: Freddy! One word. He's dead.

FREDDY: Yes. This is the very devil. We know it was a fall, an accident. But in the eyes of the law it's murder.

D'ARCY: Murder? Who by?

FREDDY: Both of us. And you know what that means?

D'ARCY: What?

FREDDY: The rope.

*He goes off.*

*D'ARCY remains.*

D'ARCY: Rope. *(Imagines a noose round his neck, gulps with terror.)*

*CURTAIN*

# Act Three

*The Office of Chief Constable GRIERSON, Scotland Yard. Door down L. two writing-tables, one downstage R., one up R. C.; the latter having a large album and some files on it. A small armchair and several smaller chairs set to face the R. C. writing-table, also a chair on the other side of the writing-table.*

*Chief Constable GRIERSON is sitting at the writing-table. He is an elderly and quite benevolent-looking man of ordinary class. He is examining two towels – a bath towel and a face towel. While he is doing so Chief Detective Inspector SIBLEY enters with a sheet of paper. SIBLEY is a sharper type, a few years younger than GRIERSON and rather more aggressive in his methods. A PC in uniform is at door without belt or helmet.*

SIBLEY: Here's that statement, sir.

GRIERSON: Oh. That one made by Mrs Orlock.

SIBLEY: Yes. The later statement.

GRIERSON: *(Taking and looking at it.)* Yes. It was this point I wanted to check – when she saw Tuck run out of the front door.

SIBLEY: He made for the garage. He had the stuff with him then.

GRIERSON: She didn't see that. That's just your idea.

SIBLEY: I shall prove it. Unless I'm mistaken. And very shortly.

GRIERSON: Have you got 'em here?

SIBLEY: Yes. They've both turned up.

GRIERSON: Tuck and Malone?

SIBLEY: Yes.

GRIERSON: They're nicely up to time.

SIBLEY: No reason why they shouldn't be. We haven't let them know they're under suspicion.

GRIERSON: Think you can get 'em to talk?

SIBLEY: Oh, I think so. Tuck, anyhow.

GRIERSON: H'm. About time too. Three weeks gone by, you know. Pity *you* weren't on it at the start.

SIBLEY: Thank you, sir. It's clearing up nicely now. You see the job *must* have come from inside the house. This statement's correct. Nobody *did* follow down that ladder. And nobody did run down that drive.

GRIERSON: Well, then, the bolted door?

SIBLEY: Malone stayed in the bedroom while the old lady woke up.

GRIERSON: Nerve.

SIBLEY: Yes. But if what Marchant thinks about Malone is right, he doesn't suffer from lack of nerve.

GRIERSON: No. By the way, we'll have Marchant in here for this.

SIBLEY: Yes, sir. *(To CONSTABLE at door.)* Davis! Sergeant Marchant.

DAVIS: Yessir.

*Disappears.*

GRIERSON: What date was it Malone went abroad?

SIBLEY: Fifteenth. The day after the inquest was adjourned. Came back on the twenty-first.

GRIERSON: Too bad, you know. No doubt he got away with the pickin's.

SIBLEY: That's his game, according to Marchant. Look here now. *(Crosses round back of table to GRIERSON, places notes on table, referring to notes.)* Malone goes to Africa, September 1925. That was just after that Brook Street Hotel case. And we never got down to that.

GRIERSON: Doesn't follow. Here's his last trip – about the fifth of February to Monte Carlo. There was nothing at that time.

SIBLEY: There was – a big job out there – at Monte Carlo, soon after he got there.

GRIERSON: There's always big jobs *there*. It's a public hobby.

*As SIBLEY is about to speak.*

I'm not going against you. Just making sure.

*DAVIS opens door as MARCHANT appears.*

Yes, come in, Marchant.

*MARCHANT is quiet, thorough type of man. At the moment his manner is pleased and eager.*

MARCHANT: I was just coming to see you, sir. I've hit on something else.

SIBLEY: About Malone?

MARCHANT: Yes, sir. I knew I'd seen him before somewhere. That's what made me so confident.

GRIERSON: Well – who is he?

MARCHANT: You remember that Leatherhead case – the Honourable Mrs Trelawny's stuff. I was on that.

SIBLEY: Was he there?

MARCHANT: One of the house-party. Not only that. Ten days after it happened he went to Paris.

GRIERSON: How d'you know that?

MARCHANT: Mrs Orlock, sir. You'll find it there. *(Indicates notes.)* Excuse me. Yes. *(Looks over notes on table.)* Here he goes. End of last June – to Paris.

GRIERSON: How does Mrs Orlock know these dates?

SIBLEY: Why, because her husband had to forward things – reports from the stables and so on. There's a book with all the dates in.

GRIERSON: I see. Oh yes; it looks quite promising.

SIBLEY: *(To MARCHANT.)* Well – anything else for me, before I see them?

MARCHANT: No sir. Nothing I haven't given you. *(Looking at notebook.)* His mode of living – extravagance and that, and no occupation.

SIBLEY: Yes, yes –

GRIERSON: But you told me he'd got a private income.

MARCHANT: His father left him twenty thousand pounds.

GRIERSON: That's a thousand a year.

SIBLEY: Yes, and he lives at the rate of ten and earns nothing.

GRIERSON: Well –

MARCHANT: Then the sister. Only had one sister and she died in South Africa nineteen-eighteen.

SIBLEY: Yes. Ethel Vera Malone.

MARCHANT: Correct, sir. This Prudence isn't his sister at all.

SIBLEY: Yes. I've got all that.

GRIERSON: Of course, there again. That's highly suspicious – but not in itself a crime. If you could hang a man for saying a girl's his sister when she isn't – maybe some of *us* wouldn't be where we are.

SIBLEY: *(Slightly impatient.)* Well, are you ready for them, sir?

GRIERSON: D'Arcy Tuck – nothing known.

MARCHANT: No, sir. Looks like his first job. But with *him* of course there's the *motive* – this Hewlett property.

GRIERSON: Quite so, quite so. Yes, all right – go ahead. Send for Bryant.

*He rises and SIBLEY takes his place at the table. GRIERSON goes to a chair apart from the others. MARCHANT to the door, where he speaks to DAVIS and returns. GRIERSON puts the towels away.*

SIBLEY: *(As he takes GRIERSON's place.)* Thank you, sir.

MARCHANT: *(To DAVIS.)* Tell Bryant to come along.

GRIERSON: It looks to me as if you might find this Malone a pretty tough nut to crack.

SIBLEY: Yes, quite possibly. But you wait till you see his pal.

*BRYANT, a Sergeant-writer, in plain clothes, enters with his materials.*

GRIERSON: I shall want you to take this down, Bryant.

BRYANT: *(Quite used to this.)* Yes, sir. *(Sits at other table.)*

SIBLEY: I'll have Malone first. *(To MARCHANT.)*

MARCHANT: Yes, sir *(Cross to door, opens it and tells DAVIS to call Malone.)*

SIBLEY: *(Turning, rather abruptly, to GRIERSON.)* Of course, there's to be no question what we're out for here?

GRIERSON: Certainly not – not if you can land 'em with it.

SIBLEY: If I can bring home the robbery to them, we're going to run them for murder.

GRIERSON: Absolutely.

*FREDDY is shown in. He is serious, but without any apprehension whatever, it appears.*

FREDDY: Good evening, Mr Sibley.

SIBLEY: Good evening. This is Chief Constable Grierson.

FREDDY: How do d'you do?

SIBLEY: And Sergeant Marchant you know. *(Over left shoulder.)*

FREDDY: *(To MARCHANT.)* Yes. Funny thing – when I met you the other day I couldn't place you. You came to the Trelawny's at Leatherhead when there was that burglary there. I was staying there at the time.

MARCHANT: *(Non-committal.)* Oh, yes, sir? *(Exchange looks with GRIERSON and SIBLEY.)*

GRIERSON: Take a chair, Mr Malone. That's a comfortable one.

FREDDY: *(Sitting in armchair.)* Thank you. *(Looks round room with interest.)*

SIBLEY: Well, we're still very busy on this case.

FREDDY: I'm glad of that.

SIBLEY: We're trying to eliminate. We get hold of all those who – possibly – might be guilty; and make quite sure they're not.

FREDDY: I'm glad of that.

SIBLEY: We're trying to eliminate. We got hold of all those who – possibly – might be guilty; and make quite sure they're not.

FREDDY: Oh, I see. Oh, then I'm here to be eliminated.

SIBLEY: *(Without a change of manner.)* We hope so.

FREDDY: *(With a laugh.)* So do I, I'm sure. Really, this is quite an interesting experience.

SIBLEY: This man is here to take notes. Have you any objection?

FREDDY: None whatever.

SIBLEY: Now – about yourself, please, a few details. You're very well off?

FREDDY: Very. I've made a lot of money.

SIBLEY: How?

FREDDY: Stock exchange. Speculating, mostly. I've made a fortune. Well – two – *(To BRYANT.)* Make it two.

SIBLEY: H'm. You travel a lot?

FREDDY: Yes. All over the shop – shooting, you know. I go to the Continent, too. I was there last week – Paris.

SIBLEY: What did you go to Paris for?

FREDDY: *(Hesitating a moment.)* Has that got to be taken down?

*SIBLEY smiles.*

Well, I had a business excuse. I went to see some people who deal in big game trophies – Mornay and Co., Rue Suisse.

SIBLEY: Does that business take you a week to do?

FREDDY: No. But once in Paris – it usually takes me a week.

SIBLEY: Besides, you haven't been big game shooting lately.

FREDDY: No, but I'm going again next month.

SIBLEY: That is, if you're through with this affair.

FREDDY: You mean, if *you* are. You won't want me.

SIBLEY: Oh, we might. *(Short pause.)* How many sisters have you got?

FREDDY: One. Prudence. The one you've met.

SIBLEY: *(A statement, not a question.)* Just the one.

FREDDY: *(After a pause.)* I had another. Ethel. She died in South Africa ten years ago. So I haven't got *her* have I?

*GRIERSON looks at FREDDY, then.*

SIBLEY: *(Quickly.)* Is this one really your sister?

FREDDY: Who – Pru?

SIBLEY: Yes.

FREDDY: Yes, of course – why not? Both my parents were entirely respectable.

SIBLEY: Her birth was never certified.

FREDDY: *(Looking genuinely surprised.)* Wasn't it? That's odd. Still, I'm afraid I can't answer for that. I was at school at the time.

SIBLEY: And she was never mentioned in your father's will.

FREDDY: No. My father died before she was born. He died in nineteen hundred – *(Sees SIBLEY glancing at a note.)* February, wasn't it?

SIBLEY: Well?

FREDDY: Yes – and Prudence was born in June. Still, you can take it from me. Prudence is certainly my sister. I don't know why you should think she wasn't – or what that's got to do with it. However – go on.

SIBLEY: Unfortunate that you should have had workmen's ladders about when there was this valuable jewellery in the house.

FREDDY: There's often valuable jewellery in my house.

SIBLEY: Someone knew the ladder was handy and the right window to put it to. Who would have known that?

FREDDY: Oh, lots of people.

SIBLEY: Right. Now to narrow it down. Who, in addition, could have known which was the jewel-case, and whereabouts it was in the room?

FREDDY: Yes, who?

SIBLEY: Your sister was with Mrs Hewlett while she undressed.

299

FREDDY: My sister was, yes. But – look here, you keep on about my sister – what are you – ? *(Pauses.)*

SIBLEY: Yes?

FREDDY: Are you suggesting that my sister told somebody where this jewel-case was?

SIBLEY: Yes. *(His tone is quiet and conversational.)*

FREDDY: What!

SIBLEY: *(As before.)* Yes. If it points to that.

FREDDY: *(Jumping up.)* Look here -!

SIBLEY: Well?

FREDDY: *(Subsiding.)* Oh, I – suppose I must control myself, but this is ridiculous.

SIBLEY: Did your sister tell *you* where the jewel-case was?

FREDDY: Me? Oh it's me now? Oh, don't be so dammed silly.

SIBLEY: I've told you I must eliminate. Can I eliminate you on the evidence?

FREDDY: What evidence? A man broke in. He burst the window. He cut the telephone wire.

SIBLEY: Couldn't you have done that?

FREDDY: Oh – yes, I suppose so. I don't quite know what with.

SIBLEY: The broken window was a blind.

FREDDY: Oh, was that me, too? I'm an ingenious bloke, aren't I? Then I broke open the jewel-case without disturbing the sleeping beauty?

SIBLEY: Well, somebody did.

FREDDY: Look here. That bedroom door was bolted on the inside. Whoever did it got away down that ladder. Surely to goodness you don't need to be told that.

SIBLEY: Can you produce anyone who saw you come out of your own bedroom when the alarm was given?

FREDDY: No, I was the first out.

SIBLEY: Oh, I understood Mr Tuck was the first out.

FREDDY: Well, he says so – yes. I didn't see him, he didn't see me. But all this is an absolute waste of time. The burglar was seen by my sister.

SIBLEY: I don't believe that.

FREDDY: What?

*SIBLEY shakes his head.*

Oh! Well, I suppose you're entitled to say what you like in here. But you seem to have forgotten, as well as being seen by my sister, the man was heard in the hall by Miss Hewlett.

SIBLEY: I hadn't forgotten. The man was detected by two persons – *your* sister and the fiancée of Mr Tuck.

FREDDY: Exactly.

SIBLEY: Exactly. And this job was done by two men.

FREDDY: Two. *(Suddenly seems amused.)* Excuse my smiling. I don't think I should shine as a burglar, but I should love to see D'Arcy Tuck being one.

SIBLEY: *(Rather more intensely.)* Tell me this, please. Why did you ever make friends with Mrs Hewlett? She's not your class at all.

FREDDY: Her son wanted to marry my sister.

SIBLEY: Did you approve?

FREDDY: No, I did not. *(To BRYANT.)* Underlined, please.

SIBLEY: Mrs Hewlett says you *did* approve.

FREDDY: I temporized, that's all. You know what sisters are. If you say to your sister, 'You're not to marry that man,' what happens? She goes up like a rocket, and next time you see her she's looking at bassinet catalogues.

SIBLEY: *(After a brief pause, with finality.)* Mr Malone, as you may have realized, we know a good deal.

FREDDY: No, I can't say I've realized that at all.

SIBLEY: One of the things we know is that you're not telling the truth.

301

FREDDY: Thank you. I'm almost sorry to say I can't lose my temper with you. It's all too dammed ludicrous for that.

SIBLEY: It may be found that the death of Simon Veal was accidental. I can't hold out any promise, but it's possible. Now you've got an idea of how much we know, don't you think it might be worth your while to make a statement? Think carefully.

FREDDY: I don't need to. Here's my statement. If you think I've got anything whatever to do with this affair, you're wrong. *(Looking at BRYANT.)* That'll do. Put that down.

SIBLEY: *(To MARCHANT.)* Send for Mr Tuck.

MARCHANT: *(To DAVIS.)* Mr Tuck.

*DAVIS exits.*

*SIBLEY again turns to FREDDY – GRIERSON passes note to SIBLEY – SIBLEY grunts satisfaction.*

SIBLEY: I ask you this. Why did you invite Mrs Hewlett and Mr Tuck together to your house?

FREDDY: Knowing Mr Tuck I thought that was the best way to annoy Mrs Hewlett.

SIBLEY: With Mr Tuck's full knowledge and cooperation?

FREDDY: Yes.

*D'ARCY is shown in. His manner is effusive in order to hide any apprehension. The door is closed.*

D'ARCY: Hallo, Inspector – how's everything?

SIBLEY: Mr Tuck. Before we go any further, answer me this question.

D'ARCY: Which one?

SIBLEY: The one I'm going to ask you.

D'ARCY: Oh, that one? Rather. Anything I can do to help.

SIBLEY: With what motive did you arrange to meet Mrs Hewlett at Mr Malone's house?

D'ARCY: He asked me to.

SIBLEY: Why did he?

D'ARCY: Well, you'd better ask him.

SIBLEY: I want to know what reason he gave for asking you.

D'ARCY: I asked him to ask me.

SIBLEY: You've just said he asked *you.*

D'ARCY: Well, he did. I asked him to ask me, so he asked me.

SIBLEY: Why did you ask him to ask you? That's what I want to now.

D'ARCY: Well, say so. It makes it so much easier. *(Pause.)* So that's that.

SIBLEY: Oh, no, it isn't. Answer my question, please.

D'ARCY: Which one?

SIBLEY: Why did you want to be there at the same time as Mrs Hewlett?

D'ARCY: I didn't want to be. He wanted me to be.

SIBLEY: But you distinctly said you requested him to invite you.

D'ARCY: Well, of course. He said, 'I want you to be there,' so I said, 'Then ask me' – so he asked me.

SIBLEY: Mr Tuck – this is Chief Constable Grierson.

GRIERSON: Sit down, Mr Tuck.

*D'ARCY sits.*

SIBLEY: Sergeant Bryant is here to take notes. Have you any objection?

D'ARCY: Have I?

FREDDY: I don't suppose so – why should you have?

D'ARCY: No! – of course not.

SIBLEY: Mr Tuck. You and Mr Malone have been sent for because you're suspected of knowing something about this crime. Now, do you wish to make any statement?

D'ARCY: Yes.

SIBLEY: Ah! Well, think it over. Don't be in a hurry.

D'ARCY: It won't take long. It's only one syllable.

FREDDY: Now, D'Arcy. Don't be vulgar.

D'ARCY: I don't care. I'm going to say it. Rats!

SIBLEY: You'd be well advised to be a *little* less discourteous.

D'ARCY: Very well then – mice!

SIBLEY: I must put some questions to you, that's all.

D'ARCY: I warn you – I may not answer.

SIBLEY: Any refusal to answer may be brought up in court.

*Short pause.*

You don't seem at all surprised at being suspected.

D'ARCY: Don't I? *(Off his guard.)* I thought I did. I meant to be.

SIBLEY: Come, come, Mr Tuck. Everything will be taken into account. Why don't you tell us all you know?

D'ARCY: I can't. It's impossible. You know what I mean? I don't know anything, so it's impossible.

SIBLEY: *(Resignedly.)* All right – if you won't take my advice – *(Consults papers.)*

*A brief menacing pause.*

*D'ARCY takes an obviously careless glance at FREDDY, who remains absolutely stolid.*

Your motive in running round to the garage that night was, I suppose, to see if the burglar was there?

D'ARCY: *(Turning to GRIERSON.)* Naturally, I thought he might be trying to pinch a car.

SIBLEY: I see. So you admit you *did* run round to the garage?

D'ARCY: Yes, I did.

*Pause.*

When?

SIBLEY: Directly the alarm was given – if not before.

D'ARCY: Ah! Yes. No. I went there but when I went there – wasn't –

SIBLEY: Wasn't what?

D'ARCY: Wasn't when you think.

SIBLEY: What?

D'ARCY: Our whens are different. I went there afterwards. With a footman for the police. To get a car with a footman. For the police – I – with a footman went.

SIBLEY: You just said you went because you thought a car might have been stolen.

D'ARCY: *(To GRIERSON, ignoring SIBLEY.)* I did. I *said* to the footman, I said, 'Footman, I shouldn't be surprised if we find a car had been stolen.'

SIBLEY: And he replied what?

D'ARCY: No. He didn't. He didn't hear not even enough to make him say what.

SIBLEY: I can prove you ran downstairs, out of the house and straight into the garage. Now, definitely, did you or did you not?

D'ARCY: I did. *(Pause.)* Unless –

SIBLEY: Unless what?

D'ARCY: Unless you meant when I did.

SIBLEY: In any case why were you down in the hall so soon?

D'ARCY: So soon as what?

SIBLEY: Well, so soon as you *were*?

D'ARCY: But that's ridiculous – I mean, if I were there as soon as I was there – I mean – naturally – there I was.

SIBLEY: *(Tapping the table impatiently.)* Don't trifle with me. Mrs Hewlett came straight downstairs. By the time she got to the hall you'd run down and outside. Explain that.

D'ARCY: She was screaming. Her sounds travel a great deal faster than she does.

SIBLEY: Why did you run downstairs so quickly and out of the house?

D'ARCY: To look.

SIBLEY: To look for what?

D'ARCY: To look to see. To see the man.

SIBLEY: How did you know there was a man?

D'ARCY: I didn't. If I'd known there was a man I shouldn't have had to look to see.

SIBLEY: So this was it – you were asleep. You were awakened by a scream. Immediately you jumped out of bed, ran downstairs, unbolted the front door, and dashed out after some imaginary burglar. Very brave of you, wasn't it!

D'ARCY: I'm a Tuck.

*A pause. D'ARCY thinks he is doing pretty well and takes a self-satisfied glance at FREDDY.*

SIBLEY: *(Deliberately.)* Even before you got downstairs – Miss Joan Hewlett – was already there.

D'ARCY: Yes, and why? Because *she* heard someone in the hall. Which only *proves* – something.

SIBLEY: Why didn't she express surprised at seeing you?

D'ARCY: She did.

SIBLEY: Oh, very well then – why *did* she? *(Pause.)*

D'ARCY: What? I don't know – I mean – why ask about *her*? This had nothing to do with *her*. *(Losing a good deal of his confidence.)*

SIBLEY: How d'you know it hadn't?

D'ARCY: What? Well – good Lord – are you saying it had?

SIBLEY: When she saw you in the hall – did she know *then* you had the jewels with you?

D'ARCY: Of course she didn't.

SIBLEY: Oh, she found that out later?

D'ARCY: She – she didn't know at all. Of course she didn't – I mean, because I hadn't. How dare you? *(Anxiously looking at FREDDY for inspiration.)*

SIBLEY: The jewels were wrapped in Mrs Hewlett's petticoat which has been missing since. They were taken out of the house. You were the first out of the house. You were seen returning from the garage by Mrs Orlock. A few minutes later Mr Malone deliberately sent you back to the garage. We know all that. *(Rising.)* But *now*, what about Miss Joan Hewlett's position? It very much depends on what you say.

D'ARCY: *(Looks at FREDDY.)* I – I absolutely refuse to – to have her lugged into this.

SIBLEY: Well, I make no conditions – but if she can be cleared, so much the better.

D'ARCY: *(Rising.)* Cleared? She? What are you trying to make out about her?

SIBLEY: She was standing there in the hall with the lights up. How could you have passed her and opened the front door, carrying those things in a petticoat, without her seeing?

*As D'ARCY hesitates.*

Come on, show me. Demonstrate to me how you could have. If you want to state her innocence now's your chance.

D'ARCY: Well, if I – if I – if I carried them like this – *(With his hands in front.)*

SIBLEY: I'm her. Standing here. There's the staircase, where you come from – there's the front door. Now, show me.

D'ARCY: Well – these are the stairs – if I had them like this *(Hands behind this back.)* would you notice?

*GRIERSON looks at FREDDY and D'ARCY during this.*

SIBLEY: H'm – possibly not – if you went out like that. Is that how you did carry them?

D'ARCY: No, I didn't. Because you know quite well if I'd had them at all she must have noticed *(D'ARCY regains confidence and sits.)* Pooh! Of course she'd have noticed. A great big bundle like that.

SIBLEY: And how do you *know* it was a big bundle?

D'ARCY: *(Nonplussed; then suddenly inspired.)* Well, it *must* have been a big bundle, you've just said yourself – it was Mrs Hewlett's petticoat.

*SIBLEY shrugs and resumes his seat.*

FREDDY: May I say something?

D'ARCY: Yes.

SIBLEY: Well?

FREDDY: The garage was locked. The key was in a drawer; only the butler, my sister and myself knew which drawer. I took the key out the drawer and handed Mr Tuck the key in front of the whole household.

SIBLEY: *(In contempt.)* Duplicate.

FREDDY: Duplicate be blowed! Where is another key? Who made another?

SIBLEY: *(To FREDDY, waiving him.)* Excuse me, please. *(To D'ARCY.)* Mr Tuck, this involves a man's death. If you want to clear yourself about that man's death, I warn you again, you'd better tell us all you know.

D'ARCY: Why ask me about it? It's *you* who know things. There's only one thing about the whole concern you *don't* know – and that is who did it.

FREDDY: Yes, now look here, Mr Grierson. The time has come to speak out. You're casting around pretty desperately for a – a victim. You've rigged up some plausible sort of a case against us. You could have made out just as likely-sounding a case against any member of the household, from Sir George Chudleigh down to the scullery-maid.

D'ARCY: Yes. What was the scullery-maid doing that night? Do you know? No! Nor do I. So there you are.

FREDDY: *(To D'ARCY.)* Shut up. *(To GRIERSON.)* It's not without its funny side to a man in my position. Only a few weeks ago I was playing bridge with your Chief Commissioner.

D'ARCY: And in my position too. I play bridge with all sorts of people.

FREDDY: *(Rising.)* There were some questions you *had* to ask, I admit. But your zeal has led you into making the most ridiculous accusations. Against me and against my friend, Tuck – a nervous man.

D'ARCY: I'm not. Not very.

FREDDY: Now, look here, You think it over carefully – as you're fond of saying. You're worried; you're groping. You see a line of queer little possibilities leading to us. You follow blindly along that line and you'll hit up against a stone wall.

D'ARCY: And break it. The wall, I mean, not your head.

FREDDY: Don't be rude. No occasion for that. But time's getting on. Three weeks gone by. You're snapping at any clue like a trout at a fly. This woman Orlock let fall some little malicious hint and you grab and swallow it. Three hours before this affair took place I gave that woman the sack. Did you know that?

GRIERSON: *(To MARCHANT.)* Have you any information about that.

MARCHANT: She's still there, sir.

FREDDY: She was under notice at the time for cheek to me. And that's the woman whose word you take against the word of my sister and Miss Hewlett.

D'ARCY: Yes – we don't mind your accusing us – well, not so much.

FREDDY: No, but when you try and worm some false admission out of us by making hasty threatening little innuendoes against those ladies – my God, you must be pretty hard up for a case.

D'ARCY: Yes, I quite agree. *(To BRYANT.)* Put me down as saying that.

FREDDY: You've *no* case. Where's the jewellery? Where's the smallest particle of evidence? I want your help. This dammed thing happened in my house. Instead of which, this is what we get. I can't answer for Tuck, of course –

D'ARCY: I can. Anything you like.

FREDDY: I'm not trying to pull any bluff or any nonsense of that sort. I couldn't do it. It isn't in my nature. But I say this. If after what's happened we stay here at all, we stay here under arrest.

D'ARCY: Or not. Which?

GRIERSON: *(Standing – after a pause.)* I think you'd better bid the gentleman good evening. *(Goes up to the windows, looks out.)*

SIBLEY: *(Very subdued.)* Certainly, sir. Thank you, Mr Malone. You must understand I was merely trying to do my duty.

D'ARCY: That's all right. We don't want to be nasty about it.

FREDDY: Very well then. Good evening. If I can be of any assistance to you, I shall be at my house at Walton Heath. So will Mr Tuck. Won't you?

D'ARCY: Yes, old boy, thanks, for the present. I like the golf.

FREDDY: Good evening. *(Goes to door.)*

D'ARCY: *(Following him. Nods to each in turn – finally to BRYANT.)* Good evening, and thank you very much. *(Makes to tip DAVIS. FREDDY stops him.)*

*They go, closing the door.*

*A brief pause.*

SIBLEY: Well, sir. *(To GRIERSON.)*

*Old GRIERSON, smiling, nods his agreement looking over notes on table.*

GRIERSON: You'll get 'em all right, they did it.

*Big Ben strikes half-hour. MARCHANT crosses to BRYANT, looking over his notes.*


*CURTAIN*


## SCENE 2

*At FREDDY's house next day. The scene is the same as in Act II.*

*The front door bell rings and BUCKLEY enters and crosses up to open it. MRS HEWLETT and OSWALD are the visitors. Their mourning for SIMON is not very conspicuous.*

MRS HEWLETT: Is Mr Malone at home?

BUCKLEY: Yes, Madam.

MRS HEWLETT: He 'phoned and asked us to call here.

*She enters followed by OSWALD.*

BUCKLEY: Yes, madam. If you'll take a seat I'll tell him you've arrived.

*Goes off.*

MRS HEWLETT: *(Seating herself and turning to OSWALD, who is standing about nervously.)* Can't you take a seat?

OSWALD: I don't care to.

MRS HEWLETT: *(Sits on settee.)* Go on. Take it. Standing there looking goosey.

*FREDDY enters.*

FREDDY: Oh! *(In an unfriendly manner.)* Good afternoon.

OSWALD: *(Trying to appear genial.)* Hallo! How are we?

FREDDY: How are we? I think some of us are going to feel a bit off-colour. *(Calls.)* D'Arcy! Come on.

*D'ARCY enters.*

MRS HEWLETT: What, are you here, too?

D'ARCY: Yes, no thanks to you.

FREDDY: *(To D'ARCY.)* Leave it to me. Now then. Are you aware that I've been sent for by Scotland Yard and practically accused of this crime?

D'ARCY: What about me?

FREDDY: Oh yes. Him too. And all owing to you.

MRS HEWLETT: To me?

FREDDY: Yes. You made insinuations to the police. They said so. Just think of it. Think of the insult – to a man like me.

D'ARCY: And another man – like me. Sending me through life with a blotted copy-book.

MRS HEWLETT: *(To FREDDY.)* I never said anything against *you*, Mr Malone.

D'ARCY: *(Crosses to MRS HEWLETT.)* There you are. You admit you *did* against me.

FREDDY: That's how it started. You accused Mr Tuck. They looked at him and said, 'Oh, *he* couldn't have done much without help.' So they picked on me.

OSWALD: *(To MRS HEWLETT.)* I told you you'd gone a bit far, you know.

D'ARCY: There! Did you hear that admission? Straight from this horse's mouth.

MRS HEWLETT: Well, they came along and said, 'Tell us the truth, the 'ole and nothing but.'

FREDDY: The two girls are suspected as well.

OSWALD: What – Pru? *(To MRS HEWLETT.)* Oh, what have you done?

D'ARCY: *(To OSWALD.)* If you'll just listen, you're being told what she's done.

FREDDY: I know this. You're going to withdraw any insinuations against anyone.

MRS HEWLETT: I am certainly not! What I said I stand to and stick by.

OSWALD: No, Mother. *(To D'ARCY.)* I'm sure at heart she regrets and withdraws.

D'ARCY: Never mind about that. Let her say it.

OSWALD: What do you want her to say?

D'ARCY: Say this – 'I don't accuse D'Arcy Tuck.'

FREDDY: Hi! Steady! I'll tell her what to say.

MRS HEWLETT: *(Rises.)* You may tell me, but say it you won't catch me do.

D'ARCY: *(To MRS HEWLETT, taking OSWALD across.)* This is your son. That is a drawing-room. Take him in and hear him out.

MRS HEWLETT: Even so, I'll speak nothing truthless.

*She goes into the drawing-room with OSWALD.*

FREDDY: There you are – I told you. Pru's our strong card. I'll get her here.

D'ARCY: But why all these precautions? We're clear, aren't we?

FREDDY: You never know. There's no harm in having that ace in your shirt! *(Exit.)*

*JOAN comes downstairs.*

JOAN: D'Arcy, does Mrs Veal suspect you?

D'ARCY: I don't know. I don't care. I'm free now. They dismissed me with flying colours.

JOAN: I've been so nervous about you these three weeks. D'you know why I came here today?

D'ARCY: Of course I do. Because you thought I was in danger.

JOAN: Yes, darling. But you are sure you're safe now?

D'ARCY: Of course. I've got them baffled.

JOAN: Well, then, let's go away somewhere and get married. And we'll forget all about it.

D'ARCY: Yes, darling, and only remember other things.

JOAN: But what have you done with what you took? Where is it?

D'ARCY: That's so like a girl. You say 'Never speak of it again' and in the next breath you say 'Tell em the lot'.

JOAN: But I want it to be given back.

D'ARCY: I can't. If I give it back they'll run me in for pinching it.

JOAN: You needn't put on a card 'With compliments from D'Arcy Tuck'.

D'ARCY: Well, do you want it or not?

JOAN: No, I wouldn't touch an ounce of it.

D'ARCY: Then why worry where it is?

JOAN: I believe there's someone else in it you're sharing it with.

D'ARCY: Joan! You'd hate to think a thing like that of me.

JOAN: Yes, I should.

D'ARCY: Then don't.

*FREDDY and PRUDENCE enter.*

FREDDY: *(To PRUDENCE.)* Ozzy's in there with the old woman. Pop in and tick them off.

PRUDENCE: I should think so. The idea of Freddy being accused.

JOAN: And D'Arcy.

D'ARCY: Thank you, darling. Yes, and me.

PRUDENCE: Well, *that*, of course, is a scream.

*She goes into the drawing-room.*

JOAN: Well, *I'm* not going to see the Veals. I'll come back when they've gone.

D'ARCY: Yes, darling. I shall look forward to seeing you again.

*JOAN goes off.*

*OSWALD enters from drawing-room.*

OSWALD: I say – re this. You don't think any worse of me, do you?

FREDDY: I couldn't. D'you know that Pru herself has been accused?

OSWALD: What?

FREDDY: Yes. The police say Pru never saw the man and that Joan never heard anyone in the hall.

OSWALD: Here! What if I can prove there *was* someone in the hall?

D'ARCY: What d'you mean?

OSWALD: It's quite true. There was someone down here.

FREDDY: How d'you know?

OSWALD: I was down here myself.

D'ARCY: What, at the time of the burglary?

OSWALD: Yes. Now tell Pru that.

FREDDY: That doesn't prove Pru saw the burglar. That only confirms Joan's story.

OSWALD: Oh – yes – I didn't think of it that way.

FREDDY: And anyhow, what were *you* doing down in the hall at that hour?

D'ARCY: And why have we only just heard of it?

FREDDY: Were you down here when your uncle fell?

OSWALD: I – I can't say.

D'ARCY: You've got a mouth, haven't you?

OSWALD: Yes – but –

D'ARCY: All right. I don't want to see it. Just use it.

FREDDY: Answer my questions. Were you down here when your uncle fell?

D'ARCY: *(As OSWALD hesitates.)* Were you?

OSWALD: Yes – I – suppose so.

*FREDDY and D'ARCY exchange a look and turn up stage. They hold a brief consultation and return down-stage.*

D'ARCY: Would you care to make a statement?

OSWALD: No, thanks. *(Cross between them.)*

D'ARCY: All right. If you won't take my advice I shall have to ask you some questions, that's all.

FREDDY: Take a chair, Mr Veal. That's a comfortable one.

OSWALD: *(Subsiding with a murmur.)* Thank you.

FREDDY: Now then. Your uncle was wandering about the place at night. So were you. *(To D'ARCY.)* There's something at the back of this.

D'ARCY: Yes. Put it in front.

OSWALD: It was only I – I said I'd see him. *(Facing them.)* Just – to give him something. He wanted something.

D'ARCY: But what could be want at three in the morning?

FREDDY: That *you* could give him, anyway?

OSWALD: I'd rather not say.

D'ARCY: Any refusal to answer may be brought up in court.

OSWALD: *(Uncomfortably.)* Court?

FREDDY: Oh, yes. The inquest's only been adjourned, you know. What was it your uncle wanted?

OSWALD: Well – money. Some money.

FREDDY: Money? What money? What for?

OSWALD: He – was going next morning, you see.

FREDDY: Now, look here, Veal. Your uncle wouldn't go until you or our mother had come across with some money. You had to agree. You were meeting him to pay the money when he met his death.

D'ARCY: Very brave of you, wasn't it?

FREDDY: He's a Veal. This man was blackmailing you, wasn't he?

OSWALD: I absolutely refuse to say another word.

D'ARCY: Right, then think carefully before you speak.

FREDDY: *(Behind OSWALD to D'ARCY.)* D'Arcy, ring up Scotland Yard and ask Chief Inspector Sibley to come down here at once. *(Signs to him to hold down telephone-spring.)*

D'ARCY: *(Crosses to 'phone. )* Right you are. I shall very, very much like to see Old Sibley again.

*FREDDY crosses to OSWALD.*

*(On 'phone, obviously disconnected with exchange.)* Hallo. Give me Scotland Yard. Thanks very much.

FREDDY: *(To OSWALD.)* You'd better speak up. By Gad, if Sibley gets hold of you in that room of his he'll soon have it out of you.

D'ARCY: Hoo! Rather! I'd hate to be a man with a guilty conscience among those devils. *(Speaking into 'phone.)* Hallo! Is that Scotland yard? How are you? Never mind about that. Give me Chief Inspector Sibley.

FREDDY: *(To OSWALD.)* You'd much better throw yourself on our mercy than on his.

D'ARCY: His? He's got none. Sibley's an absolute swine. Hallo, is that you, Sibley, old boy? It's D'Arcy Tuck speaking.

OSWALD: *(Agitated.)* No, I say – hold on a moment.

D'ARCY: *(On 'phone.)* Did you hear that? Hold on a moment.

OSWALD: It's to do with my mother. You wouldn't wish her any harm.

D'ARCY: Who wouldn't? *(On 'phone.)* I'm at Freddy Malone's. If you care to come at once –

FREDDY: Tell him to hold on a minute.

D'ARCY: *(On 'phone.)* No. Hold yourself again.

FREDDY: *(To OSWALD.)* Why should your mother be afraid of a man who's dead? Is it something your mother's done?

OSWALD: What? Well – Oh, give me time to think.

FREDDY: Tell us or the Inspector. Which?

D'ARCY: *(On 'phone.)* Keep on holding yourself but be ready to start.

OSWALD: It's nothing to do with my uncle's death, nothing.

FREDDY: *(To D'ARCY.)* All right. Have him along.

D'ARCY: Start.

OSWALD: No, no.

D'ARCY: Hallo? Too late. He says he's started. *(Puts down receiver.)*

FREDDY: Then now you *are* for it. Speak up. What did Simon Veal know about your mother?

OSWALD: If I tell you, swear you won't tell the police?

FREDDY: I won't do anything that isn't honest.

D'ARCY: But as friends, we shall do our best to save you.

OSWALD: Well, it's only – Simon Veal was my father's brother you see. He knew something about Dad.

D'ARCY: What's the matter? Dad's dead, too, isn't he?

OSWALD: Oh – I – ah –

FREDDY: *(Feet on chair – as OSWALD hesitates.)* Is your father still alive then?

FREDDY: Has your mother been divorced?

*OSWALD looks up at FREDDY.*

We can easily find that out.

OSWALD: No. She hasn't.

*Drawing-room door opens.*

*MRS HEWLETT appears with PRUDENCE.*

D'ARCY: Dad's alive. They've not been divorced. She married old Hewlett –

FREDDY: By Gad! She's a bigamist.

*D'ARCY and FREDDY shake hands.*

MRS HEWLETT: Ozzy! What have you been saying?

*FREDDY and D'ARCY resume their attitude as inquisitors. MRS HEWLETT is shown to a chair.*

D'ARCY: *(Crosses to MRS HEWLETT.)* Now! *Your* statement please.

MRS HEWLETT: It's all a lie. I don't know he's alive. I haven't seen him for years.

D'ARCY: Then he's all the more likely to be alive.

FREDDY: *(Cross to MRS HEWLETT.)* Stop all that flap-doodle. Where's your husband now?

MRS HEWLETT: I don't know where he is or even *if.*

FREDDY: Simon Veal knew.

D'ARCY: And so does Osram.

FREDDY: Yes. And he came to *you* to get money for keeping quiet! Ugly!

D'ARCY: Oh, very ugly.

MRS HEWLETT: I feel queer.

PRUDENCE: I'll get you some water.

MRS HEWLETT: No, thank you. This is no time for water. It's all a lie.

FREDDY: Anyhow, they give you a good stretch for bigamy.

D'ARCY: Mind you, Freddy, we may take a lenient view of this.

FREDDY: I think we ought to tell the police.

MRS HEWLETT: No, no. You wouldn't do a thing like that on me.

FREDDY: *(Pointing to drawing-room.)* Well, go back in there.

*MRS HEWLETT crosses to door.*

I'll think it over. *(To OSWALD.)* You too.

MRS HEWLETT: *(To OSWALD, who has crossed to door R.)* A nice son you've turned out to be.

OSWALD: I couldn't help myself. They dragged it out of me.

MRS HEWLETT: And to think of the trouble I once took to keep you alive.

*She goes indignantly into the drawing-room R. with OSWALD.*

D'ARCY: This is fine. Quick! Where's Joan?

FREDDY: Hold on! I want you.

*Holding D'ARCY's arm.*

*(To PRUDENCE.) You* tell Joan.

PRUDENCE: All right. *(To D'ARCY.)* Seems almost a pity you ever pinched the jewellery at all.

*She goes off.*

FREDDY: Now you can get your own back if you like. But you'd better let me handle it for you. You'll muck it up if I don't.

D'ARCY: Really! Let me tell you, regarding this partnership, I wish to resign.

FREDDY: Don't you worry. I wouldn't have you as a partner at clock-golf. If it hadn't been for me, you'd have been in gaol by this time.

D'ARCY: Gaol! Freddy, I won't boast but it was I who saved the situation at Scotland Yard. All that bluff of yours was no good. Look at the way you sneaked out, as if you'd just escaped – like this.

FREDDY: If they didn't arrest you it was only because you looked such a prize ass.

D'ARCY: Oh no. It was my light and airy manner that did the trick. Did I creep out like you? No, I stayed and jollied them. They liked me very, very much. I said 'Well, boys –'

*Knock at door.*

*D'ARCY goes up to door, opens it and discovers SIBLEY, MARCHANT and another plain-clothes man. D'ARCY immediately turns and goes off. SIBLEY enters. The other two remain behind him in the doorway.*

FREDDY: What do you want here?

SIBLEY: That man, D'Arcy Tuck. I've a warrant for his arrest.

FREDDY: *(Coolly.)* Oh! Going to arrest *him*, are you?

SIBLEY: Yes, only him for the present.

FREDDY: Oh! Got some fresh evidence?

SIBLEY: I *have.*

*Goes towards door.*

FREDDY: Hold on. I've something to tell you.

SIBLEY: *(Pausing.)* Ah! You think *you'd* better speak?

FREDDY: Yes. *Now* I can tell you who stole that jewellery.

SIBLEY: Well, I can caution you –

FREDDY: Caution your grandmother. Mrs Hewlett has come here to see me. She admits the burglar was Simon Veal.

SIBLEY: Indeed!

FREDDY: She saw him take the stuff and throw it out of the window in the petticoat.

SIBLEY: Is she here now?

FREDDY: Yes. In the drawing-room. She'll tell you all about it. Leave her to me. I'll bring her along.

*FREDDY goes out slamming door.*

SIBLEY: *(To MARCHANT.)* He's up to something. Keep an eye outside the house.

MARCHANT: Right, sir.

*Goes out.*

SIBLEY: *(To other man.)* You – drawing-room window. I'll see to Tuck.

*Man goes out at front door. SIBLEY goes out at door down L.*

*D'ARCY reappears at head of stairs. He steals down and seeing the hall empty sneaks through door up R. and comes out again next moment with his hat and overcoat in his hand. As he turns to front door MARCHANT reappears. D'ARCY crosses down L. and SIBLEY reappears from there. D'ARCY starts upstairs again.*

Mr Tuck.

D'ARCY: Oh! Come in.

SIBLEY: I shall want you.

D'ARCY: Well, I'm very, very busy. What?

SIBLEY: Mr Malone has just told me who committed the crime.

D'ARCY: Oh no, he hasn't. I know him too well for that. He wouldn't say anything against anybody unless it was false.

SIBLEY: If *he* knows who did it so do *you*. I've a warrant for your arrest. Now. Your last chance. Who did it?

D'ARCY: Ah, I see. Oh, no, you don't. He thinks I did it, so he's told you *he* did, to save me. And you're trying to make me say *I* did it, in case I think *he* did, to save him. Well, the answer to you is a stuffed tomato.

*He goes out again quickly.*

SIBLEY: *(As he attempts to run after D'ARCY, to MARCHANT.)* All right. I'll get him. You stay outside.

*MARCHANT goes out at front door. SIBLEY goes off after D'ARCY.*

*FREDDY enters from drawing-room with MRS HEWLETT.*

FREDDY: Good! He's not here. Now remember. Your one hope, if we're to keep quiet about that bigamy. You'll say exactly what I told you.

MRS HEWLETT: I must. You've got me.

FREDDY: Yes. And you remember what you might get.

*SIBLEY returns with D'ARCY. MARCHANT and Plain Clothes Policeman in front doorway.*

Oh, here you are, Mr Sibley. *(To MRS HEWLETT.)* Now then, out with it.

MRS HEWLETT: I saw Simon Veal in my bedroom take my jewellery and throw it out of the winder in me petticoat.

D'ARCY: Oh, this is the first I knew of it. Go on!

*FREDDY gives him a look.*

MRS HEWLETT: I got out of bed. He saw me and fell into the conservatory.

D'ARCY: I'm not surprised.

FREDDY: You told me he had the big towel over his head.

MRS HEWLETT: Yes. So as I shouldn't see who he was, I suppose.

D'ARCY: Ah! And he had the little towel no doubt in case she had to be doused.

SIBLEY: Why haven't we heard all this before?

MRS HEWLETT: Because I was terribly afraid you'd say I shoved him off the ladder.

SIBLEY: But you told me you suspected Mr Tuck.

MRS HEWLETT: I never. You made me say that, the way you questioned me.

FREDDY: Hallo! I don't like the sound of that, Mr Sibley.

*JOAN appears on stairs. Comes to foot.*

SIBLEY: *(To FREDDY.)* That's ridiculous. Are you prepared to sign a statement that this story's true?

D'ARCY: Yes. *(To MRS HEWLETT.)* Aren't you?

MRS HEWLETT: Yes.

SIBLEY: I see. Yes, this throws a very different light on it.

D'ARCY: *(To SIBLEY.)* Yes. Well, now we shan't really want you any more.

SIBLEY: *(Turning to D'ARCY.)* Oh, won't you? Then account for this bracelet marked on the clasp Mary Hewlett. And found in your room in town this morning.

JOAN: That's mine.

SIBLEY: Oh! Yours.

JOAN: Yes. I gave it to Mr Tuck to have copied.

FREDDY: That's quite true. I was at Marvin Court when she took her own personal possessions away. That bracelet was among them. She showed it to me.

D'ARCY: And to me. *(To MRS HEWLETT.)* And to you, too, I think?

MRS HEWLETT: Perfectly true. It's hers.

SIBLEY: Oh, confound this.

FREDDY: Why confound it? When at last you've discovered the truth.

SIBLEY: Well, but this case has all gone to blazes.

D'ARCY: Then follow it.

SIBLEY: *(To MARCHANT.)* We can't make this arrest.

JOAN: Well, I shall be obliged if you'll give me back my bracelet.

SIBLEY: Oh, you may take it. *(Hands it to JOAN.)*

JOAN: Thank you. *(Turns to stairs.)*

D'ARCY: That's right, darling. Take it somewhere safe, away from all these people.

*JOAN goes upstairs.*

SIBLEY: Well, I can't proceed any further with this, of course. *(To his men.)* Get along. *(They go. He turns to MRS HEWLETT.)* I'll call on you tomorrow for that statement. You've run a very grave risk, keeping this back about Simon Veal.

*D'ARCY goes up stage to door.*

MRS HEWLETT: Yes, but if you say I did him in, I'll have the law on you.

SIBLEY: Well – good-day.

D'ARCY: Oh, very.

*SIBLEY goes out leaving door open.*

OSWALD: *(Opening drawing-room door.)* Oh, Mother!

*OSWALD enters.*

FREDDY: *(Speaks to D'ARCY.)* Shut the door.

D'ARCY: *(To OSWALD.)* You hear? Shut the door.

OSWALD: Oh, certainly. *(Goes and shuts door.)*

FREDDY: Now. You'll have to come to some arrangement about this property. You'll hear about that.

D'ARCY: You'll hear a lot.

FREDDY: And – I don't want to preach. We can't all be perfect. We each have our little shortcomings.

D'ARCY: Some shorter than others.

FREDDY: But do let this be a lesson to you in future. Be honest. It pays in the end.

D'ARCY: *(To OSWALD.)* Are *you* listening to this?

OSWALD: Yes.

FREDDY: Be honest. It pays in the end. That's all.

D'ARCY: *(To OSWALD.)* That's all. Stop listening.

FREDDY: And now – get out.

D'ARCY: *(To OSWALD.)* Open the door.

*He does so.*

MRS HEWLETT: Well, anyhow I had a run for my money. If I'd known it'd end like this I'd have blown the lot. *(Pushes OSWALD.)* Get out!

*She goes out with OSWALD, bangs the door.*

FREDDY: Be honest. It pays in the end. I suppose, that applies to you too.

D'ARCY: You bet it does. I've done with this sort of thing. Never again me.

FREDDY: Then you won't want to know what I got for the stuff?

D'ARCY: What! Did you sell it?

FREDDY: Of course I sold it.

D'ARCY: Oh! *(Sitting as he speaks.)* Would you care to make a statement?

*CURTAIN*

THE BED BEFORE YESTERDAY

A COMEDY

# Characters

*The Bed Before Yesterday* was first presented by H. M. Tennent Ltd in association with Eddie Kulukundis at the Lyric Theatre, London, on 9 December 1975, with the following cast:

| | |
|---|---|
| VICTOR KEENE | John Moffatt |
| ALMA | Joan Plowright |
| MRS HOLLEY | Gabrielle Daye |
| AUBREY | Frank Grimes |
| ELLA | Helen Mirren |
| LOLLY TUCKER | Patsy Rowlands |
| FELIX | Leonard Fenton |
| FRED CASTLE | Royce Mills |

The Play directed by Lindsay Anderson
Setting by Alan Tagg

The action takes place in Alma's house in Brompton Mews.

# Act One

*ALMA's house in Brompton Mews. Four o'clock on a late spring afternoon in 1930.*

*The front door to the street opens into a very small recess between it and the room, with just space for a hat-and-coat-stand with umbrella-stand and doormat. Beside the front door is an oblong window with permanent lace curtains and practical side curtains. Other doors lead to the kitchen and the dining-room. A short staircase leads to a landing on to which opens three further doors. The furniture, with some period pieces, and decoration of the room are in keeping with the taste of an owner who is precise and houseproud as well as being very well-to-do. The whole action of the play is during spring and summer, and the chintzes, etc., are in keeping with this. The pieces of furniture essential to the action are a sofa, a writing-table with telephone either on the writing-table itself or on a smaller table close by, complete with the fat, one-volume London Directory of the period. There is also a tea-table in two of the scenes, but this can be folded and placed aside during the rest of the action. This tea-table is in evidence at the opening, with two upright chairs placed on either side in readiness. It is set for two with everything ready, including a lidded muffin-dish and a cake-stand. Only the teapot and hot-water jug are missing.*

*VICTOR Keene is standing up-stage of the table. He is in his late fifties, a gentleman fallen on evil days. He has made his well worn suit and shoes look as presentable as possible for the occasion. His manner and attitude are self-conscious and rather intimidated; on his best behaviour and anxious to please. ALMA enters from the kitchen, carrying a little tray on which are the teapot and hot-water jug. She is forty-five to -six. She too has made the best of herself for the occasion, although she is always well-dressed. She is by no means a beauty and very conscious of the fact. She has a most difficult temperament, being liable to fly into uncontrollable fits of anger. At the opening her nervous efforts to face an important, self-imposed situation make her appear possessive and petulant, as she herself explains later on.*

ALMA: *(As she comes to the table and deposits the teapot and jug.)* There we are. Sit down, Mr Keene.

VICTOR: Oh – thank you.

*He waits until she sits, then seats himself. A brief pause. Then ALMA gives a little nervous, meaningless laugh.*

ALMA: *(With this laugh.)* Her-her…

VICTOR: *(Responding in like fashion.)* Her-her…

ALMA: Milk?

VICTOR: Please.

ALMA: Before or after the tea?

VICTOR: Oh – whichever you – do.

ALMA: *(Decisively.)* After. If you put the milk in first you have to guess how much tea. *(Sharply.)* Don't you?

VICTOR: Oh, I see, yes. But surely if you put the tea in first you have to guess how much milk?

ALMA: No, no. tea first lets you judge the right blend from the colour you get from the milk.

VICTOR: *(Giving way.)* Ah. Yes. I – see your point.

ALMA: Sugar?

VICTOR: Please.

ALMA: One lump or two?

VICTOR: Oh whichever – one will do, thank you.

ALMA: I never think one is enough to sweeten the tea.

VICTOR: Oh, very well; if you take two –

ALMA: I don't take any. Well? One or two?

VICTOR: Two, please. I mean one. One. Thank you.

*She hands him his cup.*

Thank you.

ALMA: *(Pouring her own cup.)* It's very kind of you to come and have tea with me.

VICTOR: It's very kind of you to ask me.

ALMA: I got your address from your sister.

VICTOR: Yes. She wrote to me too.

ALMA: *(Sharply again.)* About me? What did she say about me?

VICTOR: Oh, just – she thought I'd like to keep up the acquaintance sort of thing.

ALMA: *(Lifting the muffin-dish lid and offering.)* Have one of these. Do you call them scones or scons?

VICTOR: *(Guardedly.)* Which do you?

ALMA: Scons

VICTOR: *(As he takes one.)* Yes, I knew it was one or the other. Thank you.

ALMA: *(Starting the genuine conversation.)* Mr Keene..?

VICTOR: Yes?

ALMA: When you came to that hotel at Southbourne a fortnight ago..?

VICTOR: Yes?

ALMA: Why did you come?

VICTOR: *(Obviously.)* Why? To visit my sister. Just for a few days. She thought the change might do me good.

ALMA: When she invited you, did she say anything about *my* staying there?

VICTOR: *(Surprised.)* No. Why should she? I mean – I'd never even heard of you.

ALMA: Because she went out of her way to tell me about *you.* Before you arrived, that is.

VICTOR: About me? What about me?

ALMA: About – well – your past history.

VICTOR: Past history? I haven't got one. *(A little chuckle and he takes a bite of his scone.)* Why, what did she tell you?

ALMA: That you were a widower and – not doing anything and… *(She pauses.)*

VICTOR: *(With a little frown.)* And what?

ALMA: Well – living on a very modest income, she said.

331

VICTOR: *(Resentfully.)* That's true enough. But why should my sister want to tell you that?

ALMA: *(With nervous irritation.)* Do please eat your scon over your plate, do you mind.

VICTOR: Oh. *(Taking the plate.)* Sorry.

ALMA: Scons make the worst kind of crumbs because they have butter in them.

VICTOR: *(Examining his scone innocently.)* Oh, have they?

ALMA: I remember when I first saw you in the hotel. You and your sister were having tea with my step-mother in what they call the sun-lounge.

VICTOR: Yes. You came in from giving your little dog a run on the leash.

ALMA: My step-mother's little dog.

VICTOR: *(Resignedly.)* Step-mother's little dog.

ALMA: Personally I dislike little dogs.

VICTOR: So do I. Oh, your step-mother's is quite a nice little dog…

ALMA: It's a horrible little dog.

VICTOR: Oh, is it? I didn't get to know it at all well. *(Amiably.)* But if you dislike it why take it for a run on the leash?

ALMA: Because my step-mother was having one of her bad feet days. *(With nervous irritation.)* Besides, it wasn't a run on the leash. How can anybody give a dog a run on the leash?

VICTOR: Oh, a little dog like that, surely? It could run even on the leash. Sort of patter, patter, patter.

ALMA: You stood up to say how-do-you-do still holding your teacup in your right hand.

VICTOR: *(Innocently.)* Did I? I suppose I was taken aback or something.

ALMA: You got in a terrible muddle putting the teacup down and slopping it and having to wipe your hand before you shook with it.

VICTOR: *(Fighting resentment.)* I don't know why you should remember that.

ALMA: It gave me time to have a good look at you.

VICTOR: *(Jokingly.)* Did you want to?

ALMA: Yes, I was interested after what your sister had told me.

VICTOR: Why, what more had she told you?

ALMA: About your first marriage.

VICTOR: My first? I've only had one.

ALMA: Then it was your first, wasn't it? She said your wife died about ten years ago.

VICTOR: Yes, in nineteen-twenty. Soon after I got back from the war.

ALMA: I know. Your sister told me all about her.

VICTOR: *(Genuinely annoyed.)* She had no right to.

ALMA: You needn't think I asked her. She just told me.

VICTOR: Told you what?

ALMA: That your wife ruined you by her extravagance. And that's why you're so badly off.

VICTOR: I'll have something to say to my sister.

ALMA: Well, it's true, isn't it?

VICTOR: Whether it's true or not …

ALMA: Don't be snappish with me, Mr Keene. I'm only sympathizing.

VICTOR: *(Relenting somewhat.)* Oh. Then it's very kind of you and all that; but I really don't see…

ALMA: That it's my concern?

VICTOR: No. Yes.

ALMA: Don't you want it to be? *(A moment's pause.)* I sympathized because I had much the same experience myself. In a sort of way.

VICTOR: Really? But nobody ruined *you,* surely?

ALMA: Not in that way. *(Pause.)* Aren't you going to drink your tea?

VICTOR: Oh. Yes. It's still quite hot. *(He drinks for the first time.)* I prefer it cool.

ALMA: You must find life very depressing. Because you were so well off at one time, weren't you?

VICTOR: *(With a sudden change of candour.)* Well, since you know so much about me, Mrs Millet, yes, I was. I had quite a good private income but – it all went.

ALMA: Your wife gambled, didn't she?

VICTOR: This is my sister again, I suppose? Well, yes, it's true enough. My wife was a born gambler. It was just part of her nature.

ALMA: *(Sincerely and bitterly.)* Yes, I know what a curse one's nature can be.

VICTOR: *You* do?

ALMA: Never mind about me yet. What happened about your wife?

VICTOR: Well, there she was – at it the whole time. Stock Exchange – horses – she used to take trips to Monte Carlo. It was her whole life. She was Australian, you see.

ALMA: Oh, how sad.

VICTOR: By the time I came back from the war I was pretty well ruined. I'd never done any sort of job and I felt too old to start.

ALMA: *(Pleased.)* Yes. How old *are* you? Never mind, I can guess.

VICTOR: I don't mind your knowing. I'm getting on for sixty.

ALMA: Oh, is that all?

*He does not know quite how to take this. There is a brief pause.*
More tea?

VICTOR: No, thank you.

ALMA: There's some cake if you…

VICTOR: No, thank you. I don't as a rule have any tea at all.

ALMA: Poor Mr Keene. *(Rising.)* Well, let's sit over here. *(She moves to the sofa.)*

VICTOR: *(Rising.)* I'm afraid I mustn't stay too long.

ALMA: *(With sudden vehemence.)* You've only just finished your
tea – not that you've had any. Of course, if you want to
go…

VICTOR: *(Anxiously.)* No, no – if you really wish to talk to
me…

ALMA: *(As before.)* What do you think I asked you here for?
*(Checking herself.)* No, I'm sorry. I mustn't be like that. I
promised myself I wouldn't.

VICTOR: *(Appeasingly.)* Like what?

ALMA: Like I am. Like I've been ever since you came.
Nervous and edgy and abrupt. I did so want to be pleasant.
It's sort of over-anxiety. Do forgive me.

VICTOR: That's all right, Mrs Millet. It's best to be oneself.

ALMA: Not in my case. *(She sits on the sofa.)* Do sit down.

*VICTOR: sits in the armchair. ALMA goes on evenly but always with
impatience just below the surface.*

Yes, I do want to talk to you. About myself. I've led an
unusual sort of life. I had a very peculiar childhood to
begin with. I was born a Bull.

*He looks blankly puzzled. She notices this and takes him up,
impatiently.*

One of the Bull family. Bull's potted meat.

VICTOR: *(To himself.)* Good Lord.

ALMA: My mother died when I was born. They did that
half the time in those days. My father wanted a son. He
detested me for being a girl. Besides, I was hideously ugly.
I always have been.

VICTOR: Oh, come come…

ALMA: Please don't interrupt me all the time. Oh, there I go
again. I'm sorry. But that was your fault.

*VICTOR makes a reassuring gesture.*

I never saw much of my father. He married again. That old
Southbourne hotel one. Poor thing, she's got very old and
silly. I try to be nice to her; not that I'm nice to anybody

335

for long. Then my father died too. I was brought up by an aunt. Very strictly. I was sent to a convent school. They wanted me to become a nun. *(Angrily and scornfully.)* I soon saw to that. Insidious gammon. They were after my money, of course. *(With challenge.)* You're not a Roman Catholic, I hope?

VICTOR: Me? No. I'm just a common-or-garden C. of E. sort of thing.

ALMA: My father left most of his fortune to my step-mother – in trust for me, that is. At the time I only got a hundred thousand pounds.

VICTOR: *(Involuntary.)* Gosh!

ALMA: *(Sharply.)* What?

VICTOR: Nothing – I wasn't interrupting.

ALMA: I was a very innocent young woman. I never thought of getting married.

VICTOR: Why not? I'd have thought – *(Checking himself.)* – no. Please, go on.

ALMA: Then, when I was nineteen, a young man came along – an absolute scoundrel. Oh, of a very good family – heir to a title, and so on. And I married him. But he was as bad as the nuns – he only wanted my money. Oh, I had a shocking experience. Thank goodness it didn't last long. He very soon got drunk and fell out of an aeroplane.

VICTOR: What a happy release. I hope he didn't spend too much of your money before he – fell out.

ALMA: He didn't have long enough. *(With a shrewd look at VICTOR.)* So that's still all right, Mr Keene.

VICTOR: So what did you do then?

ALMA: What could I do? A widow of twenty. My aunt was dead by then, thank goodness. I wasn't going to live with my step-mother. A little of her went a very long way; it still does. So I decided to try again – with George Millet. He was my official guardian. He was twenty-five years older than I was.

VICTOR: Twenty-five? No?

ALMA: *(In a minor flare-up.)* What do you mean 'no'? When I say twenty-five I mean twenty-five.

VICTOR: *(Hastily.)* Yes, yes; I only meant fancy.

ALMA: *(Calming down.)* We lived at Reigate for twenty-odd years. He died six months ago.

VICTOR: Oh, I'm sorry.

ALMA: No, you're not: why should you be? I'm the only person entitled to be sorry and I'm not either.

VICTOR: *(Stung into retaliation.)* Was *he*?

ALMA: *(Unconscious of any sarcasm.)* No; I think he was glad to die. He'd got old and crotchety and he had bad feet.

VICTOR: Oh, these bad feet.

ALMA: *(Sharply.)* Why? Don't tell me *you* have bad feet?

VICTOR: No; I meant your step-mother.

ALMA: Oh, hers are just bunions. George Millet's feet had got past belief. It was all this ridiculous golf. Do you play golf?

VICTOR: Good heavens, no. I can't afford anything like that.

ALMA: So then I sold the Reigate house and came to live here in London, in this mews.

VICTOR: That's a bit of a come-down, isn't it? Oh, it's very nice and all that. But you say you've still got – well, ample means...

ALMA: You seem very concerned about that, Mr Keene.

VICTOR: I? No. I only meant – is this house big enough for you?

ALMA: Quite big enough, thank you. It's got two bedrooms.

VICTOR: So I should hope. You surely must have a spare room for a friend.

ALMA: I have no friends. *(Rising.)* I'm a friendless woman. Or, rather, unfriendly. Aren't I?

*VICTOR rises.*

VICTOR: *(Guardedly murmuring.)* You're being very friendly to me.

ALMA: I've got this dreadful sort of nature – hostile to people – almost, oh, I don't know – rancorous. I've had it ever since I grew up, since my first marriage anyhow. I'm embittered. I look for opposition everywhere; I anticipate it. You needn't think I want to be like it. I struggle against it sometimes. But it's difficult to fight against what's – *(She thumps her chest.)* – there, inside you; part of you.

VICTOR: *(After a thoughtful pause.)* But your husband...? I mean, while he was alive – did he – come in for it?

ALMA: He learnt to turn his back and ignore it.

VICTOR: D'you know what I'd have done? I'd have known you didn't really mean it and tried to make *you* see that too. Sort of laugh it off.

ALMA: *(Thoughtfully.)* No one has ever done that.

VICTOR: Then it's time they did.

ALMA: But I get like it with shopkeepers and servants. People like that can't laugh at me. All the same, I think you've been very clever.

VICTOR: *(With a chuckle.)* First time I've ever been accused of that.

ALMA: I'll try laughing at myself instead of hating myself. Poor Mr Keene, I'm sorry to inflict myself on you like this. I know the impression I've made on you and oh, I wanted so much not to. You think I'm an absolute shrew, don't you?

VICTOR: Indeed I don't.

ALMA: *(Angrily.)* Oh, don't lie to me.

VICTOR: *(Reprovingly.)* Now, now...

*He gives a little laugh. ALMA doesn't join in the laugh but pulls herself together and speaks quietly.*

ALMA: You *must* think I'm a shrew.

VICTOR: No. Well – perhaps I may have, a tiny bit, to begin with. But against that, I think you've got... *(He pauses.)*

ALMA: *(Rather challenging.)* Got what?

VICTOR: *(Very tentatively.)* Well, charm… *(Hastily.)* In a funny sort of way, of course.

ALMA: *(Greatly softening.)* You really mean that?

VICTOR: I do. I daresay it's hard to believe.

ALMA: *(Sharply again.)* Why is it?

VICTOR: No, I shouldn't have said that?

ALMA: Shouldn't have said I had charm?

VICTOR: No; shouldn't have said it's hard to believe.

ALMA: Why not, if you really think so. *(A moment's pause.)* Well? Shall I go on?

VICTOR: Oh, please do.

ALMA: *(Gentle again and appealing.)* Well, what do you suppose I get like, here alone and like I am? I'm lonely. Wretchedly lonely.

*Even the rather stupid VICTOR is wise now to what's up. He decides to play it cautiously.*

VICTOR: No one to visit you? No relations?

ALMA: My only relation is some sort of distant cousin named Lolly Tucker. She's divorced and lives in Ealing and takes lodgers. I'm afraid she's not quite our class.

VICTOR: Oh. Well, what about a companion?

ALMA: *(Suddenly fierce again.) Companion?* You mean a female one? Some vicar's daughter with chronic adenoids?

VICTOR: *(Meekly.)* Couldn't you find one without?

ALMA: No. They all have them. *(Sitting in the armchair.)* In any case, another woman? No, thank you. *(Getting down to it forcibly.)* I want two things, Mr Keene. I want someone to help me overcome this accursed disposition and I want company; agreeable company. A man.

VICTOR: *(Sitting on the sofa.)* What – sort of man?

ALMA: Don't pretend you don't understand.

VICTOR: Mrs Millet, what is this leading up to?

ALMA: And don't pretend either that you didn't come here today hoping that this might happen.

VICTOR: *(In protest.)* Oh, Mrs Millet...

ALMA: Because of my money.

VICTOR: Oh, but I had no idea that you were so prosperous.

ALMA: Your sister knew.

VICTOR: *(More boldly, in self-defence.)* She didn't. She gathered that you were well-off but neither of us had an inkling that you were Bull's potted meat.

ALMA: Oh, I know that my money is the only possible attraction...

VICTOR: No, but...

ALMA: What do you mean 'no'? Of course it is.

VICTOR: *(Appealingly.)* Oh, please – you don't want me to pretend I've fallen in love with you?

ALMA: No. Any more than I have with you. It's simply that you happen to be the right sort of man. A gentleman. And of the right age.

VICTOR: But, Mrs Millet...

ALMA: Alma, my name is. Yours in Victor, isn't it? Very appropriate too.

VICTOR: No, but hold on...

ALMA: *(Incredulously.) Hold on?*

VICTOR: No, but please listen. *(He rises.)* Here I am, living on a piffling little annuity – two hundred and thirty a year – in a miserable basement flat off the Earl's Court Road. No decent clothes, no decent food. Hardly enough for tobacco. None of the old pleasures of life – no clubs, except my membership of the M.C.C.; I've always stuck to that. Then suddenly this incredible thing happens. *You* come along. I'm given the choice between carrying on the way I am – and you.

ALMA: You needn't make it sound like a choice of evils.

VICTOR: No – I expressed myself badly. I only mean – ought one to get married just for the money and nothing else; well, nearly nothing. Would it be ethical?

ALMA: What does that matter?

VICTOR: Oh, so long as you don't think it does. *(He sits on the sofa.)*

ALMA: I want your company; you want a share of my money. What has being ethical got to do with it?

VICTOR: Well, if you put it like that how can I refuse?

ALMA: *(Rising.)* Then don't refuse. *(Softening greatly.)* Oh, please – please, Victor. *(She sits by him on the sofa.)*

VICTOR: After all, I don't suppose it would be so – I mean it might turn out wonderfully. I did mean that about your having charm.

ALMA: *(Eagerly, and growing quite emotional.)* I can stop myself being like I am; morose and lonely and – blank. I can be happy; we both can. I can get rid of my flying-up and be pleasant and gentle. I'll try so hard to be.

VICTOR: Perhaps I may be able to help about that.

ALMA: Oh, you will; I know you will. The money won't be the first thing with you for long.

VICTOR: No, it's beginning not to be already. I'm sorry I said I wanted you only for the money.

ALMA: At least it showed you're honest.

VICTOR: But the way I put it – I made it sound as if you were revolting.

ALMA: *(Almost coyly.)* And I'm not?

VICTOR: Good heavens, no; of course not. Not really.

ALMA: You make me feel happy already. Kiss me, Victor.

VICTOR: What? Oh, yes. I forgot that.

*He kisses her formally and briefly on the cheek. She becomes gay and enthusiastic.*

ALMA: *(Rising.)* We can get married at once. In a registry office. I'm not going to be gawped at coming out of a church. We won't need a honeymoon. We can come straight back here and settle down. Oh, Victor – how soon can you be ready?

VICTOR: I can give up my flat anytime. *(Rising.)* Oh. *(The 'oh' is because he suddenly realizes that there is a snag which he has entirely overlooked.)* Oh, Lord. There's something else. Oh, confound it – I got so carried away.

ALMA: *(Shocked, challengingly.)* Why, what do you mean?

VICTOR: There's someone I'd forgotten about.

ALMA: Another woman?

VICTOR: No, no, Aubrey. Oh, gosh.

ALMA: Aubrey? Who is Aubrey?

VICTOR: My son.

ALMA: Oh, you have a son.

VICTOR: Yes, I'm afraid so. He's dependent on me.

ALMA: Why? He can't still be an infant.

VICTOR: No, he's quite grown-up – twenty-two, in fact. But he's never – how can I put it? – he's never quite developed.

ALMA: A midget.

VICTOR: No, I mean developed mentally.

ALMA: *(Less aggressively.)* Oh, dear – an imbecile.

VICTOR: Yes. *(Hastily correcting himself.)* No, no. No. You couldn't put him away or anything like that. He's just – silly.

ALMA: You mean he can't feed himself or –

VICTOR: *(Cutting in.)* – Oh, yes; he's quite active. In fact he's often a great nuisance.

ALMA: Does he work?

VICTOR: He has worked. In little odd jobs. But never for long.

ALMA: Well, he can find somewhere to live and look after himself, I take it?

VICTOR: He'll have to, won't he? *(Tentatively.)* I mean, he can't very well come along here too.

ALMA: *(Threatening to flare up.)* What?

VICTOR: No, I'm saying he can't. But you see, I'm his father. I feel responsible for him. Besides, I'm very fond of him in a way. Don't worry; I'll do something about him. We can't let anything interfere with our – future

ALMA: *(Very decisively.)* Nothing's going to interfere with mine so you needn't think so.

VICTOR: Quite, quite.

*ALMA pulls herself together with an effort and becomes amiable and practical.*

ALMA: Very well then – do you want to be shown your new home?

VICTOR: Oh, yes, please.

ALMA: *(Pointing.)* Through there is the kitchen and back door.

VICTOR: Oh yes?

ALMA: *(Going up and opening the dining-room door.)* And this – this is my dining-room.

VICTOR: *(Glancing into the room.)* Oh, that's very nice and compact.

*ALMA points upwards at the door nearest up-stage.*

ALMA: That front room up there – that will be your bedroom.

VICTOR: Oh, that's very nice, I'm sure. You mean – all to myself?

ALMA: *(Ignoring this; indicating the middle door.)* In the middle there, that's the bathroom. *(Pointing to the third door.)* And that's *my* bedroom. There's no point in my showing you that.

VICTOR: *(With one of his little chuckles.)* Her-her. Not yet, anyhow.

*A pause. ALMA turns and looks at him, deliberating. He notices this and his jocular manner leaves him immediately. After taking thought ALMA speaks as if to herself.)*

ALMA: I'd better tell you now and get it over and done with.

VICTOR: Oh, please don't say anything you don't want to.

ALMA: *(Half flaring.)* I *never* say what I don't want to.

VICTOR: *(Appeasingly.)* No, no. I think I can guess what you have in mind

ALMA: *(Still angrily.)* What, then?

VICTOR: Well, the – shall I say – bedroom side of it?

343

*VICTOR hesitates.*

ALMA: What *do* I have in mind?

VICTOR: All I mean is – a woman like yourself – a widow and still fairly young – that is, compared with women who are a bit older and past it…

ALMA: *(Impatiently.)* What are you trying to say?

VICTOR: Simply that no doubt one of your reasons for wanting to get married again is that you may still be feeling – how can I put it nicely? – feeling the need of a husband not only in the day time.

*ALMA reacts with a little shudder. He compromises quickly.*

Occasionally, anyhow.

ALMA: And is that what is in your mind, too? As well as the money?

VICTOR: No, no. With me it's entirely the money. I mean it was to begin with.

ALMA: *(Softening again.)* Come and sit here.

*She sits on the sofa and pats the seat beside her. VICTOR obeys.*

I told you about my first marriage, I was nineteen. I went into it without the slightest knowledge of what happened to a girl on her wedding night.

VICTOR: Oh, I say. You mean nobody told you?

ALMA: They didn't tell brides in those days. They observed the Victorian tradition that it wasn't a respectable thing to talk about. Girls had to find out for themselves. *(Bitterly.)* I found out. My husband had no consideration or compassion or restraint.

VICTOR: The rotter.

ALMA: I was forced down and outraged and terribly hurt. Oh I resisted, of course. I had a will of my own already. I scratched his face so badly that he couldn't show it in public for the rest of the honeymoon. But that wasn't for long. He went away almost at once.

VICTOR: *(Guardedly.)* Well, don't be afraid that *I'd* try to do anything – unpopular – no, what's the word? – discourteous.

ALMA: *(Greatly relieved.)* I'm so glad you feel like that, Victor. That was my one and only experience of it; but that was enough.

VICTOR: *(Also relieved, perking up.)* Oh, well; if that's how you feel, that suits me. But how about your husband – I mean the other, golfing one – Millet?

ALMA: He was quite willing not to from the first. With me, anyhow. I know he consoled himself here and there. I didn't mind.

VICTOR: There'll be nothing like that with me. I don't want to have anything more to do with a woman even if she isn't you.

ALMA: You only say that to please me.

VICTOR: No, I don't.

ALMA: Because, judging by George, quite elderly men still hanker for it.

VICTOR: Not in my case.

ALMA: *(Hardening suddenly and rising.)* Because I'm so undesirable?

*VICTOR rises.*

VICTOR: No, no. that isn't the reason at all. It's simply I've – shot my bolt.

ALMA: You needn't be sordid. I can't think how any man could ever want to go through that disgusting rigmarole but apparently they do.

VICTOR: *(Meekly.)* It's his nature. Besides, the world has got to be populated.

ALMA: *(Defiantly.)* Why?

VICTOR: Oh, please; there's nothing to argue about. We're in perfect agreement. You don't want to sleep with me; I don't want to sleep with you.

ALMA: Only because I'm like I am.

VICTOR: You said that before. It isn't true.

ALMA: *(Flying up.)* If you're going to contradict me the whole time we'd better not start at all.

VICTOR: *(Boldly.)* Oh, yes we had. I'm not going to give you up in a hurry.

ALMA: That's for me to say, not you.

VICTOR: *(Holding up a warning forefinger.)* Now, Olga…

ALMA: *(In a horrified tone.)* Olga?

VICTOR: I mean…

ALMA: Al-ma.

VICTOR: Alma, yes, of course. Now, Alma…

*He wags the forefinger at her and laughs a false laugh. After a moment she relapses completely and laughs too. She takes him by the shoulders.*

ALMA: Oh, Victor – I *knew* you were the one I was looking for. *(She releases him and turns towards the staircase.)* Come along: I'll take you and show you your own little bedroom.

VICTOR: Oh, *rather*, yes – thank you.

*ALMA leads the way upstairs. VICTOR follows her, his hands decorously clasped behind his back, as –*

*The CURTAIN falls.*


## SCENE 2

*The same. Four months later; a morning in August.*

*The room is just as it was before. When the Curtain rises, MRS HOLLEY, a daily woman of about fifty, is using a carpet-sweeper and singing as she works. After a moment the doorbell rings, she goes and opens it.*

*AUBREY is at the door. He wears an old suit and no hat. His manner is furtive. AUBREY's silliness takes the form of being offensive with the pleasantest of natures and accepting reproach with a fatuous grin. He enjoys using expressions and words which were in those days considered obscene. Beneath his slovenly appearance he is well-bred and not altogether an unsympathetic character.*

AUBREY: *(Secretively.)* Is she out?

MRS HOLLEY: *(Who dislikes AUBREY.)* Do you mean Mrs
    Keene?

AUBREY: Yes, of course. Is she?

MRS HOLLEY: She's gone shopping.

AUBREY: *(Advancing confidently.)* Oh, good egg. What about the
    old man?

MRS HOLLEY: I beg your pardon?

AUBREY: My father. I suppose he's had to go, too. To carry the
    parcels, poor old sod.

MRS HOLLEY: You'll kindly not use words of that sort to me. If
    you wish to see Mr Keene he's in his bedroom.

AUBREY: What, isn't he up yet?

MRS HOLLEY: Of course he's up. *(Dusting the desk.)* Long ago.
    It's just he likes to sit up there of a morning and smoke his
    pipe.

AUBREY: *(Laughing.)* I get it. Not allowed to smoke it down
    here. *(He sits in the armchair.)*

MRS HOLLEY: *(Aloof.)* That don't concern me and it's not for
    me to say even if it do.

    *VICTOR comes from his room upstairs onto the landing. He is wearing
    a much better tweed suit. He speaks as he opens the door.*

VICTOR: Who's that down there? My God, Aubrey! *(He
    comes downstairs, speaking as he does so.)* That's all right, Mrs
    Holley; thank you.

MRS HOLLEY: I was jest about to go, sir, unless there's
    anything else.

VICTOR: Nothing I know of. Only don't say I said so.

MRS HOLLEY: *(With an amiable smile for VICTOR.)* Not me, sir. I
    know better than that.

    *MRS HOLLEY goes off to the kitchen.*

AUBREY: *(As MRS HOLLEY goes.)* Bye-bye, Pussy.

VICTOR: Will you stop behaving like that?

AUBREY: Like what? *(He rises.)*

VICTOR: And I told you not to come here, didn't I?

AUBREY: Not when she's in, you said.

VICTOR: How were you to know?

AUBREY: Know what?

VICTOR: That she wasn't in, of course.

AUBREY: Well, is she?

VICTOR: No, thank goodness.

AUBREY: Then what are you bellyaching about?

VICTOR: I told you always to find out first.

AUBREY: *(Pitiably.)* But I have found out, haven't I?

*AUBREY's tone softens VICTOR, whose affection for AUBREY is never far from the surface.*

VICTOR: All right, all right, my dear boy. But you know what it is.

AUBREY: What what is?

VICTOR: I'm being careful not to put her out. She's been considerate and cheerful; in fact quite gay at times, especially since her stepmother died. So long as she doesn't see *you* everything's fine. I'm absolutely in clover.

AUBREY: Well, I'm bloody well not. *(He sits.)*

VICTOR: Now steady with that language. And don't be ungrateful, either. I've spent a lot of my own money in helping you along. I got you a decent room to live in. I found you a good job.

AUBREY: I've chucked that.

VICTOR: What? Aubrey, you haven't got the sack again?

AUBREY: No, I tell you; I chucked it. It was a lousy job, Dad – buggering about trying to sell cars.

VICTOR: *(Losing patience.)* My God, Aubrey, I don't know how I stick you. You are the biggest chump I ever... So what are you going to do now? Nothing, as usual/

AUBREY: I *am* doing something.

VICTOR: You are? What?

AUBREY: I'm an extra.

VICTOR: An extra what?

AUBREY: At film studios. It's a damn good job. I get a quid for every day I'm there.

VICTOR: And how often is that?

AUBREY: *(Gloomily.)* Not frightfully often.

*AUBREY's depressed tone softens VICTOR again.*

VICTOR: Oh, my dear boy, I'm sorry I spoke like that. *(He pats his shoulder.)* I know you do your best. I think about you a great deal, you know. Anyhow you've got your room. I've paid your rent on that a month ahead.

AUBREY: I know. I wish you hadn't, Daddy.

VICTOR: *(Heartily.)* No, that's all right. I'm glad to.

AUBREY: No, but I've quit.

VICTOR: *(Reacting again.)* You've what?

AUBREY: *(Rising.)* I've got another room pretty nearly as cheap.

VICTOR: Where?

AUBREY: The room you got was a lousy one anyhow, and the bloke who kept it is a frightful shit.

VICTOR: But he was paid in adv… *(He gives up.)* Oh, well, where are you now?

AUBREY: Just along there. In Eaton Place. *(He jerks his thumb.)*

VICTOR: *(Incredulously.)* Eaton Place?

AUBREY: It's a top room, a sort of attic. I think it's really meant for a skivvy but it's quite all right. It's got a basin and all that.

VICTOR: But Eaton Place? How did you come to go there?

AUBREY: That's really what I came to see you about. A girl found it for me.

VICTOR: *(Alerted.)* A girl? What's all this? Haven't I told you to be careful about women?

AUBREY: You speak for yourself, old feller me lad.

VICTOR: That'll do. Now – what have you been up to?

AUBREY: Nothing. You can see for yourself. She said she wanted to meet you so I brought her along.

VICTOR: What? Where is she?

AUBREY: Outside. She was waiting while I had a look-see. I'll call her in. *(He opens the front door.)*

*VICTOR is anxious but curious.*

VICTOR: Well, we mustn't be too long.

AUBREY: *(Calling.)* Hi – come in – it's okay.

VICTOR: Still I'd better find out about this.

*ELLA comes to the front door.*

AUBREY: *(As ELLA appears and passes him.)* She isn't in. Only the old man.

*ELLA comes down to VICTOR. AUBREY closes the front door. ELLA is an attractive and sexy girl of twenty-one. She is of provincial middle-class but bright and confident. She wears a neat and becoming but inexpensive summer dress and hat. AUBREY announces her from the doorway as she enters.*

Here she is, Papa.

VICTOR: *(Surprised by ELLA's appearance.)* Oh. How-do-you-do? *(He shakes hands with ELLA.)*

ELLA: How do you do, Mr Keene. My name is Ella – Ella Reed.

VICTOR: Well, well. You mean to tell me you're a friend of Aubrey's?

ELLA: *(With little laugh.)* Yes. Why not?

VICTOR: I'm very glad to hear it. Fancy poor old Aubrey getting off with a girl like you.

ELLA: *(Seriously defensive.)* It depends what you mean by getting off.

VICTOR: Oh, no, no, no. I expressed myself badly.

ELLA: We're just friends, that's all. And I'm very glad we are. Aubrey's different from the others.

VICTOR: I can well believe that. But where did you meet each other?

ELLA: At a Lyons tea-shop, actually. It was full-up and we shared a table and got talking.

VICTOR: H'm. That was a bit forward, wasn't it? On somebody's part?

ELLA: Mine. I suppose I'm rather a forward girl. *(She smiles briefly.)*

*VICTOR begins to smile back but checks himself.*

AUBREY: Well, come on, Pop.

VICTOR: What d'you mean, come on?

AUBREY: What you're always telling me – manners. Ask her to sit down.

VICTOR: Yes, but you'd better not be here for too long. Very well; just for a minute… *(He indicates a chair.)*

ELLA: Thank you. *(She seats herself.)*

VICTOR: *(Sitting.)* So you met and talked at Lyons. *(To AUBREY.)* You must have got to know her very quickly.

AUBREY: *(Patting VICTOR on the shoulder.)* I'll bet you would have too. *(He laughs, then sits.)*

VICTOR: What did you talk about?

ELLA: Oh, jobs and things. I'm by way of being an actress; or wanting to be.

VICTOR: Are you, though? Have you been in anything lately?

ELLA: I've never been in anything at all. I get an odd day's crowdwork at Elstree or somewhere.

VICTOR: Ah – on the films – an extra. So that's how Aubrey got on to that.

ELLA: Yes, I gave his name to my agent. But he's only done it about once. Poor Aubrey simply can't manage to get their early enough.

VICTOR: *(Beginning to get definitely hostile.)* If you'll tell me something that poor Aubrey *can* manage…

AUBREY: It isn't me we're talking about. *(He rises.)*

VICTOR: Yes, it is. *(To ELLA.)* He was in a perfectly good job…

AUBREY: It was a lousy job…

VICTOR: *(Still to ELLA.)* You've taken him to a new room too, I hear. In Eaton Place. As if he could afford to live in this part of the world.

ELLA: Well I couldn't either. But I know the man who owns the house.

VICTOR: Oh, so that's it?

ELLA: No, it's not. There's nothing like that about it. *(With a quick smile.)* Not with him, anyhow.

*This brings a sharp glance from VICTOR. ELLA goes on resignedly.*

And I'm being turned out of the flat, in any case.

VICTOR: Oh, and why's that?

ELLA: It's just the old story, Mr Keene.

VICTOR: What old story?

AUBREY: Wake up, Dad. She's broke.

ELLA: *(Reprovingly.)* Aubrey…

AUBREY: Well, he's got to be told sometime. And he's not very quick off the mark.

VICTOR: Ah, now I have it. *(To AUBREY.)* So that's why you brought her here?

AUBREY: Yes.

VICTOR: Have you been taking money off Aubrey?

ELLA: No – well – we sort of help each other out when we can.

VICTOR: *(Rounding on AUBREY.)* That twenty pounds I gave you the other day for a new suit and shoes and things? Where's the new suit? Where is it? That isn't it.

*The front door opens. VICTOR turns with an alarmed exclamation.*

Oh, good Lord. *(He rises.)*

*ALMA enters, carrying a shopping bag of the period. She wears a dress of good quality but of quiet taste and a hat. She shuts the door.*

ALMA: There. I'm back in good time.

VICTOR: Yes, dear; better than I…

ALMA: *(Seeing AUBREY.)* What's he doing here?

VICTOR: He brought this girl.

ALMA: Oh? Who's she?

*ELLA rises. She does not appear in awe of ALMA.*

ELLA: Good morning, Mrs Keene. My name's Ella. I'm a friend of Aubrey's.

*AUBREY moves slowly towards the front door whenever ALMA is not looking.*

ALMA: Really? I'm surprised to hear he's got one.

ELLA: Aubrey wanted me to meet his father. Actually, we were just going.

ALMA: You looked to be sitting pretty squat. *(Controlling herself.)* No. But why did you want to meet my husband?

VICTOR: All right, dear. I'll tell you when they've gone.

ALMA: But I'd like to know now.

VICTOR: Well, you can guess – any friend of Aubrey's. They came to try and get some money.

ALMA: I see. *(To ELLA.)* And what's Aubrey to you, may I ask?

ELLA: *(Bolding.)* Someone to be with, that's all. *(She goes and takes AUBREY's hand.)* I'm fond of Aubrey. I look on him as a sort of pet.

ALMA: Well, that's honest enough, but you must have very unwholesome tastes.

ELLA: I don't think so. Besides, he's such a pleasant change.

ALMA: What from? *(She puts her shopping bag on the table below the sofa.)*

ELLA: Oh, never mind. Come on, Aubrey, we'll go.

VICTOR: No, wait a minute. *(To ELLA.)* I'm afraid this has got to be put a stop to.

ELLA: *(Challenging.)* What has?

VICTOR: I'm sorry, but I don't think you're the right friend for Aubrey.

ELLA: That's exactly what I am. And he for me.

AUBREY: *(Laughing.)* I believe poor old Popsy thinks you're a tart.

VICTOR: Aubrey – will you?

ALMA: *(Genuinely puzzled.)* A tart? What does he mean, a tart?

VICTOR: It's a common term, dear – for prostitute.

ALMA: *(In a shocked tone.)* Victor…

VICTOR: Well, you asked.

ALMA: *(To ELLA.)* And is that what you are?

ELLA: *(Mildly.)* No, I don't think so. No, of course not. I mean, I don't get paid for it, or walk out on the streets or anything like that.

ALMA: Then what *do* you do?

VICTOR: Yes, well, never mind, dear. She told me she was trying to be an actress.

ELLA: That was the idea six months ago when I first came to London.

ALMA: Where from?

ELLA: Gloucestershire. My father's a house agent. My mother died and he married again. To a woman I hate. I had a terrible row with my father and left home. I wanted to go on the London stage because I'm good at acting. I played the lead in all the local amateur shows. *(To ALMA.)* You know – *Paddy-the-next-best-thing. (Dramatically.) All-of-a-sudden-Peggy.*

ALMA: *(Recoiling.)* Good gracious. *(She sits of the sofa.)*

ELLA: But I never realized how hopeless it would be. *(She sits in the armchair.)*

ALMA: And so now you've come here trying to get help?

ELLA: Oh, if only you'd let me tell you all about myself – but I suppose I'd only shock you.

ALMA: You've done that already. Because so far as I can understand you are telling me that you allow men to seduce you.

ELLA: Yes, well…

ALMA: It's a very distasteful subject and one which I know very little about…

AUBREY: *I'll* bet. *(He sits.)*

VICTOR: *(In a savage aside to AUBREY.)* You keep your mouth shut.

ALMA: But is that true?

ELLA: Yes. Well, no. Not seduce me exactly, because…

ALMA: Because what?

ELLA: Well, I don't object, you see. Well, to be perfectly honest with you, I enjoy it like everybody else. So long as it's with somebody I like.

VICTOR: Alma, I don't want you to listen to this.

ALMA: *(Snubbing him flat; with a trace of a flare-up.)* Do be quiet. Go on.

*VICTOR is so squashed by ALMA that he lets this go. ELLA is anxious to be allowed to tell her story.*

ELLA: It all began when I had a terrible disappointment. I got spotted in the film-crowd by a very well-known actor. He sent for me to see him in his dressing-room on the set.

VICTOR: Who was he?

ELLA: I don't know that I ought to tell you.

AUBREY: It was Fred Castle.

ELLA: Aubrey.

VICTOR: *(Impressed.)* Fred Castle, good Lord. *(To ALMA.)* Even you have heard of Fred Castle.

ALMA: *(Indignantly.)* What do you mean, 'even I'? I've seen him several times. George never missed one of the farces he's always doing. He's supposed to be very attractive to women. *(To ELLA.)* So you went to his room, did you? What did he say?

ELLA: *(With a little laugh.)* I remember his first words. I'd better not tell you what *they* were.

ALMA: You'll tell me what I ask you. What did this Castle man say to you?

ELLA: He just sat and pointed at me and said, 'You look to have a very good pair of charlies.'

ALMA: *(Again puzzled.)* Charlies? What did he mean?

AUBREY: Tits.

ALMA: Charlies? Tits? What are you talking about?

VICTOR: Tits, dear; short for teats – or rather the same thing. *(Illustrating with cupped hands.)* You know…

ALMA: Don't be so disgusting, Victor.

VICTOR: *(Roused.)* Don't go on at me – it's not *me. (To ELLA.)* Keep it clean, can't you?

ALMA: *(To VICTOR.)* Don't keep interrupting. *(To ELLA.)* What did you do then? Walked out, I should hope.

ELLA: Walked out? On Fred Castle? Oh, Mrs Keene, how could I? I thought my career was made. Naturally I did what he wanted.

ALMA: But do you mean to say *you* wanted to too?

ELLA: Of course. Well, I mean – Fred Castle – who wouldn't want to? Wouldn't you?

VICTOR: Don't speak to my wife like that. *She,* of all people.

ALMA: That'll do, Victor. *(To ELLA.)* What happened then?

ELLA: He took me out that night to Eaton Place to a house run by a man called Mr Morris.

VICTOR: And what goes on there? *(Quickly and guardedly.)* No, steady – I mean if it's anything too near the knuckle…

ELLA: Oh, it's nothing improper.

AUBREY: *(Confidentially to VICTOR.)* Gambling, Papa.

VICTOR: *(In a sudden shock.)* What?

ELLA: Chemmy and roulette and things.

*VICTOR can only glare.*

Mr Fred Castle doesn't really care for gambling. He's never been there since.

VICTOR: But you have?

ELLA: Mr Morris asked me to come back to entertain his men friends; and he rented me this little flat next door.

ALMA: To entertain the men friends there as well?

ELLA: *(Nearly losing control.) Yes.*

ALMA: And you tell me you enjoy doing that?

ELLA: Well, I can pick the men friends I like, can't I? *(Turning impulsively.)* Come on, Aubrey; it's no good; we'd better go. *(She rises.)*

ALMA: We haven't heard why you came here trying to get money.

ELLA: *(Sitting.)* Well, I owe Mr Morris for the flat. He wants it all by tomorrow morning or he'll turn me out.

ALMA: And how much do you owe him?

ELLA: And I've had to get food and stockings and everything.

ALMA: How much, I asked?

AUBREY: I'll tell you. *(Rising.)* She wants a hundred and seventy quid.

VICTOR: A hundred and seventy – it's past belief.

ALMA: *(Rising.)* I'm afraid you're a very weak and immoral girl.

ELLA: *(Gently.)* I don't think I'm *weak*.

ALMA: *(Beginning to get worked up.)* There's no denying that you're immoral, is there?

ELLA: *(Rising.)* No, not if you're old-fashioned, I suppose.

ALMA: These men you take to your flat – don't they give you money?

ELLA: *(Shrugging.)* They mostly seem to think I do it for pleasure.

ALMA: And that's exactly what you do, or so you say. Why can't you take yourself in hand and resist?

ELLA: Mrs Keene, why should anybody try and resist a thing like that?

ALMA: *(Still angrier.)* But you *can* resist if you put your mind to it. You can fight against anything and overcome it. You can change your whole nature.

VICTOR: By Gad, that's very true, dear.

ALMA: *(At the flying-up stage.)* I didn't ask you to comment.

VICTOR: No, but if anybody's got a right to say that, it's you. You've proved it yourself. You've been wonderful.

ALMA: *(In a complete outburst.)* How dare you talk like that in front of people? My goodness. Victor, it's incredible sometimes how stupid you can be.

AUBREY: *(Delightedly.)* Wow.

ALMA: Take that creature away out of my sight and keep him there. Go on, go away, go out and take him with you. *(She picks up VICTOR's hat and opens the front door.)*

VICTOR: Now steady, Alma...

ALMA: Go on, do what you're told. Go away, both of you. Go on. Go for a walk. And only *you* come back.

VICTOR: I don't want to go for a walk. Now, Alma... *(He attempts his 'laughing at her' stunt, laughing falsely himself and pointing a fore-finger.)*

ALMA: Stop that nonsense and it isn't what *you* want. *(To AUBREY.)* Go on. You too.

VICTOR: *(Looking out of the door.)* I think it's going to rain.

ALMA: Then take your umbrella. *(She throws an umbrella at VICTOR.)*

VICTOR: You'll be sorry for this, you know. Come along, Aubrey.

*VICTOR takes his hat and umbrella and goes out.*

*AUBREY follows VICTOR to the front door.*

AUBREY: *(To ELLA.)* I'll see you later.

ALMA: You will not. I'll see to that.

AUBREY: I wasn't talking to you, Honeybum.

*AUBREY goes out.*

*ALMA closes the door, then goes through a little spasm of remorse, shaking her shoulders as though to shake the anger from her. She speaks as if to herself.*

ALMA: Oh, why do I have to get like that – I haven't been like it for so long. *(To ELLA.)* It's that ghastly Aubrey. Why did he have to bring you here?

ELLA: I'm sorry you dislike Aubrey so much.

ALMA: Dislike him – he makes me positively shudder.

ELLA: *(Sharply.)* You don't think I go to bed with Aubrey, do you?

ALMA: Oh, don't be so revolting and disgusting and shameless.

ELLA: Aubrey's just…

ALMA: *(Cutting in.)* Never mind Aubrey. These other men. Apparently you go with them right and left. And like it.

ELLA: But, Mrs Keene, doesn't everybody like it?

ALMA: *(Emphatically.)* No.

ELLA: But surely they ought to?

ALMA: *(With challenge.)* Ought to?

ELLA: Well, if Nature tells you…

ALMA: Nature can be a savage and brutal thing. Look at tigers.

ELLA: I'm not talking about tigers.

ALMA: I am. And some men too, for that matter.

ELLA: But it isn't only that Nature urges you on to do it. It's so gorgeous when you do do it. I don't see how it can be wrong.

ALMA: I'm not talking about rights and wrongs. It's this finding pleasure in it. *(She sits in the armchair.)*

ELLA: Well, if you don't, Mrs Keene, I'm very sorry for you. And for myself too. Because I've got in this awful mess and I was hoping for sympathy.

ALMA: *(Severely.)* Don't you tell me that I'm unsympathetic.

ELLA: No, but I took it for granted that you still went in for it like everybody else.

ALMA: That'll do, thank you. *(She rises.)*

ELLA: There are heaps of other girls like me, you know.

ALMA: I do not know and don't want to.

ELLA: I think most unmarried girls will soon be doing it as a matter of course, like men do.

ALMA: I keep telling you I am not interested. *(She sits on the sofa.)*

ELLA: *(Sincerely baffled.)* Honestly, you're awfully different from everybody else about it. *(Sitting on the sofa.)* I mean, for instance, look at my grandmother.

ALMA: Why should I look at your grandmother?

ELLA: She had a boy-friend in Bordighera, an Italian boy, a gigolo. She used to spend every winter out there with him in Bordighera. Right up to the time she was seventy.

ALMA: *(Incredulously.)* Seventy?

ELLA: Over seventy.

ALMA: Poor thing. She must have had a particularly nauseating type of aberration.

ELLA: *I* don't think she was a poor thing at all. I think she got the best out of life. I only hope *I* live to be seventy.

*VICTOR enters at the front door. He has regained his self-confidence and his manner is rather bossy. He closes the front door and speaks while hanging up his hat and disposing of his umbrella.*

VICTOR: Aubrey made off somewhere so I've come back.

ALMA: Is it raining?

VICTOR: No, but I'm not going to hang about out there. Besides, I want a word with this girl.

ELLA: *(Hopefully.)* Oh, Mr Keene. Do you? *(She rises.)*

VICTOR: Yes. About Aubrey. I'll find him somewhere to go. In fact, I've had a very good idea about that. But please understand I won't have you going about together.

ELLA: *(With spirit.)* But you don't understand – I'm good for Aubrey. I stop him from doing silly things.

VICTOR: Such as chucking his job and becoming an extra and getting mixed up with a gambling hell.

ELLA: *(Turning to ALMA.)* Oh, Mrs Keene, do please make him understand. I've got to get this money right away.

ALMA: It's no good you're looking at me like that. This is entirely my husband's concern.

VICTOR: *(Decisively.)* Come along, now; I think you'd better go. *(He moves up and opens the front door.)*

*ELLA goes up to the front door.*

ELLA: *(In the doorway.)* Yes, very well. But what a pity. Because I'm sure you're both such kind people really.

*ELLA goes out.*

*VICTOR closes the door and comes down.*

VICTOR: There goes a minx if ever there was one.

ALMA: *(Effusively penitent.)* Oh, Victor, I flew up at you. I'm so sorry. I won't ever do it again.

VICTOR: Oh, well. It may have been my fault.

ALMA: What do you mean 'may have been'? Of course it was your fault.

VICTOR: You can make amends, anyhow. I've got to find Aubrey somewhere else to live.

ALMA: *(Sharply.)* You're not going to bring him near *me*.

VICTOR: No, listen; I've had a brainwave. I had it while I was waiting out there. Mrs Tucker.

ALMA: Mrs Tuck – you mean Lolly?

VICTOR: Yes; that cousin of yours. When she called here that day she said she still had that house at Ealing and took lodgers. She might take Aubrey.

ALMA: Not if she knew him beforehand.

VICTOR: *(Moving to the desk.)* She might. And in a nice healthy domestic atmosphere like that he might reform. He's very weak-minded. Try her, do. *(He picks up the telephone directory.)*

ALMA: It wouldn't be fair on her.

VICTOR: *(Hastily.)* She could find out for herself. Please, Alma. For my sake. You said you were sorry for flying up. Look up her number.

*ALMA accepts the book.*

Oh, thank you, dear.

ALMA: I won't have Aubrey coming in here to meet her.

VICTOR: *(Picking up the shopping bag.)* Well – we'll see. I'll just take this through to the kitchen. I must get him away from that girl. Mustn't I?

ALMA: *(With a deep breath.)* I never knew such a girl existed. And there are numbers of others like her, she says. What are we coming to?

VICTOR: Oh, I dunno. This younger generation – all unsettled and restless.

*ALMA slowly turns the pages of the telephone directory as they speak.*

ALMA: These young women going to bed with men and – whatever the word for it is. What *is* the usual word for it?

VICTOR: What? Oh, I – don't think we want to go into that.

ALMA: *(On a sharper note.)* Why not?

VICTOR: The er – the polite term for it is sexual intercourse.

ALMA: Oh, rubbish. And as if there could be a polite term for that.

*VICTOR escapes with the shopping bag into the kitchen.*

*ALMA flips the pages more quickly to discover 'Tucker' in the directory as –*

*The CURTAIN falls.*

## SCENE 3

*The same. Tea-time the same day.*

*The tea-table is back in the same position as Scene I, with three places laid, and a large tray with teapot, etc.*

*ALMA, dressed as in the previous scene, is seated at the table on one side. LOLLY is seated behind it. A third chair has been occupied and is now back against the wall. The cake-stand remains alongside the table. LOLLY, who is drinking tea, is a plump, jolly, outspoken woman of ALMA's age. She is a good stage lower in the social scale than ALMA, good-looking, well-dressed, and evidently prosperous. Besides the tea-cup, she is holding a little napkin, with which she gives her mouth a quick wipe.*

ALMA: Would you like a piece of seed cake?

LOLLY: No, thank you.

ALMA: You didn't have much tea. I hope you had all you wanted?

LOLLY: Oh, more than enough, thank you. It was Victor who didn't. He was hardly here a minute.

ALMA: *(Taking LOLLY's cup.)* He's looking for this – son of his. *(She collects the tea-things on the tray.)* He's been trying to find him all the afternoon. Not that it matters. I wouldn't let you take him in, even for a night. That was Victor's idea. *(She rises and moves to the kitchen.)*

LOLLY: Yes, well, I'll wait and see him, anyhow; just for Victor's sake.

ALMA: Would you mind opening the door?

LOLLY: Of course, dear. What am I thinking of?

*ALMA exits with the tray.*

ALMA: Thank you.

LOLLY: *(Finding her lipstick and using it with a hand-mirror.)* Anyway, it's nice to see you again and have a bit of a pow-wow. It was sad about your old step-mother popping off like that.

*ALMA enters with a crumb-brush and tray.*

ALMA: Was it?

LOLLY: Oh, well. I daresay it was one of those merciful releases. *(Producing a cigarette-case and lighter.)* D'you smoke?

ALMA: No. I never have. Victor smokes his pipe sometimes. In his own room.

LOLLY: *(Lighting up.)* Ah, a pipe-smoker. Yes, I thought he looked that sort. Tweedy-suited kind of chap. Shall I sit here? *(She indicates the sofa.)*

ALMA: Where you like.

LOLLY: *(Sitting on the sofa.)* He's nice, Alma. You made a good pick.

ALMA: He's been very kind to me, and considerate. *(With deeper feeling.)* He's made me quite a different woman.

*ALMA takes the cloth from the table and folds it during the dialogue. She is in no hurry about it.*

LOLLY: Well, marriage can't have meant much to you before. Oh, not that I can talk. Fifteen years ago it is now since I bade farewell to Archie. Let's see – did you ever know Archie?

ALMA: *(Coldly.)* I saw him once; but I never had anything to do with him.

LOLLY: You must be about the only woman who didn't.

*ALMA puts the folded tea-cloth over her arm and picks up the cake-stand and crumb-brush.*

*(Continuing in a sympathetic manner.)* And your old George Millet – he was another of them, wasn't he?

ALMA: I don't quite know what you mean.

LOLLY: Well – another like Archie.

ALMA: But did you know George?

LOLLY: Yes, of course. Didn't you know I did? *(She quickly adds.)* Oh, I didn't know him as well as he wanted me to. Don't think that.

ALMA: He was never very particular.

*ALMA goes into the kitchen.*

LOLLY: *(Talking on during this.)* Mind you, I'm not saying anything against your old George. He was a dear old boy. I don't blame you for sticking to him despite it all. But I *was* a bit surprised when you told me you'd gone and taken another one on.

*ALMA returns.*

ALMA: I wanted companionship. A man's companionship. I hate women. *(She resets the desk chair.)*

LOLLY: *(Readily.)* Oh, so do I, dear. And this has turned out really well?

ALMA: *(With reserve.)* Perfectly, thank you. George did everything he liked. Victor does everything I like.

LOLLY: Aren't you lucky? Oh, well; it's never too late.

ALMA: *(As if just for something to say.)* I wonder *you* never married again. *(She sits.)*

LOLLY: After what I'd been through with Archie? No, thank you. I've done better than that.

ALMA: How do you mean?

LOLLY: Archie was all right to begin with – as a lover and all. That was his trouble, women. Like it is with all of 'em. Goodness knows he got all he could want from me.

ALMA: *(Fighting shy of the subject.)* You needn't go into any detail.

LOLLY: *(Oblivious.)* Oh, I don't mind your knowing. He was one of those chaps that just have to have variety. Quite soon after we were married, off he went, fornicating all over the shop.

ALMA: Lolly, you're spilling ash on the carpet. *(She rises.)*

LOLLY: Oh, sorry, dear. Even at home he was at it. I had to sack two of the parlour-maids. He even had a crack at the cook.

ALMA: There's an ashtray here somewhere. *(She takes an ashtray from the window table to LOLLY.)* There. *(She sits.)*

LOLLY: Oh, thank you. So after I'd divorced Archie I said to myself, 'Oh, all right, my lad. I'll take a leaf out of your book. I've got this house, plenty of rooms and no one in them. I'll take lodgers – nice, attractive gentlemen, bachelor ones.' *(Laughing.)* And that's what I've been doing ever since. I've got three there now. Life's one long razzle.

*ALMA has listened to this with growing resentment and incredulity. She exclaims almost involuntarily.*

ALMA: You too? You do that?

LOLLY: *(Taken aback.)* Well, of course. Why not?

ALMA: *(Incredulously.)* You keep men in the house and go to bed with them in turns?

LOLLY: Well, you needn't put it quite like that. It makes it sound a bit insincere.

ALMA: *(More and more worked up.)* Insincere? I think it's horrifying.

LOLLY: Oh, come off it, Alma. You ought to be the first to sympathize. Your marriage was much the same as mine – sitting there alone at home listening to the wireless while your husband was off on his own, chasing every woman in sight. Why shouldn't I make up for lost time and enjoy myself?

ALMA: That's what I can't understand – your enjoying it.

LOLLY: *(Catching some of ALMA's vehemence.)* But – God Almighty – haven't you always enjoyed it and don't you still?

ALMA: Very well, I'll tell you. I never let George touch me. He was quite willing not to. As for Victor, I told him from the start – no. And he doesn't mind either.

LOLLY: But why? What put you off it? Were you raped as a kid or something?

ALMA: Yes. On the first night of my first marriage; when I knew nothing about anything.

LOLLY: *(Genuinely enlightened.)* Oh-h, yes. I remember hearing now. Well, of course – if you get a shock like that when you lose your virginity.

ALMA: Didn't you?

LOLLY: Shock? *(Laughing.)* I went into absolute transports. I remember how I made Archie laugh. I will say for him, with all his faults, he was a marvellous hand at it.

ALMA: Transports! It's beyond me. I met another one today who's – like you about it. And she's only a girl.

LOLLY: *(Quietly and kindly.)* Darling, you're the only one I've ever heard of who's like *you* are.

ALMA: I shrink from the very thought of it; from the whole revolting messy awkwardness of what you have to do. I think the whole thing's disgusting and nauseating and that Nature or Providence or whoever is responsible ought to be thoroughly ashamed of themselves. They might at least have thought of something nicer *looking* for it to be done with. I can't think of anything more repulsive than the sight of a man with nothing on. All that hideous bundle.

LOLLY: *(Honestly sympathetic.)* Oh, you poor darling.

ALMA: You needn't pity me. I'm only too glad to have avoided all that side of life.

LOLLY: Life – you don't know what life means. You poor dear, you were scared and horrified at the start and went and cut yourself off from the loveliest thing in the whole of existence.

*LOLLY's kindly manner and words have their effect on ALMA. She softens a little.*

ALMA: I know I'm different but I'd rather you didn't tell me any more.

LOLLY: It's my duty to tell you and your duty to listen. Your duty to yourself. To say nothing of your duty to Victor.

*This really makes ALMA sit up and take thought. There is a note of uncertainty in her reply.*

ALMA: Victor's quite contented. He never thinks of that sort of thing.

LOLLY: Oh, rats. All men do. Especially at his time of life; a man gets his second wind. Oh, dear. I hope he's not doing an Archie on you.

ALMA: A what?

LOLLY: Having a bit of his own on the Q.T.

ALMA: Don't you dare say such a thing about Victor.

LOLLY: No, of course not. Then all I can say is he's being very unselfish.

ALMA: Unselfish? Do you really imagine that?

LOLLY: I don't imagine it; I know it. It means more to a man than it does even to us; though for meself I don't see how that's possible. Oh, Alma dear; if only you'd let yourself find out what it's like to be a woman. To be clasped tight to a man with him absolutely part of you and with that lovely urge growing in you all the time – on and on, more and more, nearer and nearer until ooo – it happens and you hear a glorious burst of bells and you're in Paradise – if ever Paradise could be such Paradise as that.

ALMA: *(After a moment or two; half-heartedly.)* I know most people do find it attractive.

LOLLY: I can't bear to think of you missing it all your life. Try it while you've still got plenty of time. And think what it would mean to Victor.

*Pause.*

*VICTOR enters at the front door.*

VICTOR: No good. Not a sign of him. *(He hangs his hat up and comes down.)*

ALMA: Did you go to his room?

VICTOR: Yes. The front door was open so I went right up there. Nobody about at all.

ALMA: Well, it wouldn't have mattered in any case.

LOLLY: Oh, I'd have liked to have seen the boy.

ALMA: You wouldn't.

LOLLY: *(Preparing to leave.)* I'll be getting along now. *(Rising.)* Thank you for the nice tea, dear.

ALMA: Not at all. *(She picks up the ashtray and takes it to the kitchen door.)*

VICTOR: Must you go so soon?

LOLLY: Yes, I really must. My lodgers will be getting home. Good-bye, Alma.

ALMA: Good-bye. *(Opening the kitchen door.)* And – thank you for coming.

*ALMA exits to the kitchen.*

*VICTOR escorts LOLLY to the front door and lets her out.*

VICTOR: Yes, it's been good to see you again.

LOLLY: Yes, it's nice to do each other a bit of good when we can. Ta-ta.

*LOLLY exits.*

*VICTOR closes the door and comes down.*

*ALMA enters from the kitchen.*

VICTOR: What did she mean by that? I don't want any doing good to.

*From this point ALMA's whole manner shows a marked change. She has come to a decision and is amicable, eager and persuasive; with only an occasional brief moment of impatience and irritation.*

ALMA: Victor…

VICTOR: Yes, dear?

ALMA: I want to speak to you.

VICTOR: *(Apprehensively.)* Oh? Well – yes?

ALMA: I've been meaning to tell you. I saw you in a new light this morning. I was very pleased with you.

VICTOR: *(Puzzled.)* Why? When? What?

ALMA: The way you dealt with that girl. It showed how strong-minded you can be if you choose.

VICTOR: Rather too much so, I'm afraid. Poor little fool. I didn't mean to be too aggressive.

ALMA: But I like you to be aggressive. I want you to be more aggressive.

VICTOR: I've no reason to be, Alma.

ALMA: Yes, you have. Aggressive with me too. Especially with me. I've always been the one to lay down the law. You've been so gentle and – giving-in.

VICTOR: No, no. I've tried to be helpful and – considerate.

ALMA: Yes, and I haven't.

VICTOR: Oh, you have, Alma.

ALMA: I have not. You're my husband. The husband should be the one to dictate.

VICTOR: I've had no reason to…

ALMA: Instead of which I've always been the one to dictate: 'Do this; do that. I don't want you to do this. *(Meaningly.)* I don't think we should do that,'

VICTOR: Well, but we've got along very happily. There's Aubrey, of course; but apart from him – I'm perfectly contented, Alma.

ALMA: I'm sure you're not.

VICTOR: I am.

ALMA: No. In one way – in particular – I know you've been very remiss.

VICTOR: *(Suddenly enlightened.)* Oh, that? Well, dear, that's been up to you. But perhaps now that your step-mother's dead and you've got all that much more, it may seem a trifle squinny.

ALMA: *(Put out of her stride, annoyed.)* What are you talking about?

VICTOR: What *you* are. You mean my allowance.

ALMA: *(Almost flying up with impatience.)* I do not mean your allowance. I give you your whole board and keep and three pounds a week to say nothing of paying the whole of the rates and electricity and telephone…

VICTOR: Yes, all right, all right…

ALMA: And *gas*…

VICTOR: Yes, yes, all right. Now, Alma, don't begin…

*A brief pause. ALMA becomes gentle and almost pleading in her manner.*

ALMA: Victor…

VICTOR: 'Mmm??

ALMA: Victor, I think I've been behindhand in showing you affection.

VICTOR: Oh, nonsense, dear; you've always been very affectionate.

ALMA: I mean affection in its deepest sense.

VICTOR: Your affection has always been as deep as it can go.

ALMA: *(A flash of annoyance.)* Oh, don't be dense. *(Recovering and becoming alluring again.)* Deep. *(She moves close to him.)* Deep. *(Her face close to his.)* It.

VICTOR: *(Staggered.)* It?

ALMA: It.

VICTOR: *(Incredulously.)* Oh, not it?

ALMA: It. What Nature intended for a man and wife. Part of each other. In and in. Up and up. On and on. Nearer and nearer. Bells and Paradise.

VICTOR: Good god. *(He sits on the sofa.)* But, Alma, from the very start you said...

ALMA: *(Sitting beside him.)* I was prejudiced and – ignorant and dreadfully unfair to you. *(She kisses him suddenly.)* Now! I am going upstairs to my bedroom. *(On the move.)* You come, too.

*VICTOR is utterly unprepared for this and very uncertain of his own desires and capabilities.*

VICTOR: *(Rising.)* Now, hold on, Alma.

*She halts and turns.*

This is something that Lolly has been gassing about.

ALMA: She made me realize – and she was quite right to

VICTOR: But I'd put all thoughts of that behind me.

ALMA: So had I. But now – oh, come along, I'm so inquisitive and stimulated.

VICTOR: Yes, but I mean – in the middle of the afternoon and everything...

ALMA: *(Hardening.)* Don't you want to? Aren't you eager to?

VICTOR: Yes, of course, if you are. But it's so unexpected.

ALMA: Doesn't that make it all the better for both of us?

VICTOR: Yes, but it's a thing you have to...

ALMA: *(Still more challenging.)* Have to what?

VICTOR: Well, sort of – have to think yourself into.

ALMA: Why? Because I'm undesirable and off-putting?

VICTOR: No, no, no; of course not; it isn't only that...

ALMA: Then what is it? Have you been doing an Archie on me?

VICTOR: A what?

ALMA: Going with other women behind my back?

VICTOR: Alma – how can you speak like that?

ALMA: Then why aren't you running upstairs after me? *Bounding* upstairs?

VICTOR: I am. Only give us a chance.

ALMA: *(Seizing his lapels and shaking him.)* Then come on, will you?

VICTOR: *(Making the best of it.)* Ra*ther* – you bet I will.

*ALMA changes again to glad excitement. She relaxes his lapels; puts her hands on his shoulders for a moment.*

ALMA: Oh, Victor… *(She goes quickly upstairs.)*

*VICTOR follows slowly. ALMA turns half-way up the stairs.*

Come on, Victor.

*The CURTAIN falls.*

# Act Two

*The same. Shortly after ten that night.*

*The lights are on and the curtain drawn, though it is still dusk outside.*

*VICTOR, in a darker suit and tie, is sitting in an armchair reading the evening paper, and, for the first time in this room, smoking a pipe. There is a small table beside his chair.*

*ALMA, in a stylish semi-evening dress, enters from the dining-room armed with a poured-out drink on a tray. She is in a very amiable mood. VICTOR's attitude at the opening is self-assured, and indeed rather patronizing.*

ALMA: Here, dear.

VICTOR: *(Glancing up.)* Mm?

ALMA: A whisky and water for you. I thought you might like one tonight.

VICTOR: Oh, thanks. Put it down there, will you?

*ALMA puts the tumbler on the little table. She stretches her limbs and then goes and reclines on the sofa. She smiles at her thoughts for a moment or two, then speaks.*

ALMA: Oooo – I feel so radiant, Victor. Wasn't this afternoon wonderful?

VICTOR: *(Looking up from the paper with a short smile.)* I'm very glad you found it so.

ALMA: Well, you did too.

VICTOR: *(With a brief chuckle.)* M-hm.

ALMA: Oh, Victor; it can go on and on now, can't it? There's still a long time for us ahead.

*He is reading again; she speaks rather more pointedly.*

Isn't there?

*VICTOR takes a sip of the drink and replaces the tumbler.*

VICTOR: Yes, dear, but…

ALMA: But what?

VICTOR: It's not a thing you want to have a – well, a set timetable about.

ALMA: *(Ignoring this.)* After all these years, suddenly to discover – and you were so considerate.

VICTOR: Oh. Thank you, dear. *(He gives another brief chuckle.)*

ALMA: I mean it was so thoughtful of you to take so long about it. *(Brief pause; then rhapsodically.)* I got the bells. Did you get the bells?

VICTOR: What bells?

ALMA: When it happens you seem to hear bells.

VICTOR: Do you?

ALMA: Don't *you?*

VICTOR: Well, I dunno – that sounds a bit high-falutin to me.

ALMA: Dear Victor, I know you were thinking only of me. I could tell that from what you said.

VICTOR: *(Apprehensively.)* Why, what did I say?

ALMA: You said, 'Thank God I brought it off.'

*He takes another sip, puts the tumbler back and rises.*

Oh, Victor, isn't it wonderful to know that we possess such a treat?

VICTOR: *(Putting the newspaper on the table.)* My dear Alma, I'm very glad for you; especially now when you're getting on in life. But it's not a thing you want to overdo.

ALMA: I don't see how one could possibly overdo it.

VICTOR: Oh, one can, you know.

ALMA: I can quite understand Lolly going on as she does. That girl this morning too – even at her age.

VICTOR: What I mean is it's apt to take it out of you.

ALMA: Oh, yes; but only for that lovely minute with the bells...

VICTOR: Yes, but quite apart from these bells.

ALMA: *(With a note of anxiety.)* But, Victor; you do love it. Don't say you don't.

VICTOR: I don't. I mean I don't say I don't. I do. Love it I mean.

ALMA: *(Stretching out her arms to him.)* Well, then…

*The front-door bell rings. They are both very surprised.*

Who on earth can that be?

VICTOR: I can't think. Somebody from outside wanting something.

ALMA: Someone come to the wrong house. You'd better see.

VICTOR: *(Going to the front door and calling.)* Who is it? *(He opens the door.)*

*AUBREY appears. He is dressed just as before.*

AUBREY: Oh, hallo, Pop.

ALMA: *(Rising.)* Send him away.

VICTOR: *(To AUBREY.)* What do you want?

ALMA: I won't have him in here.

VICTOR: No, hold on, Alma. I've been trying to find him ever since this morning.

ALMA: It's my house, isn't it?

VICTOR: Yes, but dash it he *is* my son.

ALMA: *(Indignantly.)* Very well, see him. So long as I don't. I'm going to my room.

*ALMA goes upstairs, but remains on the landing, listening. VICTOR admits AUBREY and shuts the front door.*

VICTOR: *(Bluntly.)* Come in, then.

*AUBREY comes down and picks up VICTOR's drink.*

AUBREY: Hallo, what's this?

VICTOR: *(Following him down.)* Leave that alone. That's my drink.

AUBREY: Good for you. I'll bet you don't often get a piss-up.

VICTOR: *(Taking the tumbler from AUBREY and putting it back on the table.)* What have you come for? And at this hour of night.

AUBREY: I had to come. It's about Ella.

VICTOR: That girl? No, thank you. I'm through with her.

AUBREY: It's frightfully urgent. She's had an offer.

VICTOR: Thank goodness for that.

AUBREY: She's in a frightful mess, and wants your advice.

VICTOR: She's had all the advice she'll get from me.

AUBREY: Oh, don't be bloody about it, Dad. She's brought a bloke along.

VICTOR: What? She's not here again, is she?

AUBREY: Yes. Outside.

VICTOR: Send her away.

AUBREY: But this bloke's here, too.

VICTOR: What bloke?

AUBREY: A bloke named Felix. He comes from Morris's place.

VICTOR: *(Indignantly.)* What are you talking about?

AUBREY: He's Morris's stick-man.

VICTOR: Stick-man?

AUBREY: You know, the bloke who rakes in the doings. *(He imitates a croupier.)*

VICTOR: *(Very incensed.)* You mean you've brought some damned hanger-on from that gambling-den to this house.

AUBREY: Ella got him to come along to show she was on the level. *(He turns towards the front door.)* I'll let 'em in.

VICTOR: *(Taking a step to prevent him.)* No. I won't have it.

ALMA: *(From the landing.)* Yes, she can come in.

AUBREY: Oh, good egg! *(He opens the front door and calls.)* Come right in.

*ALMA comes downstairs. VICTOR turns to her, protesting.*

VICTOR: But, Alma…

ALMA: I want to see her again. She interests me more than she did.

*ELLA, entering, hears this last line and responds gladly.*

ELLA: Oh, thank you, Mrs Keene.

*ELLA is followed in by FELIX and AUBREY. FELIX comes right in. ALMA speaks as AUBREY follows.*

ALMA: *(To AUBREY.)* But not you. You can wait outside.

VICTOR: *(To AUBREY.)* You hear that? You wait out there.

AUBREY: No, thanks.

VICTOR: *(Changing to sympathetic persuasion.)* Go on, Aubrey, there's a good chap.

AUBREY: *(Disgustedly.)* Oh, shit.

*AUBREY exits.*

*VICTOR closes the front door.*

ELLA: I'm awfully sorry to trouble you again, Mrs Keene, but something ghastly has cropped up.

ALMA: What is it now?

*ELLA presents FELIX. Her manner towards him is aloof and unfriendly.*

ELLA: I've brought this man…

ALMA: I heard about him, thank you. What's he got to do with it?

*FELIX is about thirty-five. He is dark – he looks as if he were a Cypriot, but if so he has lived in England most of his life, for his English is perfect, in fact profuse, with a common and just very slight accent.*

ELLA: His name's Felix.

FELIX: Pleased to meet you, madam.

ELLA: I don't know whether he's got any other name.

FELIX: *(Jokingly.)* Oh, a large selection.

*ALMA sits on the sofa.*

ELLA: And this is *Mr* Keene. *(She indicates VICTOR.)*

FELIX: Pleased to meet *you*, sir.

VICTOR: *(Glaring at him.)* You won't be for long. You help to run this gambling-den?

FELIX: That is so, yes. I'm what you might call a junior partner. Like I understand you are here.

VICTOR: If you're going to start by being insulting…

ALMA: *(Quietly.)* No, don't be aggressive, Victor.

VICTOR: *(In a hurt tone.)* Oh, it's *don't* be aggressive now.

ALMA: *(Calming him.)* Just until we've heard… *(To ELLA.)* Do you want to sit down, my dear?

ELLA: Oh, thank you. *(She sits beside ALMA.)* Shall I tell you what's happened?

ALMA: I'd like to do some talking first. *(To FELIX.)* You gave this girl a flat next to your building…?

FELIX: Not me. I didn't. That was Mr Morris. It's him that owns the property.

ALMA: But why is she being turned out now without proper notice?

FELIX: There again, that's Mr Morris. But he considers she's had ample time to settle her losses and her back rent and that. He told her so six weeks ago.

VICTOR: *(To ALMA.)* But there's something about an offer, dear, I don't know what it is.

ELLA: I can tell you that. Felix has offered me another flat to go to. *(Angrily, to FELIX.)* Go on – *you* tell them.

FELIX: I haven't offered – not me in person. It's just I have a friend who's willing to give her accommodation.

VICTOR: *(Scornfully.)* A gentleman friend, no doubt?

FELIX: A perfect gentleman. He moves in the highest circles.

ALMA: *(Optimistically.)* Oh, well… *(To ELLA.)* Is he somebody you know and like?

*ELLA shakes her head; ALMA is disappointed.*

Oh.

VICTOR: *(Challenging FELIX.)* What you mean is some man wants to keep her?

ELLA: No, it isn't that. If it was that I might... *(To FELIX as before.)* Tell them.

FELIX: *(To VICTOR.)* It isn't he wants to keep her, sir; not in the sense you mean, speaking no doubt from your own vast experience.

*VICTOR is about to protest violently; FELIX beats him to it and continues.*

More like – maintain her. In a swankey way and at a very high-class address.

ELLA: *(With emphatic scorn.)* Yes, Duke Street, St James's. They want me to become a whore.

VICTOR: *(To FELIX.)* You unutterable swine.

ALMA: No, Victor...

VICTOR: But damn it...

FELIX: *(Politely.)* Again, it is not me, sir. I don't mind what she does. I am the mere mouthpiece for my friend.

ALMA: *(Amicably to FELIX.)* I expect you're really my friend himself.

FELIX: I only wish I was, madam. He's in very much better off circumstances than me. Or Mr Morris, either. No, my friend picked on her principally by reason of her being a girl of class. Oh, looks as well, granted; but class, that's what they go for, my friend's clientele. They're very high-class themselves; guards officers and the like. Two or three MPs in their time off – Conservative ones, needless to say. Men of title even.

VICTOR: Alma, I don't like you listening to this.

ALMA: Why on earth not? It's most interesting. Quite a revelation. *(To FELIX.)* Men of title, you say?

FELIX: *(Warming to it.)* Oh, yes, madam. *(Sitting.)* In that quarter of the West End; all top-notchers.

ALMA: *(Genuinely interested.)* Goodness.

FELIX: *(Encouraged; concentrating on ALMA.)* And then country gentlemen in town for the night and rich American visitors and so on. Oh, it's a very fruitful field.

379

ALMA: I'd no idea of all this. Really, it's quite fascinating.

VICTOR: *(Barely audible in protest.)* Alma…

FELIX: And not only nights, of course. There's a very sizable afternoon clientele.

ALMA: *(For her own benefit.)* Afternoon – Oh, yes – I can quite believe that.

FELIX: Yes, there's quite a number of respectable old middle-aged-customers show their preference for matinee performances.

VICTOR: That's enough. Get out of this house!

ALMA: *(To VICTOR.)* Oh, do stop interfering. This is something I've never heard about and I want to. *(To FELIX.)* And do you mean she'd simply live in a smart flat and sit there waiting to be called on?

*ELLA, who has been sitting bottling up her indignation, now butts in angrily.*

ELLA: *(Rising.)* That's what they like to make out. It doesn't mean that at all. It means walking the streets at night with the police after you, and goggling at every vile man you meet. Doesn't it? *(She prods FELIX.)*

ALMA: Does it? *(To FELIX.)* Would she have to do that?

FELIX: Yes – it would mean she would have to walk around…

ELLA: There – you see?

FELIX: But round there, up and down Jermyn Street, it's a very exclusive beat; so long as she steers clear of the cheaper sister'ood. Some of those foreign ones can be very nasty with their handbags.

VICTOR: Now, that'll do. Alma, I simply won't…

ALMA: Wait a moment, Victor. *(To FELIX.)* Now, you.

FELIX: At your service, madam.

ALMA: Oh, not at mine too, I hope. But tell me this. If she did this, would she still have to pay what she owes at your gambling place.

ELLA: *(Vehemently.)* Yes. That's how they want me to raise the money – this filthy way.

ALMA: *(To ELLA.)* Oh. *(Rising.)* I thought perhaps you *wanted* to do it?

ELLA: Wanted to? Would you want to? Having to give yourself to the first brute of a man who came along.

ALMA: *(Still quite intrigued.)* Oh, but you could always choose only nice-looking ones.

ELLA: That's just what you can't do. *(To FELIX.)* Can you?

FELIX: *(To ALMA.)* No, madam. *(Rising.)* With all his good qualities my friend would hardly stand for that. Outside of her own clientele she'd have to accommodate whatever comes along.

ELLA: *(To ALMA, anxiously.)* There you are! You see? After what you said this morning you must be horrified?

ALMA: Never mind what I said this morning I was hasty and inconsiderate. There is that actual pleasure you spoke of.

ELLA: *(Sitting.)* Well, Mrs Keene, I don't want to be rude, but I just can't make you out.

FELIX: Of course, she'll have to face up to some formidable unpleasantness…

VICTOR: That's enough from you.

*ALMA sits.*

*(Moving to the front door.)* You get out.

FELIX: *(To ELLA.)* Well, there it is – Mr Morris says he's got to have the money tomorrow morning. *(To VICTOR.)* That's OK. I have no desire to outstay my hearty welcome.

VICTOR: *(Opening the front door.)* I ought to inform the police about you. You'll be lucky if I don't.

FELIX: No, sir. I think you will be the lucky one.

*FELIX goes out.*

*VICTOR shuts the door on him quickly and comes down, speaking as he does so.*

VICTOR: God, what skunks there are in the world. *(He quickly finishes his drink, clamps the tumbler on the table and round on ELLA.)* How dare you bring a man like that into my wife's house?

ELLA: I had to bring him; to make you believe the trouble I'm in.

VICTOR: You're in no trouble whatever, or needn't be. You can easily get a respectable job…

ELLA: Well, you've seen for yourself what may happen to me if you don't give me the money.

ALMA: All of these men you've been so friendly with – won't one of them…?

ELLA: *(Cutting in.)* I don't know where they are. Or even who they are.

ALMA: Ask your grandmother – the one that goes to…

ELLA: Bordighera?

ALMA: Bordighera.

ELLA: *(Sarcastically.)* I can't very well do that; she's dead.

ALMA: *(Thoughtfully.)* Oh, yes; I suppose she very likely is.

VICTOR: *(In an aloof, rather sneering tone.)* Why not the fellow who started you off? The man who first *took* you to this ghastly gambling place?

ELLA: *(Startled.)* Who?

VICTOR: Your friend Fred Castle.

ALMA: Of course, Victor, how clever of you.

*The suggestion has flabbergasted ELLA. She does her best to hide this.*

ELLA: Oh, but, no really – I couldn't possibly do that.

ALMA: Of course you can. And taking you to the place wasn't all he did to you, was it?

ELLA: I don't think he liked me much. He never did anything else for me. I think I disappointed him.

ALMA: *(Rising.)* Well, if you won't tell him I'll tell him myself.

ELLA: *(Rising.)* Oh, Mrs Keene, you mustn't.

VICTOR: No, steady, Alma.

ALMA: *(Rounding on VICTOR.)* Why? It was you who suggested him. Where is he acting now?

VICTOR: At the Leicester Theatre, I suppose. He always is.

ALMA: Well, he'll be there now. If we go at once we can catch him.

VICTOR: What? No, Alma, hold on. We can't do this.

ALMA: Well, if she won't go by herself we'll go with her.

*ELLA, who has been taking thought, now chimes in readily.*

ELLA: No, all right; I'll go. After all, he can't kill me.

ALMA: No, you kill him. Be firm with him. You don't know how to treat men. Except, I suppose, in bed.

VICTOR: Alma, Alma…

ALMA: Don't keep on 'Alma, Alma', and wasting time. *(To ELLA.)* Go at once and catch him. You'd better take a taxi. *(To VICTOR.)* Give her the money for the taxi.

*VICTOR resignedly searches in his pocket.*

VICTOR: Probably get there quicker by tube. Still…

ELLA: I'll do my best with Mr Castle but if he won't help me, Mrs Keene, can I come and see you again?

ALMA: *(Sitting on the sofa.)* Not tonight.

VICTOR: No, we've done what we can. You've had your chance. Here's for your taxi. *(He gives her some money.)*

ELLA: *(Quietly.)* Thank you.

*VICTOR opens the front door.*

ALMA: Now go along quickly.

*AUBREY appears in the doorway. ELLA passes him and goes.*

AUBREY: Cuckoo.

VICTOR: You go away too. Go on.

ELLA: *(From outside.)* Come along, Aubrey.

AUBREY: Gosh. D'you mean he's coughed up?

*AUBREY disappears quickly.*

*VICTOR shuts the door.*

ALMA: Bolt the door.

VICTOR: You bet I will. *(He bolts the door.)* I've had enough of that young woman. As for her bringing that swine of a fellow…

ALMA: Yes, but it was interesting to hear about prostitution. What a pity there's such a disagreeable side to it.

VICTOR: *(Sitting beside ALMA.)* Alma – honestly, I don't know what's come over you. It's that Lolly. Ever since she came you've been a different woman.

ALMA: *(At her gentlest.)* Yes, bless her for it. Oh, Victor; I wish I'd known about it all along.

VICTOR: Oh, well, better late than never, or whatever the saying is. *(He pats her hand and turns away. He wants to get off the subject.)* I wonder whether that girl will find a taxi. *(He rises.)*

ALMA: *(Changing to the practical.)* Why? You mean she won't be in time to catch Fred Castle?

VICTOR: *(Unconcernedly.)* Oh, I should think so.

ALMA: He ought to be told to wait and see her. *(She rises.)*

VICTOR: *(Rather more anxiously.)* No, no; he'll still be there.

ALMA: *(Moving to the desk.)* I think I'll just make sure. *(She sits and picks up the directory.)*

VICTOR: *(Alarmed.)* No, Alma; steady. What are you up to? *(As she begins to search the pages.)* No, Alma; think what you're doing. We don't want to get involved in this.

ALMA: *(As she turns the pages.)* Well, it was you who sent her to him.

VICTOR: But there's no need for him to know that. Do be careful, Alma.

ALMA: Leicester Theatre, Stage Door. *(During the next lines she dials, moving her eyes to and from the book.)*

VICTOR: Wait, will you. Listen, Alma. We can't get mixed up –

ALMA: *(Cutting in.)* – Will you stop interfering.

VICTOR: No. You told me to assert myself and I'm damn well going to.

*He tries to get the receiver. She pushes him back. He half stumbles and by the time he has recovered himself she has dialled and is listening.*

It may lead to some hideous row.

ALMA: *(With a violent gesture at him.)* Quiet, will you? *(On the telephone.)* Are you there? ... Yes. I want to speak to Mr Castle, please... Still what? ... On stage? You mean he's still acting?

VICTOR: Thank God for that.

ALMA: *(On the telephone.)* Well, give him a message, please.

VICTOR: No.

ALMA: *(Flapping at VICTOR and gesturing.)* He's to wait there, please, until a young lady gets there to see him... No, I can't remember her name but it's important he should see her because she's in trouble and it's really Mr Castle who's responsible.

VICTOR: *(Horrified.)* Alma. Oh, my God.

ALMA: *(With another quick flap at VICTOR.)* What do you say? ... Never mind all that; just ... Certainly, it's Mrs Keene... Yes; twenty-nine A Brompton Mews, Keene, with an 'e' on the end. Keene ... K – double e – n – e Keene... *(Sharply.)* I beg your pardon?

VICTOR: *(In a last desperate effort.)* Here, give me that. Let me speak to him.

ALMA: *(Not yielding the receiver.)* Are you there?... *(To VICTOR.)* It's no use; He's rung off.

VICTOR: I'm not surprised.

ALMA: He seemed a very ill-mannered man.

VICTOR: Do you realize what you told him to tell Castle? That the girl's in trouble and he's responsible?

ALMA: Well, so he is. *(She rises.)*

VICTOR: But, Alma, that can only mean that he's put her in the family way.

ALMA: Oh, rubbish. And what does it matter, anyhow? The girl will soon tell him if it isn't that.

VICTOR: *(Relieved.)* Oh yes, that's true. But he'll want to know what *you're* up to.

ALMA: She can tell him that too. *(She goes to the window table and pours a drink.)* I'm a friend who's trying to help her.

VICTOR: *(Half-heartedly.)* Well, let's hope so. *(He sits.)*

ALMA: Of course. *(With a benign smile.)* Stupid.

VICTOR: But listen, Alma. This is the end of it about this girl. I'll get Aubrey away from her somehow and then that's done, finish.

ALMA: *(Giving VICTOR the drink.)* I suppose she'll have to go to Duke Street.

VICTOR: She'll get there sooner or later – you said so yourself. *(Accepting the drink.)* Thank you, dear. I'm sorry for her in a way but I'm not going to have you upset. *(Thinking aloud.)* We've had enough for one day.

ALMA: *(Affectionately.)* Dear Victor – you don't call *today* upsetting, do you? *(She sits.)*

VICTOR: *(Responding.)* Oh that. I'm delighted about that. Anything to make you happy. *(In a practical tone, with a glance at his watch.)* Come on, dear; it's time we went to bed.

ALMA: Oh, rather! *(She rises.)*

VICTOR: After all that I'm feeling pretty fagged out. *(He rises.)*

ALMA: Oh, I'm not. I'm feeling quite gay. You go and get into your pyjamas and then come along to my room.

VICTOR: What?

ALMA: Well, what do you suppose?

VICTOR: Oh, but Alma dear, don't...

ALMA: Don't what?

VICTOR: Don't – don't please have any ideas about now – again.

ALMA: *(In a hurt, not angry tone.)* You mean you don't want to?

VICTOR: Tonight? Alma, it isn't possible. I mean a man of my age, it absolutely whacks him. For quite a time.

ALMA: *(Rather mischievously.)* Listen, I had a lovely hot bath this afternoon – you know, afterwards. It made me feel so wonderful, so exhilarated. Why don't you go and have a bath?

VICTOR: *(Firmly.)* I fully intend to have a bath, but not with any idea of exhilaration. I mean to have a good long soak.

ALMA: Well, do. Soak as long as you like and then come and tell me how you feel.

VICTOR: I'm sorry, Alma. Definitely not tonight.

ALMA: Oh, Victor.

*She looks suddenly fiery and he anticipates her volubly.*

VICTOR: It's just that you've had this experience now suddenly late in life or, rather, in middle-age or whatever it is, and you've found it very agreeable and exciting and all that and you want to go right ahead and carry on with it all the time – I believe women can do that much more than men. I don't know. But men can't – at any rate *I* can't. I never could.

ALMA: *(Still fiery.)* After all this time – and I came round to it – chiefly for your sake because of what Lolly said about your being unselfish about it – and now I find how wonderful it is and what I've been missing – *(Pointedly.)* – and *you too...*

VICTOR: *(Aggressively.)* There's no reason to turn it into a sort of smash and grab thing. *(More appealingly.)* It's meant for people who feel deeply for each other at the right time.

ALMA: Right time? When? When next?

VICTOR: Alma, it isn't a thing you can have a regular set schedule for. *(Compromising.)* Well, I don't know – I believe the working classes do sort of earmark Saturday nights...

ALMA: What? Only once a week?

*He shrugs.*

I must be very mistaken in my idea of the working classes.

VICTOR: I mean – people at our time of life. I think once a week is supposed to be – about it.

*ALMA makes no reply. She turns and sits on the sofa with a quick impulsive sitting action. VICTOR deliberates for a moment and decides not to continue the argument.*

Well, I'm going up now. *(He goes to the stairs.)* Are you going to bed, dear?

ALMA: *(Dully.)* Not yet. You go to your bath. I'll do the lights.

VICTOR: Oh, right you are. *(Turning on the stairs.)* Goodnight, dear.

*ALMA does not reply.*

*VICTOR goes upstairs and into his room.*

*ALMA remains on the sofa as though deliberating a desperate problem. Her lips move to her thoughts and she is scarcely heard murmuring the words 'Once a week'. Her body makes a slight swaying movement as she sits. Then comes a sudden sweeping change. She gets as intense a 'flying-up' fit as ever before. She rises, picks up a cushion, flings it to the floor. Then she kicks it, and strides upstairs, as –*

*The CURTAIN falls.*


## SCENE 2

*The same. About 11.30 the next morning.*

*MRS HOLLEY is standing in the middle of the room looking at a shopping bag. She calls up towards ALMA's bedroom.*

MRS HOLLEY: Madam! I'm going… I say I'm going, madam! Huh. None so deaf as them that doesn't want to.

*MRS HOLLEY exits to the kitchen. VICTOR enters from his bedroom, with binoculars. He calls to ALMA's closed door.*

VICTOR: Well, I'll be off to Lord's, dear.

*MRS HOLLEY enters.*

Good morning, Mrs Holley. *(He comes downstairs.)*

MRS HOLLEY: Good morning, Mr Keene.

VICTOR: Why, what's up, Mrs Holley? Why have you got your hat on?

MRS HOLLEY: I'm off.

VICTOR: Anything wrong?

MRS HOLLEY: Yes, sir, not that there's often anything right. But this morning…

VICTOR: Why, what's happened?

MRS HOLLEY: Madam comes in here with her shopping; starts in on me – why hasn't this bin been done, why hasn't that. Go on, then, she says, take this stuff into the kitchen, talking to me as if I was some sort of native.

VICTOR: Yes, well, listen, Mrs Holley. Don't take it to heart. Between you and me, she's rather upset about something that went wrong.

MRS HOLLEY: What went wrong, sir?

VICTOR: I've no idea.

MRS HOLLEY: I've done nothing to upset her.

VICTOR: No, no, she was like it before you got here. Now, please, Mrs Holley, do all you can to make her, you know, like she generally is.

MRS HOLLEY: Like she generally is who to?

VICTOR: Please, Mrs Holley, for me. *(He hugs her.)*

MRS HOLLEY: Just for you, sir.

VICTOR: Tha-at's better.

MRS HOLLEY: Thank you, sir.

*MRS HOLLEY exits to the kitchen with the basket. ALMA enters from her bedroom with a travel brochure.*

ALMA: What were you saying to Mrs Holley?

VICTOR: Oh, nothing, dear. She was just messing about in here. I'm going to Lord's now. Is that all right?

ALMA: *(Coming downstairs.)* Why shouldn't it be all right?

VICTOR: Yes, well, have a nice day, dear. *(Pausing as he goes up.)* Alma…

ALMA: Yes, what?

VICTOR: Alma, is anything the matter?

ALMA: The matter? What do you mean?

VICTOR: Only you seem rather, well, distant to me this morning.

ALMA: Do I?

VICTOR: Mrs Holley seemed a bit put out. Did you have a row with her?

ALMA: One doesn't have rows with servants. I had occasion to speak to her.

VICTOR: When I came down she was leaving.

ALMA: If she wants to leave she can. *(Calling into the kitchen.)* Mrs Holley…

MRS HOLLEY: *(Off.)* Yes, madam.

ALMA: You can go if you wish.

MRS HOLLEY: Oh, thank you, madam.

VICTOR: Just for the day that is.

ALMA: Well, of course for the day. What do you suppose?

*MRS HOLLEY enters and moves towards the front door.*

MRS HOLLEY: Good day, madam, Good day, sir.

*The front doorbell rings. MRS HOLLEY opens the door.*

*ELLA is standing there.*

ELLA: Is Mrs Keene in?

MRS HOLLEY: She is if you want her.

*MRS HOLLEY exits.*

ELLA: Thank you. Oh, Mrs Keene.

ALMA: Yes. Come in. Shut the door, Victor.

ELLA: I hope you don't mind my coming here again.

ALMA: No, I want to hear what happened with that Castle man. *(She sits.)*

VICTOR: Did you see him?

ELLA: Yes, of course.

VICTOR: What did he say about my wife?

ELLA: About who?

ELLA: About my wife. What did he say?

ELLA: Nothing. Why should he? He doesn't know you, does he?

ALMA: Never mind about me. What did he say about you?

ELLA: Oh, need you ask. *(She sits.)* He said what I knew he would. He said I was a fool to get mixed up with Morris and it was nothing more to do with him.

ALMA: So what are you going to do now?

ELLA: What can I do?

VICTOR: I told you that yesterday. Go and get yourself a respectable job.

ELLA: Oh, Mrs Keene, please make him understand. I've got to get this money straight away.

VICTOR: No you haven't. Just clear out and leave. Morris can't do a thing.

ELLA: Oh, very well then, you've got to be told the whole truth.

VICTOR: I've been told all I want to hear.

ALMA: No you haven't.

VICTOR: What? Why not?

ALMA: Because I haven't. Go on.

*A car is heard to drive up outside and sound its horn.*

ELLA: You're not going to like this.

VICTOR: Oh, that'll be a nice change.

ALMA: *(Interrupting.)* Wait a moment. What's that car doing there?

VICTOR: Car?

ALMA: *(Pointing at the window.)* There. Outside.

VICTOR: It can't be coming here.

ALMA: Then why has it stopped outside my house?

VICTOR: Half a tick – I'll see. *(He steps to the window and lifts a corner of the lace curtain. He looks out then reacts violently.)*

Good God; it's Fred Castle.

ELLA: *(In sudden panic.)* Oh, no. *(She rises.)*

ALMA: *(In a satisfied tone.)* Then he did get my message.

ELLA: Your message?

ALMA: *(Rising.)* About you. Last night. I telephoned him.

ELLA: But I didn't see him. I lied to you. Oh, don't let him know I'm here.

*The doorbell rings.*

I'll tell you everything after he's gone. I was just going to. Oh please don't tell him. I'll wait in here.

*ELLA scoots into the dining-room. The dining-room door remains a crack open.*

VICTOR: *(In a dither.)* Oh, good Lord, Alma…

ALMA: *(Calmly.)* Let him in, can't you?

*VICTOR opens the door, revealing FRED CASTLE. He is about forty – very trim and well-turned-out. He is autocratic, completely the boss and not to be argued with; but with a sense of humour and a candour which are entirely sympathetic. He is at first in a very challenging mood.*

FRED: Is there a Mrs Keene living here?

VICTOR: Yes. I'm her husband.

FRED: *Are* you though?

VICTOR: Please come in.

FRED: You bet I'll come in.

*FRED walks in. VICTOR closes the door.*

ALMA: I am Mrs Keene.

FRED: Really. My name is Fred Castle.

VICTOR: *(Gushing.)* Yes, yes. You need no introduction.

FRED: *(To ALMA.)* Was it you sent me that telephone message last night?

ALMA: Certainly it was. Why?

*FRED looks slightly puzzled but is still on the offensive. He turns and looks at VICTOR.*

FRED: That's an M.C.C. tie you've got there.

VICTOR: That's right, yes. I'm a member.

FRED: Oh. I didn't know they admitted blackmailers.

VICTOR: *(More alarmed than affronted.)* What? Really, Mr Castle – blackmail – that's a very ugly word.

FRED: Ah. I see you know the right dialogue, too. Yes, it *is* an ugly word. *(Looking at ALMA.)* And it applies to some very ugly people.

VICTOR: My wife didn't mean what she said on the 'phone.

ALMA: Victor, how dare you say that? Of course I meant it.

VICTOR: Oh, do shut up.

ALMA: *(Angrily.)* What?

VICTOR: *(To FRED.)* I heard what she said about your getting a girl into trouble. Of course to you that can only mean one thing.

FRED: Oh, thank yer.

VICTOR: She didn't mean it that way at all.

FRED: Then why didn't you stop her saying it?

VICTOR: *(With desperation.)* Have you ever tried to stop a telephoning woman?

ALMA: *(Sitting on the sofa.)* I'll tell you what I meant, Mr Castle. You took a girl to a gambling place kept by a man named Morris.

FRED: Did I? When? And why shouldn't I, I'd like to know?

ALMA: Did you or did you not?

FRED: Don't you question me. I've come to do that to you. You said this girl was coming to see me last night.

VICTOR: Yes, but now she says she didn't.

FRED: I know she didn't – why not?

VICTOR: There's something very fishy about this.

FRED: *(Indignant.)* I'll say there is. Why d'you think I've come here?

VICTOR: *(Passing FRED to get to the dining-room door.)* Excuse me.

FRED: *Excuse* you – that's a good one. Come on, what *is* this little game?

VICTOR: *(Opening the dining-room door.)* Come out here.

*ELLA comes in.*

*ELLA and FRED face each other in silence for a moment; FRED with a frown as if searching his memory.*

ELLA: I don't suppose you remember me?

FRED: Eh? Oh, yes. I do. It wasn't so long ago.

ALMA: You saw her in a film studio and told her she had a nice pair of charlies.

VICTOR: *(Alarmed.)* No, Alma – really.

ALMA: Well, that's what began it; according to her.

FRED: Yes, I daresay I did. And I don't think I was far wrong.

ALMA: Then you took her to this Morris's and then took her home and had social intercourse.

FRED: *(With a glance at the despairing VICTOR.)* I'm glad I was so refined about it. *(Indignantly again.)* And what the devil has that got to do with you? Are you her parents or something?

ELLA: No, they're only trying to be kind. Only I'm desperately wanting some money and they thought I'd better ask you first. Only I didn't dare.

FRED: No, but it seems you got around telling people about me.

ELLA: No, only them. It's not a thing I boast about. Because I'm afraid I must have been rather a flop.

FRED: *(More amicably.)* You needn't think that. I like to mix it, you know. I don't go in for permanent attachments.

ALMA: That's true of all men who have made reputations as great lovers.

VICTOR: Alma, be careful what you're saying. You can't talk to Mr Castle like that.

ALMA: But it's a compliment. Everyone knows that Mr Castle is very attractive to women. Aren't you?

FRED: Well, that's my good fortune, isn't it? *(Guardedly.)* In some cases. *(Breaking off, to ELLA.)* What's all this, this trouble you're in? What happened to you?

ELLA: That night Mr Morris asked me to come back. So I did. Then he sort of took me up and rented me a flat next door, to entertain his men friends. So I did that too. But not for money. And I got awfully into debt.

ALMA: So now she's being turned out of the flat.

FRED: *(Not over-concerned.)* Oh, dear.

ALMA: But she has got an offer to go to Duke Street and become a tart.

VICTOR: Prostitute, dear.

ALMA: Oh, don't be so pernickety. *(FRED sits.)*

ELLA: I only told you that as a sort of last effort to get the money. I got Felix to come along and help.

VICTOR: You're the most unscrupulous girl I've ever heard of.

ELLA: Yes, I expect I am. *(She sits.)* Because, if you must know, I don't need the money for the flat, I paid Mr Morris a week ago.

*VICTOR and ALMA are open-mouthed.*

VICTOR:⎫ Paid him? How could you?}

ALMA: ⎬ Paid him with what?} *(Speaking together.)*

*ELLA is silent for a moment; then speaks as though against her will.*

ELLA: Aubrey got the money for me.

VICTOR: *(Incredulously.) Aubrey?*

ELLA: From the car place he had a job at.

VICTOR: You mean to say they let him have it?

ELLA: No. Some customer paid a hundred and forty pounds for a car in cash. And Aubrey kept it.

VICTOR: Stole it?

ELLA: Yes.

VICTOR: Oh, my God.

FRED: Who's Aubrey?

ALMA: His abominable son. Not mine, thank you.

VICTOR: He's simple-minded.

FRED: He sounds pretty capable to me.

ELLA: His boss was away at the time. He came back two days ago. I knew he'd find out so I went and talked to him.

VICTOR: Walker?

ELLA: Yes. He was very angry of course. But I got him to give me till today to pay him back. But he's going to run Aubrey in if the money isn't paid by this morning.

VICTOR: But, good heavens, it's nearly twelve now. *(In a great flap.)* Hold on – I'll phone Walker. No, that's no good; he calls himself something motor depot. The what motor depot? Oh, damn it, I've forgotten. Do you remember?

ELLA: I'm afraid not. I wrote it down but I haven't got it here.

VICTOR: Why not? Oh, hell.

FRED: *(Rising and taking VICTOR aside, confidentially.)* Steady, now. You seem to be in what is commonly known as a bugger's muddle. You know where this motor place is, anyhow?

VICTOR: Yes, very close to here, thank God. End of Brompton Road by the Oratory. I'll go there at once.

ALMA: *(Who has been regarding VICTOR's flap rather disdainfully.)* Take your cheque-book.

VICTOR: Yes, yes; I have it on me; but… *(He pulls up, faced by a snag.)*

ALMA: *(With quiet command.)* Pay the man.

VICTOR: *(Effusively.)* May I do that? Oh, thank you, Alma.

ALMA: Then don't waste any time.

VICTOR: No fear. I'll run all the way.

FRED: You can take my car if you like.

VICTOR: Oh, thank you, but it's no distance.

FRED: It'll save you getting apoplexy. Come on; I'll tell me feller.

*FRED goes to the front door. VICTOR hurries after him.*

VICTOR: *(As he goes.)* This is immensely kind of you.

FRED: Oh, that's nothing.

*FRED and VICTOR disappear leaving the door ajar.*

*ELLA turns to ALMA. ELLA does not appear very penitent.*

ELLA: *(Rising.)* Oh, Mrs Keene, I hardly know what to say.

ALMA: You don't often have that trouble, do you? Tell me this, did you ask Aubrey to steal it for you?

ELLA: Well, it was sort of – between us…

ALMA: All these lies – that other nonsense about Duke Street…

ELLA: *(With great assertion.)* No, that was true. I did get that offer. It still holds good.

*A car is heard starting up and driving away.*

ALMA: Then that is where you'll finish, I should think. Wretched girl. *(She turns aside angrily.)*

*ELLA tries a bit of blarney.*

ELLA: Oh, Mrs Keene, if ever it looks as if I might have to go to Duke Street, do you think I could come and see you again then?

*ALMA turns as if to rend her. She glares at ELLA and speaks angrily.*

ALMA: Yes.

*FRED enters through the open doorway and comes down.*

ELLA: *(To ALMA.)* Shall I wait until Mr Keene comes back?

ALMA: No, certainly not. *(She rises.)*

ELLA: Then I'll go now. Thank you, Mrs Keene. Good-bye. Good-bye Mr Castle.

FRED: *(Airily.)* Oh, good-bye, my dear. Glad to have seen you again.

ELLA: *(Without any sarcasm; rather artificially coy.)* Oh, I'm so glad you're glad. Good-bye.

*ELLA goes.*

ALMA: *(As ELLA goes.)* Close the front door, please.

*FRED closes the front door.*

Thank you for lending my husband your car. It was very thoughtful.

FRED: Well, he seemed a bit het up. I don't mind waiting a few minutes. This is all a rather unusual experience for me.

ALMA: It certainly is for me – to have a little while alone here with you of all people. *(Pointedly.)* With your reputation.

FRED: *(Quite sincerely.)* I just happen to be what I am. One thing, thank goodness – I don't need flattery. I never flatter *myself.* In fact, it gets rather a bore at times being so much better than anyone else.

ALMA: Oh, I didn't mean your reputation as an actor.

FRED: *(With instinctive resentment.)* Why, what more d'you want? *(Quickly urbane again.)* Ohh, you mean the horses? *(Surprised.)* Why, are you a race-goer?

ALMA: No, no, Mr Castle; I mean what I said before – your reputation as a ladies' man.

FRED: *(Laughing.)* Oh, so that's it? Well, I'm not supposed to have many rivals in that field either. *(Leg-pulling.)* So that's where your tastes lie, is it?

ALMA: *(Dead seriously.)* Yes. That's why it's so helpful to be able to consult an expert. You see, I've only just become interested in the physical side of it.

FRED: Why, have you been in a nunnery or something?

ALMA: Yes. For over twenty-five years. In a nunnery of my own making.

FRED: Pity you left it so late to come out.

ALMA: *(Sitting on the sofa.)* Not too late. But I don't suppose a man like you would want to be bothered with my case; odd though it is.

FRED: I like oddities. I didn't know there were any left.

ALMA: Please don't laugh at me. I know I'm middle-aged and undesirable.

FRED: I didn't mean it that way.

ALMA: Yes, you did. It serves me right for talking to you like this.

*ALMA is genuinely upset with herself. FRED sees this and becomes gentle and sympathetic.*

FRED: Now, now – don't upset yourself. *(Confidentially.)* I'll tell you something. I've had pretty nearly every desirable young woman who's available and quite a few who aren't. I don't say I get tired of them, but just now and then, there's something about a middle-ager – well, say forty-odd – which offers a new sort of kick.

ALMA: A beautiful woman though…

FRED: Doesn't follow. As a rule the lovelier a woman looks the dumber she comes. It's personality that counts.

ALMA: Oh, Mr Castle. I think it's wonderful of you to be so versatile. Do you think I've got personality?

FRED: You bet you have.

ALMA: *(Brightening.)* You mean I might possibly be one of these middle-agers who could offer a new sort of kick?

FRED: *(Slightly compromising.)* Well, let's say – I didn't think there was much novelty left. But if there is you're certainly a starter.

ALMA: You're really laughing at me the whole time, aren't you?

FRED: Not at all. I'm always ready to encourage an enthusiast.

ALMA: Then you're just being kind to me.

FRED: Well, why not? Come on – snap out of this droopy stuff. It's a thing to be bright about and – sporty.

ALMA: Oh, Mr Castle. You're making me feel more optimistic every moment.

FRED: I'll tell you something else. *(Sitting beside her.)* Women who are past the early stages have got another consolation.

ALMA: Oh, what?

FRED: *(Putting his arm round her.)* They're always the most passionate.

ALMA: Oh, Mr Castle, are they?

FRED: Always.

ALMA: Oh, Mr Castle; you've got your hand on my charlie.

FRED: It's just making itself at home. *(Removing his hand and sitting up.)* But I don't quite get this – have you been married long?

ALMA: A few months.

FRED: Is that all? It seems a bit soon for you to be on the general rampage like this. Isn't he up to the job?

ALMA: *(Rather incoherently.)* No. Oh, yes. At the time it was wonderful and I got the bells and he brought it off thank God and everything. But he's no good about wanting and enthusiasm and oftenness enough.

FRED: A bit past it, eh? Poor devil. I hope I never get that way. You must have a heart, you know. Don't tick him off about it. If you want to bring him up to scratch do it gently and fondly – you know – a little monkey business.

ALMA: Monkey business? Oh Mr Castle; what do monkeys do?

FRED: *(Laughing to himself.)* Oh, good Lord, we're back in the kindergarten. Here – turn your face here. *(Taking her face he brings it to his.)* Open your mouth a little.

*ALMA opens her mouth.*

No, just a little crack.

*A silent scene follows in which he plays on her lips with his tongue. She opens her mouth and he inserts his tongue. ALMA works herself up into a passionate state. She grips his hand and takes it to her breast. At length, with an effort he frees himself and laughs.*

There you are. That's what's generally referred to as the guzzle. Does it give you ideas?

ALMA: *(Exclaiming wildly.)* Ideas. *(She seizes him.)*

FRED: Steady now.

ALMA: Guzzle me again. Guzzle me.

*They kiss.*

FRED: *(Getting himself disengaged.)* My word. You're that novelty all right.

*A car horn is heard. The shadow reappears at the window. FRED turns his head towards it.*

But you'd better return to normal. *(Rising.)* Your old man's back.

ALMA: Bolt the door.

FRED: No, thank you.

ALMA: Oh, how exasperating.

FRED: Your hair's a bit wonky.

ALMA: I don't care. *(Nevertheless she tidies it as she goes on.)* Well, at least I can say I've been guzzled by Fred Castle. *(She rises and goes to the mirror.)*

FRED: *(With assumed severity.)* Now, don't *you* start.

*VICTOR enters hurriedly, leaving the door open.*

VICTOR: It's all right – it's settled. He was pretty nasty about it but he took my cheque. *(To FRED.)* I'm very grateful to you, Mr Castle.

FRED: That's OK. I've got to get along now.

VICTOR: Thank you for waiting. I'm sure it's been a great treat for my wife.

FRED: For me too. *(He gives VICTOR a mischievous dig.)* You don't realize how lucky you are.

VICTOR: Oh, I do indeed.

FRED: *(To ALMA.)* You keep him up to that. Good-bye.

ALMA: *(Almost inaudibly.)* Good-bye.

*FRED turns to the door.*

VICTOR: I'm sorry I've been such a bad host. I ought to have offered you something.

FRED: Your wife did that.

*FRED goes.*

*VICTOR follows into the porch and gives him a wave of the hand. Then closes the door and turns, as the car is heard going and the shadow disappears.*

VICTOR: My word, what an awfully nice chap.

ALMA: How much did Aubrey steal?

VICTOR: A hundred and forty pounds.

ALMA: I'll tell the bank to pay it to your account.

VICTOR: Oh, thank you, dear Alma. Doing this for my sake – it's wonderful.

ALMA: So long as you guarantee that I never see Aubrey again. *(She sits on the sofa.)*

VICTOR: Absolutely. What a business all round. To think that Fred Castle would ever come to this house. I must say he was awfully agreeable and helpful, wasn't he?

ALMA: *(Flatly.)* Very.

VICTOR: How did you get along with him?

ALMA: We just chatted. He was very pleasant. Aren't you going to your cricket?

*ALMA is only half-listening; she is trying to decide whether to tell him something.*

VICTOR: Righto then. *(Picking up his binoculars.)* I'll be off. *(Getting up.)* Good-bye, dear, and thank you again for what you did.

ALMA: *(As he gets to the door.)* No, Victor. *(Rising.)* Wait a moment.

VICTOR: *(Turning back.)* Yes, what?

ALMA: You were quite right about me this morning, I was in a very bad mood. It was because of last night – your not wanting to – go on.

VICTOR: Well, never mind that now. That's all... *(He breaks off with a gesture.)*

ALMA: Let's be honest about it. You don't really ever want to do that, do you?

VICTOR: Well, Alma, we were very happy before it – cropped up.

ALMA: But don't you really ever have any sort of – *(Making an urging gesture.)* feeling that way?

VICTOR: Well, I'm a normal man, of course. One occasionally – thinks about it.

ALMA: Haven't there been any times since we married when you wanted?

VICTOR: Oh yes, I suppose – mildly.

ALMA: But you've never done it? I mean with anybody else?

VICTOR: Of course not.

ALMA: Why of course? I would have, if I'd been you.

VICTOR: *(Nettled.)* I don't mind telling you I nearly did once.

ALMA: *(Keenly enthusiastic.)* Oh Victor, when?

VICTOR: I was on top of a bus. It came over me unexpectedly, like a sort of itch. It happens that way. Especially on the tops of buses.

ALMA: Poor Victor. But you resisted?

VICTOR: Oh, it passed off. I forgot it when I got to Lord's. I saw Duleep make a hundred.

ALMA: You're quite right about how we were getting to be happy together. I don't want to upset that. So I've decided something. I'm going away.

VICTOR: *(In great surprise.)* Away? Where?

ALMA: I don't know where. Just for three or four weeks perhaps.

VICTOR: But why on earth – what's the id…? *(With sudden challenge.)* Alma – what's the idea?

ALMA: *(Decisive and practical.)* Mrs Holley will see to you – I'll arrange all that. And I'll give you quite enough to keep you going.

VICTOR: What's behind all this? I can't help suspecting something and I don't at all like it.

ALMA: I can't help that. I've got to do something about myself.

VICTOR: No listen, Alma. If this is what I think I won't stand for it.

ALMA: Are you the one to say? *(Brief pause.)* Go on – go to your cricket. *(She sits on the sofa.)*

*VICTOR again turns towards the front door; pauses in thought. He takes a step down towards ALMA and speaks gently.*

VICTOR: Alma, just sit and think it over quietly. Don't go and ruin our whole life together. You don't seem to realize how fond I am of you.

*ALMA rises.*

ALMA: *(Flying up.)* Do you suppose I'm not fond of *you*?

*VICTOR gives up. He takes his hat and walks out, closing the front door.*

*ALMA deliberates for a moment, then goes to the desk with the travel brochure. She picks up the telephone, sits, finds a number in the brochure, and dials.*

ALMA: *(After listening for a moment.)* Are you there? … Is that Messrs Thomas Cook and Sons?

*The CURTAIN falls.*

## SCENE 3

*The same. Ten o'clock at night, three weeks later.*

*All the lights are on, and the curtains are drawn.*

*VICTOR, wearing a dressing-gown and pyjamas, is standing by the window table drinking a glass of brandy. He pours another glass. A taxi is heard approaching. VICTOR looks out of the window, then finishes his drink hurriedly, moves down to a table and empties the ashtray into the wastepaper basket. He replaces the ashtray, then takes the drinks tray into the dining-room. The taxi door slams. VICTOR hastens to the stairs, switches off the lights, then runs upstairs, switches off the landing lights, and goes into his bedroom.*

*ALMA enters from the front door carrying a coat and vanity case. She switches on the lights by the front door, then puts the case by the window. A Taxi-driver enters with a hatbox and suitcases.*

ALMA: Just put them down there, please.

*He puts the cases by the window. She pays him.*

Thank you.

*The Taxi-driver inspects what she has given him, gives a slight jerk of the head, and goes.*

*ALMA shuts the front door and draws the bolts.*

*VICTOR enters on to the landing and switches on the landing light.*

VICTOR: Alma – good Lord – you've come back home again. *(He starts down the stairs.)*

ALMA: That's fairly obvious, isn't it? Well, Victor?

VICTOR: Good Lord, this is beyond anything.

ALMA: What is?

VICTOR: Your sudden turning up after all this time.

ALMA: It's only been three weeks and a bit.

VICTOR: Yes, but I'd have come and met you. If only you'd have let me know you were coming.

ALMA: It's just as well I didn't. I'm about three hours late. Something went wrong with the cross-Channel boat. They had to go and get another.

VICTOR: Poor Alma, You must be fagged out.

ALMA: No, not in the least. I just sat and waited.

VICTOR: Have you had any dinner?

ALMA: Oh, yes; a very good one. They saw to all that.

VICTOR: Oh, good. But will you want something else before you turn in? A cup of tea or anything?

ALMA: *(Casually removing her hat and coat and laying them aside as they talk.)* No, thank you. And I'm not going to turn in just yet.

VICTOR: Well, I'd better take your things upstairs, anyhow.

ALMA: No, leave them alone for now. I want to sit and hear all about you.

VICTOR: Me? Oh, I've got along all right – as best I could.

ALMA: You've been looked after properly? Has Mrs Holley been behaving herself?

VICTOR: Oh, fine. I've been going out for my evening meals. I did tonight. Then I came back and was reading in bed and heard you arrive.

ALMA: And Aubrey? What have you done about him?

VICTOR: Nothing. That girl's still looking after him. I've just let it rip. I don't know what else to do.

ALMA: *(Sitting on the sofa.)* Well, now about *myself* – I've decided to tell you everything. I want to tell you all that happened to me straight away. I feel I should sleep better.

VICTOR: *(Sardonically.)* I wonder if I will.

ALMA: No, I'm afraid you won't.

VICTOR: For heaven's sake. Let's keep it till tomorrow.

ALMA: No. Now sit down, Victor.

VICTOR: *(Greatly against his will.)* Oh, all right then. *(He sits on the armchair.)* Let's have it.

ALMA: You can smoke your pipe if you like.

VICTOR: No, no; I've finished with all that for tonight. I've cleaned my teeth and everything.

ALMA: Then just listen and don't keep fidgeting. Well, you know what my motive was in going abroad, to Bordighera.

VICTOR: Yes, but – go on.

*She glances at him sternly.*

ALMA: I didn't like it at first.

VICTOR: Why only at first?

*She gives a quiver of impatience at him. He makes a gesture of apology.*

No. All right. Carry on.

ALMA: There weren't many people in the hotel. A few American married couples and one old permanent Englishman. It was hopeless for me there, hopeless. I thought I'd come on a wild goose chase. I got almost frantic...

VICTOR: Oh, Alma, do you have to tell me all this?

ALMA: Yes. I want you to realize what happened to me, and to try and understand. Just to show you the sort of – turmoil – I was in; there was a valet in the hotel that did the shoes. A regular valet, quite a smart, well-mannered young man. I got him to bring my shoes into my room in the morning. On the second morning he brought them in, I came out of my bathroom by mistake on purpose with nothing on.

VICTOR: *(Staring and shaking his head.)* It's beyond me. What happened then?

ALMA: He ran away, screaming.

VICTOR: I expect he thought *he'd* surprised *you*, and was screaming in apology.

ALMA: Don't try to be kind, Victor. It made me despair of myself. Then suddenly, ten days ago, it came my way – the complete fulfilment I was looking for.

VICTOR: *(Rising quickly.)* That's enough. I don't want to hear any more. A wife coming home and telling her husband –

ALMA: *(Cutting in sharply.)* – Well, you knew what I'd gone for. You must listen.

VICTOR: I will not.

ALMA: You must.

VICTOR: *(Moving to the cases.)* I'll take these things upstairs and go to my room. And you too. To yours.

ALMA: *(Rising.)* Not yet, Victor, until I've told you everything – I want you to take pity on me and help me to decide.

VICTOR: *(With challenge.)* Decide what?

ALMA: What's going to happen to me now. And to you. Please, Victor.

*He gives in without saying anything. She goes on as before.*

I hired a car to have a drive around the country. The driver was a young Italian, very bronzed and handsome and speaking very good English. I asked him whether he was married and he said no, he had too many girl friends to want to get married. I told him he ought to try going with a plain, middle-aged woman because I'd heard from a friend of mine who was a great connoisseur, that they were the women who were the most exciting and passionate and gave kicks.

VICTOR: Alma, this is incredible; it simply isn't you. What in God's name has happened to you?

ALMA: He took me for miles to an empty farmhouse he knew of. It was all locked up but there was a nice clean barn.

VICTOR: A barn? *(He sits on the sofa.)* Good God, Alma, this is the most degraded thing I ever heard of. Like a dirty French farce.

ALMA: *(Sitting in the armchair.)* I couldn't help that. I'd found what I'd been longing for and it was even more wonderful than I'd hoped. I left the hotel and rented a little furnished villa by the week. He came in his car every afternoon. It was – *(Closing her eyes.)* – oh – beyond all words. *(Opening her eyes.)* The great thing was he appeared to be quite inexhaustible.

VICTOR: Thank you; it's bad enough without any sarcasm. I wonder how much you had to pay this bastard.

ALMA: I gave him what he wanted – I didn't care. But that was really the trouble; that's what led to it.

VICTOR: Led to what?

ALMA: It was three days ago – it seems like weeks…

VICTOR: What does?

ALMA: He came to the villa as usual, all gay and debonair and paying my compliments. He started to undress me…

VICTOR: You can spare me the details…

ALMA: Then he began whispering about how he'd got into money trouble, and would have to sell his car and wanted me to give him a great deal more and when I said no he began shouting and threatening me; I thought he was going to kill me. And it was all so shaming because besides being frightened I had nothing on above the waist. I was like one of those Greek women from some vulgar piece of old statuary, struggling with some heathen male creature who is trying to get at her handbag.

VICTOR: *(Rising, forgetting himself in indignation.)* The stinking Dago brute – by gad, I wish I'd been there.

ALMA: Oh, Victor, I wish you had. He threw me on the bed and got my bag and threw my traveller's cheques at me and took all my Italian lire and dashed off in his car. So I went straight to the telephone – that is, directly I'd got my camisole on again…

VICTOR: And phoned the police…

ALMA: Police? No, of course not. I gave up the villa and booked to come back here today. *(Brief pause.)* So here we are. *(Sharply.)* And don't go on being angry with me; that won't do any good.

VICTOR: Oh well – I don't suppose I've any right to be.

ALMA: Yes, you have. But please keep it to yourself, because if you're going to stay on with me after this...

VICTOR: We'll thrash all that out tomorrow. *(Going up to the cases.)* Now, for goodness sake, go to bed. *(He takes up the two suitcases.)* I'll take these up.

ALMA: But, Victor, I want to get things settled about ourselves.

VICTOR: Yes, but not tonight.

ALMA: You're ashamed of me, aren't you?

VICTOR: No. What you do is up to you. It always has been. Don't forget your coat and things. *(He goes to the bottom of the stairs.)* Don't bother about the lights; I'll see to them.

ALMA*: (Picking up her coat and hat.)* You needn't think I'm ashamed. Yes, I am. But I'm only ashamed of being so vain as to think any man would really want me like that.

*She starts upstairs, VICTOR following.*

I suppose my bed's made?

VICTOR: *(On the landing,.)* Oh Lord, I hope so. Yes, I expect Mrs Holley will have seen to that.

ALMA: *(Opening her bedroom door.)* It looks to be all right.

*ALMA goes into the bedroom.*

VICTOR: *(Speaking into the room.)* Well, there you are. *(He puts the cases inside.)* Don't be too long getting to bed. Goodnight. *(He turns away.)*

*ALMA comes out of the bedroom.*

ALMA: Leave the landing light on. I'm going to the bathroom.

VICTOR: Oh, are you? Yes, of course. Right you are.

*ALMA goes into the bathroom and shuts the door.*

*VICTOR starts downstairs and stops half-way, looking anxious. LOLLY, fully dressed and carrying a hat and handbag, comes quickly, and in a very surreptitious manner, from VICTOR's bedroom. There is some dumbshow, LOLLY wanting to escape and VICTOR signalling that ALMA is only in the bathroom and for LOLLY to go back to his room. LOLLY, despite this, comes impetuously down, pushing past*

*VICTOR and making for the front door. She unlocks this, but does not realize that it has been bolted. She then tries to unbolt it, but finds it difficult. VICTOR goes to her aid, getting LOLLY out of the way and pulling back the bolt.*

*ALMA comes out of the bathroom, her toothbrush in her hand, and stands watching.*

*VICTOR opens the front door.*

*LOLLY hurriedly escapes.*

*VICTOR finishes bolting the door. He looks over his shoulder, and sees ALMA. She comes downstairs slowly and calmly and does not speak until she is at the bottom and face to face with VICTOR.*

ALMA: Was that Lolly?

VICTOR: Yes.

ALMA: Has this been happening often?

VICTOR: No, this is only the second time. Soon after you went away Lolly rang up. I said you'd gone abroad for a little change. So she asked me to take her out to dinner. And – oh, well…

ALMA: Why did you say yes?

VICTOR: Well, dash it, I was lonely. I wanted company and she was friendly and we had rather a lot to drink and there it was.

ALMA: And now again a second time.

VICTOR: She invited herself again. I couldn't very well say no. You wouldn't want me to hurt her feelings.

ALMA: What about my feelings?

VICTOR: *(Boldly.)* Well, think what you were doing.

ALMA: You didn't know what I was doing.

*He makes a hapless gesture. She continues volubly.*

I've been completely open with you – poured out my troubles. You weren't going to tell me a word about yourself and Lolly.

VICTOR: *(Lamely.)* The husband isn't supposed to.

ALMA: You're really just as bad as I am and even worse.

VICTOR: You began it.

ALMA: Never mind who began it. Can't you see what this means? I come home to you and make a clean breast of all that happened to me, half expecting you to turn away in disgust and leave me. And now what do I find? That you're as bad as I am and even worse and we're back where we were before.

VICTOR: *(Hopefully.)* Oh, Alma; can we be?

ALMA: It isn't can we be, it's what we're going to have to be. Of course it will be much easier for you than for me. You only did what you did out of silly weak-mindedness. You never think of that sort of thing as a rule. You said so yourself.

VICTOR: Now and then, I said. *(Meekly.)* Well, but we've still got affection. At least, I have.

ALMA: Haven't we both? Are you accusing me of not being affectionate?

VICTOR: No, no. But that'll help, won't it? Because affection really counts for more than the other thing, doesn't it?

ALMA: I daresay it *does*. Yes, of course it does. Except at the actual time.

VICTOR: Try to overcome this other thing, Lolly.

ALMA: *(Fiercely.)* What?

VICTOR: I mean, Alma. Try to overcome it.

ALMA: I'm going to. I've got to, haven't I – if there's nothing else for it?

VICTOR: And if there's anything I can do…

ALMA: The only thing you can do is never never to let the subject be mentioned between us again.

VICTOR: No. We'll be like we were before any of this ever happened.

ALMA: I've said so already, haven't I? *(Moving to the stairs.)* Now – I'll go and start my unpacking. You go to bed. I'll bring you your tea in the morning as I always used to.

VICTOR: *(Relieved and pleased with himself.)* Thank you, dear Alma.

*ALMA mounts two stairs and turns.*

ALMA: Just one thing.

VICTOR: *(Amiably.)* What is it, dear?

ALMA: Don't ever let Lolly know that I know.

VICTOR: Know what?

ALMA: Don't be stupid, Victor. Don't ever let Lolly know that I know what you did with her tonight.

VICTOR: Of course not. As a matter of fact, I didn't. You came barging in before we'd even started.

ALMA: *(With slow, joyful surprise.)* Ohhh – oh, then you're still...

*She runs down at him, throwing her toothbrush in the air. He catches her in his arms.*

Oh, Victor – how splendid. Come along.

*They both run upstairs, VICTOR leading ALMA. As they disappear into his bedroom –*

*The CURTAIN falls.*